McGRAW-HILL READING

Contributing Authors

Barbara Coulter, Frankie Dungan, Joseph B. Rubin, Shirley Wright

Contributors

The Princeton Review, Time Magazine

The Princeton Review is not affiliated with Princeton University or ETS.

McGraw-Hill School Division

A Division of The McGraw-Hill Companies

McGraw-Hill School Division
Two Penn Plaza
New York, New York 10121

Printed in the United States of America

ISBN 0-02-184738-X/4
6 7 8 9 [006/043] 04 03 02 01

Macmillan/McGraw-Hill Edition

McGRAW-HILL READING

Authors

James Flood
Jan E. Hasbrouck
James V. Hoffman
Diane Lapp
Angela Shelf Medearis
Scott Paris
Steven Stahl
Josefina Villamil Tinajero
Karen D. Wood

UNIT 1

Reflections

UNIT 2

Something in Common

UNIT 3

UNIT 4

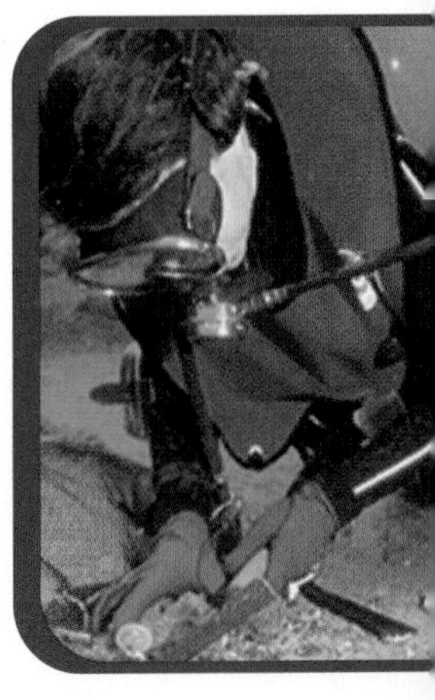

UNIT 5

UNIT 6

Sorting It Out

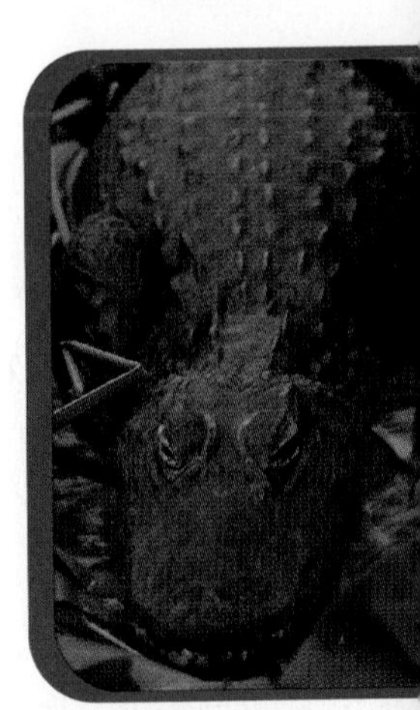

Reflections

UNIT 1

To
make
this world
a whole lot
brighter

when
I
grow up
I'll
be
a writer.
I'll
write about
some things
I know—

how to bunt
how to throw . . .
a Christmas wish
a butter dish . . .
a teddy bear
an empty chair . . .
the love I have inside
to
share . . .

Yes.

To
make
this world
a whole lot
brighter,

when
I grow up
I'll
be
a
writer.

by Lee Bennett Hopkins

Like a story, a painting can show you time and place. It can also describe characters in a setting.

Look at this landscape painting. What can you tell about it? How does the artist create a quiet scene? How do the people feel in this setting? What makes you think so?

Close your eyes. What part of the painting do you remember? Why?

Gathering Watercress on the River Mole
by William F. Witherington
Owen Edgar Gallery, England

THE Lost Lake

by Allen Say

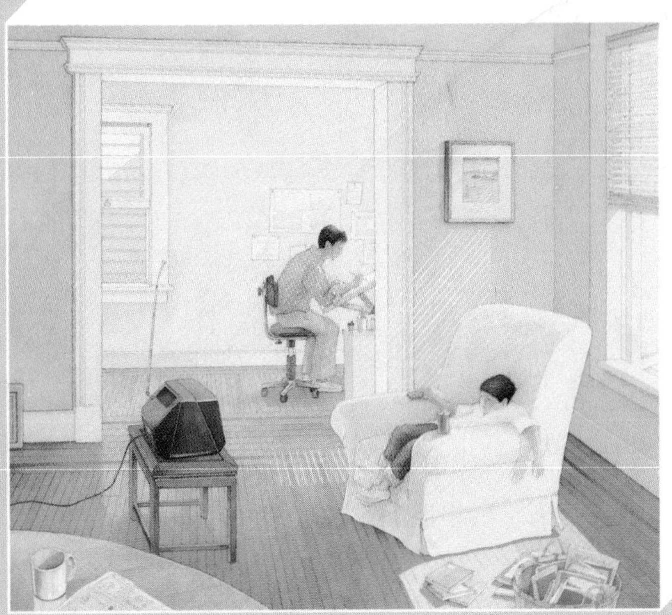

I went to live with Dad last summer.

Every day he worked in his room from morning to night, sometimes on weekends, too. Dad wasn't much of a talker, but when he was busy he didn't talk at all.

I didn't know anybody in the city, so I stayed home most of the time. It was too hot to play outside anyway. In one month I finished all the books I'd brought and grew tired of watching TV.

One morning I started cutting pictures out of old magazines, just to be doing something. They were pictures of mountains and rivers and lakes, and some showed people fishing and canoeing. Looking at them made me feel cool, so I pinned them up in my room.

Dad didn't notice them for two days. When he did, he looked at them one by one.

"Nice pictures," he said.

"Are you angry with me, Dad?" I asked, because he saved old magazines for his work.

"It's all right, Luke," he said. "I'm having this place painted soon anyway."

He thought I was talking about the marks I'd made on the wall.

That Saturday Dad woke me up early in the morning and told me we were going camping! I was wide awake in a second. He gave me a pair of brand-new hiking boots to try out. They were perfect.

In the hallway I saw a big backpack and a knapsack all packed and ready to go.

"What's in them, Dad?" I asked.

"Later," he said. "We have a long drive ahead of us."

In the car I didn't ask any more questions because Dad was so grumpy in the morning.

"Want a sip?" he said, handing me his mug. He'd never let me drink coffee before. It had lots of sugar in it.

"Where are we going?" I finally asked.

"We're off to the Lost Lake, my lad."

"How can you lose a lake?"

"No one's found it, that's how." Dad was smiling! "Grandpa and I used to go there a long time ago. It was our special place, so don't tell any of your friends."

"I'll never tell," I promised. "How long are we going to stay there?"

"Five days, maybe a week."

"We're going to sleep outside for a whole week?"

"That's the idea."

"Oh, boy!"

We got to the mountains in the afternoon.
"It's a bit of a hike to the lake, son," Dad said.
"I don't mind," I told him. "Are there any fish in the lake?"
"Hope so. We'll have to catch our dinner, you know."
"You didn't bring any food?"
"Of course not. We're going to live like true outdoorsmen."
"Oh..."

Dad saw my face and started to laugh. He must have been joking. I didn't think we were going very far anyway, because Dad's pack was so heavy I couldn't even lift it.

Well, Dad was like a mountain goat. He went straight up the trail, whistling all the while. But I was gasping in no time. My knapsack got very heavy and I started to fall behind.

Dad stopped for me often, but he wouldn't let me take off my pack. If I did I'd be too tired to go on, he said.

It was almost suppertime when we got to the lake.

The place reminded me of the park near Dad's apartment. He wasn't whistling or humming anymore.

"Welcome to the *Found* Lake," he muttered from the side of his mouth.

"What's wrong, Dad?"

"Do you want to camp with all these people around us?"

"I don't mind."

"Well, I do!"

"Are we going home?"

"Of course not!"

He didn't even take off his pack. He just turned and started to walk away.

Soon the lake was far out of sight.

Then it started to rain. Dad gave me a poncho and it kept me dry, but I wondered where we were going to sleep that night. I wondered what we were going to do for dinner. I wasn't sure about camping anymore.

I was glad when Dad finally stopped and set up the tent. The rain and wind beat against it, but we were warm and cozy inside. And Dad had brought food. For dinner we had salami and dried apricots.

"I'm sorry about the lake, Dad," I said.

He shook his head. "You know something, Luke? There aren't any secret places left in the world anymore."

"What if we go very far up in the mountains? Maybe we can find our own lake."

"There are lots of lakes up here, but that one was special."

"But we've got a whole week, Dad."

"Well, why not? Maybe we'll find a lake that's not on the map."

"Sure, we will!"

We started early in the morning. When the fog cleared we saw other hikers ahead of us. Sure enough, Dad became very glum.

"We're going cross-country, partner," he said.

"Won't we get lost?"

"A wise man never leaves home without his compass."

So we went off the trail. The hills went on and on. The mountains went on and on. It was kind of lonesome. It seemed as if Dad and I were the only people left in the world.

And then we hiked into a big forest.

At noontime we stopped by a creek and ate lunch and drank ice-cold water straight from the stream. I threw rocks in the water, and fish, like shadows, darted in the pools.

"Isn't this a good place to camp, Dad?"

"I thought we were looking for our lake."

"Yes, right..." I mumbled.

The forest went on and on.

"I don't mean to scare you, son," Dad said. "But we're in bear country. We don't want to surprise them, so we have to make a lot of noise. If they hear us, they'll just go away."

What a time to tell me! I started to shout as loudly as I could. Even Dad wouldn't be able to beat off bears. I thought about those people having fun back at the lake. I thought about the creek, too, with all those fish in it. That would have been a fine place to camp. The Lost Lake hadn't been so bad either.

It was dark when we got out of the forest. We built a fire and that made me feel better. Wild animals wouldn't come near a fire. Dad cooked beef stroganoff and it was delicious.

Later it was bedtime. The sleeping bag felt wonderful. Dad and I started to count the shooting stars, then I worried that maybe we weren't going to find our lake.

"What are you thinking about, Luke?" Dad asked.

"I didn't know you could cook like that," I said.

Dad laughed. "That was only freeze-dried stuff. When we get home, I'll cook you something really special."

"You know something, Dad? You seem like a different person up here."

"Better or worse?"

"A lot better."

"How so?"

"You talk more."

"I'll have to talk more often, then."

That made me smile. Then I slept.

Dad shook me awake. The sun was just coming up, turning everything all gold and orange and yellow. And there was the lake, right in front of us.

For a long time we watched the light change on the water, getting brighter and brighter. Dad didn't say a word the whole time. But then, I didn't have anything to say either.

After breakfast we climbed a mountain and saw our lake below us. There wasn't a sign of people anywhere. It really seemed as if Dad and I were all alone in the world.

I liked it just fine.

MEET ALLEN SAY

For Allen Say, who writes and illustrates many of his own stories, pictures always come first. When he makes up a story, he begins by drawing pictures without having words or even ideas to go with them. *The Lost Lake* grew out of pictures Say drew of a camping trip. He unexpectedly remembered hiking to a mountain lake many years before and finding the area completely ruined by litter.

Say has been an artist almost all of his life. He originally dreamed of being a cartoonist. At thirteen he already had a job drawing backgrounds for a famous cartoonist in Japan. Say eventually came to the United States. He never lost his interest in art and later began to write and illustrate stories.

Other books by this writer and illustrator that you might enjoy are *El Chino,* a book about Bill Wong, the first Chinese bullfighter, and *Tree of Cranes*, a book Say dedicated to the man he learned from and first worked for, the Japanese cartoonist Noro Shinpei.

Story Questions & Activities

1. Where does the story take place?
2. How do the characters act in the two different settings?
3. How can you tell that Luke's father cares about him? Explain.
4. What is this story mostly about?
5. Imagine that Luke stepped into the painting on pages 18–19. What do you think he would tell the people about his camping trip?

Write a Personal Narrative

Luke's camping story is drawn from his own experience. Write a personal narrative of your own about a time when you and your family took a trip somewhere. Where did you go? What did you do? Why is the trip still important to you? Use *I* when telling your story.

Use a Compass

Luke's father found his way in the mountains by using a compass. Try using a compass to find out in which direction from your home you would go to get to certain places in your community. Make a list of these places, such as your school, a park, or a friend's house. Then use a compass. Jot down the results.

Look at a Map

Where would you go to find a private place of your own? Look at a map to find a "lost lake." Use the map scale. Figure out how far you would have to travel to find a place where there are no roads or people. How would you get there?

0 2 mi.
0 2 km

Find Out More

In the story, Luke and his father hike through bear country. Use an encyclopedia or a library book to find out more about bears. For example, what kinds of bears live in your part of the country? What are their habits? What should you do if you come in contact with a bear while camping? Use what you learn to give a report to your class.

Use Parts of a Book

Where would you look in this book for the page on which "The Lost Lake" begins? The answer is the table of contents. Like many of your books, this book has different parts.

In the front of the book, you will find the table of contents. The **table of contents** lists the titles of the units or chapters and the selections. It also gives the page on which each of these begins. At the back of the book, the **glossary** gives the meaning of important words in the book. The **index** gives a list of topics and names.

Use the sample parts of a book to answer these questions.

1. Where would you look to find out how many chapters a book has?
2. Where would you look to find the meaning of *backpack*?
3. Where would you look to find out how to use a compass?
4. Why do you think a book has a glossary?
5. How do book parts help you understand a book?

TEST POWER

Test Tip

Always answer all questions.

DIRECTIONS

Read the sample story. Then read each question about the story.

SAMPLE

Robert Plays Kickball

Robert wandered into the schoolyard where the other children were playing a fast-paced game of kickball. He had just moved to town and felt shy because he didn't know any of the children on the team.

A girl about his age walked up to him and said, "My name is Katie. I don't remember seeing you here before. Are you new here?"

Robert blushed. "Yes."

"Do you know how to play kickball?" The girl did not give him a chance to answer. "Because we play all the time. Would you like to be on my team?" Katie urged.

"That would be great," Robert responded happily.

1 What is the main idea of this passage?

A Robert makes friends with Katie.

B Robert just moved to town.

C Katie plays kickball.

D Robert felt shy.

2 At the beginning of the story, Robert was shy because—

F he didn't like school

G the new school was bigger

H he couldn't play kickball

J he didn't know anyone

Like real life, a painting can present a problem. It can also give you clues to help you find a solution.

Look at this twisting road. Where does it go? How does the artist use it to lead your eye through the picture? What might this painting be saying about the road you travel through life?

Imagine that you are walking on this road. What problems will you meet along the way? How will you reach your destination?

Broadbottom, Near Glossop
by Edward Alexander Wadsworth, 1922
Bradford Art Galleries and Museums, West Yorkshire, England

Meet
Linda Jacobs Altman

Linda Jacobs Altman was born in North Carolina and went to college in California. Her career as an author comes from her desire to spend her life doing what she likes best—writing. Through her writing, she hopes to explore and share her own ideas.

Altman often writes about the difficult lives of migrant workers. These are the people who move from one harvest to another, picking fruit and vegetable crops. She has also written many books for young people. These books include the life stories of important political, sports, and entertainment personalities such as Cathy Rigby and Natalie Cole.

Meet
Enrique O. Sanchez

Enrique O. Sanchez was born in Santo Domingo in the Dominican Republic. He studied architecture and art there. In the 1960s, Sanchez moved to New York City, where he worked as a designer of sets for the "Sesame Street" television series.

The first book that Sanchez illustrated, *Abuela's Weave*, was a 1993 Parents' Choice Award Honoree. Sanchez often works on books with Mexican-American characters and themes. In fact, many of his books have been published in both English and Spanish.

Amelia's Road

Written by Linda Jacobs Altman
Illustrated by Enrique O. Sanchez

Amelia Luisa Martinez hated roads. Straight roads. Curved roads. Dirt roads. Paved roads. Roads leading to all manner of strange places, and roads leading to nowhere at all. Amelia hated roads so much that she cried every time her father took out the map.

The roads Amelia knew went to farms where workers labored in sunstruck fields and lived in grim, gray shanties. *Los caminos*, the roads, were long and cheerless.

They never went where you wanted them to go.

Amelia wanted to go someplace where people didn't have to work so hard, or move around so much, or live in labor camps.

Her house would be white and tidy, with blue shutters at the windows and a fine old shade tree growing in the yard. She would live there forever and never worry about *los caminos* again.

It was almost dark when their rusty old car pulled to a stop in front of cabin number twelve at the labor camp.

"Is this the same cabin we had last year?" Amelia asked, but nobody remembered. It didn't seem to matter to the rest of the family.

It mattered a lot to Amelia. From one year to the next, there was nothing to show Amelia had lived here, gone to school in this town, and worked in these fields. Amelia wanted to settle down, to belong.

"Maybe someday," said her mother, but that wonderful someday never seemed to come.

"Mama," Amelia asked, "where was I born?"

Mrs. Martinez paused for a moment and smiled. "Where? Let me see. Must have been in Yuba City. Because I remember we were picking peaches at the time."

"That's right. Peaches," said Mr. Martinez, "which means you were born in June."

Amelia sighed. Other fathers remembered days and dates. Hers remembered crops. Mr. Martinez marked all the important occasions of life by the never-ending rhythms of harvest.

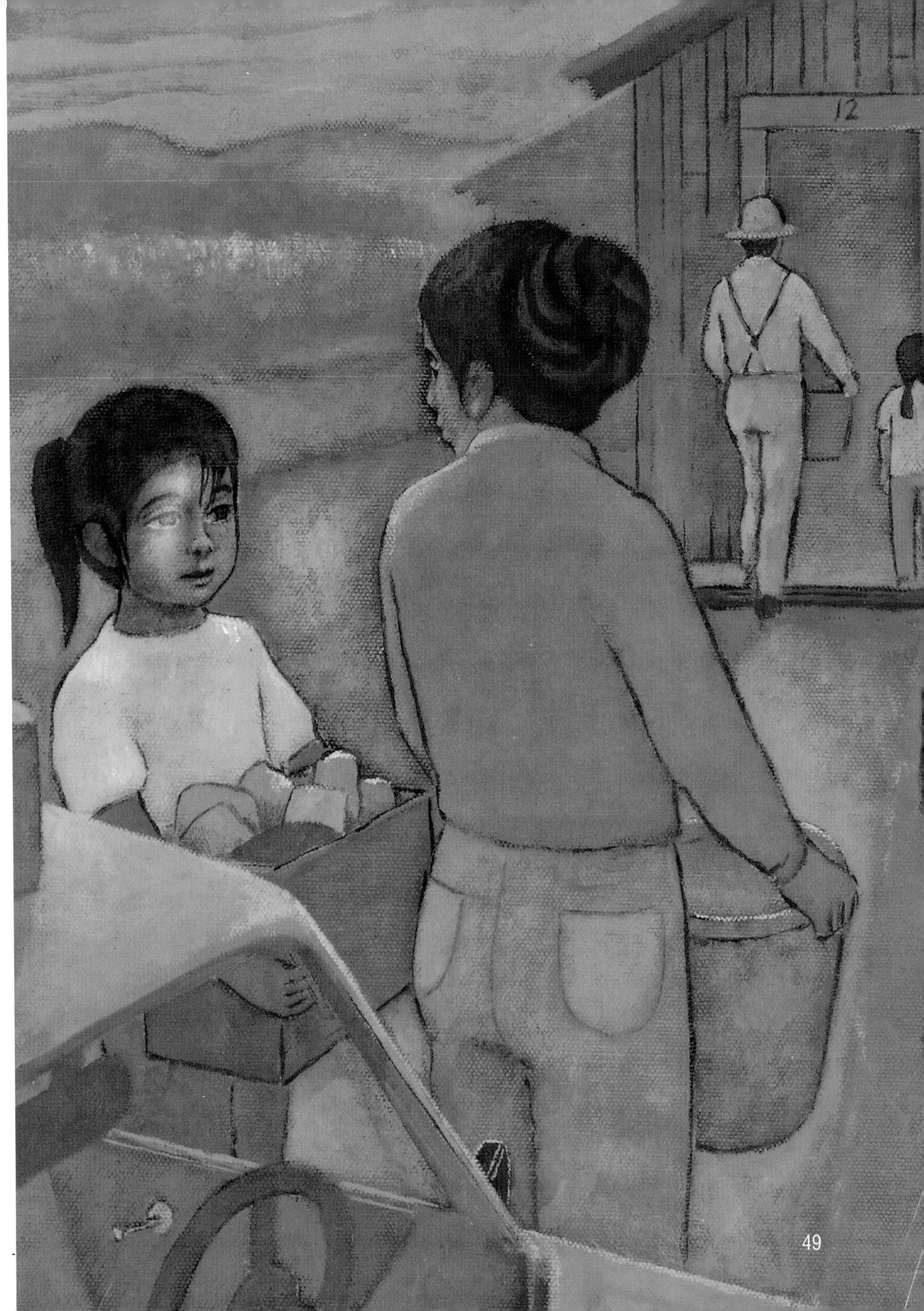
12

The next day, everybody got up at dawn. From five to almost eight in the morning, Amelia and her family picked apples. Even though she still felt sleepy, Amelia had to be extra careful so she wouldn't bruise the fruit.

By the time she had finished her morning's work, Amelia's hands stung and her shoulders ached. She grabbed an apple and hurried off to school.

MRS.
RAMOS
AMELIA
Amelia

Last year, Amelia spent six weeks at Fillmore Elementary School, and not even the teacher had bothered to learn her name.

This year, the teacher bothered. She welcomed all the new children to her classroom and gave them name tags to wear. She wore a name tag herself. It said MRS. RAMOS.

Later, Mrs. Ramos asked the class to draw their dearest wishes. "Share with us something that's really special to you."

Amelia knew exactly what that would be. She drew a pretty white house with a great big tree in the front yard. When Amelia finished, Mrs. Ramos showed her picture to the whole class. Then she pasted a bright red star on the top.

By the end of the day, everybody in class had learned Amelia's name. Finally, here was a place where she wanted to stay.

Amelia couldn't wait to tell her mother about this wonderful day. Feeling as bright as the sky, she decided to look for a shortcut back to camp. That's when she found it.

The accidental road.

Amelia called it the accidental road because it was narrow and rocky, more like a footpath that happened by accident than a road somebody built on purpose.

She followed it over a grassy meadow, through a clump of bushes, and down a gentle hill. There, where the accidental road ended, stood a most wondrous tree. It was old beyond knowing, and quite the sturdiest, most permanent thing Amelia had ever seen. When she closed her eyes, she could even picture it in front of her tidy white house.

Amelia danced for joy, her black hair flying as she twirled around and around the silent meadow.

Almost every day, when work and school were over, Amelia would sit beneath the tree and pretend she had come home.

More than anywhere in the world, she wanted to belong to this place and know that it belonged to her.

But the harvest was almost over, and Amelia didn't know what she'd do when the time came for leaving.

She asked everyone for advice—her sister Rosa, her parents, her brother Hector, her neighbors at camp, and Mrs. Ramos at school, but nobody could tell her what to do.

The answer, when it came, was nearly as accidental as the road.

AMELIA
amelia
Amelia Road

Amelia found an old metal box that somebody had tossed into the trash. It was dented and rusty, but Amelia didn't care. That box was the answer to her problem.

She set to work at once, filling it with "Amelia-things." First she put in the hair ribbon her mother had made for her one Christmas; next came the name tag Mrs. Ramos had given her; then a photograph of her whole family taken at her last birthday; and after that the picture she'd drawn in class with the bright red star on it.

Finally, she took out a sheet of paper and drew a map of the accidental road, from the highway to the very old tree. In her best lettering, she wrote *Amelia Road* on the path. Then she folded the map and put it into her box.

When all the apples were finally picked, Amelia's family and the other workers had to get ready to move again. Amelia made one more trip down the accidental road, this time with her treasure box.

She dug a hole near the old tree, and gently placed the box inside and covered it over with dirt. Then she set a rock on top, so nobody would notice the freshly turned ground.

When Amelia finished, she took a step back and looked at the tree. Finally, here was a place where she belonged, a place where she could come back to.

"I'll be back," she whispered, and then she turned away.

Amelia skipped through the meadow, laughed at the sky, even turned cartwheels right in the middle of the accidental road.

When she got back to the camp, the rest of the family had already started packing the car. Amelia watched them for a moment, then took a deep breath and joined in to help.

For the first time in her life, she didn't cry when her father took out the road map.

Author's Note

Amelia Luisa Martinez and her family, and thousands like them, are often referred to as migrant farm workers. This is because they usually have to move from one harvest to another, and they do not have stable homes. Many of the migrant workers come from different parts of the world, such as Mexico, South America, or the Caribbean. But many of them are American citizens, born in the United States.

Some of the male workers travel by themselves and return to their families after the harvest. Others travel with their families. Out of necessity, even their children work in the fields.

The constant work and moving about make it very difficult for the children to get to know a place or to make friends. In this story about Amelia, my hope is to show how one girl finds a favorite place.

Story Questions & Activities

1. What kind of work does Amelia's family do?
2. Why is Amelia unhappy about moving?
3. What makes the "accidental road" Amelia's special place? Explain.
4. In your own words, describe Amelia's problem in the story. Explain how she solves it.
5. How are Amelia and Luke in "The Lost Lake" like each other?

Write a Diary Entry

Think about a place that is special to you. Write a diary entry about the first time you went to that place. Be sure to explain how you felt while you were there.

Use a Product Map

Mrs. Martinez knows that Amelia was born in Yuba City, California. It must have been there because she remembers that her family was picking peaches. Where do crops grow in your state? Look at a product map. Make a list of the crops and the places where they grow.

Draw Your Dream House

Amelia drew the house that she would like to live in. Now it's your turn. Draw your own dream house and yard. Include all the features you would like your special house to have.

Find Out More

Amelia and her family were migrant farm workers. They picked different crops and moved from one harvest to another. What do you think life is like for Amelia's family? Start by looking up "migrant labor" in an encyclopedia. Use what you learn to list some problems that migrant farm workers and their families have.

Use a Glossary

Do you know what a *footpath* is? What are *shanties*? The writer of this story uses some words you may not know. For help, you can look up these words in the glossary.

The **glossary** is in the back of the book. It is like a small dictionary, but it contains only words from the stories. A glossary tells you how to pronounce a word. It also gives you the word's meaning as it is used in the story. Glossary words are listed in alphabetical order.

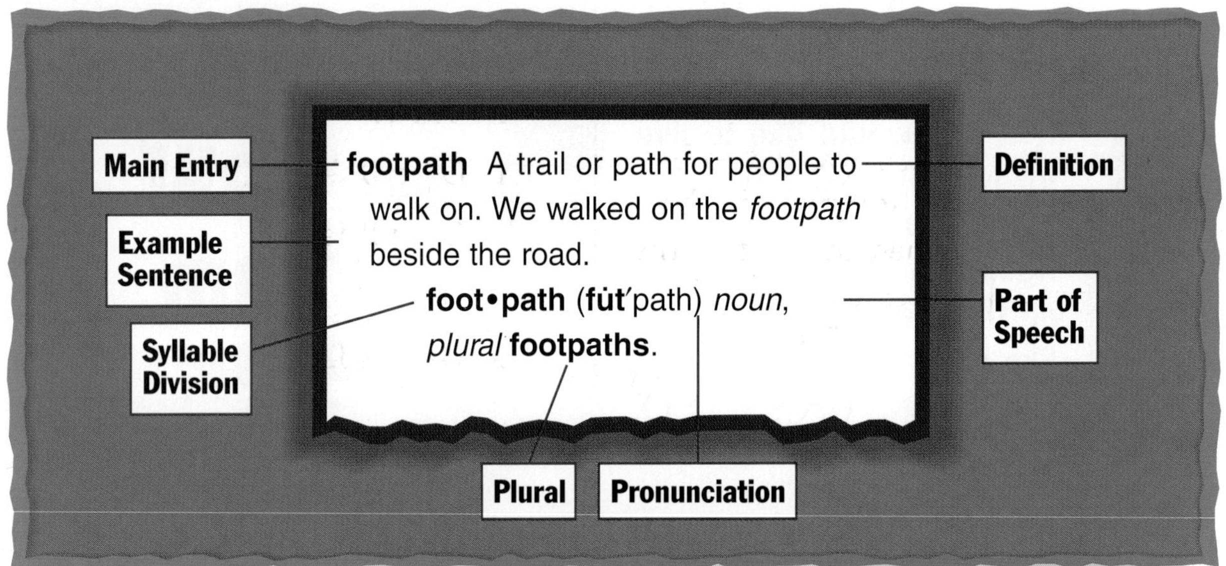

Use the sample glossary entry to answer these questions.

1. What is the meaning of *footpath*?
2. What part of speech is the word *footpath*?
3. Is the word *footpaths* singular or plural?
4. How many syllables does the word *footpath* have?
5. When would you use a glossary instead of a dictionary?

TEST POWER

Test Tip

Pay attention to short words. Question #2 asks which is *NOT* offered.

DIRECTIONS

Read the sample story. Then read each question about the story.

SAMPLE

A Day at the Fairgrounds

Kee and Lin jumped out of the car and ran across the parking lot. Each wanted to be first inside the fairgrounds, but first they stopped in front of the fairground poster to see what they wanted to do first.

Green County FAIR

Blue Rides: Cost $2
Roller Coaster
Giant Steps

Green Rides: Cost $1
Ferris Wheel
Fun House
Bumper Cars

You must be over three feet tall to go on the rides.

The last ride is at 5:30 P.M.

1 How tall must you be to go on the rides?

A Over 3 feet

B Over 2 feet

C Over 1 foot

D Over 4 feet

2 Which of these is NOT offered at the fairgrounds?

F Roller Coaster

G Giant Steps

H Fun House

J Horseback Riding

Every painting tells a story. Some things you see right away. Other things you have to figure out by studying the painting for a while.

Look at this setting and these people. How does the artist tell you about time? How do you think the people feel? Are they starting a new life? Why do you think so?

Imagine that you are inside this house. Is it fun to explore? Would you like living here? What would your life be like?

Admiring the New House
by Jane Wooster Scott
Living American Collection of Ed McMahon

FOR
SA
SOLD
Admiring the New House
© Wooster Scott

illustrated by Burton Silverman

Sarah, Plain and Tall

by Patricia MacLachlan

Anna and Caleb's mother died the day after Caleb was born. Papa and Anna miss Mama, and Caleb longs for a mother to love and care for him. When Papa decides to advertise for a wife, Sarah Elisabeth Wheaton answers the advertisement from Maine. After trading a few letters with Papa, Anna, and Caleb, Sarah decides to visit them in their prairie home for a month. She writes that they will recognize her at the train station because she is "plain and tall." Sarah brings Seal, her cat, and gifts from the ocean she loves so much. Papa, Caleb, and Anna wonder if Sarah will be content to stay and make her new home with them, so far from the sea.

The dandelions in the fields had gone by, their heads soft as feathers. The summer roses were opening.

Our neighbors, Matthew and Maggie, came to help Papa plow up a new field for corn. Sarah stood with us on the porch, watching their wagon wind up the road, two horses pulling it and one tied in back. I remembered the last time we had stood here alone, Caleb and I, waiting for Sarah.

Sarah's hair was in thick braids that circled her head, wild daisies tucked here and there. Papa had picked them for her.

Old Bess and Jack ran along the inside of the fence, whickering at the new horses.

"Papa needs five horses for the big gang plow," Caleb told Sarah. "Prairie grass is hard."

Matthew and Maggie came with their two children and a sackful of chickens. Maggie emptied the sack into the yard and three red banty chickens clucked and scattered.

"They are for you," she told Sarah. "For eating."

Sarah loved the chickens. She clucked back to them and fed them grain. They followed her, shuffling and scratching primly in the dirt. I knew they would not be for eating.

The children were young and named Rose and Violet, after flowers. They hooted and laughed and chased the chickens, who flew up to the porch roof, then the dogs, who crept quietly under the porch. Seal had long ago fled to the barn to sleep in cool hay.

Sarah and Maggie helped hitch the horses to the plow, then they set up a big table in the shade of the barn, covering it with a quilt and a kettle of flowers in the middle. They sat on the porch while Caleb and

Matthew and Papa began their morning of plowing. I mixed biscuit dough just inside the door, watching.

"You are lonely, yes?" asked Maggie in her soft voice.

Sarah's eyes filled with tears. Slowly I stirred the dough.

Maggie reached over and took Sarah's hand.

"I miss the hills of Tennessee sometimes," she said.

Do not miss the hills, Maggie, I thought.

"I miss the sea," said Sarah.

Do not miss the hills. Do not miss the sea.

I stirred and stirred the dough.

"I miss my brother William," said Sarah.

PAPA

"But he is married. The house is hers now. Not mine any longer. There are three old aunts who all squawk together like crows at dawn. I miss them, too."

"There are always things to miss," said Maggie. "No matter where you are."

I looked out and saw Papa and Matthew and Caleb working. Rose and Violet ran in the fields. I felt something brush my legs and looked down at Nick, wagging his tail.

"I would miss you, Nick," I whispered. "I would." I knelt down and scratched his ears. "I miss Mama."

"I nearly forgot," said Maggie on the porch. "I have something more for you."

I carried the bowl outside and watched Maggie lift a low wooden box out of the wagon.

"Plants," she said to Sarah. "For your garden."

"My garden?" Sarah bent down to touch the plants.

"Zinnias and marigolds and wild feverfew," said Maggie. "You must have a garden. Wherever you are."

Sarah smiled. "I had a garden in Maine with dahlias and columbine. And nasturtiums the color of the sun when it sets. I don't know if nasturtiums would grow here."

"Try," said Maggie. "You must have a garden."

We planted the flowers by the porch, turning over the soil and patting it around them, and watering. Lottie and Nick came to sniff, and the chickens walked in the dirt, leaving prints. In the fields, the horses pulled the plow up and down under the hot summer sun.

Maggie wiped her face, leaving a streak of dirt.

"Soon you can drive your wagon over to my house and I will give you more. I have tansy."

Sarah frowned. "I have never driven a wagon."

"I can teach you," said Maggie. "And so can Anna and Caleb. And Jacob."

Sarah turned to me.

"Can you?" she asked. "Can you drive a wagon?"

I nodded.

"And Caleb?"

"Yes."

"In Maine," said Sarah, "I would walk to town."

"Here it is different," said Maggie. "Here you will drive."

Way off in the sky, clouds gathered. Matthew and Papa and Caleb came in from the fields, their work done. We all ate in the shade.

"We are glad you are here," said Matthew to Sarah. "A new friend. Maggie misses her friends sometimes."

Sarah nodded. "There is always something to miss, no matter where you are," she said, smiling at Maggie.

Rose and Violet fell asleep in the grass, their bellies full of meat and greens and biscuits. And when it was time to go, Papa and Matthew lifted them into the wagon to sleep on blankets.

Sarah walked slowly behind the wagon for a long time, waving, watching it disappear. Caleb and I ran to bring her back, the chickens running wildly behind us.

"What shall we name them?" asked Sarah, laughing as the chickens followed us into the house.

I smiled. I was right. The chickens would not be for eating.

And then Papa came, just before the rain, bringing Sarah the first roses of summer.

The rain came and passed, but strange clouds hung in the northwest, low and black and green. And the air grew still.

In the morning, Sarah dressed in a pair of overalls and went to the barn to have an argument with Papa. She took apples for Old Bess and Jack.

"Women don't wear overalls," said Caleb, running along behind her like one of Sarah's chickens.

"This woman does," said Sarah crisply.

Papa stood by the fence.

"I want to learn how to ride a horse," Sarah told him. "And then I want to learn how to drive the wagon. By myself."

Jack leaned over and nipped at Sarah's overalls. She fed him an apple. Caleb and I stood behind Sarah.

"I can ride a horse, I know," said Sarah. "I rode once when I was twelve. I will ride Jack." Jack was Sarah's favorite.

Papa shook his head. "Not Jack," he said. "Jack is sly."

"I am sly, too," said Sarah stubbornly.

Papa smiled. "Ayuh," he said, nodding. "But not Jack."

"Yes, Jack!" Sarah's voice was very loud.

"I can teach you how to drive a wagon. I have already taught you how to plow."

"And then I can go to town. By myself."

"Say no, Papa," Caleb whispered beside me.

"That's a fair thing, Sarah," said Papa. "We'll practice."

A soft rumble of thunder sounded. Papa looked up at the clouds.

"Today? Can we begin today?" asked Sarah.

"Tomorrow is best," said Papa, looking worried. "I have to fix the house roof. A portion of it is loose. And there's a storm coming."

"We," said Sarah.

"What?" Papa turned.

"*We* will fix the roof," said Sarah. "I've done it before. I know about roofs. I am a good carpenter. Remember, I told you?"

There was thunder again, and Papa went to get the ladder.

"Are you fast?" he asked Sarah.

"I am fast and I am good," said Sarah. And they climbed the ladder to the roof, Sarah with wisps of hair around her face, her mouth full of nails, overalls like Papa's. Overalls that *were* Papa's.

Caleb and I went inside to close the windows. We could hear the steady sound of hammers pounding the roof overhead.

"Why does she want to go to town by herself?" asked Caleb. "To leave us?"

I shook my head, weary with Caleb's questions. Tears gathered at the corners of my eyes. But there was no time to cry, for suddenly Papa called out.

"Caleb! Anna!"

We ran outside and saw a huge cloud, horribly black, moving toward us over the north fields. Papa slid down the roof, helping Sarah after him.

"A squall!" he yelled to us. He held up his arms and Sarah jumped off the porch roof.

"Get the horses inside," he ordered Caleb. "Get the sheep, Anna. And the cows. The barn is safest."

The grasses flattened. There was a hiss of wind, a sudden pungent smell. Our faces looked yellow in the strange light. Caleb and I jumped over the fence and found the animals huddled by the barn. I counted the sheep to make sure they were all there, and herded them into a large stall. A few raindrops came, gentle at first, then stronger and louder, so that Caleb and I covered our ears and stared at each other without speaking. Caleb looked frightened and I tried to smile at him. Sarah

carried a sack into the barn, her hair wet and streaming down her neck. Papa came behind, Lottie and Nick with him, their ears flat against their heads.

"Wait!" cried Sarah. "My chickens!"

"No, Sarah!" Papa called after her. But Sarah had already run from the barn into a sheet of rain. My father followed her. The sheep nosed open their stall door and milled around the barn, bleating. Nick crept under my arm, and a lamb, Mattie with the black face, stood close to me, trembling. There was a soft paw on my lap, then a gray body. Seal. And then, as the thunder pounded and the wind rose and there was the terrible crackling of lightning close by, Sarah and Papa stood in the barn doorway, wet to the skin. Papa carried Sarah's chickens. Sarah came with an armful of summer roses.

CALEB

Sarah's chickens were not afraid, and they settled like small red bundles in the hay. Papa closed the door at last, shutting out some of the sounds of the storm. The barn was eerie and half lighted, like dusk without a lantern. Papa spread blankets around our shoulders and Sarah unpacked a bag of cheese and bread and jam. At the very bottom of the bag were Sarah's shells.

Caleb got up and went over to the small barn window.

"What color is the sea when it storms?" he asked Sarah.

"Blue," said Sarah, brushing her wet hair back with her fingers. "And gray and green."

Caleb nodded and smiled.

"Look," he said to her. "Look what is missing from your drawing."

Sarah went to stand between Caleb and Papa by the window. She looked a long time without speaking. Finally, she touched Papa's shoulder.

"We have squalls in Maine, too," she said. "Just like this. It will be all right, Jacob."

Papa said nothing. But he put his arm around her, and leaned over to rest his chin in her hair. I closed my eyes, suddenly remembering Mama and Papa standing that way, Mama smaller than Sarah, her hair fair against Papa's shoulder. When I opened my eyes again, it was Sarah standing there. Caleb looked at me and smiled and smiled until he could smile no more.

We slept in the hay all night, waking when the wind was wild, sleeping again when it was quiet. And at dawn there was the sudden sound of hail, like stones tossed against the barn. We stared out the window, watching the ice marbles bounce on the ground.

And when it was over we opened the barn door and walked out into the early-morning light. The hail crunched and melted beneath our feet. It was white and gleaming for as far as we looked, like sun on glass. Like the sea.

It was very quiet. The dogs leaned down to eat the hailstones. Seal stepped around them and leaped up on the fence to groom herself. A tree had blown over near the cow pond. And the wild roses were scattered on the ground, as if a wedding had come and gone there. "I'm glad I saved an armful" was all that Sarah said.

Only one field was badly damaged, and Sarah and Papa hitched up the horses and plowed and replanted during the next two days. The roof had held.

"I told you I know about roofs," Sarah told Papa, making him smile.

Papa kept his promise to Sarah. When the work was done, he took her out into the fields, Papa riding Jack who was sly, and Sarah riding Old Bess. Sarah was quick to learn.

"Too quick," Caleb complained to me as we watched from the fence. He thought a moment. "Maybe she'll fall off and have to stay here. Why?" he asked, turning to me. "Why does she have to go away alone?"

"Hush up, Caleb," I said crossly. "Hush up."

"I could get sick and make her stay here," said Caleb.

"No."

"We could tie her up."

"No."

And Caleb began to cry, and I took him inside the barn where we could both cry.

Papa and Sarah came to hitch the horses to the wagon, so Sarah could practice driving. Papa didn't see Caleb's tears, and he sent him with an ax to begin chopping up the tree by the pond for firewood. I stood and watched Sarah, the reins in her hands, Papa next to her in the wagon. I could see Caleb standing by the pond,

one hand shading his eyes, watching, too. I went into the safe darkness of the barn then, Sarah's chickens scuttling along behind me.

"Why?" I asked out loud, echoing Caleb's question.

The chickens watched me, their eyes small and bright.

The next morning Sarah got up early and put on her blue dress. She took apples to the barn. She loaded a bundle of hay on the wagon for Old Bess and Jack. She put on her yellow bonnet.

"Remember Jack," said Papa. "A strong hand."

"Yes, Jacob."

"Best to be home before dark," said Papa. "Driving a wagon is hard if there's no full moon."

"Yes, Jacob."

Sarah kissed us all, even my father, who looked surprised.

"Take care of Seal," she said to Caleb and me. And with a whisper to Old Bess and a stern word to Jack, Sarah climbed up in the wagon and drove away.

"Very good," murmured Papa as he watched. And after a while he turned and went out into the fields.

Caleb and I watched Sarah from the porch. Caleb took my hand, and the dogs lay down beside us. It was sunny, and I remembered another time when a wagon had taken Mama away. It had been a day just like this day. And Mama had never come back.

ANNA

Seal jumped up to the porch, her feet making a small thump. Caleb leaned down and picked her up and walked inside. I took the broom and slowly swept the porch. Then I watered Sarah's plants. Caleb cleaned out the wood stove and carried the ashes to the barn, spilling them so that I had to sweep the porch again.

"I *am* loud and pesky," Caleb cried suddenly. "You said so! And she has gone to buy a train ticket to go away!"

"No, Caleb. She would tell us."

"The house is too small," said Caleb. "That's what it is."

"The house is not too small," I said.

I looked at Sarah's drawing of the fields pinned up on the wall next to the window.

"What is missing?" I asked Caleb. "You said you knew what was missing."

"Colors," said Caleb wearily. "The colors of the sea."

Outside, clouds moved into the sky and went away again. We took lunch to Papa, cheese and bread and lemonade. Caleb nudged me.

"Ask him. Ask Papa."

"What has Sarah gone to do?" I asked.

"I don't know," said Papa. He squinted at me. Then he sighed and put one hand on Caleb's head, one on mine. "Sarah is Sarah. She does things her way, you know."

"I know," said Caleb very softly.

Papa picked up his shovel and put on his hat.

"Ask if she's coming back," whispered Caleb.

"Of course she's coming back," I said. "Seal is here." But I would not ask the question. I was afraid to hear the answer.

We fed the sheep, and I set the table for dinner. Four plates. The sun dropped low over the west fields. Lottie and Nick stood at the door, wagging their tails, asking for supper. Papa came to light the stove. And then it was dusk. Soon it would be dark. Caleb sat on the porch steps, turning his moon snail shell over and over in his hand. Seal brushed back and forth against him.

Suddenly Lottie began to bark, and Nick jumped off the porch and ran down the road.

"Dust!" cried Caleb. He climbed the porch and stood on the roof. "Dust, and a yellow bonnet!"

Slowly the wagon came around the windmill and the barn and the windbreak and into the yard, the dogs jumping happily beside it.

"Hush, dogs," said Sarah. And Nick leaped up into the wagon to sit by Sarah.

Papa took the reins and Sarah climbed down from the wagon.

Caleb burst into tears.

"Seal was very worried!" he cried.

Sarah put her arms around him, and he wailed into her dress. "And the house is too small, we thought! And I am loud and pesky!"

Sarah looked at Papa and me over Caleb's head.

"We thought you might be thinking of leaving us," I told her. "Because you miss the sea."

Sarah smiled.

"No," she said. "I will always miss my old home, but the truth of it is I would miss you more."

Papa smiled at Sarah, then he bent quickly to unhitch the horses from the wagon. He led them to the barn for water.

Sarah handed me a package.

"For Anna," she said. "And Caleb. For all of us."

The package was small, wrapped in brown paper with a rubber band around it. Very carefully I unwrapped it, Caleb peering closely. Inside were three colored pencils.

"Blue," said Caleb slowly, "and gray. And green."

Sarah nodded.

Suddenly Caleb grinned.

"Papa," he called. "Papa, come quickly! Sarah has brought the sea!"

We eat our night meal by candlelight, the four of us. Sarah has brought candles from town. And nasturtium seeds for her garden, and a book of songs to teach us. It is late, and Caleb is nearly sleeping by his plate and Sarah is smiling at my father. Soon there will be a wedding. Papa says that when the preacher asks if he will have Sarah for his wife, he will answer, "Ayuh."

Autumn will come, then winter, cold with a wind that blows like the wind off the sea in Maine. There will be nests of curls to look for, and dried flowers all winter long. When there are storms, Papa will stretch a rope from the door to the barn so we will not be lost when we feed the sheep and the cows and Jack and Old Bess. And Sarah's chickens, if they aren't living in the house. There will be Sarah's sea, blue and gray and green, hanging on the wall. And songs, old ones and new. And Seal with yellow eyes. And there will be Sarah, plain and tall.

Although Patricia MacLachlan did not write as a child, she made up stories in her head. She imagined kings and queens, heroes and villains. When MacLachlan became an adult, kings and queens no longer captured her imagination. Instead, her children and the relatives she had known and heard about as a child became models for her characters.

MacLachlan becomes old friends with the people in her stories before she begins to write. "I . . . have all sorts of conversations with myself and with characters I make up. . . . I talk with characters in the car, over a sink full of dishes, in the garden."

MacLachlan's story ideas may begin with people, but she also thinks a lot about the setting. Because she was born in Wyoming and raised in Minnesota, she says, "the western landscape has always been a powerful force in my life."

In the Newbery Award-winning story *Sarah, Plain and Tall*, character and place cannot be separated. Sarah, a mail-order bride—like one of MacLachlan's distant relatives—leaves her home on the eastern seacoast to begin a new life in the West. To the prairie she brings her love of Maine and her longing for the sea.

Other books by MacLachlan that you might enjoy are *The Facts and Fictions of Minna Pratt* and *Arthur, for the Very First Time.*

Story Questions & Activities

1. Who are the main characters in the story?
2. Why does Sarah miss Maine so much?
3. What makes you think that Sarah is adventurous? Explain.
4. How would you sum up the events in this story?
5. Compare the work done by Anna and Caleb's father with the work done by Amelia's father in "Amelia's Road." How is the work alike? What makes it different?

Write a Letter

Have you ever been caught in a storm? Write a letter to a friend about a time when the weather turned bad. Be sure to describe how you felt before, during, and after the storm. Use the correct form for writing a friendly letter.

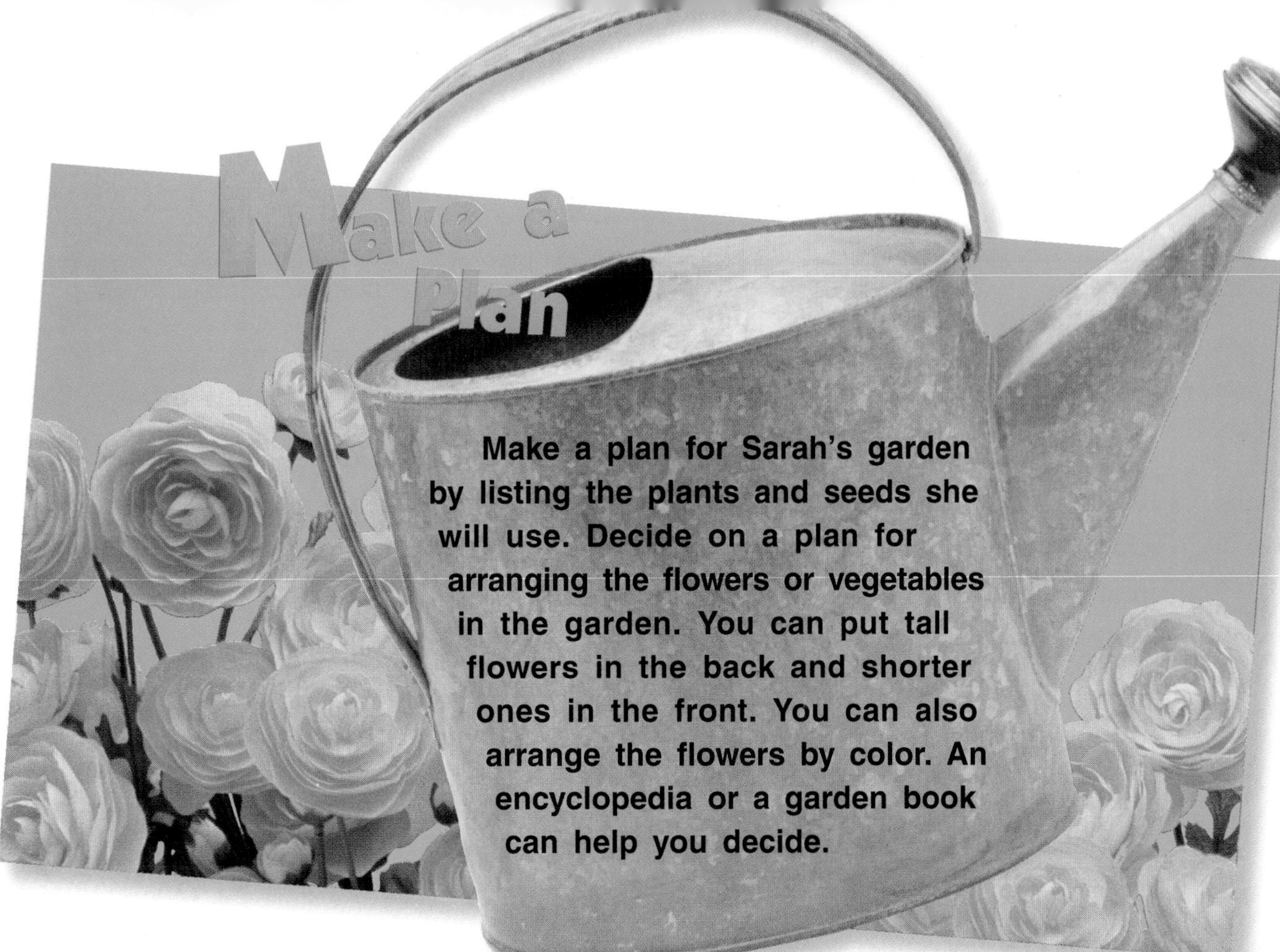

Make a Plan

Make a plan for Sarah's garden by listing the plants and seeds she will use. Decide on a plan for arranging the flowers or vegetables in the garden. You can put tall flowers in the back and shorter ones in the front. You can also arrange the flowers by color. An encyclopedia or a garden book can help you decide.

Paint a Picture

Many famous artists have painted the sea. Find a picture of the sea that you like. Then paint your own picture. Use watercolors to show the water. Give your painting a title, and sign it in one corner.

Find Out More

When a bad storm comes, the family members in the story have to stay in the barn until the storm passes. Use an encyclopedia or a science book to find out how a thunderstorm forms. Make a diagram of what you discover.

Use a Table of Contents and Headings

"Sarah, Plain and Tall" is one selection in a much longer book. Longer books often have different parts. The **table of contents** is one of these parts. It lists the name of each unit, chapter, selection, and article. It also tells the page on which these begin. A chapter may be divided into sections. Each of these sections may begin with a heading. A **heading** is like a title. It tells what the section is about.

Page Number

TABLE OF CONTENTS

Chapter Number

Chapter Title

Chapter 4

RECREATION

Heading

The Maine Coast

Maine has many miles of coastline. It has both sandy and rocky beaches. The coast of Maine is beautiful. It attracts photographers, painters, and people who just want to see the scenery.

Winter Sports — Heading

Maine has nearly 60 ski areas. Each year, thousands of people travel from all over the country to take advantage of the beautiful slopes. Even when weather

Use the table of contents and chapter headings to answer these questions.

1. How many chapters are there in the book?
2. What is the title of Chapter 2?
3. On what page does Chapter 3 begin?
4. What is the first part of Chapter 4 about?
5. Why would you check the table of contents before reading a book?

TEST POWER

Test Tip

Check your understanding as you read the story.

DIRECTIONS

Read the sample story. Then read each question about the story.

SAMPLE

Whales

The largest creature on land or in the ocean is the blue whale. The blue whale can weigh up to 150 tons and can be 100 feet long. Although a newborn whale already weighs about 1.8 tons, it will double its weight within its first week.

Whales live in the ocean, but they are not fish. Like humans, whales are mammals. Whales breathe air through lungs, give birth to live young rather than lay eggs, and are warmblooded.

A whale breathes through its "blowhole," two nostrils at the top of its head. Some whales can stay underwater for two hours before they need more air.

1 How large can a blue whale become?

A 1.8 tons

B 100 tons

C 150 tons

D 2 tons

2 Which is a **FACT** from the story?

F Whales eat fish.

G A whale is not a fish.

H A whale can weigh up to 550 tons.

J Whales are the smallest creatures on Earth.

Like stories or essays, a work of art can have a main idea and details that support it.

Look at this early American quilt. What do you see? What story might the quilt be telling? What does it say about a place and its people? What is the story's main idea?

Look at each of the squares in the quilt. How does each square add a detail to the story being told in the quilt? If you could step into one of the squares, which square would you choose? Why?

***Burdick-Childs Family Quilt*, 1876**
The Shelburne Museum, Shelburne, VT

MEET
Richard and Jonah Sobol

Richard Sobol followed the battle to end the seal hunt for many years. On a trip to Canada, bad weather kept him from photographing the seals. He knew he would return.

On his next trip, Sobol took along his son Jonah. They spent a day on the ice with the seals. Jonah had many thoughts and questions. These ideas formed the heart of *Seal Journey.*

Sobol also created a book for children about the African elephant. He hopes his books will help children respect wildlife.

SEAL JOURNEY

by Richard and Jonah Sobol ▪ photographs by Richard Sobol

The life cycle of the harp seal is one of the great wonders of nature. Each autumn the seals begin a remarkable journey that carries them over three thousand miles. At a steady flow throughout the winter months, hundreds of thousands of mature harp seals swim through iceberg-filled waters from their summer homes in the northwest Atlantic, just below the North Pole, to the solid ice packs in the Gulf of St. Lawrence in eastern Canada. Once they reach the great sheets of winter ice, each female harp seal will claim her own space on which to give birth to a single pup. Thousands upon thousands of harp seal pups, more than anyone could ever count, are born and nurtured here each spring, transforming this frozen wilderness into a vast nursery.

At the same time a second breeding population gathers on pack ice in the Barents Sea off the northern coast of Russia, while a third and smaller group comes together east of Greenland.

This year I had come to Charlottetown, Prince Edward Island, which is used as a base camp for scientists to observe the newborn harp seal pups. This was the third time that I had made this journey on assignment for a French photo agency. The first trip had been in 1981 when I set out to show the cruelty of the seal hunt that was then taking place. Now I was here to tell the story of the seals' survival and to photograph the beginnings of life out on the ice.

My eight-year-old son, Jonah, had been dreaming of seeing the seals, and I invited him to come along with me. "Can I really come with you?" he said in disbelief when I first asked. After that his questions were endless. "Will I get to see newborn seals?" "How cold will it be?" "How will we get onto the ice?" I answered as many questions as I could until finally I assured him that the best answers would come from his own observations out on the ice.

The seal colony was located about a hundred miles north of Prince Edward Island and the only way to reach it was by helicopter. Jonah sat in the front next to the pilot. After we took off, the pilot held up his map, showing Jonah the spot where we would find the

seals. The map, though, showed an ocean of blue, not miles and miles of white jagged ice, looking like a moonscape, that we had been flying over all this March morning. The snow-covered farmlands of Prince Edward Island had quickly faded from view. We now flew over wide swatches of packed ice sandwiched between small strips of open water. Searching the horizon, we eagerly waited for our first glimpse of the seals. The pilot smiled as he pointed outside and said, "Look down now, there they are. The seals have returned once again." Below us tiny brown specks dotted

the ice, first a few, then more and more, looking like chocolate sprinkles scattered on top of a huge bowl of vanilla ice cream.

As soon as we stepped out of the helicopter, we could hear the soft cries of hungry newborn pups. These were the only sounds that drifted through the stillness of this frozen landscape. It was springtime but the air was very cold—five degrees below zero. The wind bit into our skin. As we walked toward the seals, the snow swished and swirled under our clunky survival boots. We were careful to avoid the smooth round holes in the ice—bobbing holes—that the mother seals dive in and out of to return to the water to feed on small shrimp or fish, or just to swim.

Seals are great swimmers but, like other mammals, they require air to breathe. They are able to hold their breaths for long periods of time and dive deep into the water. Every few minutes they pop up through bobbing holes onto the ice to fill their lungs with air and to check on their pups.

As we walked closer to a small group of seals, we heard a sharp, deep cry, like a cat screeching in the night. We climbed along a large ridge of ice to get a better look. Up ahead, we spotted a female seal twisting one way,

then another, again and again. There was a sense of great excitement in her movements and cries. Jonah tugged at my sleeve and pointed to a newborn pup, only minutes old, that was lying beside the mother seal. It was still wet and yellow from its birth.

He did not look at all like the cuddly white ball of fur that we were expecting. It will take a day or two in the sun for this birth-stained scraggle to be transformed into a lush baby known as a "whitecoat." Jonah said he felt sorry for the tiny pup, outside on frozen ice, having just left the warmth of his mother's womb. Now, as the steam rose up from his scruffy, gooey coat the mother moved closer to him, to reassure him and share her warmth. As they nestled together in the warm glow of the sunlight, it was easy to see the dark markings on the mother seal's back. They were indeed the familiar curves of a harp, the musical instrument for which these seals are named.

To survive in this new world, harp seal pups are born with a small amount of baby fat which they immediately start to burn in order to give their bodies heat. But, they need their mothers' milk to grow the thick layer of blubber that will continue to protect them from the deep freeze that they are born into. We watched with wonder as the mother rolled onto her side, and the pup slid up toward her searching for the milk. The pup lay perfectly still, nursing without a break for ten minutes, as he would need to do five or six times each day.

The mother seals' milk is ten times richer than either cows' or humans' milk, and a well-fed pup will grow from twenty pounds at birth to almost eighty pounds by the time he is weaned at twelve days old.

Before the pup finished nursing, the mother rubbed noses with him. This "kiss of recognition" was her way of familiarizing herself with the smell of her pup. A mother seal is often surrounded by dozens of pups and she must be able to identify her own by its unique scent or it will not survive. She has only enough milk for one pup and she will only nurse her very own.

A few feet away we saw what appeared to be a mother seal giving her pup a swimming lesson. The mother nudged him toward the water, while the pup squealed and squealed. And then the pup was in the water, floating and bobbing like a little cork. The pup had so much fat that he couldn't sink. "It's like he is wearing a life jacket," Jonah said, as the mother jumped in the water too. It was almost as if they were playing a game of tag. First the mother disappeared under the water. A few seconds later, she popped up in a different place. The pup squirmed and paddled to catch up to her. Then they rubbed noses.

Pups have to learn to swim well. Their home for most of the remainder of their lives is in the water, since harp seals spend only

four to six weeks a year on the ice. By the time the pup is two weeks old, it is weaned from its mother's milk and has to find its own food in the chilly waters of the Atlantic. The weaning is sudden—without any warning, the mother slides into the water between nursings as she normally does, only this time she leaves forever, never to return to her pup. The two of them will always be part of the same seal herd, but the pup must quickly adjust to life on its own.

While the pups are being born and nursed, the males keep their distance, gathering in groups around breaks of open water. Once the pups are weaned, the female harp seals join the males for mating. The complete cycle of birth, nursing, and mating takes place in about two weeks, incredibly fast for such a large animal.

In April when the ice melts and breaks up, the entire seal colony will join together again to journey back north to their summer feeding grounds in the Arctic seas. The young pups, having lost their fine white coats by now, will straggle behind the main herd, feeding as they go on small shrimp. As they grow stronger and their swimming skills improve, they will be able to dive and catch small fish to add to their diet. When fully grown, these harp seals will weigh up to three hundred pounds.

Home for the pups for the next few years will be in the North Atlantic feeding grounds, just below the Arctic Circle. The pups will feed, grow, and develop their swimming skills until they are old enough to mate. In their fifth or sixth year of life, when autumn comes, they will know that it is their time to join the mature seals on the long swim south. Together, they will return to the ice where they were born. By the time that their lives come to an end, some twenty-five years later, most harp seals will have travelled over 75,000 miles, round and round through the ocean.

Jonah and I saw hundreds of seals. We spent hours and hours exploring on the ice. The sky grew dark in the late afternoon, and the pilots started warming the helicopter engines. Our day would soon be over. But there was still one thing Jonah wanted to do. "Dad," he said in a quiet voice, "could I please hold one seal before we go?"

We should have headed toward our helicopter, but instead, we walked in the other direction, over the long sloping ice ridge, in search of a friendly pup. There we found her—a beautiful whitecoat, round and contented with her first week of life. Slowly, Jonah approached her. When he was close he lay down to pet her. I went over and picked the seal up and placed her on Jonah's lap. "I can feel her breathing," Jonah said through the wide smile that now covered his face. "Her whiskers tickle and the soft white fur is like a warm blanket covering me."

It is sad to think that this same fur was what the hunters were seeking when they stalked the ice to slaughter these seals. The fur that they stripped from the whitecoats was turned into slippers, gloves, and even dolls. For twenty years people who cared about saving seals came out onto the ice to challenge

the hunters and to make them stop. They let people throughout the world know about this cruelty and asked them not to buy anything made from seal fur. As more people knew what was happening to the seal pups they joined together and stopped buying seal products. The hunters had no place to sell the fur. Only then did the killing stop here. In other places though, some seal hunting does continue, as hunters still stain the ice with the blood of these lovely animals. These harp seal pups, born in the Gulf of St. Lawrence, are the lucky ones. Now protected by laws, for the first time in hundreds of years this seal nursery is filled only with the cries of the hungry pups and not the thuds of the hunters' clubs.

It was now time to go. Jonah gently put the seal back down and gave her a soft pat. As he walked away he turned back toward her for one final look.

"Good-bye, seal," he said. "Now I know that dreams can come true."

As we flew back toward Prince Edward Island and looked down at the ice, its sharp edges began to soften and the harsh white glare turned into water-color splashes of pink and gray in the fading light. Soon the ice will melt and the seals will return north. During the hot summer months people will be sailing and swimming in this same wide channel. Next winter the ice will form again, calling the harp seals back. The magic of nature will bring more people here, too. Each year more and more adventurous tourists are journeying out onto the ice to experience the beauty of the seals. During these few short weeks people and seals can bring their worlds together. Somehow these seals seem to know that the people they encounter now are their protectors and there is no need to be afraid. This is how it should be.

More Seal Facts

Harp seals belong to the mammal group called pinnipeds. Pinnipeds are divided into three families:

Family Otariidae, which includes fur seals and sea lions, also known as "eared seals."

Family Odobenidae, which includes the walrus.

Family Phocidae, which includes all true seals.

True seals are monk seals, elephant seals, Antarctic seals, and northern true seals. They have rear flippers that extend behind their bodies. They are also known as "earless seals." The openings to their ears are small holes on the sides of their heads.

Harp seals are classified as northern true seals and their scientific name is *Phoca groenlandicus.*
Average adult weight—300 pounds
Average adult length—5 1/2 feet
Average lifespan—30 years

Harp seals live in three areas in the North Atlantic—the east coast of Canada near Newfoundland, in the White Sea off the coast of Russia, and between Yan Mayan and Svalbard, east of Greenland. Estimates of world population today vary from 2.25 million to 3.5 million.

Sea Lion

Walrus

Elephant Seal

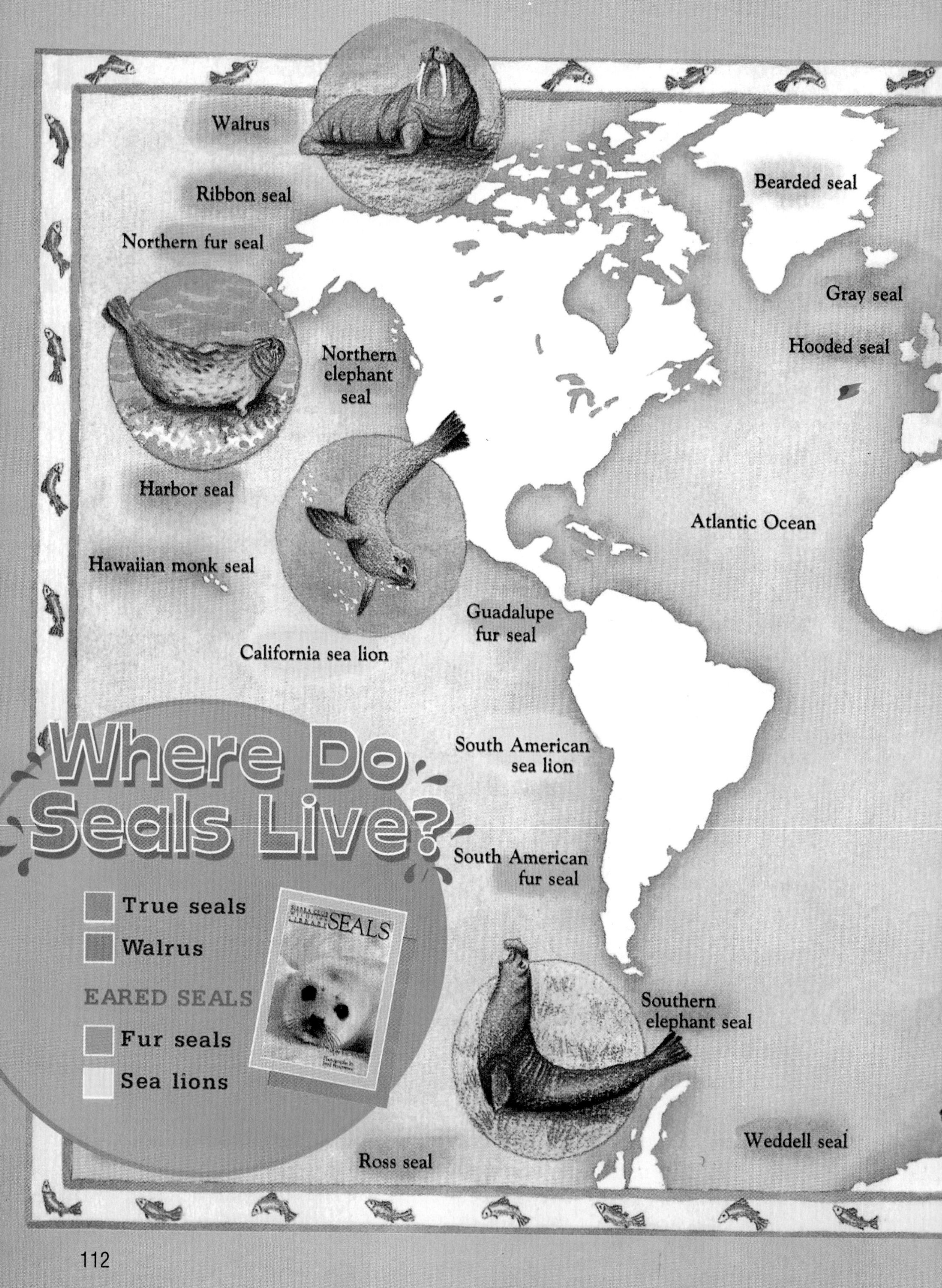
Walrus
Ribbon seal
Northern fur seal
Bearded seal
Gray seal
Hooded seal
Northern elephant seal
Harbor seal
Atlantic Ocean
Hawaiian monk seal
Guadalupe fur seal
California sea lion
South American sea lion
South American fur seal
Southern elephant seal
Weddell seal
Ross seal
Where Do Seals Live?
True seals
Walrus
EARED SEALS
Fur seals
Sea lions
SEALS

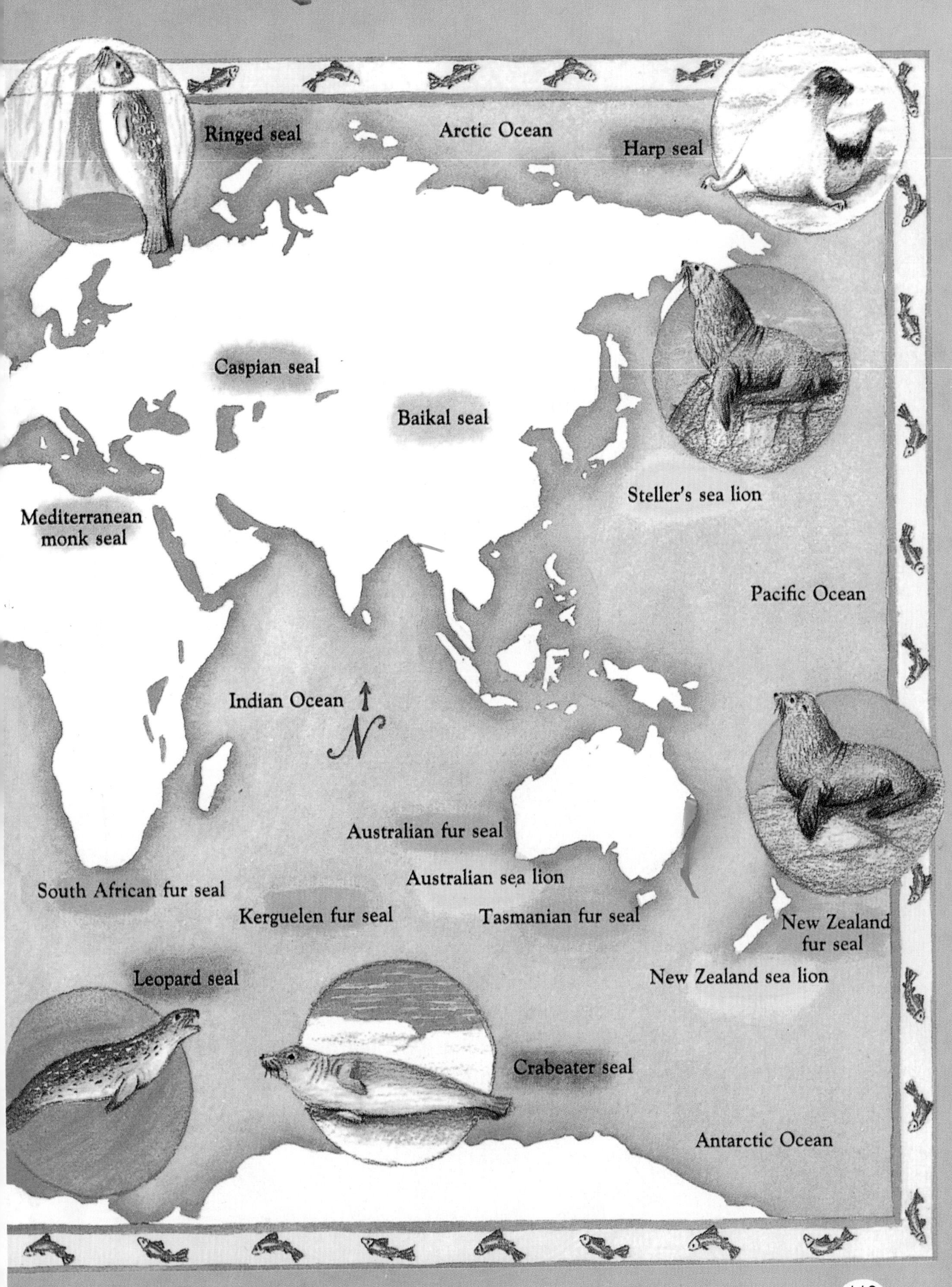

Ringed seal
Arctic Ocean
Harp seal
Caspian seal
Baikal seal
Steller's sea lion
Mediterranean monk seal
Pacific Ocean
Indian Ocean
N
Australian fur seal
Australian sea lion
South African fur seal
Kerguelen fur seal
Tasmanian fur seal
New Zealand fur seal
New Zealand sea lion
Leopard seal
Crabeater seal
Antarctic Ocean

Story Questions & Activities

1. Why do Jonah and his father go to Canada?
2. How have the seals' lives improved since 1981?
3. How do the photographs give more information?
4. What is the main idea of this selection?
5. What do Jonah and Luke in "The Lost Lake" have in common? Explain your answer.

Write a Photo Essay

Jonah and his dad took a trip to see seals. Write about a trip you have taken. Describe where you went, what you did, and what you learned. Tell about events in order. Attach photos if you have them, or draw illustrations.

Make a Poster

Every year, animal lovers gather to protest the hunting of baby seals for their fur. Make a poster to support their cause. Write a "catchy" slogan that will attract people's attention.

Read a Map

Use a map of Canada to find the place where Jonah and his father went to see the harp seals. To find the place, use the map's scale. Remember: It was about one hundred miles north of Prince Edward Island. Tell a partner what you think this place in Canada is like.

Find Out More

Jonah and his father went to Canada to learn more about harp seals. Choose a wild animal you would like to know more about. The animal might be a whale, a tiger, or a bear, for example. Look in an encyclopedia or a library book to find out about the animal's life, home, and habits.

Use an Index

Suppose that you are reading a library book for a report about seals. You don't have much time, and you really want to know about one kind of seal—the harp seal. Where would you look in the book to find information quickly? You would look in the index.

The **index** is at the back of a book. It lists all the book's topics in alphabetical order. Next to each topic are the page numbers on which you will find information about your topic.

Use the sample index to answer these questions.

1. On which pages would you find information about harp seals?
2. Where would you look to find out what a *whitecoat* is?
3. On which page would you find information about Greenland?
4. On which pages might you find information on how to travel to see the harp seals?
5. How can an index help you find information quickly?

TEST POWER

Test Tip

Always read the directions carefully.

DIRECTIONS

Read the sample story. Then read each question about the story.

SAMPLE

Jim's Big Decision

Jim knew very little about raising tropical fish. But his friend Manny said he had been studying about them.

"Tropical fish live in a warmer climate than most other fish," Manny noted. "That's why you have to keep the water in their tank at a higher temperature."

"That makes sense," Jim said. He was afraid that caring for fish was going to be more complicated than he thought. He wasn't really sure if fish were the right pets for him to have.

"I can lend you the book I have," Manny said. He could see that Jim was unsure about getting a fish.

1 What is the main idea of the second paragraph?

A The water is warm.

B Manny has a book about fish.

C Jim wants a fish.

D Tropical fish need to live in a warm climate.

2 According to the story, why was Jim unsure about getting a fish?

F He really wanted a dog.

G He knew very little about them.

H He didn't like fish.

J He didn't know how to read.

When you first look at this Japanese painting you might see a fierce tiger. If you look again, you might see a landscape and crashing waves.

Look at this painting. What details do you notice about the tiger? Is the tiger ready to spring? If so, what problem could it bring to the land? To the people? How could the people solve the problem? Notice the waves. How could the rising water cause a problem?

Look at the painting again. How does it make you feel? Explain why.

Tiger
by Kishi Ganku, c. 1784
E. A. Barton Collection, England

岸駒

TIME FOR KIDS

SPECIAL REPORT

Open Wide, Don't Bite!

It Won't Hurt, Honest!

Meet a dentist who fixes sore fangs and tusks

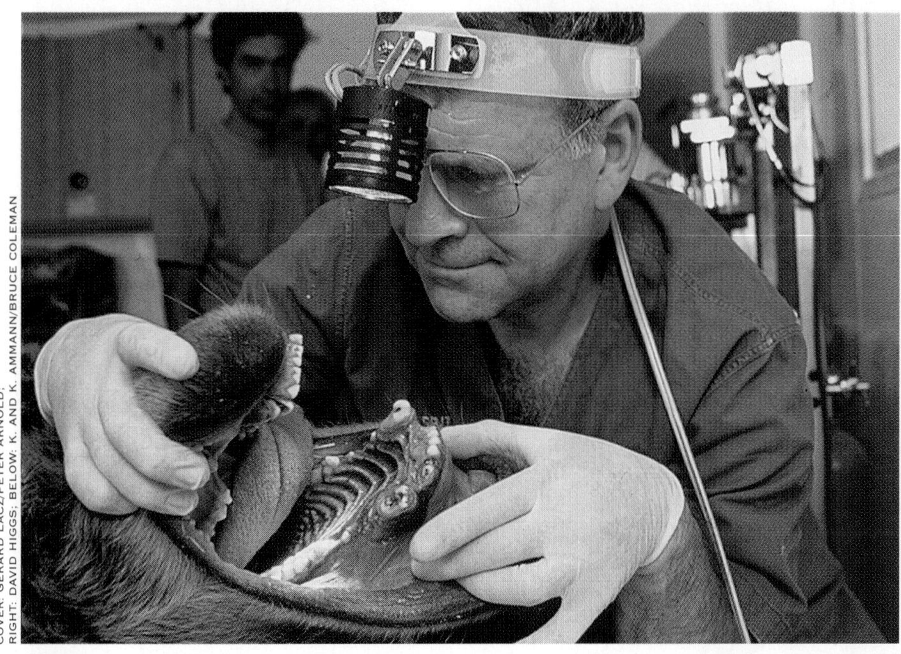

COVER: GERARD LACZ/PETER ARNOLD; RIGHT: DAVID HIGGS; BELOW: K. AND K. AMMANN/BRUCE COLEMAN

Dr. Peter Kertesz examines a former dancing bear named Mitsos.

Dentist Peter Kertesz of London, England, has the wildest patients in the world. On Fridays, after a week of treating humans, Dr. Kertesz sees four-legged patients. And almost every one of them has *very* large teeth.

Kertesz belongs to a rare breed of dentists who treat animals, from aardvarks to zebras.

It all started when an animal doctor called the dentist to pull teeth from a housecat. Kertesz agreed to pull the cat's teeth. Soon he was taking on bigger cats—like lions, tigers, and jaguars.

The dentist didn't stop there, however. He went on to elephants (which have molars the size of bricks), camels, bears, monkeys, wolves, and even whales. He has treated about 50 kinds of animals in all. The dentist gives the animals medicine to keep them calm and pain-free.

When apes pull back their lips, they're smiling.

Hand-holding calms this gorilla when it visits the dentist.

RIGHT AND FAR RIGHT: DAVID HIGGS; OPPOSITE PAGE: GEORGE LEPP/CORBIS

Dr. Kertesz shows off his dental equipment.

DID YOU KNOW? SINK YOUR TEETH INTO THESE FACTS

- Reptiles lose and replace their teeth all the time.
- Vegetable-eating animals, such as elephants, giraffes, and sheep, have very broad, flat teeth. They use their teeth to mash up the plants they eat.
- Meat-eating animals (lions, tigers, and wolves) have long, pointed teeth. The sharp teeth make it easier for them to bite into their food.
- Cats and dogs have both kinds of teeth: sharp ones to bite into food and flat ones to crush or grind it.
- Rats' and beavers' teeth are always growing. Since they are always chewing on something, their teeth stay filed down to just the right size.
- Elephants grow six separate sets of teeth between birth and age 60.

Kertesz says that large animals are the easiest patients to work with. That's because there is so much room in their mouths. The toughest patients: insect-eating aardvarks. Their mouths may be long, but they open only about an inch wide.

LIONS AND TIGERS AND BEARS . . . OH MY!

Kertesz has taken his dental skills to many countries. Most of his work is done for zoos. Circuses and animal hospitals also call on him. Kertesz has worked on Siberian tigers in Russia, an elephant in Spain, and a gorilla, a jaguar, badgers, deer, and foxes in England.

One bad tooth can keep a beast from hunting, eating, and even mating. Take a tiger, for example. It's one of the hungriest, meanest cats in the jungle—until it breaks a fang. This can mean big trouble. If a tiger can't eat, it will become weak and may become someone else's dinner.

Kertesz's dental work helps animals live longer and healthier lives. Even zoo animals, which are safer than animals in the wild, need healthy mouths. After all, diseases can start in the teeth or gums and spread throughout an animal's body. (And that's the whole "tooth"!)

The mountain lion's sharp teeth help it eat other animals.

FIND OUT MORE
Visit our website:
www.mhschool.com/reading

*inter***NET** **CONNECTION**

Based on an article in *TIME FOR KIDS.*

Story Questions & Activities

1. What unusual work does Dr. Peter Kertesz do?
2. Why would animals need a dentist?
3. What kinds of problems does Dr. Kertesz have to solve in order to do his work?
4. What is the main idea of this article?
5. Suppose that Dr. Kertesz met Dr. Dolittle. Dr. Dolittle is the doctor in books and movies who talks to the animals. What do you think the two men would say to each other? Why might Dr. Kertesz envy Dr. Dolittle's ability to understand animals?

Write About an Experience

Dr. Kertesz has had many interesting experiences with animals. Write about an experience you have had with an animal. Give details about what happened. Include how you felt about the experience.

Create a Job Box

Dr. Kertesz is a trained dentist who works on people as well as on animals. How does someone become a dentist? What does a dentist do? Interview your dentist, or invite a dentist to speak to your class. Then create a job box with a group of other students. Use an index card to write a description of a dentist's job and training. Put the card in the box. Add other job descriptions as you read about them.

Draw a Poster

Everyone needs a good dentist. Draw a poster for an advertisement. Urge people and their pets to visit the dentist regularly. Look back at the article to get ideas for your ad.

Find Out More

Some of Dr. Kertesz's patients live in zoos. What are zoos like today? Start by visiting a local zoo to see how the animals live. If that isn't possible, use an encyclopedia, a video, or a book to learn more about modern zoos. Share what you learn with your classmates.

Use Headings, Captions, and Sidebars

Hippos and dancing bears aren't the only ones who need to take care of their teeth. Look at this page from a book on dental health. Notice how the information is organized. **Headings** help you find information. **Captions** and **sidebars** contain additional facts.

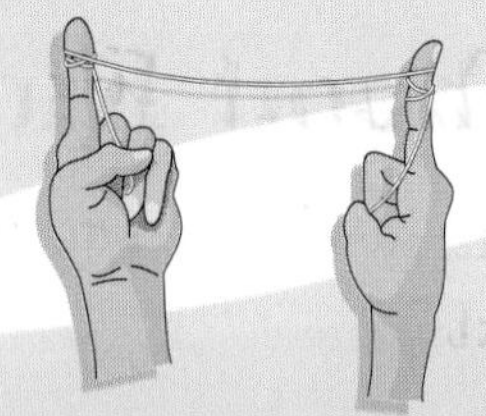

Use an 18-inch piece of floss. Wrap the ends around one finger on each hand.

Cleaning Your Teeth

If possible, brush teeth after every meal. Floss between and around your teeth once a day.

How to Brush Your Teeth

1. Use a soft toothbrush.
2. Angle the brush against your teeth.

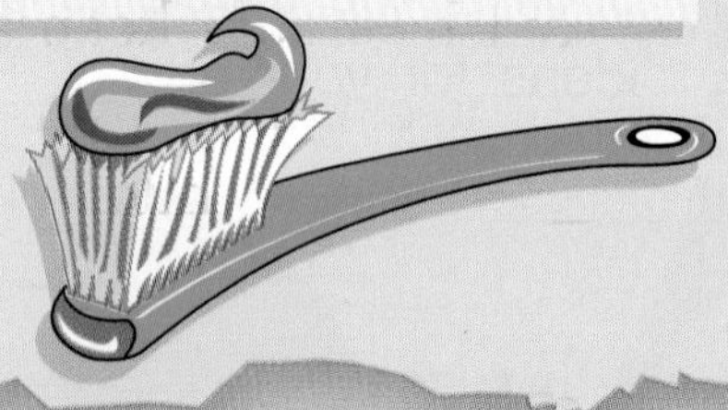

Use the sample page to answer these questions.

1. How many steps are listed for brushing your teeth?
2. How many headings are on this page? What are they?
3. Look at the drawing and read the caption. What additional information does the caption give you?
4. Why is information on brushing teeth in a sidebar?
5. How do headings, captions, and sidebars make reading easier?

TEST POWER

Test Tip

Put the passage in your own words.

DIRECTIONS

Read the sample story. Then read each question about the story.

SAMPLE

Attention: Neighborhood Kids

Mr. Kim needed assistance in fixing up his house. He offered neighborhood children a chance to complete chores and to earn points toward an outing. Mr. Kim said he would keep a record of the number of points <u>accumulated</u> by each child.

POSSIBLE OUTINGS:

The Beach:	90 points
The Fair:	60 points
The Theater:	40 points

POSSIBLE CHORES:

Wash Windows:	25 points
Paint Garage:	90 points
Paint Porch:	35 points

Kids can share chores and points. Three kids can go on each trip.

1 What is the story mostly about?

A How kids can share points

B How to go to the beach

C How Mr. Kim finds helpers for his chores

D How to wash the porch

2 In this story the word <u>accumulated</u> means—

F wanted

G earned

H asked for

J finished

Why are these answers the best choices? Give reasons.

I Ask My Mother to Sing

She begins, and my grandmother joins her.
Mother and daughter sing like young girls.
If my father were alive, he would play
his accordion and sway like a boat.

I've never been in Peking, or the Summer Palace,
nor stood on the great Stone Boat to watch
the rain begin on Kuen Ming Lake, the picnickers
running away in the grass.

But I love to hear it sung;
how the waterlilies fill with rain until
they overturn, spilling water into water,
then rock back, and fill with more.

Both women have begun to cry.
But neither stops her song.

by Li-Young Lee

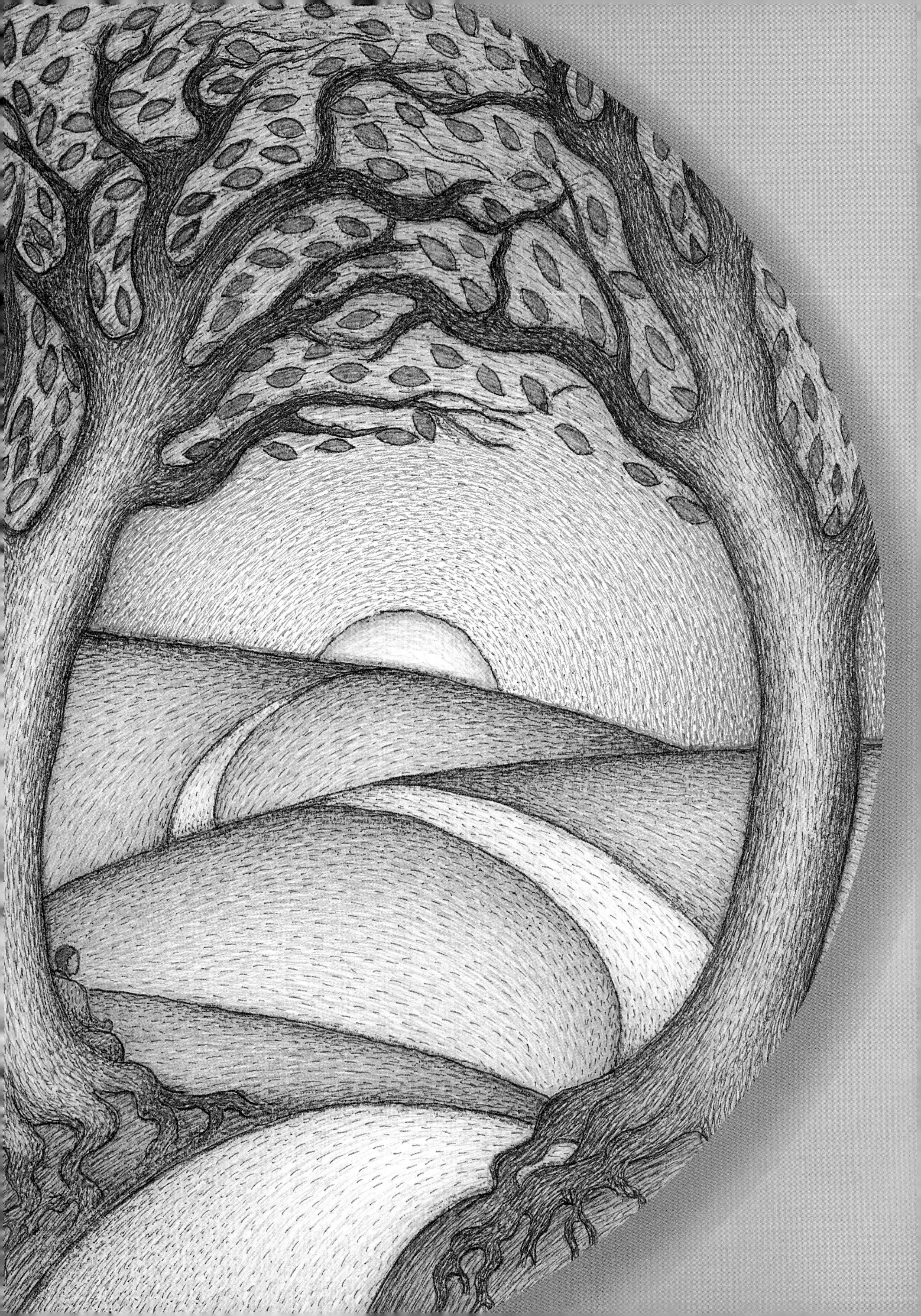

UNIT 2

Something in Common

The Arrow and the Song

I shot an arrow into the air,
It fell to earth, I knew not where;
For, so swiftly it flew, the sight
Could not follow it in its flight.

I breathed a song into the air,
It fell to earth, I knew not where;
For who has sight so keen and strong,
That it can follow the flight of song?

Long, long afterward, in an oak
I found the arrow, still unbroke;
And the song, from beginning to end,
I found again in the heart of a friend.

by Henry Wadsworth Longfellow

Stories in Art

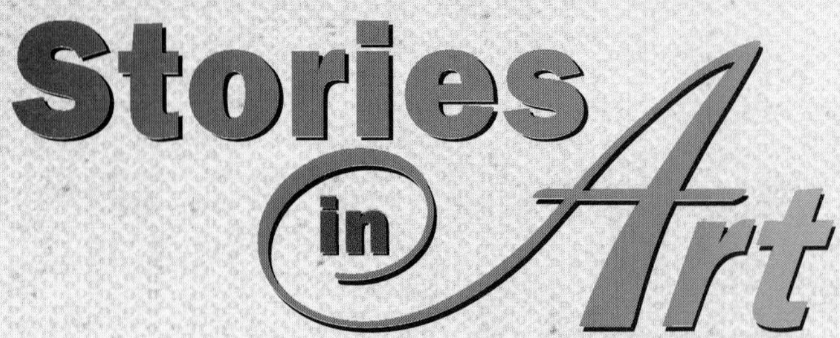

Some artists work with cloth and colored yarn instead of paint. They are called textile artists.

Look at this Navajo rug. What details do you notice? How do these details describe life in a Navajo village?

Look at this rug again. How can you tell that weaving wool is important to the Navajo way of life? What do you think will happen to the wool on the sheep? Notice the car near the center. Do you think it will change life in this Navajo village? How?

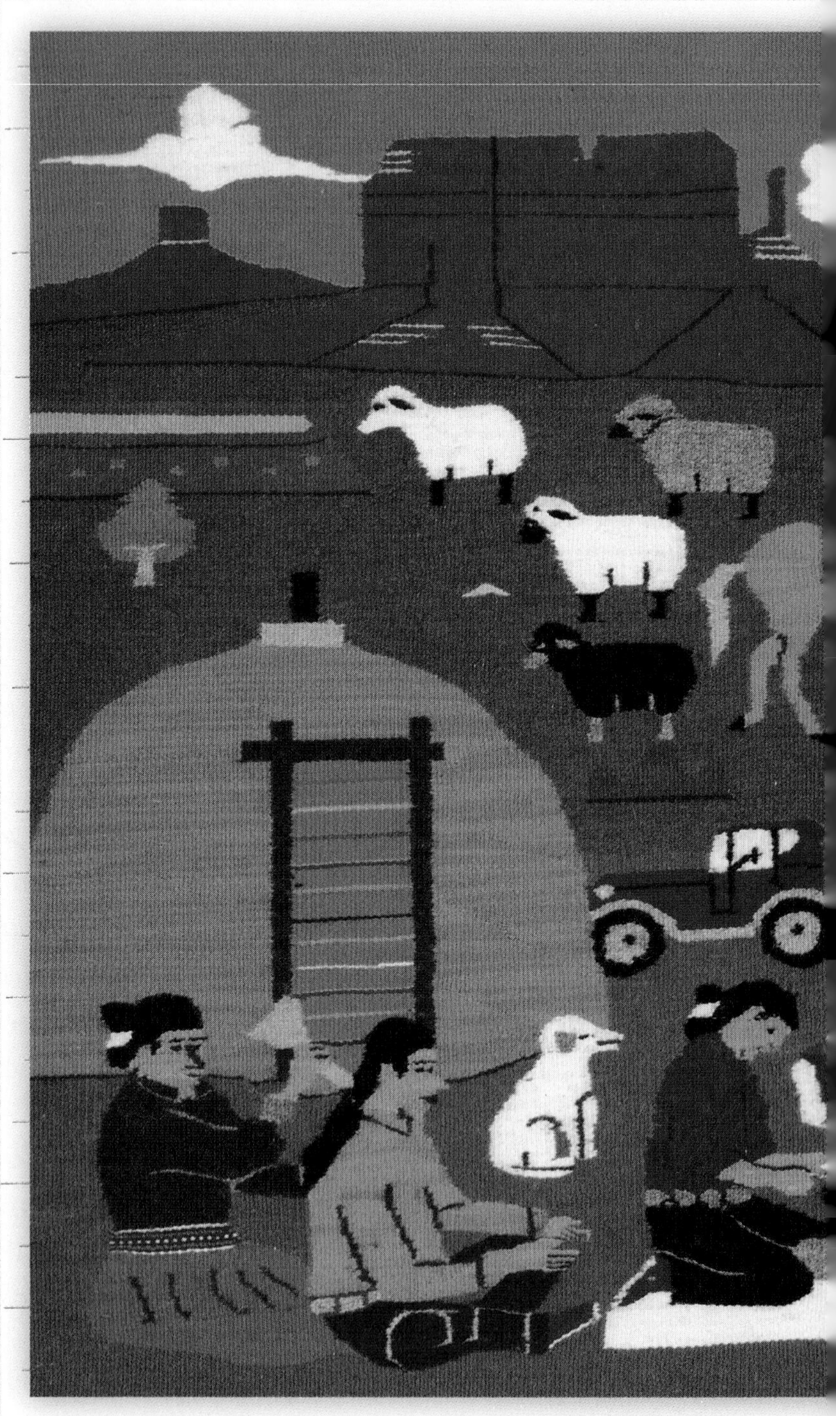

Pictorial Navajo Rug
by Betty Patterson

JUSTIN and the BEST BISCUITS in the WORLD

by Mildred Pitts Walter

Ten-year-old Justin lives with his mother and two sisters. Justin's family expects him to help with the household chores, but he thinks cooking and cleaning are women's work. He would rather play ball with his friend Anthony. When Justin's cowboy grandfather invites him to visit his ranch, Justin is delighted. Justin is certain that he and his grandfather will do real men's work together, like riding the range. But Justin's grandfather is full of surprises. Before his visit is over, Justin learns a lot more from his grandfather than he ever imagined.

illustrated by Floyd Cooper

The smell of coffee and home-smoked ham woke Justin. His grandpa was already up and downstairs cooking breakfast. Justin jumped out of bed and quickly put on his clothes.

Grandpa had hot pancakes, apple jelly, and ham all ready for the table. Justin ate two stacks of pancakes with two helpings of everything else.

After breakfast, Grandpa cleared the table, preparing to wash the dishes. "Would you rather wash or dry?" he asked Justin.

"Neither," Justin replied, quickly thinking how little success he had with dishes.

Grandpa said nothing as he removed the dishes from the table. He took his time, carefully measuring liquid soap and letting hot water run in the sink. Then he washed each dish and rinsed it with care, too. No water splashed or spilled. Soapsuds were not all over. How easy it looked, the way Grandpa did it.

After washing the dishes, Grandpa swept the floor and then went upstairs.

Justin stood around downstairs. He had a strange feeling of guilt and wished he had helped with the dishes. He heard Grandpa moving about, above in his room. Justin thought of going outside, down into the meadow, but he decided to see what was going on upstairs.

When he saw his grandpa busy making his own big bed, Justin went into his room. His unmade bed and his pajamas on the floor bothered him. But he decided that the room didn't look too bad. He picked up his pajamas and placed them on the bed and sat beside them. He waited.

Finally Grandpa came in and said, "Are you riding fence with me today?"

"Oh yes!"

"Fine. But why don't you make your bed? You'll probably feel pretty tired tonight. A well-made bed can be a warm welcome."

Justin moved slowly, reluctant to let Grandpa see him struggle with the bed. He started. What a surprise! Everything was tightly in place. He only had to smooth the covers. The bed was made. No lumps and bumps. Justin looked at Grandpa and grinned broadly. "That was easy!" he shouted.

"Don't you think you should unpack your clothes? They won't need ironing if you hang them up. You gotta look razor sharp for the festival." He gave Justin some clothes hangers.

"Are we *really* going to the festival every day?" Justin asked.

"You bet, starting with the judging early tomorrow and the dance tomorrow night." Grandpa winked at him.

Justin's excitement faded when he started unpacking his rumpled shirts. "They sure are wrinkled, Grandpa," he said.

"Maybe that's because they weren't folded."

"I can't ever get them folded right," Justin cried.

"Well, let's see. Turn it so the buttons face down." Grandpa showed Justin how to bring the sleeves to the back, turning in the sides so that the sleeves were on top. Then he folded the tail of the shirt over the cuffs, and made a second fold up to the collar. "Now you try it."

Justin tried it. "Oh, I see. That was easy, Grandpa." Justin smiled, pleased with himself.

"Everything's easy when you know how."

Justin, happy with his new-found skill, hurriedly placed his clothes on the hangers. He hoped the wrinkles would disappear in time for the festival.

"Now you'll look sharp," Grandpa said.

Justin felt a surge of love for his grandpa. He would always remember how to make a bed snug as a bug and fold clothes neatly. He grabbed Grandpa's hand. They walked downstairs, still holding hands, to get ready to ride fence.

Riding fence meant inspecting the fence all around the ranch to see where it needed mending. Riding fence took a great deal of a rancher's time. Justin and Grandpa planned to spend most of the day out on the plains. Grandpa said he'd pack a lunch for them to eat on the far side of the ranch.

Justin was surprised when Grandpa packed only flour, raisins, shortening, and chunks of smoked pork. He also packed jugs of water and makings for coffee.

The horses stood in the meadow as if they knew a busy day awaited them. While Grandpa saddled Pal, he let Justin finish the saddling of Black Lightning. Justin tightened the cinches on Black, feeling the strong pull on his arm muscles. With their supplies in their saddlebags, they mounted Pal and Black, leaving Cropper behind to graze in the meadow.

The early sun shone fiery red on the hilltops while the foothills were cast in shades of purple. The dew still lingered heavily on the morning. They let their horses canter away past the house through the tall green grass. But on the outer edge of the ranch where the fence started, they walked the horses at a steady pace.

The fence had three rows of taut wire. "That's a pretty high fence," Justin said.

"We have to keep the cattle in. But deer sometimes leap that fence and eat hay with the cattle." When it got bitter cold and frosty, Grandpa rode around the ranch dropping bales of hay for the cattle. It took a lot of hay to feed the cattle during the winter months.

"I didn't think a cow could jump very high," Justin said.

"Aw, come on. Surely you know that a cow jumped over the moon." Grandpa had a serious look on his face.

"I guess that's a joke, eh?" Justin laughed.

Justin noticed that Grandpa had a map. When they came to a place in the fence that looked weak, Grandpa marked it on his map. Later, helpers who came to do the work would know exactly where to mend. That saved time.

Now the sun heated up the morning. The foothills were now varying shades of green. Shadows dotted the plains. Among the blackish green trees on the rolling hills, fog still lingered like lazy clouds. Insects buzzed. A small cloud of mosquitoes swarmed just behind their heads, and beautiful cardinals splashed their redness on the morning air. Justin felt a surge of happiness and hugged Black with his knees and heels.

Suddenly he saw a doe standing close to the fence. "Look, Grandpa!" he said. She seemed alarmed but did not run away. Doe eyes usually look peaceful and sad, Justin remembered. Hers widened with fear. Then Justin saw a fawn caught in the wire of the fence.

Quickly they got off their horses. They hitched them to a post and moved cautiously toward the fawn.

The mother rushed to the fence but stopped just short of the sharp wire. "Stay back and still," Grandpa said to Justin. "She doesn't know we will help her baby. She thinks we might hurt it. She wants to protect it."

The mother pranced restlessly. She pawed the ground, moving as close to the fence as she could. Near the post the fence had been broken. The wire curled there dangerously. The fawn's head, caught in the wire, bled close to an ear. Whenever it pulled its head the wire cut deeper.

Grandpa quickly untangled the fawn's head.

Blood flowed from the cut.

"Oh, Grandpa, it will die," Justin said sadly.

"No, no," Grandpa assured Justin. "Lucky we got here when we did. It hasn't been caught long."

The fawn moved toward the doe. The mother, as if giving her baby a signal, bounded off. The baby trotted behind.

As they mounted their horses, Justin suddenly felt weak in the stomach. Remembering the blood, he trembled. Black, too, seemed uneasy. He moved his nostrils nervously and strained against the bit. He arched his neck and sidestepped quickly. Justin pulled the reins. "Whoa, boy!"

"Let him run," Grandpa said.

Justin kicked Black's sides and off they raced across the plain. They ran and ran, Justin pretending he was rounding up cattle. Then Black turned and raced back toward Grandpa and Pal.

"Whoa, boy," Justin commanded. Justin felt better and Black seemed calm, ready now to go on riding fence.

The sun beamed down and sweat rolled off Justin as he rode on with Grandpa, looking for broken wires in the fence. They were well away from the house, on the far side of the ranch. Flies buzzed around the horses and now gnats swarmed in clouds just above their heads. The prairie resounded with songs of the bluebirds, the bobwhite quails, and the mockingbirds mimicking them all. The cardinal's song, as lovely as any, included a whistle.

Justin thought of Anthony and how Anthony whistled for Pepper, his dog.

It was well past noon and Justin was hungry. Soon they came upon a small, well-built shed, securely locked. Nearby was a small stream. Grandpa reined in his horse. When he and Justin dismounted, they hitched the horses, and unsaddled them.

"We'll have our lunch here," Grandpa said. Justin was surprised when Grandpa took black iron pots, other cooking utensils, and a table from the shed. Justin helped him remove some iron rods that Grandpa carefully placed over a shallow pit. These would hold the pots. Now Justin understood why Grandpa had brought uncooked food. They were going to cook outside.

First they collected twigs and cow dung. Grandpa called it cowchips. "These," Grandpa said, holding up a dried brown pad, "make the best fuel. Gather them up."

There were plenty of chips left from the cattle that had fed there in winter. Soon they had a hot fire.

Justin watched as Grandpa carefully washed his hands and then began to cook their lunch.

"When I was a boy about your age, I used to go with my father on short runs with cattle. We'd bring them down from the high country onto the plains."

"Did you stay out all night?"

"Sometimes. And that was the time I liked most. The cook often made for supper what I am going to make for lunch."

Grandpa put raisins into a pot with a little water and placed them over the fire. Justin was surprised when Grandpa put flour in a separate pan. He used his fist to make a hole right in the middle of the flour. In that hole he placed some shortening. Then he added water. With his long delicate fingers he mixed the flour, water, and shortening until he had a nice round mound of dough.

Soon smooth circles of biscuits sat in an iron skillet with a lid on top. Grandpa put the skillet on the fire with some of the red-hot chips scattered over the lid.

Justin was amazed. How could only those ingredients make good bread? But he said nothing as Grandpa put the chunks of smoked pork in a skillet and started them cooking. Soon the smell was so delicious, Justin could hardly wait.

Finally Grandpa suggested that Justin take the horses to drink at the stream. "Keep your eyes open and don't step on any snakes."

Justin knew that diamondback rattlers sometimes lurked around. They were dangerous. He must be careful. He watered Black first.

While watering Pal, he heard rustling in the grass. His heart pounded. He heard the noise again. He wanted to run, but was too afraid. He looked around carefully. There were two black eyes staring at him. He tried to pull Pal away from the water, but Pal refused to stop drinking. Then Justin saw the animal. It had a long tail like a rat's. But it was as big as a cat. Then he saw something crawling on its back. They were little babies, hanging on as the animal ran.

A mama opossum and her babies, he thought, and was no longer afraid.

By the time the horses were watered, lunch was ready. *"M-mm-m,"* Justin said as he reached for a plate. The biscuits were golden brown, yet fluffy inside. And the sizzling pork was now crisp. Never had he eaten stewed raisins before.

"Grandpa, I didn't know you could cook like this," Justin said when he had tasted the food. "I didn't know men could cook so good."

"Why, Justin, some of the best cooks in the world are men."

Justin remembered the egg on the floor and his rice burning. The look he gave Grandpa revealed his doubts.

"It's true," Grandpa said. "All the cooks on the cattle trail were men. In hotels and restaurants they call them chefs."

"How did you make these biscuits?"

"That's a secret. One day I'll let you make some."

"Were you a cowboy, Grandpa?"

"I'm still a cowboy."

"No, you're not."

"Yes, I am. I work with cattle, so I'm a cowboy."

"You know what I mean. The kind who rides bulls, broncobusters. That kind of cowboy."

"No, I'm not that kind. But I know some."

"Are they famous?"

"No, but I did meet a real famous Black cowboy once. When I was eight years old, my grandpa took me to meet his friend Bill Pickett. Bill Pickett was an old man then. He had a ranch in Oklahoma."

"Were there lots of Black cowboys?"

"Yes. Lots of them. They were hard workers, too. They busted broncos, branded calves, and drove cattle. My grandpa tamed wild mustangs."

"Bet they were famous."

"Oh, no. Some were. Bill Pickett created the sport of bulldogging. You'll see that at the rodeo. One cowboy named Williams taught Rough Rider Teddy Roosevelt how to break horses; and another one named Clay taught Will Rogers, the comedian, the art of roping." Grandpa offered Justin the last biscuit.

When they had finished their lunch they led the horses away from the shed to graze. As they watched the horses, Grandpa went on, "Now, there were some more very famous Black cowboys. Jessie Stahl. They say he was the best rider of wild horses in the West."

"How could he be? Nobody ever heard about him. I didn't."

"Oh, there're lots of famous Blacks you never hear or read about. You ever hear about Deadwood Dick?"

Justin laughed. "No."

"There's another one. His real name was Nate Love. He could outride, outshoot anyone. In Deadwood City in the Dakota Territory, he roped, tied, saddled, mounted, and rode a wild horse faster than anyone. Then in the shooting match, he hit the bull's-eye every time. The people named him Deadwood Dick right on the spot. Enough about cowboys, now. While the horses graze, let's clean up here and get back to our men's work."

Justin felt that Grandpa was still teasing him, the way he had in Justin's room when he had placed his hand on Justin's shoulder. There was still the sense of shame whenever the outburst about women's work and the tears were remembered.

As they cleaned the utensils and dishes, Justin asked, "Grandpa, you think housework is women's work?"

"Do you?" Grandpa asked quickly.

"I asked you first, Grandpa."

"I guess asking you that before I answer is unfair. No, I don't. Do you?"

"Well, it seems easier for them," Justin said as he splashed water all over, glad he was outside.

"Easier than for me?"

"Well, not for you, I guess, but for me, yeah."

"Could it be because you don't know how?"

"You mean like making the bed and folding the clothes."

"Yes." Grandpa stopped and looked at Justin. "Making the bed is easy now, isn't it? All work is that way. It doesn't matter who does the work, man or woman, when it needs to be done. What matters is that we try to learn how to do it the best we can in the most enjoyable way."

"I don't think I'll ever like housework," Justin said, drying a big iron pot.

"It's like any other kind of work. The better you do it, the easier it becomes, and we seem not to mind doing things that are easy."

With the cooking rods and all the utensils put away, they locked the shed and went for their horses.

"Now, I'm going to let you do the cinches again. You'll like that."

There's that teasing again, Justin thought. "Yeah. That's a man's work," he said, and mounted Black.

"There are some good horsewomen. You'll see them at the rodeo." Grandpa mounted Pal. They went on their way, riding along silently, scanning the fence.

Finally Justin said, "I was just kidding, Grandpa." Then without planning to, he said, "I bet you don't like boys who cry like babies."

"Do I know any boys who cry like babies?"

"Aw, Grandpa, you saw me crying."

"Oh, I didn't think you were crying like a baby. In your room, you mean? We all cry sometime."

"You? Cry, Grandpa?"

"Sure."

They rode on, with Grandpa marking his map. Justin remained quiet, wondering what could make a man like Grandpa cry.

As if knowing Justin's thoughts, Grandpa said, "I remember crying when you were born."

"Why? Didn't you want me?"

"Oh, yes. You were the most beautiful baby. But, you see, your grandma, Beth, had just died. When I held you I was flooded with joy. Then I thought, *Grandma will never see this beautiful boy*. I cried."

The horses wading through the grass made the only sound in the silence. Then Grandpa said, "There's an old saying, son. 'The brave hide their fears, but share their tears.' Tears bathe the soul."

Justin looked at his grandpa. Their eyes caught. A warmth spread over Justin and he lowered his eyes. He wished he could tell his grandpa all he felt, how much he loved him.

Meet Mildred Pitts Walter

Mildred Pitts Walter wrote her first book, *Lillie of Watts*, when she was a teacher in Los Angeles. Since then she has written a number of award-winning books about African-American children, including *Justin and the Best Biscuits in the World*, which won the Coretta Scott King Award.

Speaking about her stories, Walter says, "I like to think that the images I create will make all young people thoughtful and African Americans aware of themselves as well."

Meet Floyd Cooper

Floyd Cooper remembers drawing a lot when he was young. He also created a lot of mischief. "My earliest recollection is of drawing a nice, big, sprawling picture of a duck on the side of our house," Cooper says. "You can imagine my dad's reaction, but I have been drawing ever since."

Cooper grew up in Oklahoma. He spent time on his uncle's ranch, riding and falling from bucking broncos. Remembering this experience helped him draw the illustrations for *Justin and the Best Biscuits in the World.*

Story Questions & Activities

1. How does Justin feel about doing housework at the beginning of the story?
2. Did you expect him to change his mind about doing chores at the end? Why or why not?
3. What makes Grandpa such a good grandfather? Explain.
4. What is this story mostly about?
5. Imagine that Grandpa was asked to play a part in a movie or a television show. What character could he play? Explain your choice.

Write a Letter

Imagine you are Justin. Write a letter to your family about the chores you have done on Grandpa's ranch. Compare these chores to the chores that need to be done at home. Give supporting details.

Trace the Trail

An important job for cowboys was a cattle drive. They drove herds of cattle long distances from Texas and the Southwest to railroad towns in Kansas and Nebraska. Use an encyclopedia to learn more about cattle drives. Then draw a map showing one of the trails. Include a scale of miles to show distance.

Write a Song

Cowboys, or cowhands, often sang songs on the trail. Their songs were about freedom and loneliness, the empty range, and cattle drives. Listen to cowboy songs in the library. Then write a short song that a cowboy might sing.

Find Out More

In the story, Justin's grandfather is a cowboy. Cowboys have special clothing and equipment for their work. Find out more about cowboy gear. Start by looking in an encyclopedia. Use what you learn to draw a picture of a cowboy or a cowgirl. Then label the special gear.

Use a Dictionary

Grandpa uses some things in the story that you may not know. Grandpa's *lariat*, for example, is an important piece of cowboy gear. What is a lariat? You can look up this word in a dictionary.

A **dictionary** tells you what the word means and how to pronounce it. It also gives you the word's part of speech. Sometimes a dictionary shows you how to use the word in a sentence. It may even show you a picture of the word.

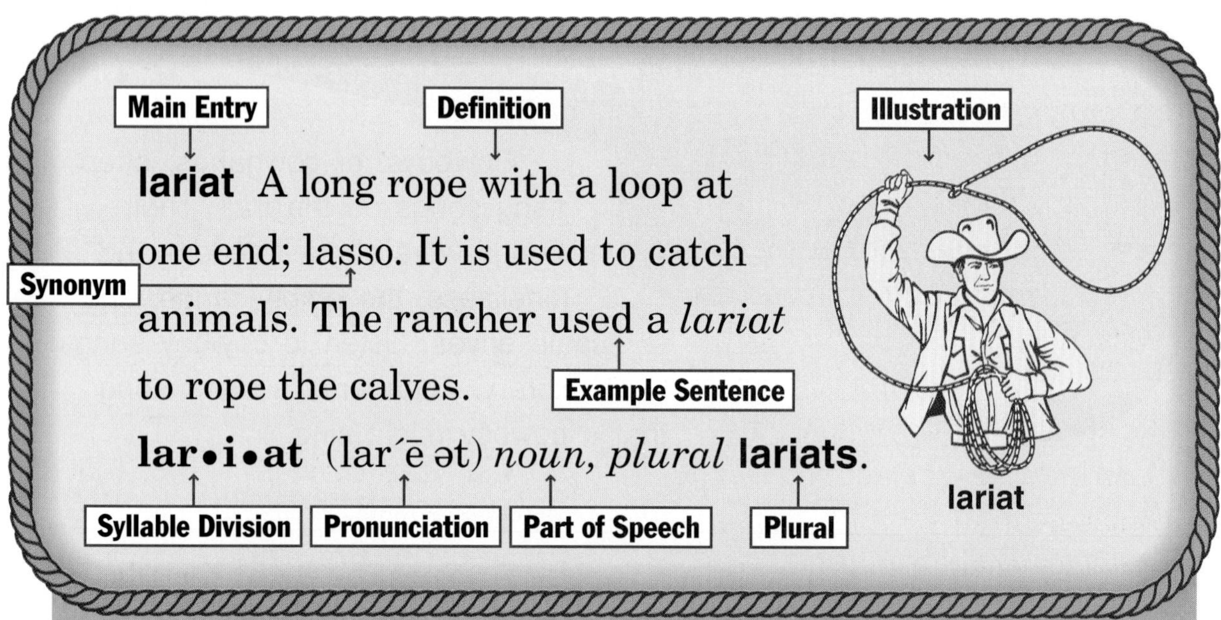

Use the dictionary entry to answer these questions.

1. What does *lariat* mean?
2. How many syllables does the word have?
3. What part of speech is *lariat*?
4. Is *lasso* another word for *lariat*? How do you know?
5. When should you look up a word in a dictionary?

TEST POWER

Test Tip

A FACT is something that is true in the passage.

DIRECTIONS

Read the sample story. Then read each question about the story.

SAMPLE

Paul's Puppy

Paul's friend Jinnie received a puppy for her birthday. The puppy had white fur and a patch of black fur over its right eye. Whenever Jinnie picked it up, it would wag its tail and lick her face.

Paul asked his mother if he could get a puppy, too. His mother thought about it for a moment and said, "A dog is a big responsibility, Paul. Dogs are fun, but they also need a lot of care. They can be great friends, but only if you are a good friend to them. Are you willing to take on that kind of challenge?"

Paul agreed that he was up to the responsibility.

1 Which of these is the best summary of this story?

A Paul liked Jinnie's puppy.

B The puppy wagged its tail.

C Jinnie's puppy was cute.

D Paul agreed to take care of a puppy.

2 Which of these is a FACT in this story?

F Dogs are great friends.

G Jinnie's puppy has white fur.

H Dogs are always cute.

J Puppies are fun.

How do you know which are facts in the story? Explain.

Movies can take us to places we can only imagine. They can lead us on adventures we have had only in dreams.

Look at this picture from the movie *The Wizard of Oz*. What is happening in the scene? What do you think will happen next? How will Dorothy and her friends get to the Emerald City? What will happen once they get there?

Look at this picture again. How can you tell that the setting and some of the characters aren't real? How do you know that the events in this scene are "just a dream"?

Scene from
***The Wizard of Oz*, 1939**
MGM Turner Entertainment

Just a Dream

Written and Illustrated by
Chris Van Allsburg

As usual, Walter stopped at the bakery on his way home from school. He bought one large jelly-filled doughnut. He took the pastry from its bag, eating quickly as he walked along. He licked the red jelly from his fingers. Then he crumpled up the empty bag and threw it at a fire hydrant.

At home Walter saw Rose, the little girl next door, watering a tree that had just been planted. "It's my birthday present," she said proudly. Walter couldn't understand why anyone would want a tree for a present. His own birthday was just a few days away, "And I'm not getting some dumb plant," he told Rose.

After dinner Walter took out the trash. Three cans stood next to the garage. One was for bottles, one for cans, and one for everything else. As usual, Walter dumped everything into one can. He was too busy to sort through garbage, especially when there was something good on television.

The show that Walter was so eager to watch was about a boy who lived in the future. The boy flew around in a tiny airplane that he parked on the roof of his house.

He had a robot and a small machine that could make any kind of food with the push of a button.

Walter went to bed wishing he lived in the future. He couldn't wait to have his own tiny plane, a robot to take out the trash, and a machine that could make jelly doughnuts by the thousands. When he fell asleep, his wish came true. That night Walter's bed traveled to . . .

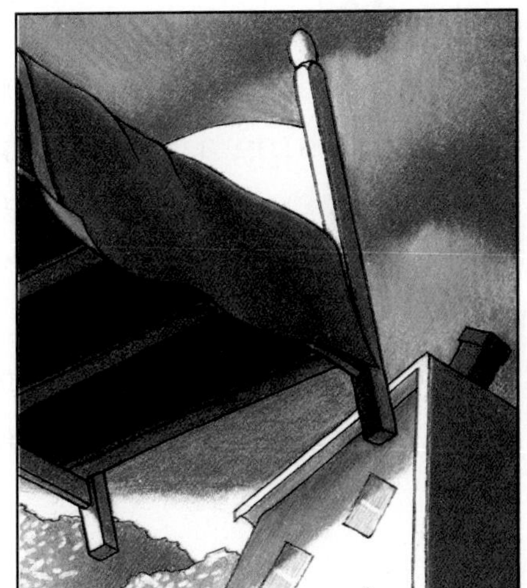

the future.

Walter woke up in the middle of a huge dump. A bulldozer was pushing a heap of bulging trash bags toward him. "Stop!" he yelled.

The man driving the bulldozer put his machine in neutral. "Oh, sorry," he said. "Didn't see you."

Walter looked at the distant mountains of trash and saw half-buried houses. "Do people live here?" he asked.

"Not anymore," answered the man.

A few feet from the bed was a rusty old street sign that read

FLORAL AVENUE. "Oh no," gasped Walter. He lived on Floral Avenue.

The driver revved up his bulldozer. "Well," he shouted, "back to work!"

Walter pulled the covers over his head. This can't be the future, he thought. I'm sure it's just a dream. He went back to sleep.

But not for long . . .

Walter peered over the edge of his bed, which was caught in the branches of a tall tree. Down below, he could see two men carrying a large saw. "Hello!" Walter yelled out.

"Hello to you!" they shouted back.

"You aren't going to cut down this tree, are you?" Walter asked.

But the woodcutters didn't answer. They took off their jackets, rolled up their sleeves, and got to work. Back and forth they pushed the saw, slicing through the trunk of Walter's tree. "You must need this tree for something important," Walter called down.

"Oh yes," they said, "very important." Then Walter noticed lettering on the wood-cutters' jackets. He could just make out the words: QUALITY TOOTHPICK COMPANY. Walter sighed and slid back under the blankets.

Until . . .

Walter couldn't stop coughing. His bed was balanced on the rim of a giant smokestack. The air was filled with smoke that burned his throat and made his eyes itch. All around him, dozens of smokestacks belched thick clouds of hot, foul smoke. A workman climbed one of the stacks.

"What is this place?" Walter called out.

"This is the Maximum Strength Medicine Factory," the man answered.

"Gosh," said Walter, looking at all the smoke, "what kind of medicine do they make here?"

"Wonderful medicine," the

workman replied, "for burning throats and itchy eyes."

Walter started coughing again.

"I can get you some," the man offered.

"No thanks," said Walter. He buried his head in his pillow and, when his coughing stopped, fell asleep.

But then . . .

Snowflakes fell on Walter. He was high in the mountains. A group of people wearing snowshoes and long fur coats hiked past his bed.

"Where are you going?" Walter asked.

"To the hotel," one of them replied.

Walter turned around and saw an enormous building. A sign on it read HOTEL EVEREST. "Is that hotel," asked Walter, "on the top of Mount Everest?"

"Yes," said one of the hikers. "Isn't it beautiful?"

"Well," Walter began. But the group didn't wait for his answer. They waved goodbye and marched away. Walter stared at the flashing yellow sign, then crawled back beneath his sheets.

But there was more to see . . .

Walter's hand was wet and cold. When he opened his eyes, he found himself floating on the open sea, drifting toward a fishing boat. The men on the boat were laughing and dancing.

"Ship ahoy!" Walter shouted.

The fishermen waved to him.

"What's the celebration for?" he asked.

"We've just caught a fish," one of them yelled back. "Our second one this week!" They held up their small fish for Walter to see.

"Aren't you supposed to throw the little ones back?" Walter asked.

But the fishermen didn't hear him. They were busy singing and dancing.

Walter turned away. Soon the rocking of the bed put him to sleep.

But only for a moment . . .

A loud, shrieking horn nearly lifted Walter off his mattress. He jumped up. There were cars and trucks all around him, horns honking loudly, creeping along inch by inch. Every driver had a car phone in one hand and a big cup of coffee in the other. When the traffic stopped completely, the honking grew even louder. Walter could not get back to sleep.

Hours passed, and he wondered if he'd be stuck on this highway forever. He pulled his pillow tightly around his head.

This can't be the future, he thought. Where are the tiny airplanes, the robots? The honking continued into the night, until finally, one by one, the cars became quiet as their drivers, and Walter, went to sleep.

But his bed traveled on . . .

Walter looked up. A horse stood right over his bed, staring directly at him. In the saddle was a woman wearing cowboy clothes. "My horse likes you," she said.

"Good," replied Walter, who wondered where he'd ended up this time. All he could see was a dull yellow haze.

"Son," the woman told him, spreading her arms in front of her, "this is the mighty Grand Canyon."

Walter gazed into the foggy distance.

"Of course," she went on, "with all this smog, nobody's gotten a good look at it for years." The woman offered to sell Walter some postcards that showed the canyon in the old days. "They're real pretty," she said.

But he couldn't look. It's just a dream, he told himself. I know I'll wake up soon, back in my room.

But he didn't . . .

Walter looked out from under his sheets. His bed was flying through the night sky. A flock of ducks passed overhead. One of them landed on the bed, and to Walter's surprise, he began to speak. "I hope you don't mind," the bird said, "if I take a short rest here." The ducks had been flying for days, looking for the pond where they had always stopped to eat.

"I'm sure it's down there somewhere," Walter said, though he suspected something awful might have happened. After a while the duck waddled to the edge of the bed, took a deep breath, and flew off. “Good luck,” Walter called to him. Then he pulled the blanket over his head. “It’s just a dream,” he whispered, and wondered if it would ever end.

Then finally. . .

Walter's bed returned to the present. He was safe in his room again, but he felt terrible. The future he'd seen was not what he'd expected. Robots and little airplanes didn't seem very important now. He looked out his window at the trees and lawns in the early morning light, then jumped out of bed.

He ran outside and down the block, still in his pajamas. He found the empty jelly doughnut bag he'd thrown at the fire hydrant the day before. Then Walter went back home and, before the sun came up, sorted all the trash by the garage.

A few days later, on Walter's birthday, all his friends came over for cake and ice cream. They loved his new toys: the laser gun set, electric yo-yo, and inflatable dinosaurs. "My best present,"

Walter told them, "is outside." Then he showed them the gift that he'd picked out that morning—a tree.

After the party, Walter and his dad planted the birthday present. When he went to bed, Walter looked out his window. He could see his tree and the tree Rose had planted on her birthday. He liked the way they looked, side by side. Then he went to sleep, but not for long, because that night Walter's bed took him away again.

When Walter woke up, his bed was standing in the shade of two tall trees. The sky was blue. Laundry hanging from a clothes-line flapped in the breeze. A man pushed an old motorless lawn mower. This isn't the future, Walter thought. It's the past.

"Good morning," the man said. "You've found a nice place to sleep."

"Yes, I have," Walter agreed. There was something very peaceful about the huge trees next to his bed.

The man looked up at the rustling leaves. “My great-grandmother planted one of these trees,” he said, “when she was a little girl.”

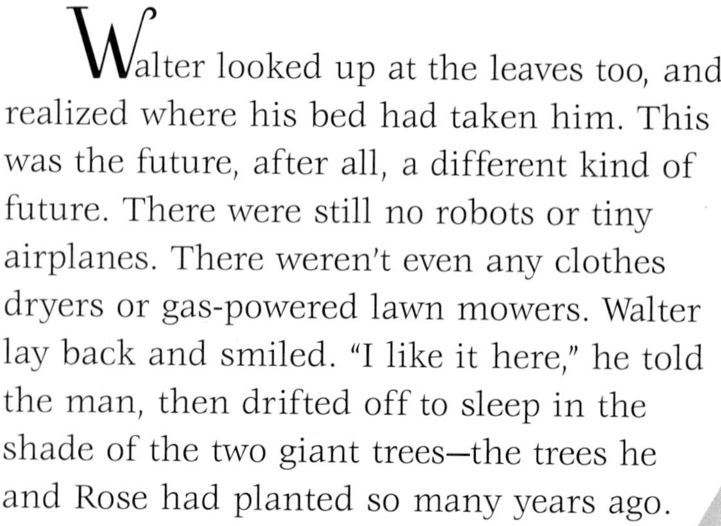

Walter looked up at the leaves too, and realized where his bed had taken him. This was the future, after all, a different kind of future. There were still no robots or tiny airplanes. There weren't even any clothes dryers or gas-powered lawn mowers. Walter lay back and smiled. "I like it here," he told the man, then drifted off to sleep in the shade of the two giant trees—the trees he and Rose had planted so many years ago.

MEET Chris Van Allsburg

Chris Van Allsburg is often asked where he gets the ideas for his books. Sometimes he says they are sent through the mail or beamed in from outer space. The truth, admits Van Allsburg, is that he isn't sure where he gets them. They just seem to arrive.

For Van Allsburg, who is both an artist and a writer, a story often begins with an image. He had just such an image in mind when he began *The Polar Express,* a book that won the Caldecott Medal. Van Allsburg pictured a boy looking at a train in front of his house and then taking trips on the train. Eventually, the train rolled all the way to the North Pole.

For *Just a Dream,* Van Allsburg pictured a polluted environment. How could he make this real problem into a good story? He decided to have a boy named Walter travel in his bed to various places. "Bed, with the covers up, is supposed to be a safe place," says the author. "But it's not safe to be in bed in a garbage dump."

Van Allsburg writes before he draws pictures for his stories. He can usually see the pictures in his mind as he writes, though. Creating a story, he says, is a little like making a film. He has to decide which parts to show in his drawings.

Story Questions & Activities

1. Where is Walter during most of the story?
2. How does Walter feel about the environment at the beginning of the story? At the end?
3. Why are Walter's dreams important?
4. What are the major events in the story? List them in order.
5. Imagine that Walter stepped into the picture from *The Wizard of Oz* on pages 158–159. What do you think he would say to Dorothy and her friends?

Write an Essay

Walter's dreams show him the importance of saving the environment. Write an essay to compare what the world may be like if we do not protect the environment and what it may be like if we do. Suggest a way you and your classmates can help bring about the better future.

Do a Science Experiment

In Walter's dream, the air became so polluted that no one could see through it. How clean is your air? To find out, hang a clean white cloth from your window. Leave it there for at least a full day. Then take it in. Is it still clean? Report the results to the class.

Draw a Cartoon

Walter's dreams showed him a pollution-filled world. Draw your own cartoon that shows what will happen if people continue to hurt the environment. Write a clever caption for your cartoon.

Find Out More

In the story, Walter's town had a plan for recycling bottles and cans. What kind of recycling plan does your community have? Start by looking in the yellow pages of your telephone book under recycling to find out the items you can recycle. Then use what you learn to make a flyer. Tell people *what*, *when*, *where*, and *how* to recycle.

Use a Thesaurus

Walter is eager to watch a TV program. The show is about a boy who flies around in a *tiny* airplane. This boy also has a *small* machine that can make food with the press of a button. Look at the words *tiny* and *small*. They are synonyms. A **synonym** is a word that has the same or almost the same meaning as another word. You can find synonyms in a book called a *thesaurus*. A **thesaurus** is often arranged alphabetically, like a dictionary. After each main word is a list of synonyms.

small *adj.* **1.** *Are you small enough to squeeze through this door?*: little, tiny, petite. **2.** *Even the small details should be checked*: minor, unimportant. **3.** *The puppy uttered a small cry:* weak, faint.

Use the sample thesaurus to answer these questions.

1. What information does a thesaurus have?
2. What are three synonyms for the first meaning of *small*?
3. How would you look up a word in a thesaurus arranged like a dictionary?
4. What part of speech is the word *small*?
5. How is a thesaurus different from a dictionary?

TEST POWER

Test Tip

Clues to the meaning of the underlined word are usually near the underlined word.

DIRECTIONS

Read the sample story. Then read each question about the story.

SAMPLE

Timothy's Gift for Matt

All of the things in Timothy's house were packed in boxes. Timothy's parents had been <u>transferred</u>, and Timothy and his family were moving away. Both Timothy and his best friend, Matt, were very upset. They had been friends since the second grade when they played on the same Little League team. It was hard for Matt to think about going to school the next day and not seeing Timothy there.

Matt blurted out, "I wish you didn't have to move!"

Timothy looked down at the box at his feet marked "baseball." He leaned down and pulled from the box his favorite baseball and gave it to his best friend, Matt.

1 What is this story mostly about?

A Being in Little League

B The friendship of two boys

C Packing boxes

D Going to school

2 In this story, the word <u>transferred</u> means—

F lied to

G moved to a different place

H asked to do a favor

J given a lot of money

When you look at this photograph, you can almost feel the empty setting. What do you think has caused the people to leave?

Study this black-and-white photograph. What do you see? What effect does the deserted house have on you? How do the empty fields make you feel?

Look at the picture again. If you could take the same photograph, would you use color film? Explain your reasons.

Tractored Out
Childress County, Texas, 1938
by Dorothea Lange

MEET ELIZABETH FRIEDRICH

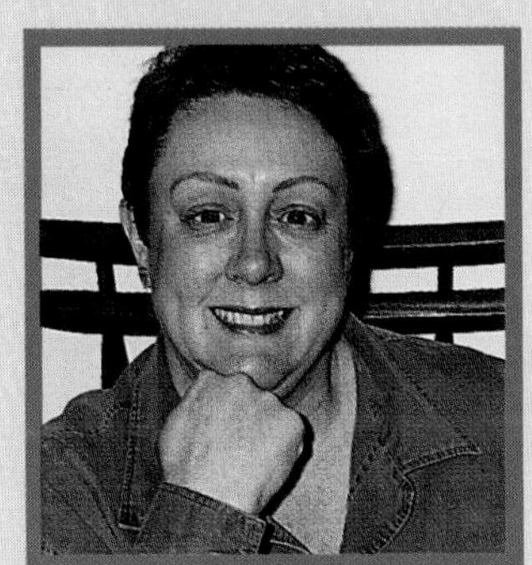

Elizabeth Friedrich was born in San Francisco, California. As a child, she loved to visit her aunt and uncle's farm in Missouri. To her, the farm was a magical place. *Leah's Pony* is based in part on what she learned there.

Today, Friedrich and her family live on a 150-year-old farm in New Hampshire, where she has a horse and six sheep. When she is not writing or working on her farm, she enjoys collecting antiques, reading, and traveling.

MEET MICHAEL GARLAND

Michael Garland was born and raised in New York City. No stranger to children's books, Garland has both written and illustrated many books for young people. His books include *Dinner at Magritte's, Circus Girl, Angel Cat*, and *My Cousin Katie*.

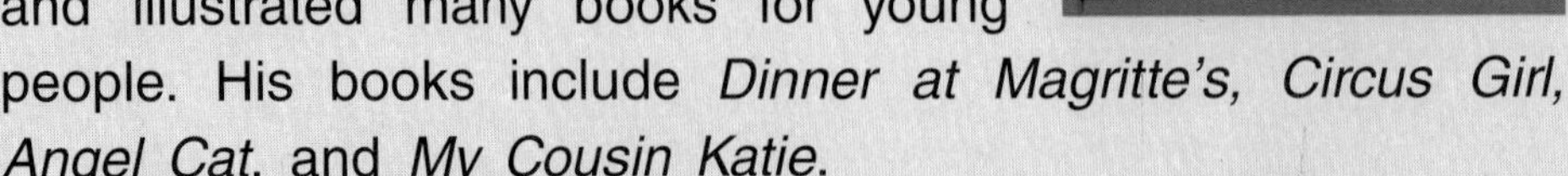

In his spare time Garland enjoys painting. He lives with his wife and three children in Patterson, New York.

LEAH'S PONY

Written by Elizabeth Friedrich   Illustrated by Michael Garland

THE YEAR THE CORN GREW TALL AND STRAIGHT, Leah's papa bought her a pony. The pony was strong and swift and sturdy, with just a snip of white at the end of his soft black nose. Papa taught Leah to place her new saddle right in the middle of his back and tighten the girth around his belly, just so.

That whole summer, Leah and her pony crossed through cloud-capped cornfields and chased cattle through the pasture.

Leah scratched that special spot under her pony's mane and brushed him till his coat glistened like satin.

Each day Leah loved to ride her pony into town just to hear Mr. B. shout from the door of his grocery store, "That's the finest pony in the whole county."

The year the corn grew no taller than a man's thumb, Leah's house became very quiet. Sometimes on those hot, dry nights, Leah heard Papa and Mama's hushed voices whispering in the kitchen. She couldn't understand the words but knew their sad sound.

Some days the wind blew so hard it turned the sky black with dust. It was hard for Leah to keep her pony's coat shining. It was hard for Mama to keep the house clean. It was hard for Papa to carry buckets of water for the sow and her piglets.

Soon Papa sold the pigs and even some of the cattle. "These are hard times," he told Leah with a puzzled look. "That's what these days are, all right, hard times."

Mama used flour sacks to make underwear for Leah. Mama threw dishwater on her drooping petunias to keep them growing. And, no matter what else happened, Mama always woke Leah on Saturday with the smell of fresh, hot coffee cake baking.

One hot, dry, dusty day grasshoppers turned the day to night. They ate the trees bare and left only twigs behind.

The next day the neighbors filled their truck with all they owned and stopped to say good-bye. "We're off to Oregon," they said. "It must be better there." Papa, Mama, and Leah waved as their neighbors wobbled down the road in an old truck overflowing with chairs and bedsprings and wire.

The hot, dry, dusty days kept coming. On a day you could almost taste the earth in the air, Papa said, "I have something to tell you, Leah, and I want you to be brave.

I borrowed money from the bank. I bought seeds, but the seeds dried up and blew away. Nothing grew. I don't have any corn to sell. Now I can't pay back the bank," Papa paused. "They're going to have an auction, Leah. They're going to sell the cattle and the chickens and the pickup truck."

Leah stared at Papa. His voice grew husky and soft. "Worst of all, they're going to sell my tractor. I'll never be able to plant corn when she's gone. Without my tractor, we might even have to leave the farm. I told you, Leah, these are hard times."

Leah knew what an auction meant. She knew eager faces with strange voices would come to their farm. They would stand outside and offer money for Papa's best bull and Mama's prize rooster and Leah's favorite calf.

All week Leah worried and waited and wondered what to do. One morning she watched as a man in a big hat hammered a sign into the ground in front of her house.

Leah wanted to run away. She raced her pony past empty fields lined with dry gullies. She galloped past a house with rags stuffed in broken windowpanes. She sped right past Mr. B. sweeping the steps outside his store.

At last Leah knew what she had to do. She turned her pony around and rode back into town. She stopped in front of Mr. B.'s store. "You can buy my pony," she said.

Mr. B. stopped sweeping and stared at her. "Why would you want to sell him?" he asked. "That's the finest pony in the county."

Leah swallowed hard. "I've grown a lot this summer," she said. "I'm getting too big for him."

Sunburned soil crunched under Leah's feet as she walked home alone. The auction had begun. Neighbors, friends, strangers—everyone clustered around the man in the big hat. "How much for this wagon?" boomed the man. "Five dollars. Ten dollars. Sold for fifteen dollars to the man in the green shirt."

Papa's best bull.

Sold.

Mama's prize rooster.

Sold.

Leah's favorite calf.

Sold.

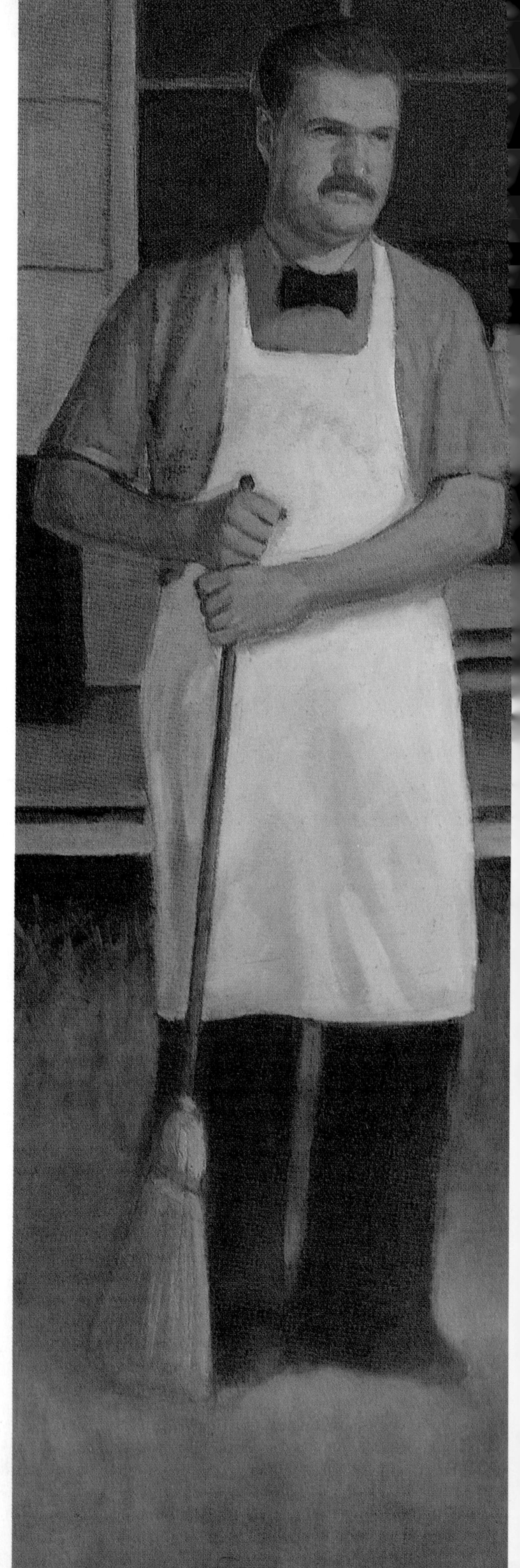

Leah clutched her money in her hand. “It has to be enough,” she whispered to herself. “It just has to be.”

“Here’s one of the best items in this entire auction,” yelled the man in the big hat. “Who’ll start the bidding at five hundred dollars for this practically new, all-purpose Farmall tractor? It’ll plow, plant, fertilize, and even cultivate for you.”

It was time. Leah’s voice shook. “One dollar.”

The man in the big hat laughed. “That’s a low starting bid if I ever heard one,” he said. “Now let’s hear some serious bids.”

No one moved. No one said a word. No one even seemed to breathe.

"Ladies and gentlemen, this tractor is a beauty! I have a bid of only one dollar for it. One dollar for this practically new Farmall tractor! Do I hear any other bids?"

Again no one moved. No one said a word. No one even seemed to breathe.

"This is ridiculous!" the man's voice boomed out from under his hat into the silence. "Sold to the young lady for one dollar."

The crowd cheered. Papa's mouth hung open. Mama cried. Leah proudly walked up and handed one dollar to the auctioneer in the big hat.

"That young lady bought one fine tractor for one very low price," the man continued. "Now how much am I bid for this flock of healthy young chickens?"

"I'll give you ten cents," offered a farmer who lived down the road.

"Ten cents! Ten cents is mighty cheap for a whole flock of chickens," the man said. His face looked angry.

Again no one moved. No one said a word. No one even seemed to breathe.

"Sold for ten cents!"

The farmer picked up the cage filled with chickens and walked over to Mama. "These chickens are yours," he said.

The man pushed his big hat back on his head. "How much for this good Ford pickup truck?" he asked.

"Twenty-five cents," yelled a neighbor from town.

Again no one moved. No one said a word. No one even seemed to breathe.

"Sold for twenty-five cents!" The man in the big hat shook his head. "This isn't supposed to be a penny auction!" he shouted.

The neighbor paid his twenty-five cents and took the keys to the pickup truck. "I think these will start your truck," he whispered as he dropped the keys into Papa's shirt pocket.

Leah watched as friends and neighbors bid a penny for a chicken or a nickel for a cow or a quarter for a plow. One by one, they gave everything back to Mama and Papa.

The crowds left. The sign disappeared. Chickens scratched in their coop, and cattle called for their corn. The farm was quiet. Too quiet. No familiar whinny greeted Leah when she entered the barn. Leah swallowed hard and straightened her back.

That night in Leah's hushed house, no sad voices whispered in the kitchen. Only Leah lay awake, listening to the clock chime nine and even ten times. Leah's heart seemed to copy its slow, sad beat.

Leah

The next morning Leah forced open the heavy barn doors to start her chores. A loud whinny greeted her. Leah ran and hugged the familiar furry neck and kissed the white snip of a nose. "You're back!" she cried. "How did you get here?"

Then Leah saw the note with her name written in big letters:

Dear Leah,

This is the finest pony in the county. But he's a little bit small for me and a little bit big for my grandson.

He fits you much better.

Your friend,
Mr. B.

P.S. I heard how you saved your family's farm.
These hard times won't last forever.

And they didn't.

Story Questions & Activities

1. What causes the family's crops to fail?
2. What effect does the crop failure have on Leah and her family?
3. How do you know that Leah's neighbors are helpful?
4. What would you say to sum up this story?
5. Imagine that Leah was the main character in "Just a Dream." What kind of dream do you think she would have? Give reasons for your answer.

Write a Newspaper Article

Good times will return to Leah's family's farm. Imagine you are a newspaper reporter. Write an article about the way life improves for the farmers in the county. In the article, compare the good times with the hard times that came before.

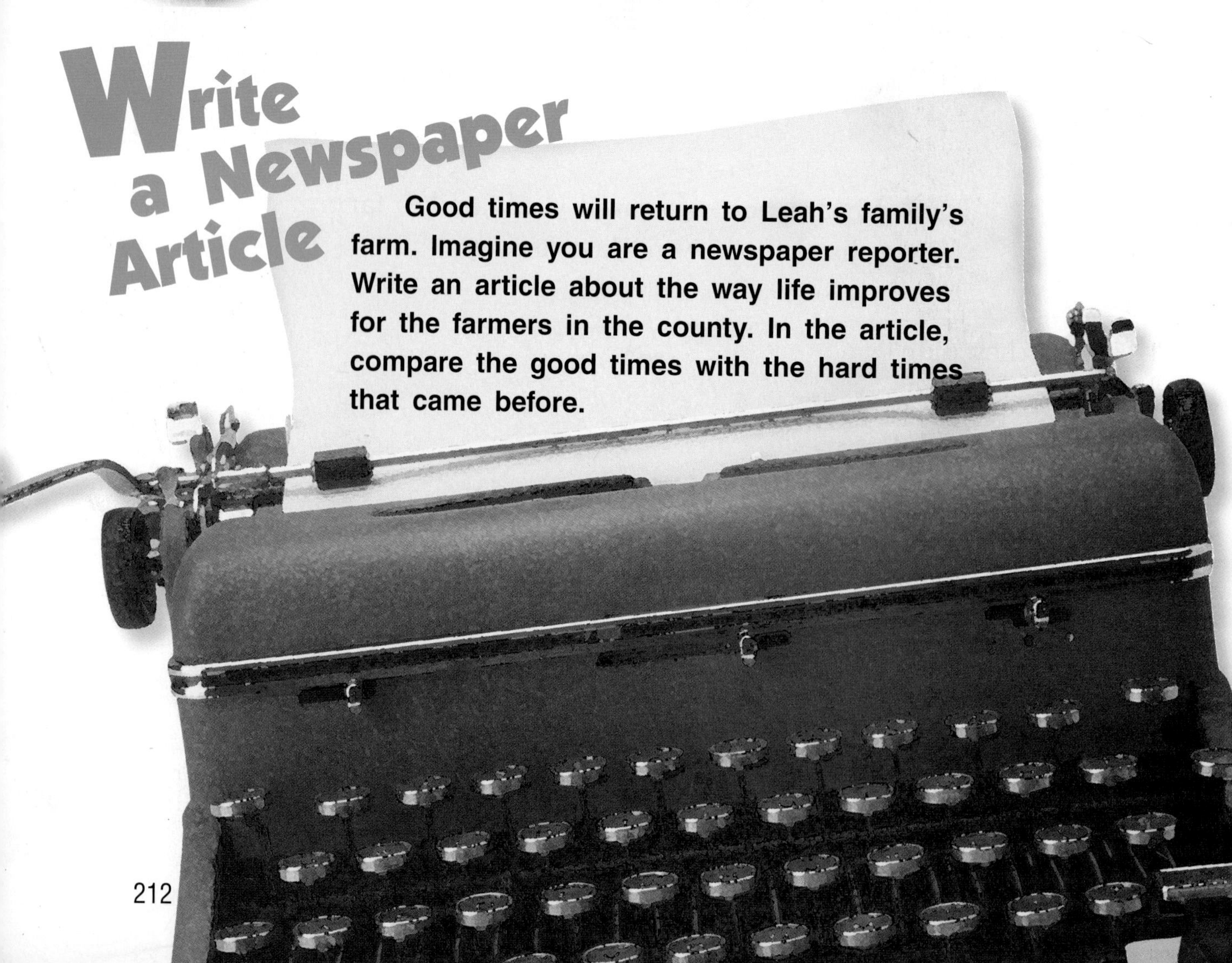

Make a Chart

A farm is a busy place, and so is a city. Use details from the story to make a chart. Draw three columns. In the column at the left, list some things about city life. In the column at the right, list some things about farm or country life. In the middle column, list the things that are about the same in the city and the country.

Draw a Diagram

Farmers like Leah's father have to know about their crops. Find out how a corn plant grows. Draw a diagram that shows its life cycle. Include the seed, the new plant, the flower, and the mature corn. On your diagram, write what the corn plant needs in order to grow.

Find Out More

In the story, there is a long dry spell, or drought, that causes everything to die. This drought really happened in the "Dust Bowl," an area in parts of Kansas, Texas, and Oklahoma. Use an encyclopedia to find out more about what happened in the Dust Bowl in the 1930s. Share what you learn with your classmates.

Choose Reference Sources

Suppose that you wanted to write a report about the Dust Bowl. Where would you look? You could start with the **dictionary**. From there, you could look in an **encyclopedia** for more information. For maps of the area, you could look in an **atlas**. Here is a description of some reference sources you could use for your report.

Almanac: has up-to-date information about people, places, and events. The information often appears in a table or a chart.

Atlas: has many different kinds of maps.

Dictionary: lists words in alphabetical order. A dictionary gives the meaning, pronunciation, and part of speech of a word.

Encyclopedia: has articles on many topics, arranged in alphabetical order.

Thesaurus: lists words with the same or almost the same meaning.

Use the reference sources to answer these questions.

1. Where would you look to find out what *glisten* means?
2. Where would you look to find out about raising chickens?
3. Where would you look to find an up-to-date chart showing how many people live in each state of the United States?
4. In which book would you look to find other words for *big*?
5. How does knowing which reference book to use save you time?

TEST POWER

Test Tip

Tell yourself the story again in your own words.

DIRECTIONS

Read the sample story. Then read each question about the story.

SAMPLE

Achilles' Pottery

One day, Achilles looked up at a row of his best pots lined up on a shelf, and said, "I have exhausted all of the possibilities for my pottery. I have made round pots, square pots, big pots and small pots. I can mold the clay into any form I wish, but there isn't another pot for me to make."

"Perhaps," his father suggested, "you should consider painting your pots. Some of the best pots are painted with figures, animals, and landscapes."

Achilles smiled as he sprang to his feet. "I'll be right back!" he cried. "I must get to the painter's shop before it closes!"

1 In the future, Achilles' pots will probably be—

A the same as before

B painted with figures, animals, or landscapes

C painted all the same color

D have only animals painted on them

2 How did Achilles feel when he looked at his best pots on the shelf?

F Furious

G Lively

H Excited

J Frustrated

Stories in Art

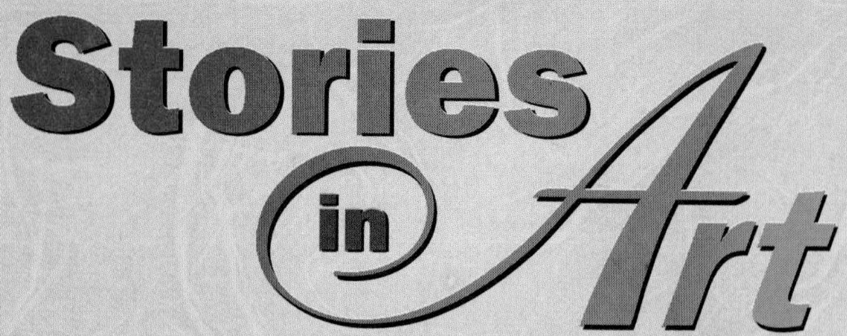

Some paintings hint at events. They do not tell the whole story. It is up to the viewer to predict what will happen.

Look at this painting. What can you tell about this race? Who is the man facing the rowers? Which team do you think will win? Why?

Look at this painting again. What do you think will happen to the winning team? How will the losers feel? If you could paint the next scene, how would it look?

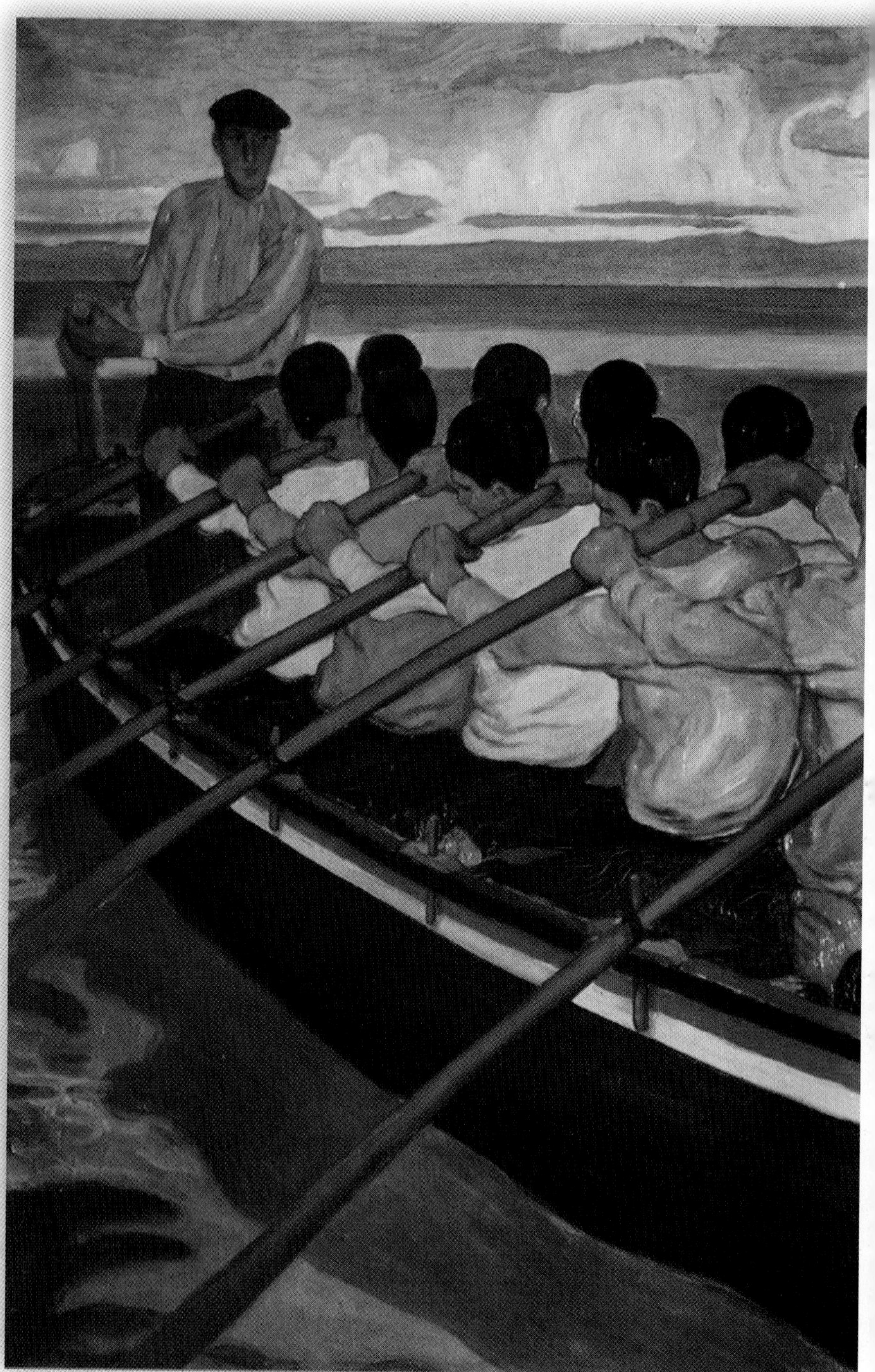

The Rowers **by Manuel Losada**
Museo de Bellas Artes, Bilbao, Spain

Meet Ken Mochizuki

Baseball Saved Us has a personal meaning for Ken Mochizuki. During World War II, his Japanese-American parents were taken from their homes and forced to live in a government "camp." By showing the camp through the eyes of the boy in the story, Mochizuki describes how the game of baseball solved many of the problems of camp life.

From this book, Mochizuki hopes to show young readers "that they should actually get to know others, rather than to assume things about them." They should also believe in what they can do, instead of believing in what others have told them they cannot achieve.

Besides writing books for young people, Mochizuki works as an actor and a journalist.

Meet Dom Lee

Baseball Saved Us is a favorite of illustrator Dom Lee. He has worked with Ken Mochizuki on several books for young people, but he has a special feeling for this one.

Lee, who was born in South Korea, does a lot of research for his books. He often looks at photographs to get ideas. For *Baseball Saved Us*, he studied the photographs of one of these camps taken by the famous American photographer, Ansel Adams.

To make the illustrations for the book, Lee first put beeswax on paper, then scratched out the images he wanted. Finally, he added oil paint and colored pencil, with remarkable results!

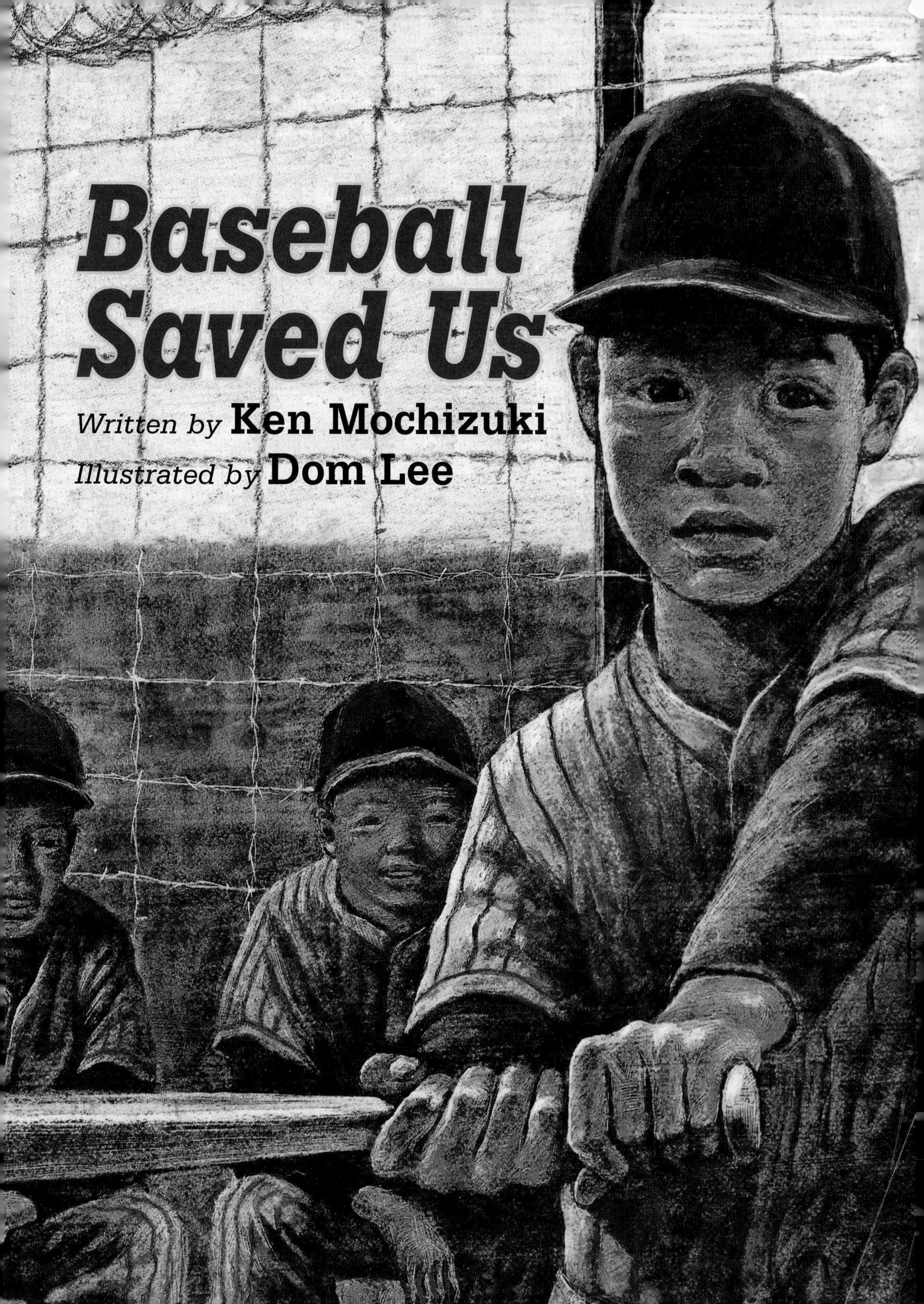

Baseball Saved Us

Written by **Ken Mochizuki**

Illustrated by **Dom Lee**

One day, my dad looked out at the endless desert and decided then and there to build a baseball field.

He said people needed something to do in Camp. We weren't in a camp that was fun, like summer camp. Ours was in the middle of nowhere, and we were behind a barbed-wire fence. Soldiers with guns made sure we stayed there, and the man in the tower saw everything we did, no matter where we were.

As Dad began walking over the dry, cracked dirt, I asked him again why we were here.

"Because," he said, "America is at war with Japan, and the government thinks that Japanese Americans can't be trusted. But it's wrong that we're in here. We're Americans too!" Then he made a mark in the dirt and mumbled something about where the infield bases should be.

Back in school, before Camp, I was shorter and smaller than the rest of the kids. I was always the last to be picked for any team when we played games. Then, a few months ago, it got even worse. The kids started to call me names and nobody talked to me, even though I didn't do anything bad. At the same time the radio kept talking about some place far away called Pearl Harbor.

One day Mom and Dad came to get me out of school. Mom cried a lot because we had to move out of our house real fast, throwing away a lot of our stuff. A bus took us to a place where we had to live in horse stalls. We stayed there for a while until we came here.

This Camp wasn't anything like home. It was so hot in the daytime and so cold at night. Dust storms came and got sand in everything, and nobody could see a thing. We sometimes got caught outside, standing in line to eat or to go to the bathroom. We had to use the bathroom with everybody else, instead of one at a time like at home.

We had to eat with everybody else, too, but my big brother Teddy ate with his own friends. We lived with a lot of people in what were called barracks. The place was small and had no walls. Babies cried at night and kept us up.

Back home, the older people were always busy working. But now, all they did was stand or sit around. Once Dad asked Teddy to get him a cup of water.

"Get it yourself," Teddy said.

"What did you say?" Dad snapped back.

The older men stood up and pointed at Teddy. "How dare you talk to your father like that!" one of them shouted.

Teddy got up, kicked the crate he was sitting on, and walked away. I had never heard Teddy talk to Dad that way before.

That's when Dad knew we needed baseball. We got shovels and started digging up the sagebrush in a big empty space near our barracks. The man in the tower watched us the whole time. Pretty soon, other grown-ups and their kids started to help.

We didn't have anything we needed for baseball, but the grown-ups were pretty smart. They funnelled water from irrigation ditches to flood what would become our baseball field. The water packed down the dust and made it hard. There weren't any trees, but they found wood to build the bleachers. Bats, balls and gloves arrived in cloth sacks from friends back home. My mom and other moms took the covers off mattresses and used them to make uniforms. They looked almost like the real thing.

I tried to play, but I wasn't that good. Dad said I just had to try harder. But I did know that playing baseball here was a little easier than back home. Most of the time, the kids were the same size as me.

All the time I practiced, the man in the tower watched. He probably saw the other kids giving me a bad time and thought that I was no good. So I tried to be better because he was looking.

Soon, there were baseball games all the time. Grown-ups played and us kids did, too. I played second base because my team said that was the easiest. Whenever I was at bat, the infield of the other team started joking around and moved in real close. The catcher behind me and the crowd for the other team would say, "Easy out." I usually grounded out. Sometimes I got a single.

Then came one of our last games of the year to decide on the championship. It was the bottom of the ninth inning and the other team was winning, 3 to 2. One of our guys was on second and there were two outs.

Two pitches, and I swung both times and missed. I could tell that our guy on second was begging me to at least get a base hit so somebody better could come up to bat. The crowd was getting loud. "You can do it!" "Strike out!" "No hitter, no hitter!"

I glanced at the guardhouse behind the left field foul line and saw the man in the tower, leaning on the rail with the blinding sun glinting off his sunglasses. He was always watching, always staring. It suddenly made me mad.

I gripped the bat harder and took a couple of practice swings. I was gonna hit the ball past the guardhouse even if it killed me. Everyone got quiet and the pitcher threw.

I stepped into my swing and pulled the bat around hard. I'd never heard a crack like that before. The ball went even farther than I expected.

Against the hot desert sun, I could see the ball high in the air as I ran to first base. The ball went over the head of the left fielder.

I dashed around the bases, knowing for sure that I would get tagged out. But I didn't care, running as fast as I could to home plate. I didn't even realize that I had crossed it.

Before I knew it, I was up in the air on the shoulders of my teammates. I looked up at the tower and the man, with a grin on his face, gave me the thumbs-up sign.

But it wasn't as if everything were fixed. Things were bad again when we got home from Camp after the war. Nobody talked to us on the street, and nobody talked to me at school, either. Most of my friends from Camp didn't come back here. I had to eat lunch by myself.

Then baseball season came. I was the smallest guy again, but playing baseball in Camp had made me a lot better. The other guys saw that I was a pretty good player. They started calling me "Shorty," but they smiled when they said it.

By the time the first game came around, I felt almost like part of the team. Everyone was laughing and horsing around on the bus. But as soon as we got out there, it hit me: nobody on my team or the other team, or even anybody in the crowd looked like me.

When we walked out onto the field, my hands were shaking. It felt like all these mean eyes were staring at me, wanting me to make mistakes. I dropped the ball that was thrown to me, and I heard people in the crowd yelling "Jap." I hadn't heard that word since before I went to Camp—it meant that they hated me.

My team came up to bat and I was up next. I looked down. I thought maybe I should pretend to be sick so I wouldn't have to finish the game. But I knew that would make things even worse, because I would get picked on at school for being a chicken. And they would use the bad word, too.

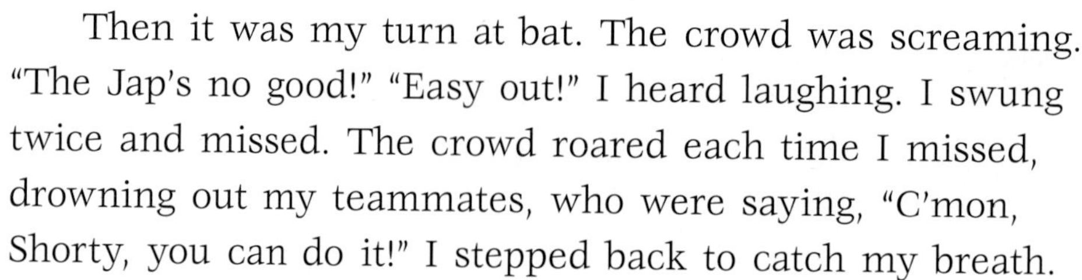

Then it was my turn at bat. The crowd was screaming. "The Jap's no good!" "Easy out!" I heard laughing. I swung twice and missed. The crowd roared each time I missed, drowning out my teammates, who were saying, "C'mon, Shorty, you can do it!" I stepped back to catch my breath.

When I stepped back up to the plate, I looked at the pitcher. The sun glinted off his glasses as he stood on the mound, like the guard in the tower. We stared at each other. Then I blocked out the noise around me and got set. The pitcher wound up and threw.

I swung and felt that solid whack again. And I could see that little ball in the air against the blue sky and puffy white clouds. It looked like it was going over the fence.

Story Questions & Activities

1. What is the "Camp" in the story?
2. Did you predict the ending of the story? Explain.
3. Why was baseball such a good idea for the people in the camp?
4. What would you tell a friend about this story?
5. Compare the boy in the story with Leah in "Leah's Pony." How are they alike? What makes them different?

Write a Sports Column

Imagine you are a wartime sportswriter reporting on games at the Japanese-American camp. Compare camp baseball to games played in other communities. Tell how and why the settings are different. Talk about how the games seem different and alike.

Design a Baseball Uniform

Everyone in the story took part in the game. For example, mothers took the covers off mattresses and used them to make uniforms. Now design your own baseball uniform. You can do this by drawing it, sewing it, or by putting together a "baseball outfit." Then have a fashion show to show off your uniforms.

Plan a Baseball Diamond

The people in the story built a baseball field. A baseball diamond has exact measurements. Look in an encyclopedia to find out what they are. Then draw a diagram of a baseball diamond. Include all of the measurements and angles.

Find Out More

The narrator became a hero by hitting a home run. Who are some of the great heroes of baseball? Look at baseball cards, interview an older friend, look in an encyclopedia, or read the sports pages of a newspaper. Find out more about baseball "greats." Share your information with the class.

Use an Encyclopedia

Where would you look to find more information about baseball? You could look in an encyclopedia. An **encyclopedia** is a set of books with articles about people, places, things, events, and ideas. The articles are arranged in alphabetical order in volumes. When you use an encyclopedia, you need a **key word**. For example, for general facts about baseball you would look under *baseball*. You could also look in the **index**. This is the last book in the encyclopedia. It gives a listing of all the topics.

Use the set of encyclopedias to answer these questions.

1. In which volume would you find the rules of baseball?
2. In which volume would you find more information about Jackie Robinson?
3. Where would you find information about the history of World War II?
4. In which volume would you look for a picture of a baseball diamond?
5. If you were not sure where to find a topic in the encyclopedia, where could you look it up?

TEST POWER

Test Tip

Look in the passage for clues about the character's feelings.

DIRECTIONS

Read the sample story. Then read each question about the story.

SAMPLE

What is Richie's new name?

Richard walked into the house, went straight to his bedroom, and closed the door.

His mother opened the door. "Richie," she asked, "is something wrong?"

"Kids are making fun of me, saying the name Richie is childish," he said sadly.

"Well, we can call you Richard or Rich, if you prefer," his mother suggested.

After his mother left his bedroom, Richard opened a book and looked through it. There he saw a famous race-car driver, Rick Astin. "Hey, Mom," Richard called, "I've found my new name."

1 What will Richard probably say next?

A That he likes the name Bob

B That he likes the name Rick

C That "Richie" is okay

D That he's hungry

2 How does Richard feel about the name "Richie"?

F Happy

G Enthusiastic

H Proud

J Embarrassed

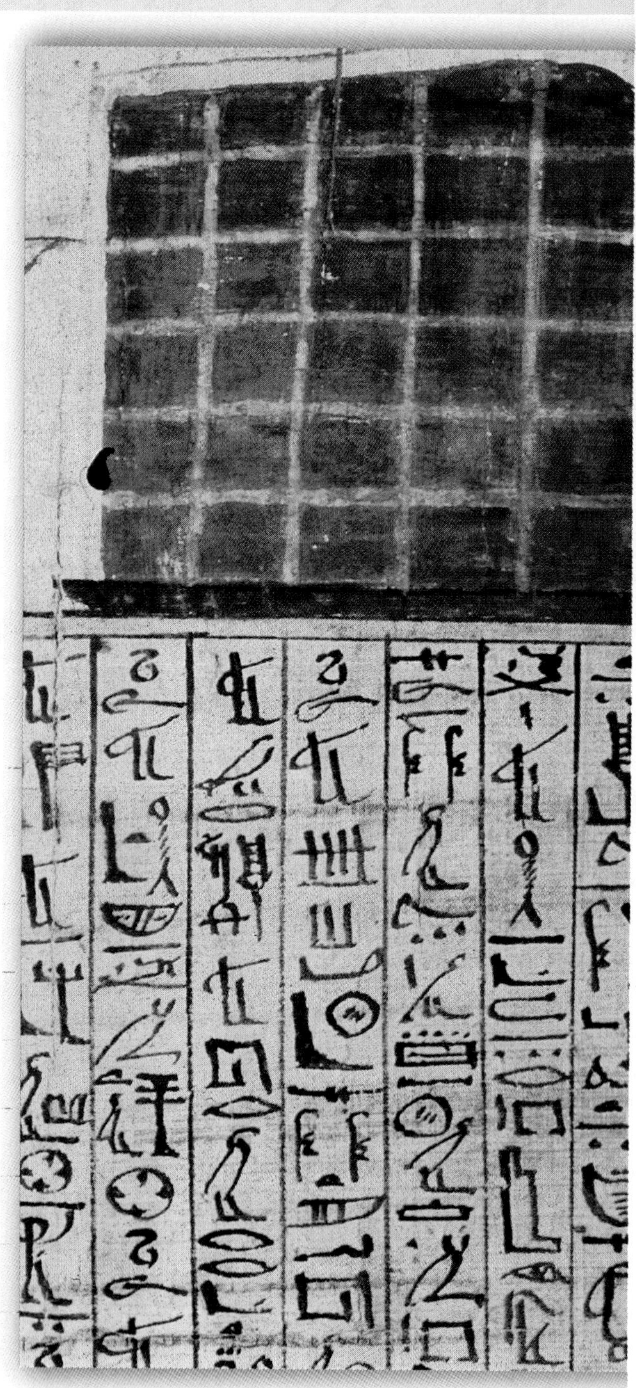

The picture writing at the bottom of this painting is called *hieroglyphics*. This writing disappeared in Egypt about two thousand years ago. What may have happened to cause it to disappear?

Look at this Egyptian painting. What are the workers doing? What do you think they are building? How does the painting use pictures and picture writing to tell a story? What effect does this painting have on you? Explain why.

Look at this picture again. If you could understand the writing, what do you think it would say? Why?

Workers Dragging Building Blocks
Egyptian, 1040–959 B.C.
British Museum, London

TIME

FOR KIDS

SPECIAL REPORT

Will Her Native Language Disappear?

Troubled Tongues

Even languages can be in danger of dying out

LeRoy Sealy's first day of first grade was probably the loneliest day of his life. He couldn't speak to any of the kids in his class. And he couldn't understand what they were saying. "I was pretty much alone, because I couldn't communicate," says Sealy, a Native American. "I didn't learn English until starting school." Sealy knew only the Choctaw language. No one else in his class could speak it.

Now grown up, Sealy teaches the Choctaw language at the University of Oklahoma. He still speaks Choctaw. So do about 12,000 other people. But Sealy worries about the future of his native language. Choctaw is on the endangered-language list.

Most Choctaw live in Oklahoma.

LeRoy Sealy helps his niece Patricia learn their native language, Choctaw.

When you hear the words *endangered* or *extinct*, you probably think of animals and other wildlife. But languages can also be endangered or extinct. People who study languages say about half the world's 6,500 languages may disappear in the next 100 years.

One group trying to change this is the Endangered Language Fund. The group prints books and makes recordings of languages that are dying out. By doing this, they may help keep some Native American languages alive.

How does a language become endangered? The most common way is that a small group of people who speak one language live among a large group of people who speak another language. The smaller group often starts to use the larger group's language and forgets its own. This has happened with Native Americans who have given up their own language to speak English.

Telephones, computers, and TV have spread languages spoken by a lot of people, such as English, across the planet.

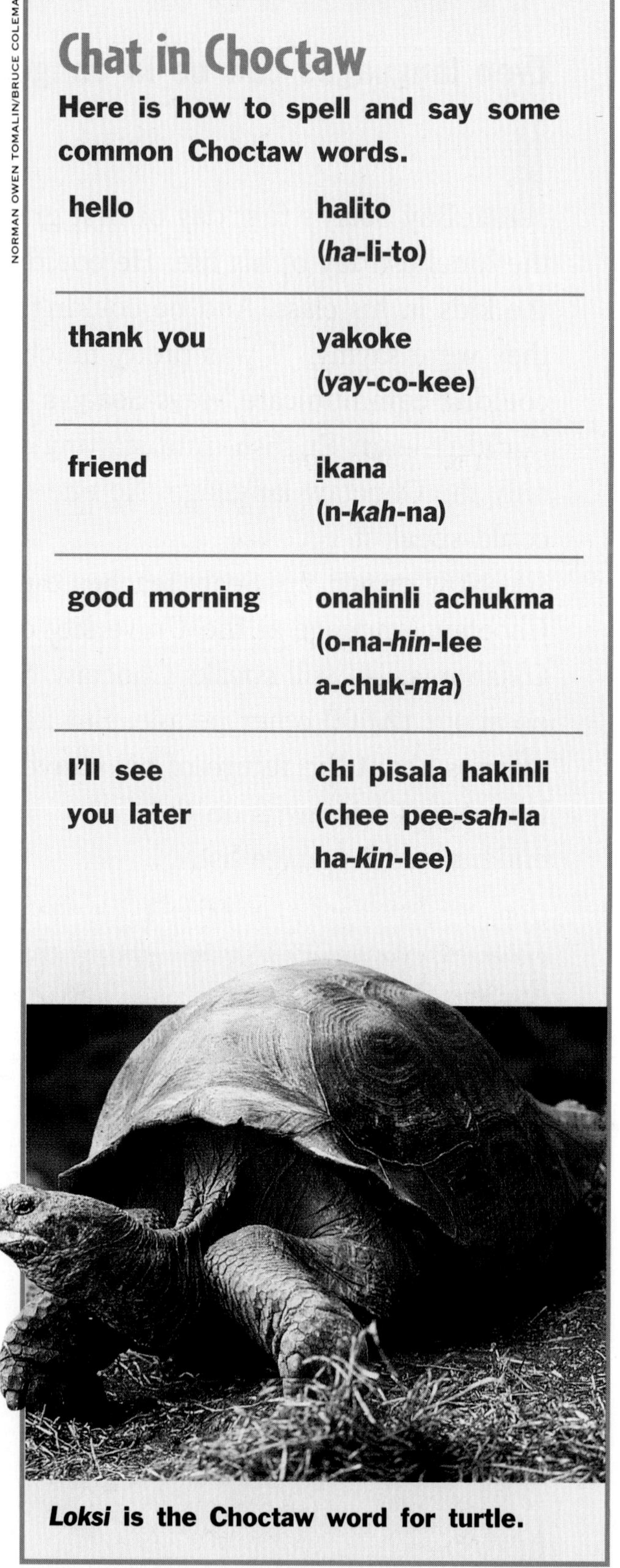

NORMAN OWEN TOMALIN/BRUCE COLEMAN

Chat in Choctaw

Here is how to spell and say some common Choctaw words.

hello	**halito (*ha*-li-to)**
thank you	**yakoke (*yay*-co-kee)**
friend	**ikana (n-*kah*-na)**
good morning	**onahinli achukma (o-na-*hin*-lee a-chuk-*ma*)**
I'll see you later	**chi pisala hakinli (chee pee-*sah*-la ha-*kin*-lee)**

***Loksi* is the Choctaw word for turtle.**

Sealy believes that sometimes governments have hurt native languages. "Native American children sent to government schools in the 1950s and '60s were told not to speak their native languages," he says. Instead, these kids spoke English and forgot their native tongues.

Some endangered languages face another problem. Many young people don't want to speak the language of their older relatives. Sealy hopes young Native Americans will learn to value their backgrounds and their language.

Sealy has taught Choctaw to his niece, Patricia Sealy. "We encourage her," he says, "because the younger generations will be the ones to carry the language into the 21st century."

FIND OUT MORE
Visit our website:
www.mhschool.com/reading

*inter***NET**
CONNECTION

Picture This!

Picture writing was used by Native Americans to record events about their lives, family histories, and the history of their tribes. Word signs were written on rocks, hides, bone, bark, and pottery. Picture writing made it possible for tribes who spoke different languages to communicate with each other.

Try picture writing yourself! Use some of the picture words here to make a story. Create your own pictures for words you would like to use.

Up **Down**

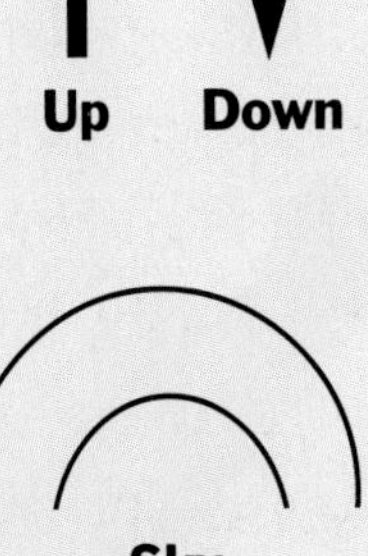
Sky

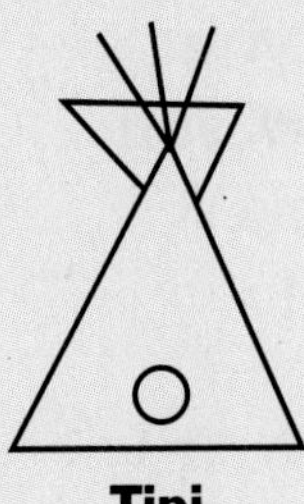
Tipi

Horse

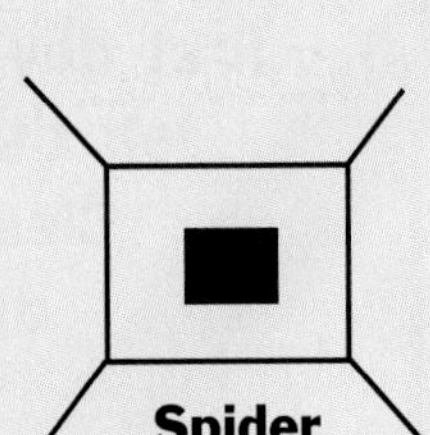
Spider

Mountain

Based on an article in *TIME FOR KIDS.*

Story Questions & Activities

1. What language did LeRoy Sealy speak as a child?
2. What might happen to the Choctaw language? Why?
3. Why is saving Native American languages important?
4. What is the main idea of this article?
5. Imagine that LeRoy Sealy met Justin's grandfather in "Justin and the Best Biscuits in the World." Do you think they would agree on why it is important to teach young people about the past? Explain.

Write a Diary Entry

LeRoy Sealy's first day of school was perhaps the loneliest day of his life. He couldn't speak English and couldn't understand anyone in his class. Write a diary entry about your first day at school. Compare how you felt then with how you feel now. Clearly state similarities and differences.

Make a Chart

LeRoy Sealy showed you how to spell and say some common Choctaw words. Now it's your turn.

Interview a friend or a family member who speaks another language. Write down in that language how to say words for such ordinary things as *school*, *coat*, and *pencil*. Make a poster illustrating the words in the other language and in English. Be sure you tell what the other language is!

Prepare a Welcome

The first day in a new school can be a lonely experience. How would you make a new student feel welcome? Get together with a small group of classmates to make a list of the things you would do to welcome the student.

Find Out More

LeRoy Sealy is a Choctaw Indian. Learn more about the Choctaw by reading about them in an encyclopedia or a book about Native Americans. What is their history? What games did they play? How did they farm? Share your information with the class.

Conduct an Interview

The writer had to interview LeRoy Sealy to get information for this article. What makes a good interview? Why is it important to know the right questions to ask? Here are some interviewing tips for you to follow.

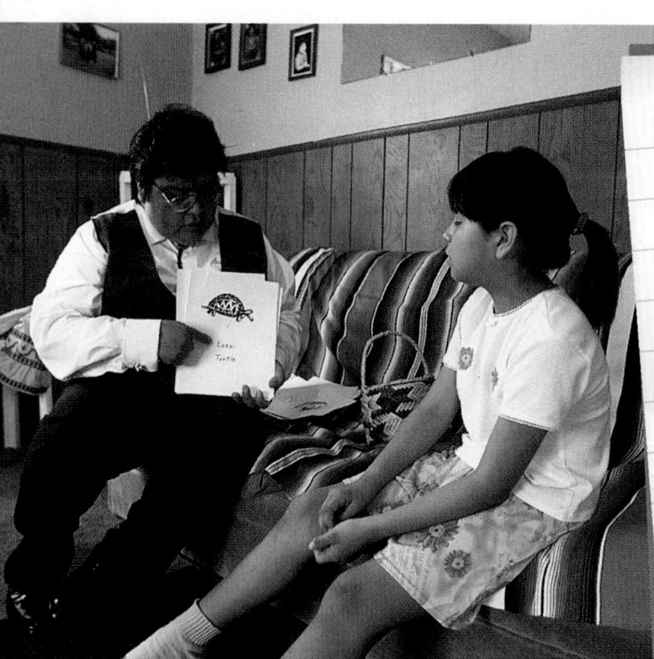

TIPS

- Make a note card of questions before the interview.
- State the purpose of your interview.
- Begin questions with these words: *Who? What? When? Where? Why? How?*
- Be polite. Ask clear, simple questions.
- Listen closely to the answers and take notes about them.
- Prepare for follow-up questions.

Use the interviewing tips to answer these questions.

1. What should you do before you interview someone?
2. With what words should most of your questions begin?
3. How should you ask questions?
4. Why is it important to listen closely to the answer?
5. Why might you ask a follow-up question?

TEST POWER

Test Tip

Enjoy what you are reading.

DIRECTIONS

Read the sample story. Then read each question about the story.

SAMPLE

The Lucky Day

Every day, Kali's bus passed the stables on its way to take her home. She hoped she would have an opportunity to learn how to ride a horse someday. She loved the way the horses charged around inside the white fence of the corral.

When Kali finished her homework, she rode her bike to the stables. She had been doing this every day for a month. Today she noticed a new woman working with the horses. The woman walked over toward Kali. "Would you like to help me groom Marco?" she asked.

"That would be great," Kali said. This was Kali's lucky day.

1 The word corral in this passage means—

A pen

B race

C kitchen

D telephone

2 What is the main idea of this passage?

F Kali enjoyed riding her bicycle.

G Kali did her homework right after school.

H Kali was a daydreamer.

J Kali wanted to learn how to ride a horse.

Did you use clues in the story to find the right answer? How?

August 8

There is no break
between
yesterday and today
mother and son
air and earth
all are a part
of the other
like
with this typewriter
I am connected
with these words
and these words
with this paper
and this paper with you.

by Norman Jordan

RIVER

UNIT 3

The Poet Pencil

Once upon a time a pencil wanted to write poetry but it didn't have a point. One day a boy put it into the sharpener, and in place of a point, a river appeared.

by Jesús Carlos Soto Morfín
Translated by Judith Infante

You might think that this picture is a photograph. But if you look closely, you will see that it is really a painting. Why do you think the artist painted the picture in this way?

Look at the picture. What do you see in the supermarket window? What information do the signs give? How do they help the shoppers decide what to buy? How do they also help you see that the picture was painted several years ago?

Look at the painting again. Would you like to see it in your home? In your school? In a museum? Does it make you think? Do you like this picture? Why or why not?

Food City
by Richard Estes, 1967
Private Collection

Meet CANDACE FLEMING

Candace Fleming discovered the music and magic of words when she learned the word "cornucopia" in second grade. "It sounded good. I loved the way it felt on my tongue and fell on my ears. I skipped all the way home from school that day chanting 'Cornucopia! Cornucopia!'"

Fleming has always admired Benjamin Franklin. She discovered *The Hatmaker's Sign* in a collection of Franklin's writings. She decided that young people would enjoy its humor and wisdom.

Fleming has won many awards for her writing. Besides her work as an author, she teaches at a college outside Chicago. When she is not working, she enjoys reading, camping, hiking, and traveling.

Meet ROBERT ANDREW PARKER

Robert Andrew Parker was born in Norfolk, Virginia. He served in the United States Army during World War II and later studied art in Chicago. Since then, he has lived in New York, Connecticut, and Ireland.

Parker's illustrations for *The Hatmaker's Sign* are an important part of the book. They help show the humor in Benjamin Franklin's story. Although he had been a painter for many years, Parker did not begin to illustrate books until after his five sons were grown. Since then, he has worked on more than fifty books! He has received many awards for his paintings and his illustrations. Parker's paintings can be found in The Museum of Modern Art, the Whitney Museum, the Metropolitan Museum of Art in New York City, and the Brooklyn Museum.

The Hatmaker's Sign

A Story by
BENJAMIN FRANKLIN

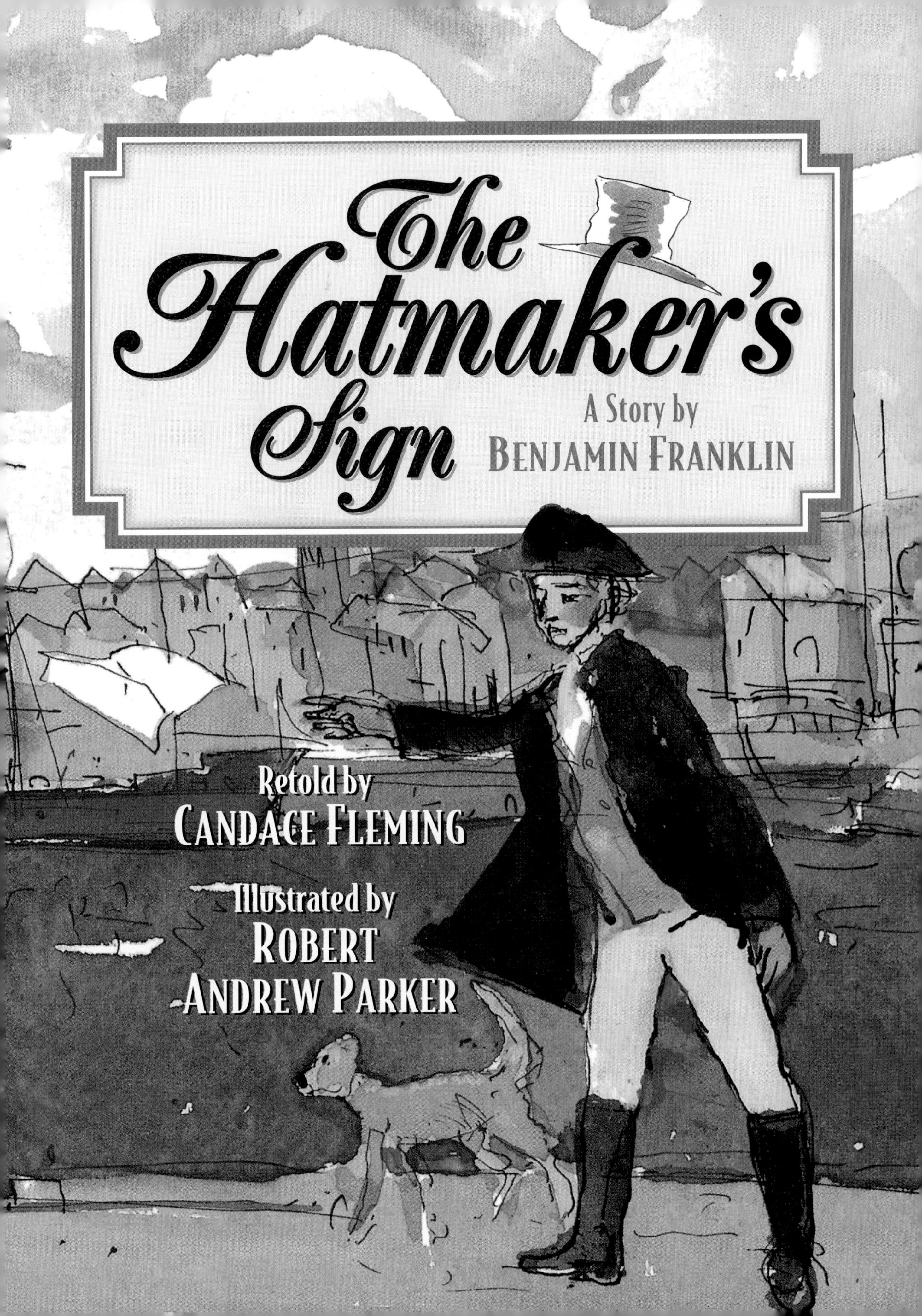

Retold by
CANDACE FLEMING

Illustrated by
ROBERT
ANDREW PARKER

At last!

After endless hours of scribbling and struggling, Thomas Jefferson had written it. And it was perfect. Every word rang. Every sentence sang. Every paragraph flowed with truth.

"It is exactly right," Jefferson exclaimed. "The Continental Congress will surely love it."

But the next morning, after Jefferson's wonderful words had been read aloud, the Congress broke into noisy debate.

"I do not like this word," quibbled one delegate. "Let's replace it."

"And this sentence," argued another. "I think we should cut it."

"What about this paragraph?" shouted still another. "It must be removed!"

While the Congress argued around him, Thomas Jefferson slumped into his chair. His face flushed red with anger and embarrassment.

"I thought my words were perfect just the way they were," he muttered to himself.

Just then he felt a consoling pat on his shoulder. He looked up and into the sympathetic eyes of Benjamin Franklin.

"Tom," Benjamin Franklin said, smiling, "this puts me in mind of a story."

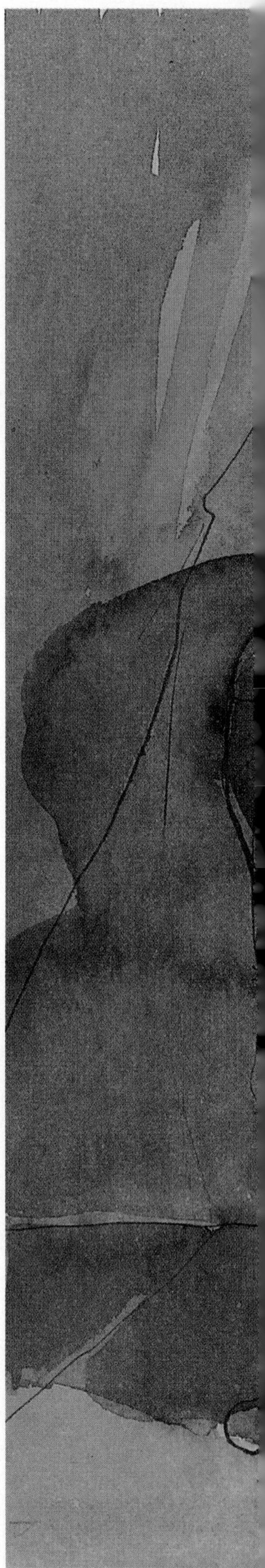

In the city of Boston, on a cobblestoned street, a new hat shop was opening for business.

All stood ready. Comfortable chairs had been placed before polished mirrors. Wooden hatboxes were stacked against one wall. And the front window was filled with tricorns and top hats, coonskins, and wool caps.

There was only one thing the hat shop did not have—a sign.

But the hatmaker, John Thompson, was working on it.

Knee-deep in used parchment and broken quill pens, John struggled to create a sign for his shop. And at long last, he wrote one. It read:

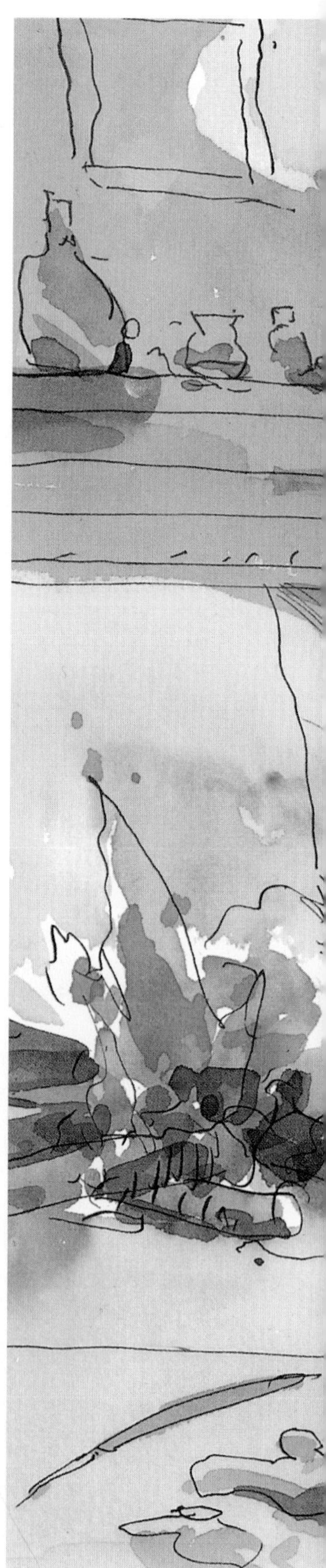

Beneath the words, John drew a picture of a hat.

"It is exactly right," John exclaimed. "Customers will surely love it."

But before hurrying to the sign maker's shop, where his words and picture would be painted onto board, John showed his parchment to his wife, Hannah.

"Oh John," Hannah giggled after reading what John had written. "Why bother with the words 'for ready money'? You're not going to sell hats for anything else, are you? Remove those words and your sign will be perfect."

"You're probably right," sighed John.

So John rewrote his sign. Now it read:

Beneath the words he drew a picture of a hat.

Parchment in hand, John headed for the sign maker's shop.

He had gone as far as the Old North Church when he met Reverend Brimstone.

"Where are you strolling on such a fine morning?" asked the reverend.

"To the sign maker's shop," replied John. He held out his parchment.

Reverend Brimstone read it.

"May I make a suggestion?" he asked. "Why don't you take out the words 'John Thompson, Hatmaker'? After all, customers won't care who made the hats as long as they are good ones."

"You're probably right," sighed John.

And after tipping his tricorn to the reverend, John hurried back to his hat shop and rewrote his sign. Now it read:

Beneath the words he drew a picture of a hat.

Parchment in hand, John headed for the sign maker's shop.

He had gone as far as Beacon Hill when Lady Manderly stepped from her carriage and into his path.

"What have you there?" asked the haughty lady. She plucked the parchment from John's hand and read it.

"Absurd!" she snorted. "Why bother with the word 'fashionable'? Do you intend to sell unfashionable hats?"

"Absolutely not!" cried John.

"Then strike that word out," replied Lady Manderly. "Without it, your sign will be perfect."

"You are probably right," sighed John.

And after kissing the lady's elegantly gloved hand, John hurried back to his hat shop and rewrote his sign. Now it read:

Beneath the words he drew a picture of a hat.

Parchment in hand, John headed for the sign maker's shop.

He had gone as far as Boston Common when he met a British magistrate.

The magistrate, always on the lookout for unlawful behavior, eyed John's parchment.

"Hand it over or face the stockades!" demanded the magistrate.

John did. He gulped nervously as the magistrate read it.

"Tell me hatter," bullied the magistrate. "Why do you write 'sold inside'? Are you planning on selling your hats from the street? That is against the law, you know. I say delete those words if you want to stay out of jail. And if you want your sign to be perfect."

"Yes, sir. No, sir. I mean I will, sir," stammered John.

And after hastily bowing to the magistrate, John hurried back to his hat shop and rewrote his sign.

Now it read:

Beneath the word he drew a picture of a hat.

Parchment in hand, John headed for the sign maker's shop.

He had gone as far as the Charles River when a brisk breeze snatched the parchment from his hand and dropped it at the feet of two young apprentices sitting on a crate of tea.

The first apprentice picked up the parchment and read it.

"Hey, mister," he said. "Why do you write 'hats' when you already have a picture of one?"

"Yes, why?" asked the second apprentice.

"It would be a much better sign without that word," suggested the first apprentice.

"It would be perfect," added the second apprentice.

"You are probably right," sighed John.

And after tossing each boy a halfpenny, John hurried back to his hat shop and rewrote his sign. Now it read:

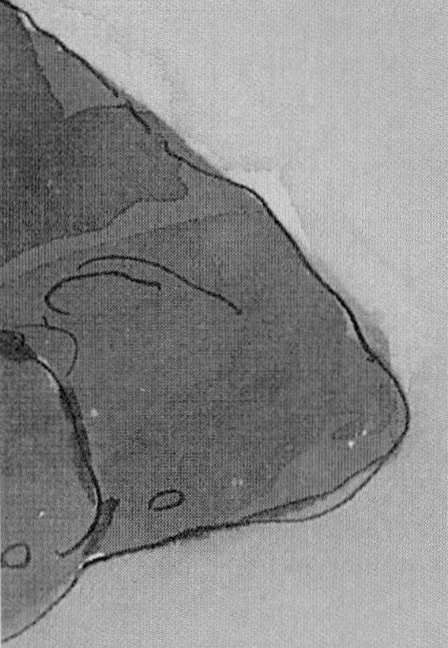

Nothing.

He drew a picture of a hat.

Parchment in hand, John headed for the sign maker's shop.

He had gone as far as Harvard College when he met Professor Wordsworth.

John shoved his parchment under the professor's nose. "Please, sir," he said. "Would you tell me what you think of my sign?"

The surprised professor straightened his spectacles and peered at the picture.

"Since you ask my opinion, I shall give it," said Professor Wordsworth. "However, I must ask you a question first. Are you displaying your hats in your shop's front window?"

John nodded.

"Then this picture is useless," declared the professor. "Everyone will know you sell hats simply by looking in your window. Eliminate the picture and your sign will be perfect."

"You are probably right," sighed John.

And after pumping the professor's hand in thanks, John hurried back to his hat shop and rewrote his sign.

Now it read nothing.

It showed nothing.

It was wordless and pictureless and entirely blank.

Parchment in hand, John headed to the sign maker's shop.

Past the Old North Church and Beacon Hill. Past Boston Common and the wharf and Harvard College.

At long last, John arrived at the sign maker's shop. Exhausted, he handed over his parchment.

"I do not understand," said the puzzled sign maker as he stared at the empty parchment. "What does this mean? What are you trying to say?"

John shrugged. "I do not know anymore," he admitted. And he told the sign maker about his new hat shop, and his sign, and how no one had thought it was perfect enough.

When he had finished, the sign maker said, "May I make a suggestion? How about:

'John Thompson, Hatmaker

Fashionable Hats Sold Inside for Ready Money.'

"Beneath the words I will draw a picture of a hat."

"Yes!" exclaimed John. "How clever of you to think of it. That is exactly right! Indeed, it's perfect!"

"So you see, Tom," concluded Benjamin Franklin. "No matter what you write, or how well you write it, if the public is going to read it, you can be sure they will want to change it."

For several moments, Thomas Jefferson pondered Franklin's story. Then sighing with acceptance, he listened as the Congress argued over the words that rang, the sentences that sang, and the paragraphs that flowed with truth.

And surprisingly, when the debate was done, and the changes were made, most believed Thomas Jefferson's Declaration of Independence was exactly right. Indeed, they thought, it was perfect!

Story Questions & Activities

1. When and where does the story take place?
2. How are the members of Congress like the people the hatmaker meets on his way to the sign shop?
3. What do you think made Benjamin Franklin a great storyteller?
4. What is the "message" of this story?
5. Imagine that the hatmaker became part of the picture on pages 256–257. What do you think he would say about the signs in the picture?

Write an Ad

Write an advertisement that will make people want to shop in the hatmaker's store. Use persuasive words and story details to support your opinions. Give three strong reasons why people should shop there.

Make a Sign

Follow the hatmaker's example and make a sign for a store you would like to own. Use a piece of construction paper to make your sign. Include the name of your store, a picture, and the kinds of things sold in it. Then display your sign in class.

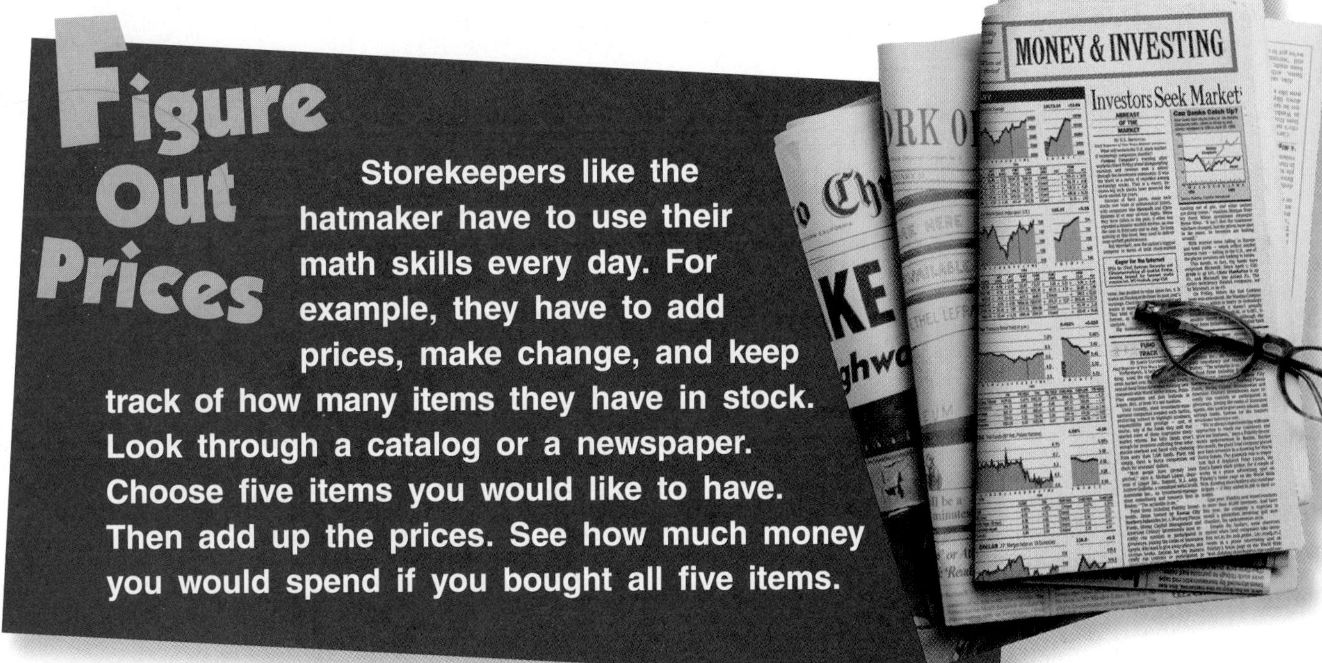

Figure Out Prices

Storekeepers like the hatmaker have to use their math skills every day. For example, they have to add prices, make change, and keep track of how many items they have in stock. Look through a catalog or a newspaper. Choose five items you would like to have. Then add up the prices. See how much money you would spend if you bought all five items.

Find Out More

In the story, Thomas Jefferson is hurt that Congress is changing his words. After all, he thought *his* Declaration of Independence was perfect. Find out more about the Declaration of Independence. Start by checking in a social studies book or an encyclopedia. Share what you find with a group or the class.

Read Signs

In Benjamin Franklin's day, **signs** on the streets of cities and towns often had pictures, just as they do today. Many signs use **symbols**, simple drawings that stand for actions, objects, or directions. For example, the symbol ⃠ means "No" or "Don't."

Use the signs to answer these questions.

1. How many of the signs have both words and symbols? What do those signs mean?
2. Which sign tells walkers not to cross the street? Describe it.
3. Why should drivers notice the School Crossing sign?
4. Why is yellow a good color for some warning signs?
5. Why do you think many signs contain symbols along with, or instead of, words?

TEST POWER

Test Tip

State the questions in your own words to make sure you understand them.

DIRECTIONS

Read the sample story. Then read each question about the story.

SAMPLE

Sally's Day at the Ballpark

Sally woke up at dawn, already grinning with excitement. She was going to a baseball game today with her cousin Jake. He was eighteen years old, and he had what seemed to Sally to be the world's best job. Jake was a hot-dog vendor.

Jake spent all summer in the park, talking with people and selling hot dogs. Sally loved the hot-dog cart. But most of all, she loved sitting with Jake—listening to him talk about funny, exciting things. She loved baseball. And she knew Jake loved baseball, too. It was no wonder Sally woke up happy. It promised to be a wonderful day.

1 The word vendor in this story means—

A friend

B brother

C seller

D teacher

2 Sally had the chance to go to the baseball game with Jake because—

F she pushed the hot-dog cart

G he played baseball

H she liked hot dogs

J he was her cousin

Did you rule out wrong answers? Tell how.

Stories in Art

It is a fact that this pastel drawing was made by the French artist Edgar Degas. Is it a good or bad drawing? That is a matter of opinion.

Look at the drawing. What can you tell about the dancers? How does the artist use line and shape to make them seem graceful? What colors does he use? What mood do they help to create? How?

Take the drawing as a whole. Do you think it is a good drawing? Give reasons to support your opinion.

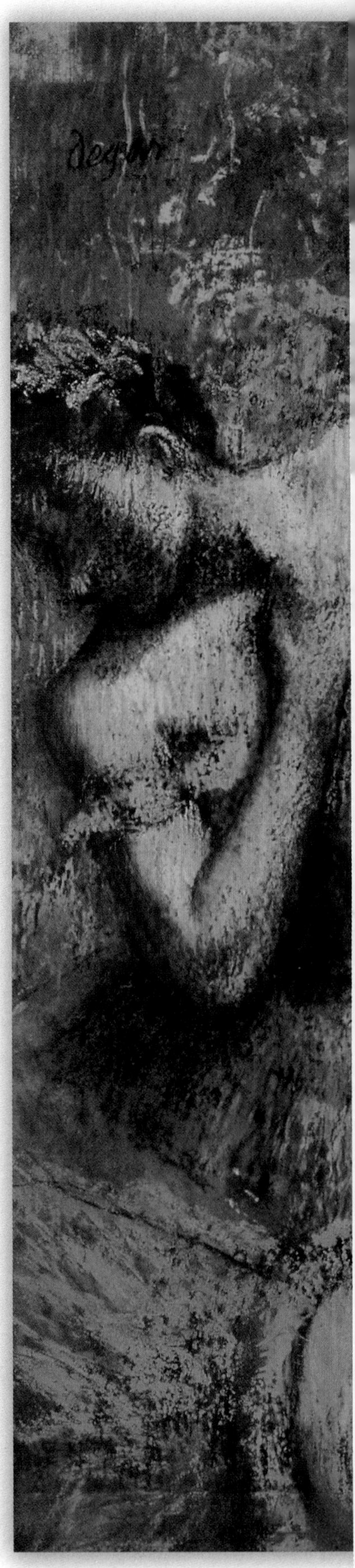

Blue Dancers **by Edgar Degas**
Hermitage Museum, St. Petersburg, Russia

PAT CUMMINGS: MY STORY

by Pat Cummings

Birthday: November 9, 1950

I've been drawing ever since I can remember. The first thing I ever drew was . . . a scribble. I would scribble all over a piece of paper and then I would go and get my box of Crayolas. I had made my mother get me the really huge, fifty-million-color size. I needed all those colors. And then I'd spend all afternoon coloring my scribbles.

I would take my drawing to my mother, and she would look at it thoughtfully and say, "What a nice *duck*!" And I would tell her, "It's not a duck, Mommy." So, she might turn the paper around and think about it and say, "Oh, I see, it's a *dinosaur*." And I would have to tell her, "It's a picture of Daddy."

yellow

It didn't take long to realize that nobody really knew what the pictures were supposed to be. But my mother would put them up on the refrigerator door, and that always made me feel good.

The first thing I remember drawing that people could recognize was the result of an adventure I had when I was about five years old.

My father was in the army and so my family moved every three years or so. At that time we lived in Kaiserslautern, Germany. My older sister, Linda, and I had decided to play outside and had taken lots of our toys and spread them out on the grass. After a while, she told me to watch all the toys while she went inside for a minute. She didn't come back.

I was getting very bored all by myself when a little bus came along and stopped at the corner. I got up, ran straight across the grass, and hopped on! I didn't know who the girls on the bus were or where they were headed and I certainly didn't speak any German, but the doors closed and we were off. After a while, we stopped at a small building and everyone got off the bus. So I got off the bus. They all ran into the building. So I ran in right behind them. Then they all got into tutus and toeshoes—it was a ballet school!

The girls were dancing around and doing stretches, so I just danced around and tried to do whatever they did. The teacher looked at me like I had just landed from Mars. All the girls were older than I was. When class ended, the teacher pinned a note on my blouse that said, "Please don't send her back until she's at least eight."

I was put back on the bus and got off when I saw my house. When I got home after a fun afternoon, I found I had worried my mother so much that I was in *huge* trouble. She had been up and down the street looking for me, knocking on neighbors' doors. She had even called the army police. I had to stay in the house for a good, long time after that and I got plenty of time to practice my drawing. And what I started drawing was . . . ballerinas, of course.

Even when I started school, I kept drawing ballerinas. I found my friends would give me a nickel for the drawings or a dime if I had really worked hard on one. Sometimes I got paid with M & M's or Twinkies. That was as good as money. Or sometimes I would trade drawings with someone else in my class who specialized in something else, maybe dinosaurs or horses. I loved to draw, and I had discovered that it could be good business, too!

Since we moved so often, my sisters and brother and I were always the "new kids" at school. I found if I joined the art club or helped make posters for other clubs, it was a way to make new friends.

Basically, I've just kept drawing because I love it, and it's never occurred to me to do anything else. I didn't know when I was growing up that there were so many types of art jobs possible. But I always felt lucky to know just what I wanted to do when I got older. I still feel incredibly lucky to be doing something I enjoy so much.

And it even pays better than the ballerinas!

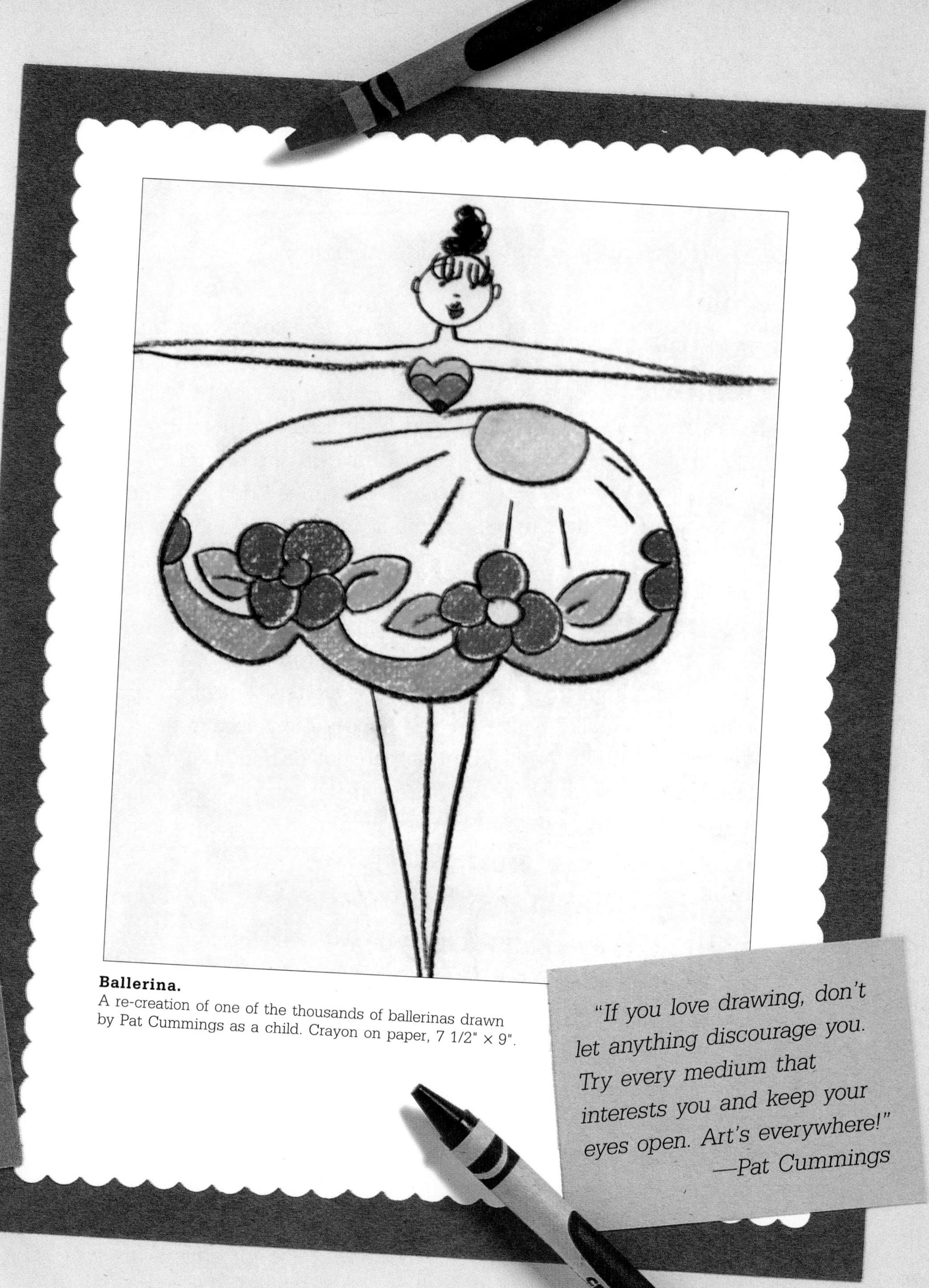

Ballerina.
A re-creation of one of the thousands of ballerinas drawn by Pat Cummings as a child. Crayon on paper, 7 1/2" × 9".

"If you love drawing, don't let anything discourage you. Try every medium that interests you and keep your eyes open. Art's everywhere!"
—Pat Cummings

Where do you get your ideas from?

Sometimes I get ideas from things I see around me, cloud formations or clothes people wear or things I've seen when I travel. One thing I really like about traveling to places where you don't speak or understand the language is that you usually look harder at things and see more. Your senses seem a little sharper.

I also get ideas from my dreams, which are usually pretty entertaining. I have great flying dreams sometimes, and that is why I usually put aerial views in my books. I'm always so disappointed to wake up and find I can't really fly, but drawing a scene from that perspective gives me back a bit of the feeling I have in the dreams.

Sometimes, ideas hit me smack in the head when I'm doing something like swimming or reading, or when I'm halfway through a drawing. Then, if I'm smart, I'll stop and write them down or sketch what I saw in my imagination. I have even jumped out of bed to paint at three in the morning because an idea won't let me sleep.

What is a normal day like for you?

I don't have any normal days because every job is different. Some days I meet with my editor, some days I get up early and work all day. Sometimes I work all night. Some days I teach a class at a local college. And sometimes I'm traveling to schools and libraries around the country. I work just about every day, and I work most of the time I'm home. If I have a deadline I am trying to meet, I might not leave the house for days at a time. I'll work until I'm sleepy, sleep until I wake up, and start again. Usually, I do try to go to the gym, and I might go to the movies to reward myself for finishing a page. There are usually thirty-two pages in a book. That can get to be a lot of movies.

Where do you work?

I live and work in a big loft in beautiful downtown Brooklyn, New York. If I look out of my back windows, I see the Statue of Liberty. Looking out of the window near my desk, I see the Brooklyn Bridge. It's great on the Fourth of July! There are fifteen windows and five skylights, so there's plenty of sunlight and, sometimes, moonlight.

My drawing table, desk, shelves, and filing cabinets are on one side of the loft, and my husband's work area is right across from mine. The whole place is one big, open space that we are always working on.

Do you have any children? Any pets?

We don't have any children, but we have talked about trying to find a twelve-year-old who likes to do dishes.

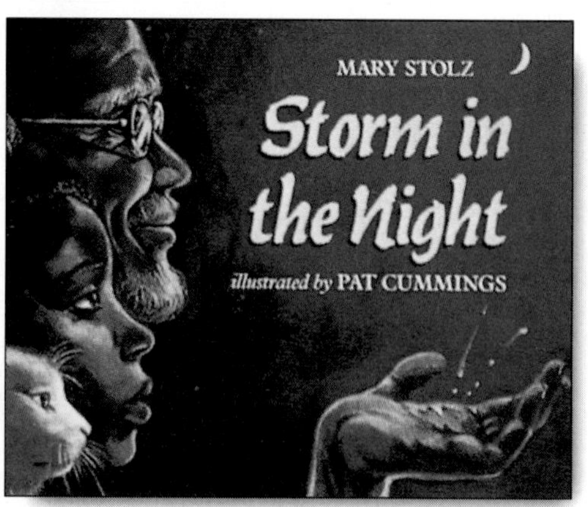

We have a cat named Cash who is very smart. She is on the cover of *Storm in the Night.* She comes when she's called, sits if you tell her to, and fetches if you throw her toy. I think she might be a dog.

C.L.O.U.D.S. 1986.
Airbrush, watercolor, and pencil, 15 1/2" × 10".
Published by Lothrop, Lee & Shepard Books.

5 What do you enjoy drawing the most?

People I know and faces in general. There is so much going on in a person's face. I like fantasy, too . . . drawing things that only exist in the imagination.

6 Do you ever put people you know in your pictures?

Definitely. Sometimes I do it to surprise the person. I might use old family photos or take new ones to use as reference. I draw my husband, Chuku, a lot. He's just about the only one who will pose for me at two-thirty in the morning. I've drawn neighbors, neighbors' pets, and friends who might even ask me to change their hairstyles or make them look thinner. I will also find models to draw who fit the image I have in my mind of the characters in the book.

I used my sister Linda and my niece Keija on the cover of *Just Us Women*. Keija told me once that her picture was the only reason people read the book! That book is filled with family: my mother, Chuku, my brother-in-law Hassan, my grandfather, my sister Barbara, and a friend or two. It makes the book more personal for me.

7 What do you use to make your pictures?

Everything. I like to use different materials. Sometimes it's big fun, but sometimes it's disastrous. I use watercolors and colored pencils most often; gouache, acrylics, pastels, airbrush, and pen and ink sometimes. I've experimented with collage and even rubber stamps, but I don't think I've tried half of the stuff I see in the art supply stores.

I also maintain a big picture file for reference. If I have to draw an armadillo, it helps a lot to have a picture to look at while I work.

8 How did you get to do your first book?

I put some illustrations from art school into a portfolio and went to see editors at publishing houses. They gave me good advice but no work. Then an editor saw my artwork in a newsletter and offered me a book to illustrate. I was so excited that when she asked if I knew what to do, I said, "Sure, no problem." I didn't have a clue how to start, but I didn't want to let her know.

I knew somebody, who knew somebody, who knew someone who used to know Tom Feelings, a children's book illustrator whose work I admired. So I looked in the phone book, called Tom up, and asked him if he would help me. He was wonderful. He gave me advice on how to pick which parts of the story to illustrate and how to decide where the pages should turn. He reminded me always to leave lots of room for the words to fit, to be sure that the character looks like the same person all the way through the book, and to try and keep important details away from the middle of the book, where the pages are sewn together. You don't want your reader pulling the book apart to see something important that's been hidden in the seam!

Tom taught me a lot that afternoon. He and many other illustrators still inspire me. I still learn from looking at their work. The most important thing I learned from Tom that day was that we have to help each other. He helped me get started, and I never forget that when someone who wants to illustrate calls me.

Story Questions & Activities

1. What event caused Pat Cummings to start drawing ballerinas?

2. Is the following statement a *fact* or an *opinion*? *I think Pat Cummings is the best artist today*. Explain why.

3. What makes Pat Cummings a good artist? Explain.

4. What is the main idea of this selection?

5. Compare Pat Cummings' attitude toward her work with John Thompson's feelings about his sign in "The Hatmaker's Sign." Who has more confidence in his or her work? How can you tell?

Write an Encouraging Note

Pat Cummings loves to draw. What do you love to do—read, dance, collect things, play a sport, or something else? Write a note encouraging a friend to try your activity. Tell why the activity is worth doing, even if it seems hard.

Do a Science Experiment

Pat Cummings gets ideas from clouds. To see how clouds form, put water in a jar. Cover it with plastic wrap. Hold it in place with a rubber band. Put ice cubes on the top. As the water warms inside the jar, it will turn into water vapor and rise to the top. The air cooled by the ice cubes turns the vapor back into water. You'll see the drops form inside the plastic wrap!

Draw a Picture

Pat Cummings often draws the people and pets she sees around her. Look around you. Draw someone or something you think would be interesting to draw. Give your drawing a title, and sign it at the bottom.

Find Out More

Pat Cummings' article is all about being an artist. How does someone become an artist? What is art school like? Start by interviewing an art teacher. Learn about some of the different jobs that artists have. Use what you learn to write an index card for each job you learn about. Then place the cards in your class's Job Box.

Read a Flowchart

Pat Cummings describes what it is like to draw pictures for children's books. In fact, she gives a step-by-step description. Look at the flowchart. A **flowchart** is a chart or a diagram that shows how to do something step-by-step. Read the steps that an artist takes to illustrate a book.

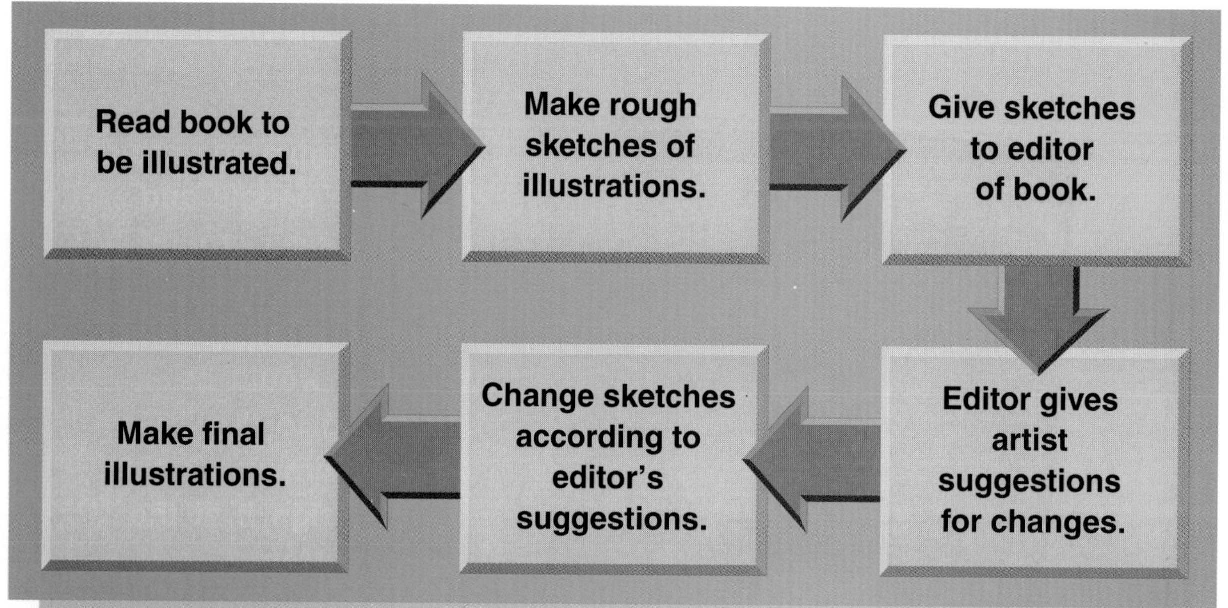

Use the flowchart to answer these questions.

1. What does this flowchart show?
2. What is the first thing an artist does to illustrate a book?
3. To whom does the artist give the rough sketches?
4. What does the editor tell the artist?
5. Which steps would an artist skip if the editor liked the rough sketches just as they were?

TEST POWER

Test Tip

Ruling out wrong answers will make it easier to find the best answer.

DIRECTIONS

Read the sample story. Then read each question about the story.

SAMPLE

The Story of Soybeans

The soybean is part of our daily lives. It is used in a broad range of products like mayonnaise, noodles, and chocolate coatings.

Soybean seeds are round or oval-shaped and come in a variety of colors. Yellow seeds are ground into meal or used for their oil, while green seeds are used to grow soybeans for food products.

Two weeks after planting, the soybeans begin to sprout. Around the sixteenth week, the seeds are fully mature, and the plant itself begins to shrivel and die. The seeds must be harvested before the pods fall to the ground. If not, the seeds will spoil and rot.

1 In order for soybeans to be harvested, the seeds must be—

A oval

B spoiled

C shriveled

D mature

2 What is the main idea of the third paragraph?

F Soybeans sprout and then mature at about 16 weeks.

G Soybeans are round or oval-shaped and colored.

H The plants will grow green leaves.

J Soybean plants blossom and produce pods.

Stories in Art

When you look at this stained glass window, you almost feel as if you, too, are going on a journey. That's because the artist has made this stained glass window from his point of view.

Look at the colored glass. How does the artist get your eye to look inside the circle? How does the circle frame the story the artist is telling? What do you think that story is about? What is the artist's purpose in telling it?

Look at the stained glass window again. How do you think it would look with the sun shining through it?

Pilgrims Going to Canterbury, **Thirteenth Century**
Canterbury Cathedral, Kent, England

Meet Dawnine Spivak

Basho's poetry is a favorite of writer Dawnine Spivak. In fact, she has taught his poetry at several different universities in New England, where she lives. Spivak, who lives in a farmhouse, has also served as a member of the Vermont Anti-Hunger Corps. Her interest in the needs of others can be seen in her writing as well.

Meet Demi

Demi's full name is Demi Hitz. She has illustrated more than 130 children's books, including *The Empty Pot*, *Liang and the Magic Paint Brush*, and *The Nightingale*, a *New York Times* Best Book of the Year. Besides book illustrations, Demi likes to make larger works of art. She has painted murals in Mexico and gold-leaf mosaics in the dome of St. Peter and Paul's Church in Wilmington, California.

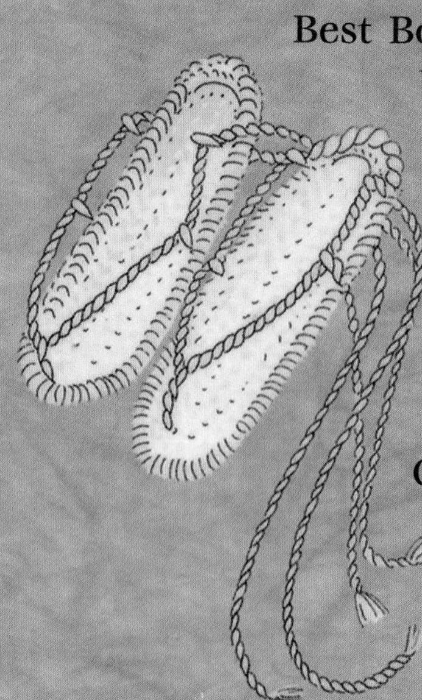

雨火友馬川山界舟月

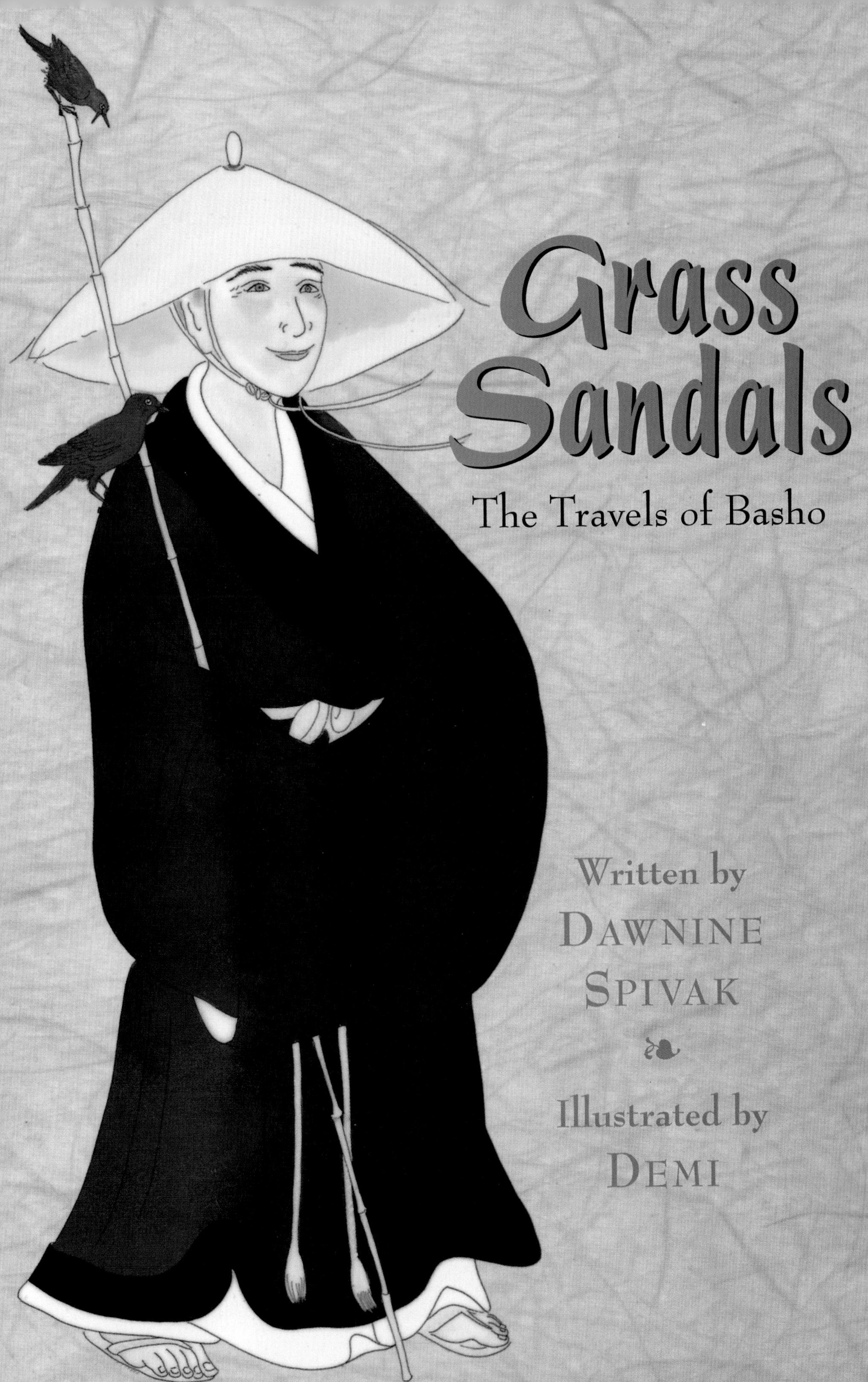

Grass Sandals

The Travels of Basho

Written by
DAWNINE SPIVAK

Illustrated by
DEMI

Traditionally, poems in the form called haiku are characterized by seventeen syllables broken into three lines with five, seven, and five syllables respectively. Each haiku includes language that appeals to two of the five senses—sight, hearing, smell, touch, and taste, or the additional sense of movement.

The characters of Japanese writing, the kanji, often follow the forms of nature. In this book, for example, the character for *mountain* can be seen to resemble the shape of a mountain, *rain* looks like rain, *river* a river, and so forth.

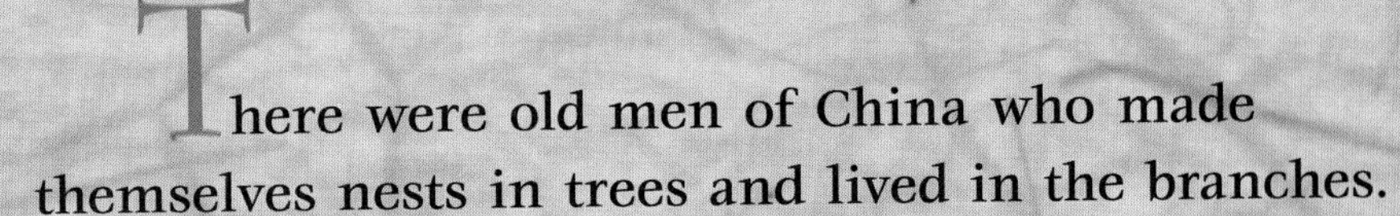

There were old men of China who made themselves nests in trees and lived in the branches.

山

YAMA
mountain

alone in my house—
only the morning glories
straggle to my door

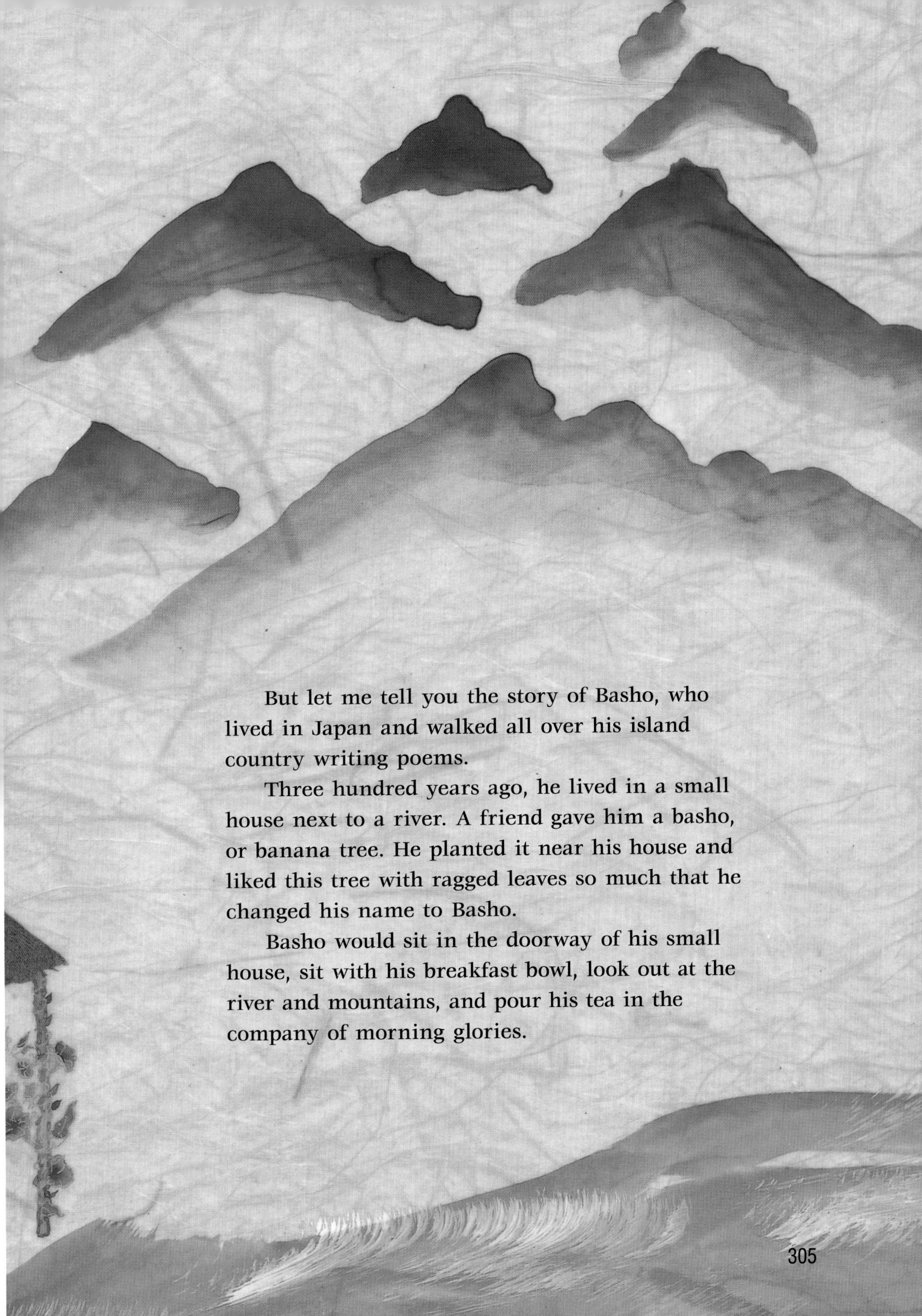

But let me tell you the story of Basho, who lived in Japan and walked all over his island country writing poems.

Three hundred years ago, he lived in a small house next to a river. A friend gave him a basho, or banana tree. He planted it near his house and liked this tree with ragged leaves so much that he changed his name to Basho.

Basho would sit in the doorway of his small house, sit with his breakfast bowl, look out at the river and mountains, and pour his tea in the company of morning glories.

But one spring day, Basho felt restless and decided to travel. He decided to walk across Japan. He didn't need much—a rainhat made of tree bark, a raincoat made of thick grass to protect his black robe. He prepared for his journey by sewing his torn pants and stitching a string on his hat so that it wouldn't fly off in the wind.

suddenly it pours—
shivering little monkey
needs a grass raincoat

AME

rain

To his hat, he said: "Hat, I will soon show you cherry blossoms."

And he scribbled on his hat: Soon, cherry blossoms. Basho closed his small house and walked to the river.

Basho began his journey on a boat, and many of his friends kept him company for a few miles on the river. His friends brought him presents for his trip: a paper coat to keep off chills, writing paper, an ink stone, and for his feet on their long walk, woven grass sandals. So little was needed for simple traveling. He carried it all with him tied up in a cloth.

川

KAWA
river

one morning at dawn
I wade in the wide river—
pants wet to my knees

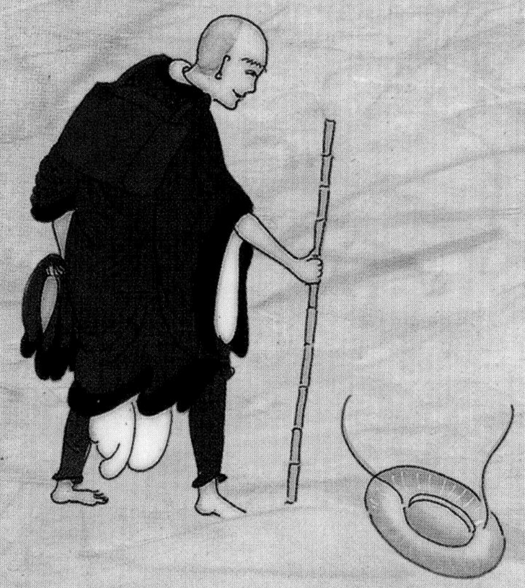

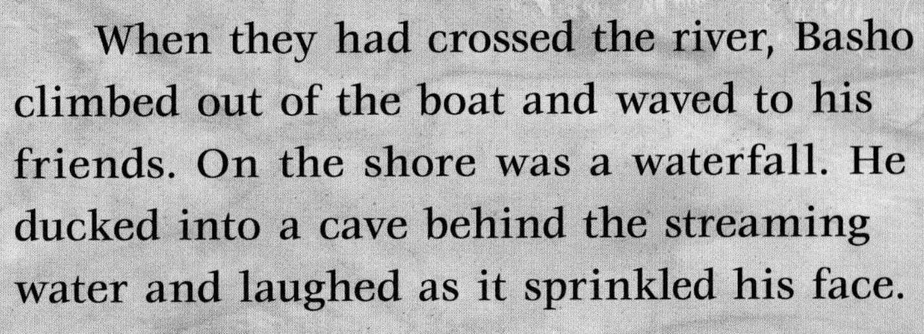

When they had crossed the river, Basho climbed out of the boat and waved to his friends. On the shore was a waterfall. He ducked into a cave behind the streaming water and laughed as it sprinkled his face.

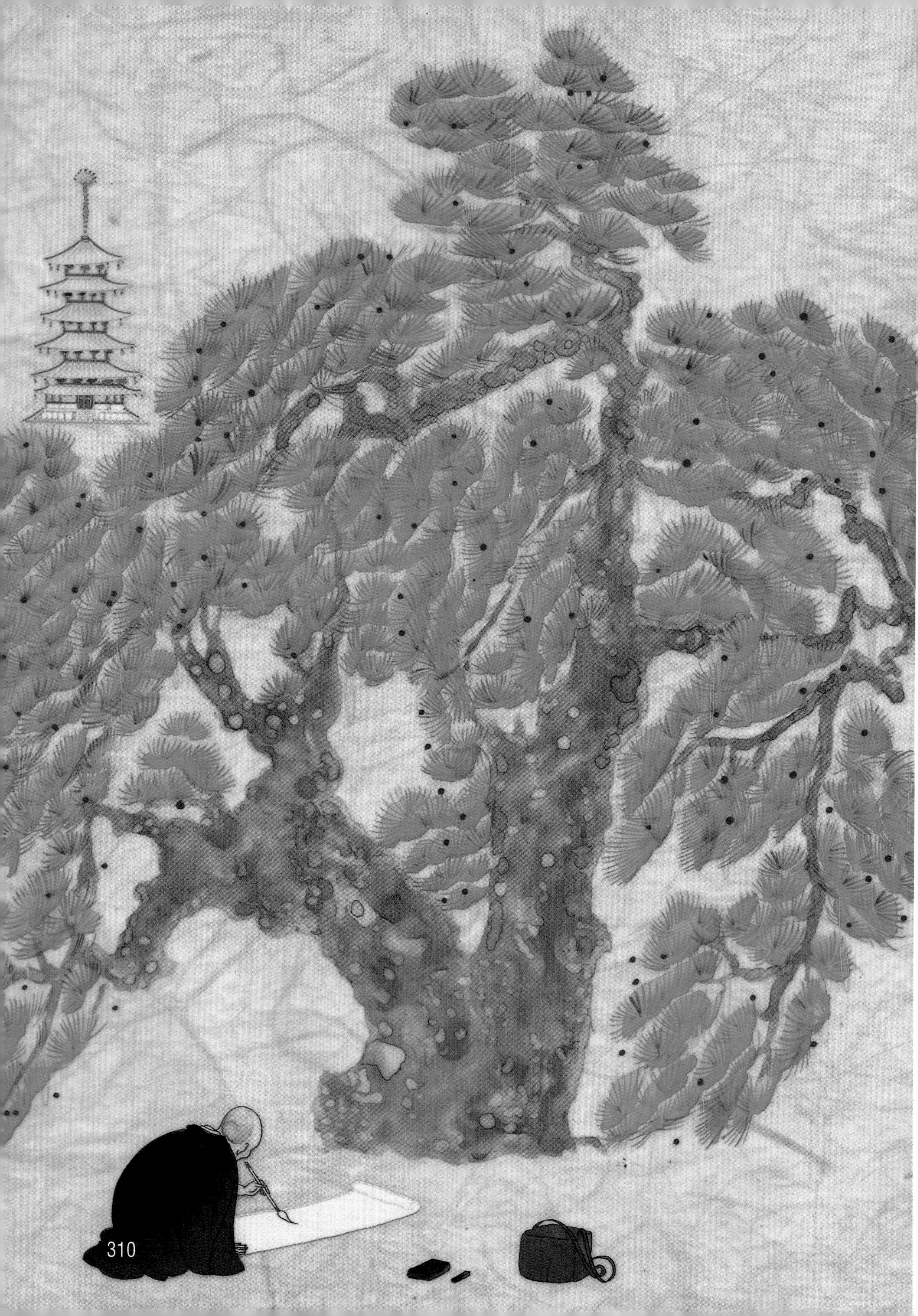

I walk to find you
sometimes five or six miles—
cherries in blossom

KI

tree

In his grass sandals and black robe, Basho walked and walked—looking like a black crow, he thought. Near an old temple he found a twin pine tree one thousand years old.

Basho sat and wrote a poem to this ancient, twisted tree.

Picking up his pack and climbing the winding paths, he was surprised by satiny red bark in a spring orchard, and to these trees, too, he chanted a poem.

For finally, he had kept his promise to his hat. He walked beneath the cherry trees in blossom and under the flowering branches met an old friend whose hair was as white as the petals.

At night he often rested his head on grass pillows. Sometimes he slept on flowers, in huts, or in paper rooms. Sometimes he rested in a horse stall or in a bed where fleas nipped him. He slept in fishing villages and smelled the fishy smells.

a tiny pink crab
tickling me climbs up my leg
from glistening sea

魚

UO
fish

Basho took his baths in hot springs, splashed in cold streams, and swam in the sea.

He ate whatever he found or was given along the way: A farmer gave him a cucumber or a radish, an old woman invited him to share her noodles.

Some days he made a fire, put water in a pot, and cooked rice and beans for his supper. Then he rolled the leftovers into rice balls to eat the next day as he journeyed.

HI
fire

let's peel cucumbers
pick up fallen red apples
for our small supper

馬

UMA
horse

Once a trusting farmer lent him a horse to ride across a wide, grassy field. The wind blew on Basho's suntanned face as the horse trotted through the clover.

hibiscus flowers
munched up in the horse's mouth
eaten one by one

When he heard a grasshopper or saw the horse eating flowers or spied a hawk circling, he took his ink brush and wrote a quick poem. Basho sent the horse back to the farmer with a poem in a pouch tied to the saddle.

In a mountain village, Basho met friends and they had a party to watch the full moon. Drinking tea, each could find a small moon reflected in the bottom of his cup. While clouds and stars and shadows lifted, they created poems together, sitting under the night sky.

winking in the night
through holes in my paper wall—
moon and Milky Way
(Issa)

月

TSUKI
moon

友

TOMO
friend

The next morning as Basho was leaving, one friend gave him new grass sandals with laces dyed blue like the iris.

"Good-bye, my friend, and thank you, thank you."

Basho hugged his friend. Crisscrossing the blue ties of his sandals around his ankles, he set out again on his walk across his island country of Japan.

stems of new iris
blooming right on my own feet—
shoelaces dyed blue

KAI
world

His blue-laced sandals carried him to distant beaches and fields and forests. Basho stopped to write a poem when he found a creature or person or plant that opened his eyes and his heart. He watched the fog curve over the hills. He noticed a cricket. Sleeping in a leaky hut, he smelled the rain. Each morning he tasted his tea.

In the evening he heard a frog leap into a pond. And so, three hundred years ago he traveled, and the world was his home.

old and quiet pond
suddenly a frog plops in—
a deep water sound

Places Basho Visited
Mogami
Kisagata
Oishida
Ryusha Kugi
Mogami River
Iwanuma
Matsushima
Nikko
Nara
Edo
Yoshino

What Basho Saw

Edo	Basho's house
Nikko	Waterfall
Iwanuma	Twin pine tree and temple
Matsushima, Kisagata	Sea coast, fishing villages
Mogami, Mogami River, Oishida	Friends composing poetry while watching the moon
Ryusha Kugi	Mountain temple
Nara	Temple
Yoshino	Cherry orchards

Matsuo Basho, the haiku poet most loved and honored in his country, lived in seventeenth-century Japan (1644–1694).

He wrote journals of his travels in *haibun*, a diary of prose and poems. The places that he loved—the shrines and mountains and villages—can still be visited, and the poems remain as fresh as new leaves.

The journey of *Grass Sandals* compresses and combines events from several of Basho's travels.

At the age of fifty, Basho sold his small house in Edo and set out on his last journey.

The haiku on the page with the Japanese character Tsuki (moon) was created by Issa, another Japanese poet who lived a century after Basho.

Story Questions & Activities

1. How did Basho get his name?
2. Why did Basho's friends give him writing paper and ink as he started on his journey?
3. Why do you think the author wrote about Basho? Explain.
4. What is this selection mostly about?
5. Both Pat Cummings and Basho enjoy the beauty around them. Compare what Pat Cummings does with the things she sees with what Basho does.

Write a Book Review

Write a book review of "Grass Sandals." Tell

- **who the main character is**
- **where and when the story takes place**
- **what happens in the story.**

Describe the pictures and the haiku poems used in the story. Then tell whether or not you would recommend the book to others to read. Give three good reasons.

Paint Japanese Characters

In the story, the author uses some Japanese symbols, or characters, and tells what they mean. Now it's your turn. Use a paintbrush, thick art paper, and black paint to draw some of the Japanese characters in the story. Below each character, write the English word for it. Share your finished product with the class.

Write a Poem

Basho walked across his country to learn and write poems about it. Imagine that you are a poet. Look at a map of your state. Make a list of the interesting places you would like to see. Then write a poem about one of them.

Find Out More

Basho traveled through Japan in the 1600s and wrote poems about his experiences. What is Japan like today? Read about Japan in an encyclopedia or a travel guide. Use what you learn to write a travel brochure. Describe a few interesting places to visit. Include photographs or pictures of Japan.

Read a Map

Basho began his journey on a boat. Then he walked across his island country of Japan. Japan lies in the North Pacific Ocean. Tall mountains and green hills cover most of the land. Like many countries today, Japan has several big cities. Edo, where Basho lived, is now called Tokyo. Tokyo is the capital and largest city in Japan.

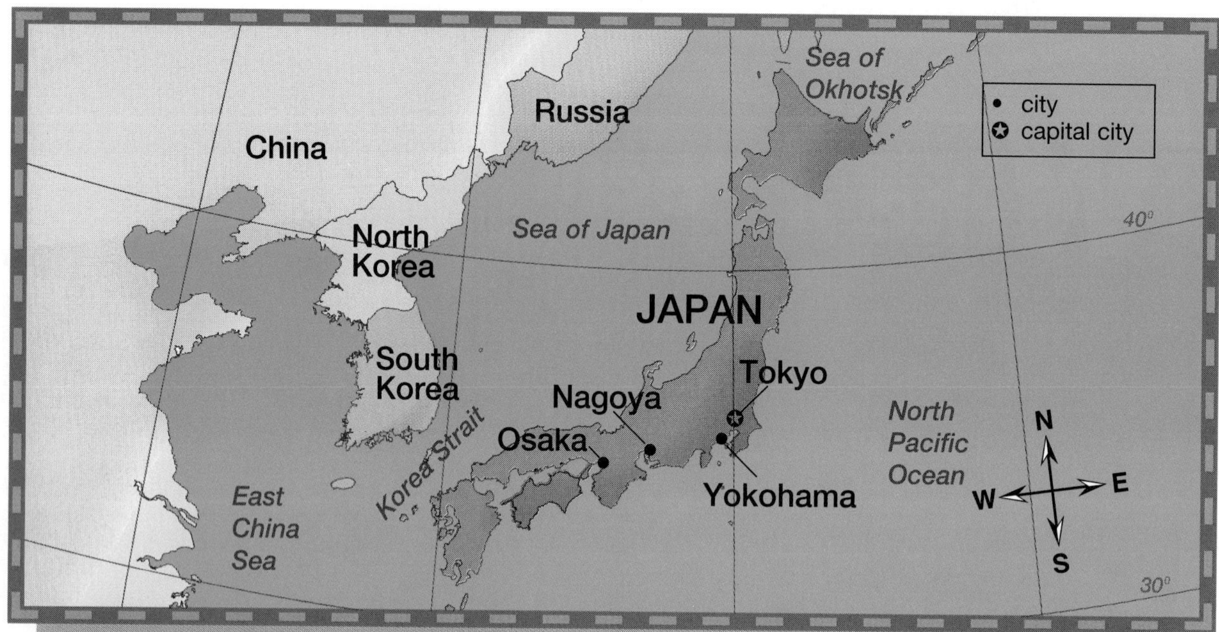

Use the map to answer these questions.

1. What is the capital of Japan?
2. Besides Tokyo, what are three other cities in Japan?
3. In which direction is Yokohama from Tokyo? How do you know?
4. Which three countries are nearest to Japan?
5. Why do you think Japan has the world's largest fishing industry?

TEST POWER

Test Tip

Keep your attention turned to your work.

DIRECTIONS

Read the sample story. Then read each question about the story.

SAMPLE

What goes in the corner?

Benoit's favorite plant, a fern with delicate, tender leaves, was sick. It had some kind of mold, and Benoit's parents said it was probably going to die.

He hurried home after school to see his fern. Benoit ran into the living room to the corner where his fern should have been. His mother came in and put a consoling arm around his shoulders.

"Your father is going to come home early today so we can go out together and buy a new plant for you. How does that sound?" she asked. Benoit looked up and said nothing. He couldn't picture anything replacing his fern.

1 Why was the fern probably going to die?

A It took up too much space in the living room.

B Benoit's parents didn't like it.

C It was too big.

D It had some kind of mold.

2 The word consoling in this story means—

F too long

G filled with caring

H hard to understand

J not very exciting

This painting tells part of a real-life story that started about 100 years ago. That story was known as the Great Migration. It was a time when African Americans moved north to find jobs in cities like Chicago, St. Louis, and New York.

Look at the painting. What facts is the artist trying to show? Why are African Americans choosing one of three gates or doors to go through? What do you think they will find on the other side? How is the artist using real life to create art? Is his painting effective? Why or why not?

Look at the painting again. Do you like it? Give reasons for your opinion.

The Migration of the Negro
by Jacob Lawrence

Meet Scott Russell Sanders

Scott Russell Sanders's three favorite things are small town life, the outdoors, and writing. He is able to put all three of these together in his work as an author. "I believe the writer should be the servant of language, community, and nature," he says. His writing is always about how many different kinds of people can get along together on our small planet.

Sanders was born in Memphis, Tennessee, and went to college in the United States and in England. Besides his work as an author, he is also a professor at a university. Sanders currently lives in Indiana with his wife and two children.

Meet Thomas B. Allen

Thomas B. Allen loved to draw when he was young. He grew up outside Nashville, Tennessee, and had to take a streetcar into town to attend art class. At the time, the only class was for adults. Yet he attended it, even though he was only nine years old!

Allen still loves to draw and paint. He says that his work studio is wherever he happens to be. Ideas for his work come "in my kitchen or while I am walking in the woods . . . in my den or the library, in a museum or out in the countryside."

Allen has taught at several art schools and universities. He is the father of three children and has two grandchildren. Currently, he lives in Kansas City.

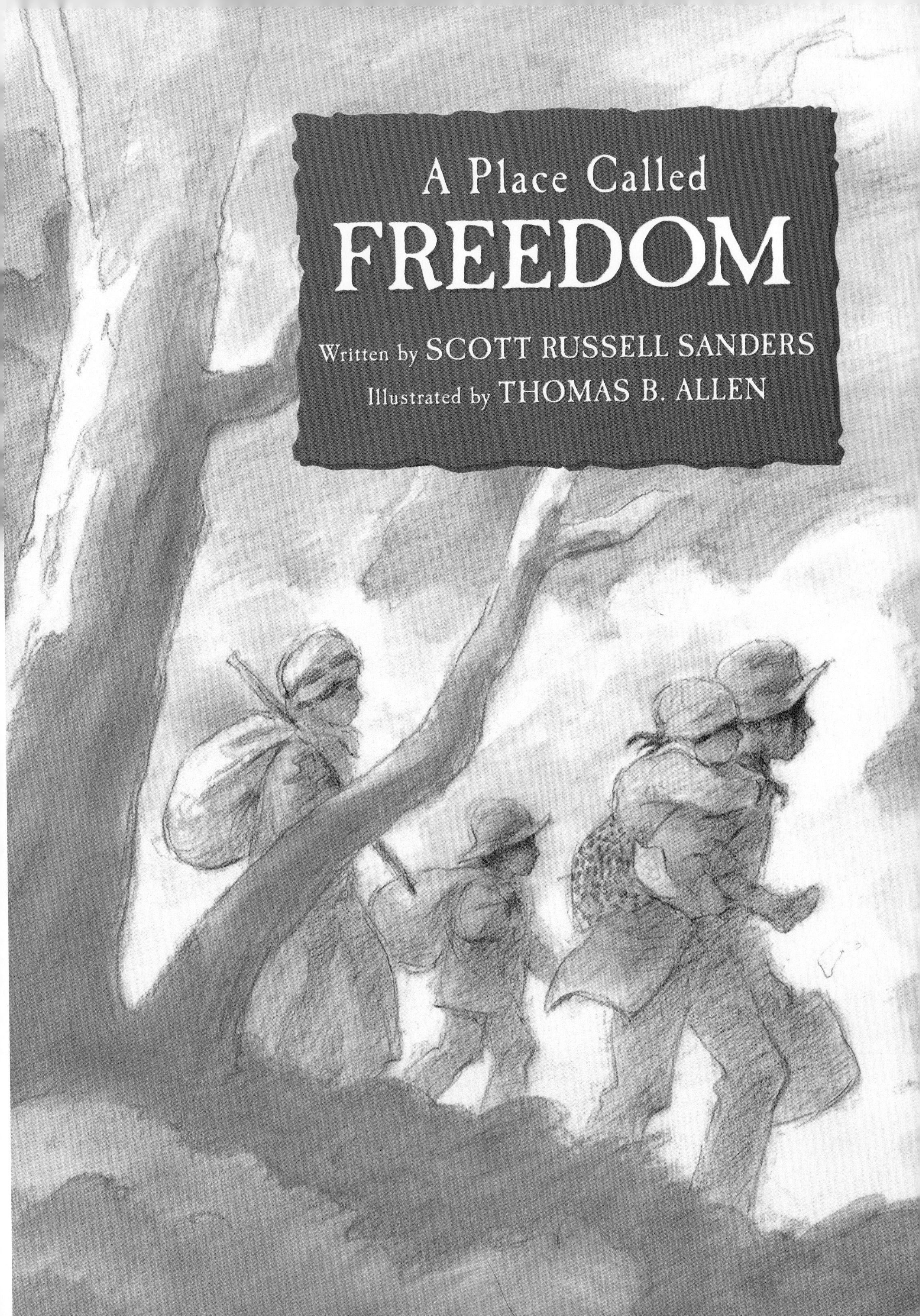

A Place Called FREEDOM

Written by SCOTT RUSSELL SANDERS

Illustrated by THOMAS B. ALLEN

Down in Tennessee, on the plantation where I was born, Mama worked in the big house and Papa worked in the fields. The master of that big house set us free in the spring of 1832, when I was seven years old and my sister, Lettie, was five.

Papa called Lettie a short drink of water, because she was little and wriggly, and he called me a long gulp of air, because I was tall and full of talk.

As soon as we could pack some food and clothes, we left the plantation, heading north for Indiana. Our aunts and uncles and cousins who were still slaves hugged us hard and waved until we were out of sight.

Papa said it would be safer to travel at night.

"How're we going to find our way in the dark?" I asked him.

"We'll follow the drinking gourd," Papa answered. He pointed to the glittery sky, and I saw he meant the Big Dipper. He showed me how to find the North Star by drawing an arrow from the dipper's lip. Papa loved stars. That's why, when he gave up his old slave's name and chose a new one, he called himself Joshua Starman. And that's why my name is James Starman.

It was a weary, long way. Night after night as we traveled, the buttery bowl of the moon filled up, then emptied again. When Lettie got tired, she rode on Papa's shoulders for a while, or on Mama's hip. But I walked the whole way on my own feet.

At last one morning, just after sunrise, we came to the Ohio River. A fisherman with a face as wrinkled as an old boot carried us over the water in his boat. On the far shore we set our feet on the free soil of Indiana. White flowers covered the hills that day like feathers on a goose.

By and by we met a Quaker family who took us into their house, gave us seed, and loaned us a mule and a plow, all because they believed that slavery was a sin. We helped on their farm, working shoulder to shoulder, and we planted our own crops.

That first year Papa raised enough corn and wheat for us to buy some land beside the Wabash River, where the dirt was as black as my skin. Papa could grow anything, he could handle horses, and he could build a barn or a bed.

Before winter, Papa and Mama built us a sturdy cabin. Every night we sat by the fire and Papa told stories that made the shadows dance. Every morning Mama held school for Lettie and me. Mama knew how to read and write from helping with lessons for the master's children. She could sew clothes that fit you like the wind, and her cooking made your tongue glad.

While the ground was still frozen, Papa rode south through the cold nights, down to the plantation in Tennessee. We fretted until he showed up again at our door, leading two of my aunts, two uncles, and five cousins. They stayed with us until they could buy land near ours and build their own cabins.

Again and again Papa went back to Tennessee, and each time he came home with more of the folks we loved.

Hearing about our settlement, black people arrived from all over the South, some of them freed like us, some of them runaways. There were carpenters and blacksmiths, basket weavers and barrel makers.

Soon we had a church, then a store, then a stable, then a mill to grind our grain. For the first time in our lives, we had money, just enough to get by, and we watched every penny.

After a few years, the railroad decided to run tracks through our village, because so many people had gathered here. If our place was going to be on the map, it needed a name. At a meeting, folks said we should call it Starman, in honor of Mama and Papa. But Mama and Papa said, "No, let's name it Freedom."

And that's how we came to live in a place called Freedom.

FREEDOM

We all celebrated the new name by building a school, where Mama could teach everyone, young and old, to read and write and do sums. She made me want to learn everything there was to know.

When Mama first told me about the alphabet, I wondered how I could ever remember twenty-six different letters. But I learned them all in a flash. It was like magic to me, the way those letters joined up to make words.

Papa's farming was also like magic. He would put seeds in the ground, and before you knew it, here came melon vines or cornstalks. He planted trees, and here came apples or nuts or shade.

For a long while, I couldn't decide whether I wanted to grow up and become a farmer like Papa or a teacher like Mama.

"I don't see why a teacher can't farm," Mama said.

"I don't see why a farmer can't teach," said Papa.

They were right, you know, because I raised the beans and potatoes for supper, and I wrote these words with my own hand.

Story Questions & Activities

1. Who is telling the story?
2. Why did people follow the "drinking gourd"?
3. How are facts important to this story?
4. What would you say to sum up this selection?
5. Thomas Jefferson's Declaration of Independence says that "All men are created equal." Do you think these words came true for the Starman family in a place called Freedom? Support your opinion with facts from the story.

Write an Editorial

What was life like for the family before they were given their freedom? Imagine that you are a newspaper editor right before the Civil War. Write an editorial for your paper. Explain why you think slavery is wrong. Support your opinions with facts. Try to persuade your readers to agree with you.

Do a Science Experiment

James Starman explains that his father could grow anything in the dark soil. Find out which soil is better for certain plants. Get two cups. Put potting soil in one cup. Put sand in the other. Then place two or three radish seeds in each cup. Give the seeds some water and put them on a sunny windowsill. Radish seeds sprout quickly. Which soil—the light-colored sand or the dark potting soil—is better for growing seeds?

Name a Town

Many of James Starman's relatives came to live near him. So many arrived that they formed their own town and gave it a name. If you formed a new town, what would you call it? Choose a name. Then draw a welcome sign for your town.

Find Out More

James Starman's father helped his relatives escape to freedom. Find out about others who helped enslaved people escape. Start by reading about Harriet Tubman and the Underground Railroad. Check for information in a social studies textbook, an encyclopedia, or another book. Compare the experiences of Harriet Tubman with the experiences of the Starman family.

Read a Line Graph

James Starman says he was born on a plantation in the South. His mother worked in the big plantation house, and his father worked in the fields. At the time of the story, most people in the North and the South were farmers. Both areas had slaves. Yet the South had large plantations. It needed more workers to care for its cotton crop. Look at the graph to see the number of enslaved workers in the South in the 1800s.

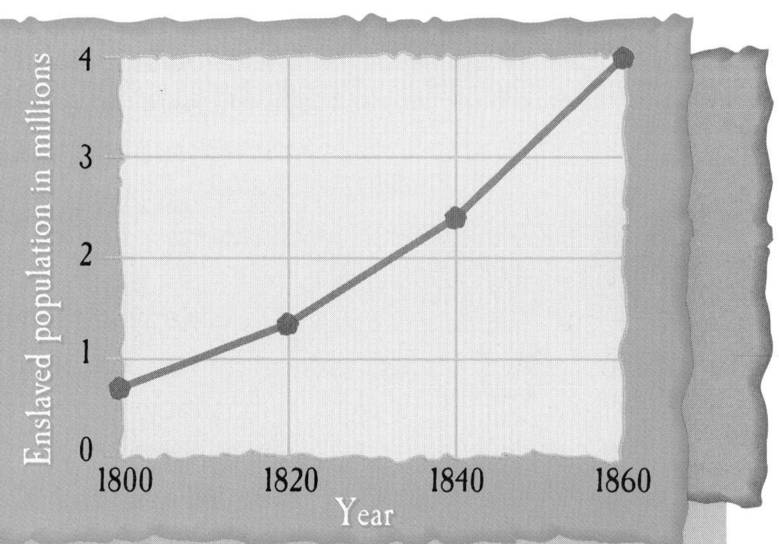

Use the line graph to answer these questions.

1. How many enslaved workers were in the South in 1800?
2. Were there more slaves in the South in 1820 than in 1810? How do you know?
3. How many enslaved workers did the South have in 1850?
4. By 1860, how many slaves were working on Southern plantations?
5. What does the graph tell you about the number of workers needed to grow and harvest cotton?

TEST POWER

Test Tip

Make sure you read each question slowly and carefully.

DIRECTIONS

Read the sample story. Then read each question about the story.

SAMPLE

Jerome's First Sail

Jerome leaned back against the side of the boat and smiled. He had always loved visiting his Uncle Henry.

Henry kept a tiny two-person sailboat ready at all times. He had been taking Jerome out on the boat as long as Jerome could remember. Jerome had learned how to trim and set the sail, steer the rudder, and tack against the wind. Jerome had become a gifted sailor, and he knew that Uncle Henry was proud of him.

His uncle looked up from a rope he was coiling and grinned. "I think you're ready for your first solo sail."

Jerome was thrilled.

1 This story mostly takes place—

A at Uncle Henry's house

B at the marina

C on the boat

D at school

2 This story is mainly about

F why Jerome was sick

G how boats can be different

H what Uncle Henry thinks about sailing

J how Jerome learned to sail

Did you reread the story to find the best answer? Tell why.

Some pictures surprise us. Others keep us guessing. Some even make us wonder what is going on.

Look at the drawing. What can you tell about the people on the stairs? Are they all moving up or down on their own staircase? Will they ever get to where they are going? Explain your reason.

Imagine that you are the person sitting down near the staircases in the picture. Can you see everything from your seat? Are the people really moving up or down—or are they going nowhere? What would you tell them? Why?

Relativity
by M.C. Escher, 1953

TIME FOR KIDS

SPECIAL REPORT

Twisted Trails

This shrub maze is in Indiana.

Meet a Maker of Mazes

From start to finish, no one knows mazes like Adrian Fisher

Adrian Fisher is A-MAZE-ING! Mr. Fisher, who lives in England, designs mazes for a living. He makes walk-through mazes that people must solve by finding a clear path from entrance to exit.

A good maze requires careful planning and a real understanding of math. Adrian Fisher's job requires him to be part scientist and part artist. "I studied math in school, and I always loved gardening," he says. "Building mazes is a way to combine these two loves."

In 1996, Fisher broke a record by making the largest maze up to that time. This Michigan corn maze was in the shape of a car. It contained more than three miles of pathways between rows of corn plants. At least 2,000 people could try to find their way through it at once.

Above: Fisher designed this Paradise, Pennsylvania, cornfield maze. Left: An outdoor maze in England.

COVER: GEORG GERSTER/PHOTO RESEARCHERS; ALL OTHER PHOTOS: ADRIAN FISHER

You'd have to swim to get through this maze at the Getty Museum in California.

"People like corn mazes," Fisher told *TIME FOR KIDS.* "They're entertaining, out in the sunshine and open air." He has been building mazes for more than 20 years, and has built more than 135 of them so far. His specialty is setting up tricky roadblocks, including fountains, mirrors, and even tanks of live crocodiles!

One of Fisher's favorites is a Beatles maze in England. The maze includes a 51-foot-long yellow submarine. The submarine honors one of the many songs the famous English singing group made popular. Fisher has also made some colorful mazes for school playgrounds.

ADULTS SOMETIMES ACT LIKE KIDS

Mr. Fisher takes pleasure in watching people walk through his mazes. "Eleven- and 12-year-old children are often better than their parents" at making their way through mazes, Fisher says. "I especially like to watch adults go through them. They get lost right away, and it forces them to act like children for half an hour."

Do grown-ups take a professional puzzlemaker seriously? You bet. A museum in Florida has shown Fisher's mazes in a special show. That makes sense to Fisher. "Maze design is very much like art," says the maze master. "There's a story behind each one."

This maze in England keeps kids and adults busy.

FIND OUT MORE
Visit our website:
www.mhschool.com/reading

inter **NET** **CONNECTION**

Path Finder

How can you get through a life-size maze if you can't see your way to the end? In many older mazes, just follow the left-hand rule: When you've entered a maze and you come to a fork, always follow the left wall. If the fork is a dead end, turn around. The wall on your left will lead you back to the correct path. Sooner or later, you'll find your way through the maze.

Remember: A good maze-maker like Mr. Fisher knows the rule, too. And he can always find a way to break it. But after all, a maze with no challenge is no fun!

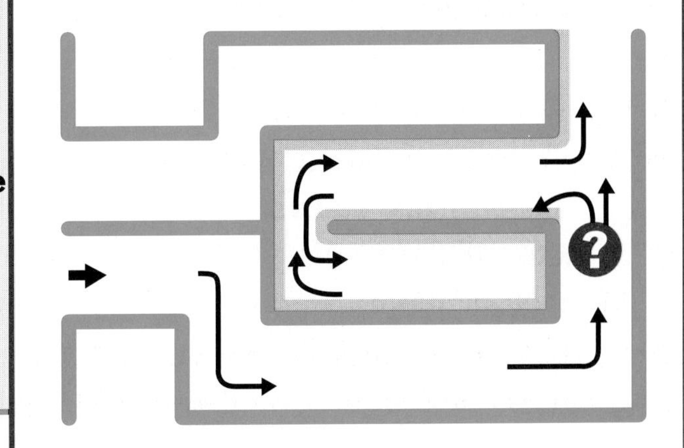

Based on an article in *TIME FOR KIDS.*

Story Questions & Activities

1. What does Adrian Fisher do for a living?
2. Why did Adrian Fisher decide to become a maze-maker?
3. What makes Adrian Fisher's mazes so interesting?
4. What is the main idea of this selection?
5. Imagine that you had a chance to show Adrian Fisher the picture on pages 360–361. Do you think he could use it for one of his mazes? Why or why not?

Write a Letter

Adrian Fisher likes to watch adults go through his mazes. The mazes make them "act like children," he says. Write a letter to an adult in your family. Persuade him or her to go with you to see one of Adrian Fisher's mazes. Give three good reasons why this grown-up should go.

Design a Maze

Adrian Fisher designs mazes for a living. Now it's your turn to design a maze. First, decide on the overall shape. Then draw the paths inside the maze. Remember to include roadblocks and dead ends. When you have finished, test your maze to make sure it can be solved in the way you had planned. Now see if a classmate can get through your maze.

Make a List

Do you remember reading about Adrian Fisher's corn maze? What happens when you make a *maze* of *maize*? Brainstorm with a partner to create a list of words that sound alike but have a different spelling and meaning. These words are called *homophones*. Use your list to write a silly sentence for each of your homophone pairs.

Find Out More

Adrian Fisher isn't the only person who designs mazes. One famous maze is in Colonial Williamsburg, in Virginia. Look for information about other famous mazes on the Internet or in activity books. Compare the mazes you learn about with the ones designed by Adrian Fisher.

Read a Diagram

Did you know that a maze is a kind of diagram? A **diagram** is a plan or a drawing that shows the parts of a thing or how the parts go together. Look at this diagram. It shows a walk-through maze, seen from above. Notice how the maze is laid out. Then walk through the maze with your pencil.

Use the maze to answer these questions.

1. In which corner do you enter the maze?
2. Where is the first fork you would come to in the maze?
3. What blocks you at the end of Path 3?
4. What is the last obstacle you might come across?
5. How many different routes can you take to walk through this maze?

TEST POWER

Test Tip

Read all answer choices for each question.

DIRECTIONS

Read the sample story. Then read each question about the story.

SAMPLE

Roger's Late Night

Today my mother dropped me off at soccer practice at the junior high school practice fields. As I was running off she said, "Your father will pick you up after practice, Roger."

By the end of practice, I was really tired. I waited for what seemed like hours, when my father pulled up, got out of the car and ran over to me. He could see that I was scared, so he gave me a big hug and apologized over and over again for being late. He had gone to the high school because he thought that my practice was there today.

We talked about it on the way home, and I said, "Dad, sometimes things just don't go the way we plan them."

1 The reader can tell from the story that when Roger was waiting, he was—

A happy

B lazy

C worried

D angry

2 Which of these happened last in the story?

F Roger was really tired.

G Roger and his father talked.

H Roger's father gave him a hug.

J Roger's mother dropped him off at soccer practice.

My Poems

I am a sun poet
sitting on a ray
of streaming light
writing
gold poems.
Quickly, my poems
shine down on
the earth
and hide
in grains of
burning sand.

I am a rain poet
under an old
gray umbrella
finishing wet, soggy
poems. As I finish,
my poems slowly
run away
and slide in
alleys and streets
of huge cities.

I am a sea poet
riding a sea
turtle while
writing poems.
My poems slither away
and have fun
swimming with fish
in the green, dark
waters.

I am a building poet
on the roof
writing poems.
My poems run into cracks
in walls
and cry out
to me.

I am a space poet
riding on a
falling star.
My poems fly
off
in the cold darkness
and are lost
forever in
twisting mysterious galaxies.

by Alan Barlow

UNIT 4

Just Curious

Final Curve

When you turn the corner
And you run into *yourself*
Then you know that you have turned
All the corners that are left.

by Langston Hughes

Stories in Art

If you look at this painting quickly, you might see a dog in a garden of flowers. Yet if you look at this painting again, you will see that there are other animals and insects hidden among the flowers and leaves.

Study this painting. What other animals do you see? How many are there? Compare two of the animals in the painting. Are they about the same size, shape, and color? If not, what are the differences? Are they both reptiles or insects? Explain.

Look at the painting again. How many different kinds of flowers do you see? How many different colors? Are all the daisies arranged together in the garden? Are they all the same color? Are there any differences? If so, what are they?

Cayle in the Border
by Hilary Jones
Private Collection

Meet Jim Brandenburg

Jim Brandenburg's interest in wolves began in 1986. That year, he went to the Arctic to photograph a wolf pack for *National Geographic*. There, he found wolves who had not developed a fear of humans. He learned that this fear in wolves comes from being hunted and trapped. During more trips to the Arctic, in 1987 and 1988, Brandenburg found that he was completely accepted by the wolves. In fact, as he was boarding a plane to leave the Arctic, the wolves gathered along the runway as if to say good-bye.

Brandenburg's respect for nature can be seen in his beautiful photographs in his magazine articles. The National Press Photographers Association has twice named him the Magazine Photographer of the Year. Brandenburg's books have also met with great success. He has won several awards, including the Minnesota Book Award. All his awards serve to honor his work as a photographer and a lover of nature.

Scruffy

A Wolf Finds His Place in the Pack

Jim Brandenburg

Scruffy finds a comfortable spot for a nap on the soft tundra.

Scruffy, a young white Arctic wolf, lives in a faraway frozen place called Ellesmere Island. He was born the year before I arrived, so he was no longer a pup. But he wasn't an adult member of his pack yet. If Scruffy had been human, he probably would have been called a teenager. He had a lot of the same problems people have trying to grow up. But he also had a bigger problem—staying alive.

The pack's home is covered with snow for most of the year.

Ellesmere Island is not far from the North Pole, so it is very cold—down to 70 degrees below zero in the winter. As if the cold isn't enough, Ellesmere also has fierce, biting winds, and it's as dry as a desert. The earth is frozen solid 1,000 feet below the surface. In the den where Scruffy and all the other pups were born, the back walls are covered with ice. There are snow fields that never melt, even during the summer. And icebergs loom nearby like white, watchful giants.

Playing king of the hill, Scruffy and a pack member climb to the top of an iceberg.

Trailing the Arctic wolf pack at 50 degrees below zero.

I arrived on Ellesmere Island during a cold, wintry spring, and I stayed through the summer. *National Geographic* magazine had sent me there to photograph all the Arctic animals. But my eyes and camera kept turning toward the wolves. Especially Scruffy.

A wolf pack is very much like a human family. In fact, many scientists believe that no other animal "family" acts more like humans than a wolf pack. Wolves mate for life, and the pack is usually made up of brothers, sisters, aunts, and uncles. Together, this family shares the duties of hunting, watching for danger, and raising the young.

Life can be difficult for the Arctic wolf pack in the winter.

Scruffy always seemed to have huge clumps of fur hanging from him.

Most young wolves strike out on their own after a year to find mates and form their own packs. It's a mystery why Scruffy stayed with this pack instead of leaving his parents. He may have been the strongest pup and driven off the others. Or he may have been the weakest one, who was not seen as a threat. Whatever the reason, he stayed and was protected by the pack.

Since my camp was near the wolf den, it wasn't long before I got to know the members of this family of wolves. Slight differences in the way each of them looked and acted helped me to tell them apart better each day. Some appeared to be stronger and bolder than the others. These *dominant* wolves were better hunters and seemed to be the most important members of the pack.

Scruffy was not one of the dominant wolves. He was timid and depended on the others to take care of him. And he was by far the messiest of the pack—that's how he got his name.

Dominant wolves move with confidence.

The leader of a wolf pack is called the alpha male (or in some cases, the alpha female). On Ellesmere Island, the pack was led by a strong alpha pair. They were always the first to attack during a hunt and the first to eat after a kill. Until these two ate as much as they wanted, none of the other wolves could get even a scrap of food.

Scruffy was the lowest-ranking member of his pack. He ate last and had to beg for food. I watched him trying to get approval and affection from his "superiors," but they usually beat him up instead.

The more dominant wolves stood tall and moved with confidence. Their beautiful white coats bristled and their tails and ears pointed upward. Scruffy and the other low-ranking wolves moved in a way that said, *please don't hurt me.* They kept their bodies low to the ground, slinking and cowering. When the dominant pack members were around, Scruffy's ears flattened and his tail curled between his legs. If he got beat up, he'd soon come back for more, as though *this* time things would be better.

But as badly as the grown-ups appeared to treat him, Scruffy seemed very lonely when the rest of the pack had gone on a hunt. He sat and howled, watching the horizon for their return.

Scruffy had a goofy way about him. He was more careless than the rest of the wolves and didn't seem to have the common sense he needed. So he usually messed up when he tried to do adult tasks. He rarely went on hunts with the pack, and the few times he did, he seemed too unsure of himself to be a good hunter.

One day, Scruffy wanted to eat the eggs from the nest of some Arctic birds called long-tailed jaegers. Adult wolves help themselves to these eggs without much trouble. But Scruffy couldn't seem to figure out how to do it. Over and over, the jaegers dive-bombed him and knocked his head with their feet. He finally gave up, with his tail between his legs and a silly, confused look on his face.

A foolish Scruffy gets dive-bombed while looking for eggs to eat.

The pups are content when the den is guarded by Scruffy.

But there was one thing Scruffy could do well. And it soon became clear that his role in the pack was very important. In July, six gray balls of fur stumbled out of the den and waddled around on oversized paws. The pups may have been big and sturdy enough to face the world outside the den, but they needed a lot of help. And Scruffy was the pups' main baby-sitter.

Two pups playfully fight for possession of a stick.

The pups always trusted Scruffy to lead them on adventures.

I was surprised by the change in Scruffy once the pups entered the picture. When the adults left on a hunt, the baby-sitter was in charge. Suddenly Scruffy became a cocky, dominant wolf. He stood and walked much taller, his tail and ears perked up. With the pups, he seemed to say, *Aha. I'm in charge now. You pups better obey or I'll beat you up.*

Scruffy played with the pups and took them on walks. He howled with them and wrestled. He even played tug-of-war with them using a piece of fur. Scruffy would sit there for a while, gently tugging and letting a pup feel powerful. Then he'd suddenly yank it back hard, forcing the pup to grow stronger and more alert.

Scruffy taught the pups to be strong with games of tug-of-war.

Scruffy was an expert bully when the pack was away hunting.

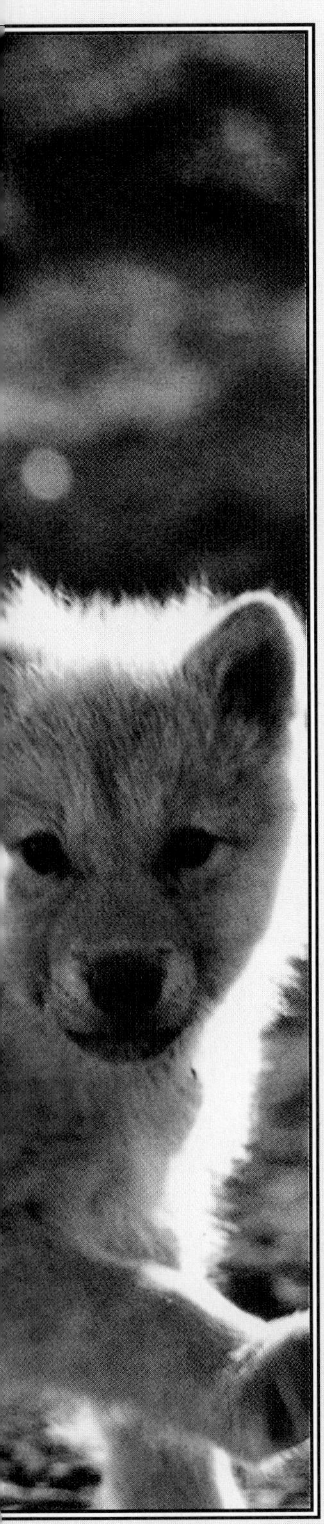

But Scruffy's job was not merely to play. It is a sad fact that at least half of the young wolves in this harsh climate die. So the most important task of any wolf in charge of the pups is to toughen them up, even if the methods seem terribly cruel. Scruffy turned out to be an expert bully. He growled and nipped at the pups, tackled and shook them until they yelped in pain. At last, Scruffy could be the "superior" one. Of course, he had to keep an eye open for the return of the pack. If he got caught acting and looking dominant, he could get punished.

Scruffy loved to make the pups beg for attention.

How did the pups feel about their baby-sitter? He seemed to be their hero. They watched his every move as though he were the best wolf who ever lived. While resting quietly, they sat at his feet and raised their small snouts toward his. And they obeyed him . . . most of the time.

The pups stand at attention while Scruffy trots by for inspection.

Scruffy, the hero of the pups, sometimes felt like a king.

The alpha female brings an Arctic fox to the pups for a hunting lesson.

Scruffy often helped the adult wolves teach the pups lessons in the art of becoming a wolf. One time, the alpha female brought an Arctic fox back to the den to give to the pups. Scruffy urged the pups to "kill" the already dead fox over and over again. In each round of this tiring game, one pup would growl, grab the fox by the throat, and shake it. The most dominant pup would eventually steal the tattered "prize" and run around and around, chased by the others.

Life for Arctic wolves is a daily life-and-death struggle. Death by disease, injury, or starvation is always a threat. This is why the ranking system in a wolf pack is important. For those who do not work and fit together well with the others, there is no room and not enough food. In spite of all his apparent faults, Scruffy's skill as a baby-sitter made him valuable to the pack.

Scruffy urges the pups to "kill" the already dead fox.

The pups during their first Arctic snow.

By August, the first snows began to fall, and I had to pack up and leave. The pups had grown a lot, and their fur, which had been gray, was now turning white like the adults' coats—for camouflage in the snow. But they still had so much to learn. I felt tremendous sadness the morning I left. How many of these pups would live? I wondered. Then I looked at Scruffy. Would he survive another winter?

Scruffy and the pups play on an iceberg.

I returned the following May to film the pack for a *National Geographic* television show. I found the pack had changed in surprising ways. Another male had taken over as leader. The calm, gentle female who had been the pups' mother the year before was now the alpha female. I still thought of her as "Mom."

Scruffy's rank in the pack hadn't changed. And neither had his role as baby-sitter. He was hovering by Mom and seemed eager to begin caring for her new litter. When he poked his head inside the den, he was greeted with a chorus of puppy growls.

The pups huddle to stay warm deep inside the frost-covered den.

Scruffy keeps a watchful eye on the den entrance.

Mom was as good-natured as before. She even let me go into the den one day to take photographs of the tiny pups. I wriggled down the narrow passageway into a cool and damp room. It smelled sweetly of puppy fur. In the beam of my flashlight I saw the four pups, shivering and clinging to each other. One of them pointed its muzzle at me and growled. At three weeks old, it was already showing signs of dominance. Maybe it would be an alpha someday. I wondered if there might be another Scruffy in that litter too.

As soon as I came out of the den, Mom disappeared inside to make sure everything was all right. Scruffy stayed by the entrance and kept a watchful eye on me. He looked ready to take on this new litter. He'd teach them a thing or two.

When I finally had to leave several days later, Scruffy trotted along with me the whole way to the airstrip. After three miles, he stopped and perked up his ears. His body pointed to a nearby herd of caribou, and he made a charge. The caribou had little trouble getting away from him, and Scruffy was soon lying on the ground, scratching. But he looked at me, in that goofy way of his, as if to say, *What do you think of me now?*

Scruffy was continually looking for approval, even from me.

Story Questions & Activities

1. Where does Scruffy live?
2. How is a wolf pack like a human family?
3. What makes Scruffy a good baby-sitter? Give three reasons.
4. What is the main idea of this selection?
5. Compare Scruffy with another animal you have read about or have seen in the movies or on television. How are Scruffy and this animal alike? What are the differences?

Write a Magazine Article

The job of the Arctic wolf is to stay alive. Suppose that you are a magazine writer. Your assignment is to write about Arctic wolves. Explain how these wolves survive the long winter. Give three examples. Add a map, a graph, or a picture to help show your facts.

Make a Diorama

Scruffy spent long days baby-sitting for the wolf pups. He played with them and taught them how to survive. The other wolves hunted for food or guarded the den. In an empty shoebox, show Scruffy and his wolf pack. Use construction paper, colored pipe cleaners, cotton, fabric, and other art supplies to show your scene.

Draw a Map

What is life like near the North Pole where Scruffy lives? Look at a map of Canada and find Ellesmere Island. Imagine what life is like there. Are there glaciers and polar bears? How cold does it get? Make a map of Ellesmere Island. Include the animals, glaciers, and mountains found there.

Find Out More

You saw many pictures of wolves in the selection. What do wolves look like? You could say they look like German shepherd dogs. Yet there are differences. Start by checking in an encyclopedia. Focus on height, weight, and habits. Use what you learn to compare dogs and wolves.

Read a Graph

Some wolves are more in danger than others. The number of Arctic wolves, for example, is getting smaller. Weather, other animals, and hunters put them in danger, making it difficult for them to survive in the places where they live. Wolves could die out if we do not save them.

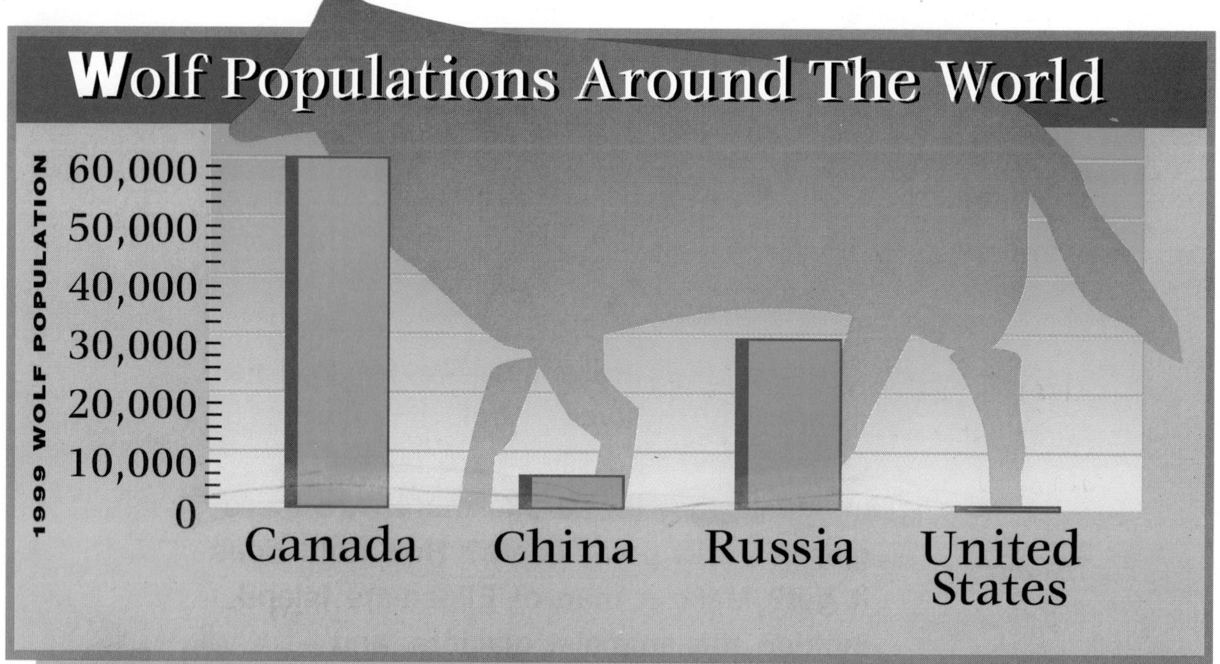

Use the graph to answer these questions.

1. Which country has the most wolves?
2. Which country has about 30,000 wolves?
3. About how many wolves live in China?
4. How many more wolves does Canada have than the United States?
5. Why do you think Canada and Russia have more wolves than the United States and China combined?

TEST POWER

Test Tip

Work slowly. Be careful.

DIRECTIONS

Read the sample story. Then read each question about the story.

SAMPLE

What It Takes

Do you know a champion? A champion is someone who works very hard and who doesn't give up. Ileana is a champion.

Ileana was only 4 years old when she started to ice-skate. Ileana decided on that first day of skating that she was going to be the fastest skater ever. By the time that she was 10, she practiced 2 hours every day. When Ileana was 11, she set a new speed-skating record. Every year, she sets new records.

Ileana hopes to join the Olympic Skating Team at the next winter Olympics. So far, she has shown that she is a champion.

1 What happened when Ileana was 11 years old?

A She joined the Olympics.

B She learned how to skate.

C She set a speed-skating record.

D She went to college.

2 Ileana practiced hard because she wanted to—

F please her mother

G be the best diver

H graduate early

J be the fastest skater

What did you do to answer each question? Explain.

Like writers, artists often like to mix the real with the unreal. If you look at this painting, you might see objects that you recognize. You might also see objects that you think you know but that the artist has drawn in a new and different way.

Look at this painting. Do you see stars? Where are they? Where is the sun? Is that how the sun really looks? Notice the different shapes and colors. How has the artist used shape and color to create a strange image of a sunset?

Close your eyes. What do you remember about the painting? Why?

New Mexico Sunset
by Linda Lomahaftewa
The Heard Museum, Phoenix, AZ

Meet Joseph Bruchac

Joseph Bruchac remembers that he started writing in the second grade. Luckily, he has never stopped. Once, while in college, his writing teacher told him to "give it up." From that time on, Bruchac was determined to be a good writer.

Nature and Native American culture play a big part in Bruchac's award-winning writing. The author has Abenaki Indian ancestors, and he often thinks of his Abenaki background and the lessons it has taught him. The main Abenaki lesson in his writing is simple: People must listen to each other and the Earth.

Meet Stefano Vitale

Stefano Vitale grew up in Padua, Italy, not far from the great artwork of Venice. He came to the United States to study politics. Yet after a short time, he realized that he could make a bigger difference in the world through art.

Although he now lives in New York City, for a while he lived in southern California. While there, he often traveled to Mexico. He fell in love with the colorful Mexican folk art he saw. Today, his illustrations use the simple folk-art style of people of many different countries. Besides books, Vitale has illustrated many magazines.

GLUSKABE AND THE SNOW BIRD

Penobscot

Told by Joseph Bruchac

Illustrated by Stefano Vitale

Wawogit Gluskabe. Here camps my story of Gluskabe, the good giant who always tried to help the people long ago.

In the old days, Skunk was one of the most beautiful of the animals. His pure white fur, as white as new snow, was long and silky. All of the animals admired him.

But Skunk was not happy. He saw how the people praised Gluskabe for doing great things.

"I, too, want to do great things," Skunk said. So he went to Gluskabe.

"Gluskabe," said Skunk, "I would like to travel with you. You know that I am a good cook. If you let me come with you, I will prepare all your meals."

Gluskabe knew this was so, and Gluskabe liked to eat good food. "My friend," Gluskabe said, "you may travel with me."

For a time, things went well. Skunk cooked all the meals, and the two of them sat together in Gluskabe's lodge. Then, one day, a messenger came from the north.

"Great One," the messenger said, "I have come to ask you for help. The snow has been falling for so long that we are unable to hunt, and we are running out of food. The snow is so deep that we are unable to gather firewood to heat our lodges. If you do not help us, we will surely die."

"I must go and speak to the Snow Bird," Gluskabe said. "He is the one who controls the snow." Gluskabe began to make ready for his journey.

Skunk packed up his cooking gear, but Gluskabe stopped him.

"My small friend," Gluskabe said, "you cannot go on this journey with me. The snow will be deep, and you will not be able to walk through it."

"I will be fine," said Skunk. "If the snow gets deep, I will just walk in your footprints."

"Are you sure this is what you wish to do? This may be a difficult journey."

"I am sure," said Skunk. So Gluskabe allowed him to come along.

As they walked toward the north, the snow grew deeper and deeper. At first it was not hard for Skunk, but soon he found himself jumping from one of Gluskabe's footprints to the next. This was not easy, because Gluskabe was so large that his footprints were far apart. Skunk began to get angry at Gluskabe. He forgot that it was his own idea to come along.

At last they came to the hilltop where a great white bird stood. As he spread his wings, snowflakes fell from them.

"Hello, Grandfather," said Gluskabe.

"Ah, Gluskabe," said the Snow Bird. "Why have you come here?"

"Grandfather, it is good that you make the snow. The snow cleans our land. It covers the plants so that they will not freeze when the weather grows cold. When the snow melts, it fills the rivers and the lakes. But now there is too much snow. If it continues to fall like this, the people will not be able to live."

Gluskabe bent down and pulled up Skunk, who was half-frozen, out of the deep snow. "See how hard it is for my little brother here?"

The Snow Bird nodded. "I see."

"Grandfather," said Gluskabe, "the snow should not fall without stopping. You should not make every snowfall a deep one. Sometimes the snow should be heavy and sometimes it should be light. Then, when the winter is over, you should close your wings. Only open them in the time between first frost and last frost."

"I shall do as you say," said the Snow Bird. He folded his wings, and the snow stopped. To this day, snow only falls for part of the year.

The snow was melting as they walked back to Gluskabe's lodge, and Skunk found it easier to walk. But he was still angry. He wanted to do something by himself that everyone would remember.

As they walked along, they passed another hilltop. A great bird stood on top of it. He held his wings open wide and light streamed out.

"Who is that?" asked Skunk.

"That is the Day Eagle," said Gluskabe. "While his wings are open, it is day all over the world. When he closes them, it will be night."

Skunk saw that this was so. The Day Eagle was just closing his wings and the evening was beginning. Soon it was dark, and they made camp for the night.

Gluskabe fell asleep, but Skunk stayed awake. He took a big ball of rawhide twine and went to the place where the Day Eagle stood. Skunk bound the great bird's wings so tightly with the twine that he would not be able to open them, no matter how hard he tried. Then Skunk sneaked back to camp and pretended to sleep.

When the next day came, there was no daylight. The birds and the animals wandered about in the dark. The people were afraid. But Skunk was not afraid. He laughed at the confusion he had caused.

Gluskabe found his way to the Day Eagle's hilltop.

"Who did this to you, Grandfather?" he asked.

"It was the white one who travels with you," said the Day Eagle.

Gluskabe tried to untie the knots Skunk had made. They were very tight, so tight that Gluskabe could not untie them all. He was only able to free one of the Day Eagle's wings. To this day, the Day Eagle can only open one wing. That is why half the world is always dark, while the other half is light. The Day Eagle must keep turning around on his hilltop to share his light with the world.

Gluskabe went back to camp, where Skunk was still pretending to sleep.

"I know what you have done," Gluskabe said. He took the ashes from the fire and emptied them over Skunk so that his white coat became all black. With his fingers, he drew two white stripes down Skunk's back to remind Skunk of how beautiful he once had been.

"Now everyone will remember what you have done," Gluskabe said. He blew smoke on Skunk, and Skunk became bad-smelling. "Now none of the people will want to be with you."

Ever since then, Skunk seldom comes out until it is dark. It is not just that he is ashamed of his sooty coat; he also fears that the Day Eagle will seek revenge for what he did long ago. Skunk also sleeps during most of the winter, for he remembers how hard it was to walk through that deep snow long ago.

To this day, the Snow Bird is careful to do as Gluskabe told him. Sometimes when the snow falls there is much snow, and sometimes there is only a little. But the snow no longer falls without stopping. The Snow Bird always closes his wings at the end of winter. He does not open them again until long after summer ends.

So it is to this day.

Story Questions & Activities

1. Where does the story take place?
2. How is snow important to the story?
3. Myths are old stories that often explain a true event in nature. What makes this story a myth?
4. What things in this story are facts? What things are not?
5. Compare Gluskabe, the good giant, with the giant in Jack and the Beanstalk, or with another giant. How are the two giants alike? What makes them different?

Write a Weather Report

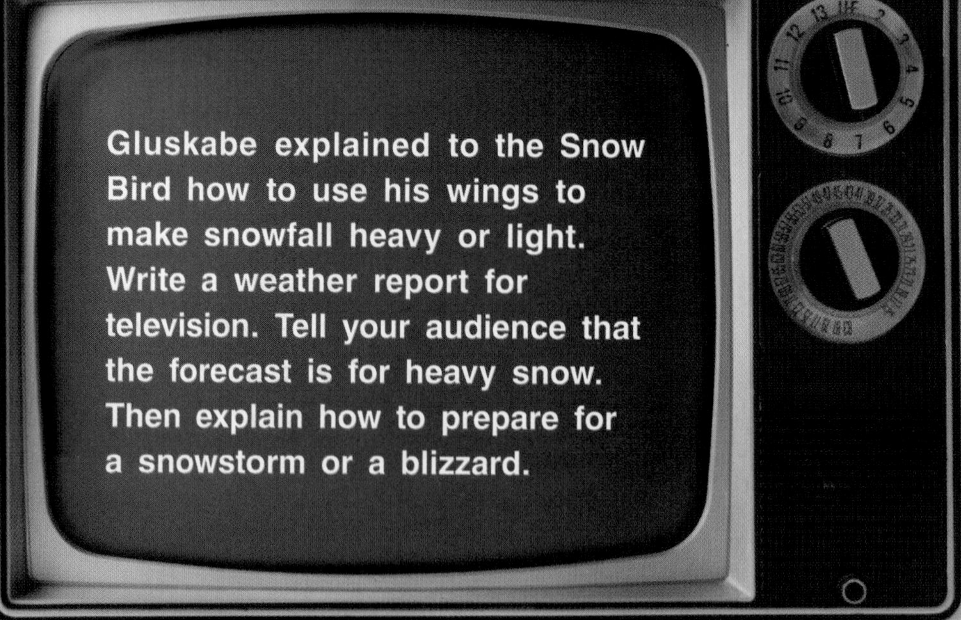

Gluskabe explained to the Snow Bird how to use his wings to make snowfall heavy or light. Write a weather report for television. Tell your audience that the forecast is for heavy snow. Then explain how to prepare for a snowstorm or a blizzard.

Draw a Cartoon

Skunk joined Gluskabe on his journey to visit the Snow Bird. On the way back, they met the Day Eagle. Draw a cartoon of one of these events in the story. Then write a caption describing your cartoon.

Create a Myth

Why do cows moo? Why do bees sting? How did the camel get his hump? Make up a myth that explains one of these. Then tell your "how" or "why" story to a group or the class.

Find Out More

In the story, the Snow Bird controls the amount of snow by opening and closing its wings. Find out which country gets the most snow, and why. Start by looking in an almanac. How is the weather in that country different from where you live?

Read a Chart

In the story, Gluskabe tells the Snow Bird it is not good to have too much snow. He explains to the bird how to use his wings to make snowfall heavy or light. People in some places in the United States would probably agree with Gluskabe. Places such as Maine, Vermont, Minnesota, the Dakotas, and Colorado get a lot of snow, maybe too much!

Look at this chart comparing the amount of snowfall in Portland, Maine, and Louisville, Kentucky. These cities are in different parts of the United States. They have different climates and different amounts of snowfall.

Average Snowfall in Inches, January–June

	January	February	March	April	May	June
Portland, Maine	19.3	17.3	12.8	3.0	0.2	0
Louisville, Kentucky	5.2	4.4	3.2	0.1	0	0

Use the chart to answer these questions.

1. How many inches of snow usually fall in Portland, Maine, in January?
2. How many inches of snow fall in Louisville, Kentucky, in February?
3. Between Portland and Louisville, how many more inches of snow does Portland have in March?
4. Which city gets more snow in a year?
5. Why does more snow fall in January than in April?

TEST POWER

Test Tip

Remember to look for the best answer to the question.

DIRECTIONS

Read the sample story. Then read each question about the story.

SAMPLE

Allowance Contract

Sammy and Sonya wanted to earn some money to buy gifts.

"Let's write up a contract. We can decide which chores should be done and how much we will pay you," their mother said.

ALLOWANCE CONTRACT

Mom agrees to: pay Sammy and Sonya five dollars each if the chores below are completed by Friday evening.

Sammy and Sonya agree to:

- Take the garbage out
- Put all newspapers, cans, and bottles in the recycling bins
- Bring dirty clothes to the laundry room
- Mow the lawn

1 Which is a FACT in this passage?

A Sammy and Sonya's mother bought a present.

B The chores are too easy.

C Sammy and Sonya made a contract with their mom.

D Sammy and Sonya may not use a lawnmower.

2 The purpose of the part of the contract called "Mom agrees to" is to tell—

F why Sonya will help

G what Mom will sign

H what will happen if the children complete their chores

J what Sammy agrees to do

Stories don't always tell you everything. Sometimes you have to make guesses about events all along the way. Art is often the same.

Look at the photograph. What can you tell about the pieces of broken glass? What clues in the photograph let you know that the glass is old? Where do you think it came from? What conclusion can you make about these glass objects?

Look at the photograph again. Why would a photographer take a picture of broken glass? Give reasons for your conclusion.

Broken Pieces of Colored Glassware
by Jonathan Blair, 1977
Serce Limani Bay, Aegean Sea

TEMPERED+

MEET AN UNDERWATER EXPLORER

Sylvia studies ocean life right where it's happening!

by Luise Woelflein

Sylvia Earle has spent more than 6000 hours under water. She has played around with friendly dolphins. She has gotten "personal" with animals that can be dangerous, such as sharks and moray eels. She has studied humpback whales by following them under water.

Once a deadly poisonous lionfish stung her. It took Sylvia an hour to get to the surface of the water, where she could get help. Another time, a shark was threatening to bite her. She kicked it, and luckily it swam away.

She flips for science! Sylvia dives into a giant basket sponge just to see what's inside. The scientist has spent more than 6000 hours under water studying ocean plants and animals.

Sylvia is a *marine biologist*—a scientist who studies ocean life. She's also one of the world's best underwater divers. And as an ocean scientist, she has done lots of firsts:

- She set new diving records and tested new equipment.
- She was the first woman to become the chief scientist for an important government group in Washington, D.C.
- She was the head of an all-woman science team that *lived* on the floor of the Atlantic Ocean for two weeks. There, she found 153 species (kinds) of plants—including 26 species that had never been seen in that area before.

Being an ocean scientist and an underwater diver fit right together. Sylvia can study life in the ocean—as it's happening.

FROM THE BEGINNING

Ever since she was a little girl, Sylvia has looked for ways to get under water. On family vacations at the New Jersey Shore, she learned the basics—how to swim past the waves and into deeper water. Then, when she was 12, her family moved to Florida.

Sylvia spent hundreds of hours playing there in the warm, clear waters of the Gulf of Mexico. "Wearing a mask, I would float for hours facedown on an inner tube, just watching," she says.

When Sylvia got to college, she tried out scuba gear for the first time. (Scuba gear is equipment for breathing under water.) "It was glorious!" she says. "It was like being a fish. My professor almost had to haul me out of the water by force, I liked it so much."

It's still hard to get Sylvia out of the water. In fact, she wants lots of people to learn how to explore the ocean. Why? Because so little is known about what's there.

TEMPERED+

Neat rock, huh? Actually, this "rock" is a scorpionfish. Look out—those sharp spines on its back are full of *poison!* So why in the world is this woman holding the creature? To study it!

WHAT IS DOWN THERE?

Sylvia points out that more than two-thirds of our planet is covered with water. But less than 10 percent of the ocean has been explored.

Most of what we know about the ocean comes from studying the things we've taken out of it with hooks and nets. Imagine exploring your neighborhood by blindfolding yourself and dipping nets from a helicopter! That's kind of how people have been exploring the ocean.

Until recently, very few people were able to go on long, deep dives. Why? Two big problems had to be overcome. You can probably guess the first—people can't breathe under water. But now there's equipment such as scuba gear that divers can use for breathing.

The other big problem is *pressure*. You probably know that water weighs a lot. (If you don't believe it, try picking up a bucketful sometime!)

When you dive down deep, a great amount of weight pushes on your body from all sides. And the deeper you go, the worse it gets. It can even crush your body if you dive too deep. To overcome this, people have invented suits and vehicles that can stand the pressure.

Sylvia was the first person to try out some of these inventions. In one of them, she set a record. She made the deepest dive in a suit that wasn't connected to a boat at the surface.

Sylvia is always trying to find ways to go deeper into the ocean. The machine—Deep Flight (left)—may be able to take her down to 4000 feet (1200 m) when it's finished. Don't worry—her dog, Blue, won't be going with her.

Dinner down under: Sylvia led this team of scientists called Tektite 2. (Sylvia is in the blue shirt.) The team spent two weeks living in a kind of "underwater hotel" and studying the ocean life around them.

INTO THE DEEP

Sylvia made that record-breaking dive off the coast of Hawaii. She was wearing a Jim Suit (named for a British diver named Jim Jarrett). It looks a bit like a space suit.

After Sylvia got into the suit, divers attached her to the front of a tiny submarine. The sub and Sylvia went down together.

She watched as the bright water at the surface slowly grew darker. The sub went down, down, down. It finally landed on the ocean floor in inky-black water 1250 feet (375 m) deep.

At Sylvia's signal, one of the people in the sub released the safety belt that was holding Sylvia in place. She stepped away from the sub and onto the ocean floor.

For 2 1/2 hours; Sylvia walked on the bottom of the Pacific Ocean. The sub followed her around, shining lights so she could see. So much was going on! A green-eyed shark swam by. Sylvia also saw strange eels, crabs, and glowing lantern fish.

Look—an underwater astronaut! Sylvia set a diving record wearing this Jim Suit. Above, she took a practice run in shallow water to get used to the suit. Then on the big day (left), she dived 1250 feet (375 m). That was the deepest dive anyone had ever made in a suit that wasn't connected to a boat at the surface.

Sylvia plays with a dolphin she calls Sandy. The scientist says she learns most about ocean animals by going where they live.

GOING DEEPER

Walking on the bottom of the ocean in a Jim Suit was exciting. But it was a slow and clunky way to get around.

That's how it is for people using Jim Suits and scuba gear. They can travel only as fast as they can walk or swim. So they can't keep up with dolphins, whales, or many other ocean animals they want to study.

Sylvia dreams of being able to dive to the deepest part of the ocean and "fly" through the sea as fast as a fish. And she's working on making that dream come true.

She and an engineer friend, Graham Hawkes, have made new one-person subs. Both Sylvia and Graham have used them to dive to 3000 feet (900 m) —deeper than anyone has ever traveled alone before. Another sub, called Deep Flight, should be able to take a person to the deepest part of the ocean and back. Sylvia can't wait to use it!

TROUBLED WATERS

During her lifetime, Sylvia has seen a lot of sad changes take place in the sea she loves. The clear Florida waters she used to explore as a child are now cloudy. Many sea creatures all over the world are endangered because of overfishing, pollution, and other people-caused problems.

Sylvia thinks that by harming the ocean, people may harm themselves. "Everything on Earth works together," she says. Tiny plants in the ocean make a lot of oxygen. If we destroy those plants, Sylvia believes, we destroy a big source of the oxygen we need to breathe. Changing the ocean may make other changes as well. In fact, she believes it may even change the Earth's weather.

"Besides," Sylvia says, "sea creatures are beautiful and precious, and they deserve to be protected just for that reason."

MANY MYSTERIES

Sylvia wishes that everyone could go under water and see the ocean as she does. Then they might better understand the importance of saving it.

Sylvia also hopes that more people will explore the ocean. "We know so little about how the ocean works," she says. "And we have no idea how many strange, new kinds of plants and animals are waiting to be discovered there.

"Some lucky kids will have the pleasure of solving these mysteries when they grow up," she says.

Sylvia, too, continues to explore and discover. There's still so much she wants to know and see. And she's willing to go to great *depths* to do it!

Sylvia collects tiny plants called algae near a Pacific Ocean island. She likes looking for new plants. And scientists have named many newly found plants after Sylvia.

MEET LUISE WOELFLEIN

Growing up on a farm in Pennsylvania, Luise Woelflein loved to explore nature. Even today, her favorite times are spent exploring nature's mysteries. Forests, mountains, seas, and even swamps are all places of wonder for her.

When not outdoors, Luise is busy writing. Her science books for children combine two loves—nature and writing. Among her books are *Forest Animals* and *The Ultimate Bug Book.* She has also written lessons to help teachers make science fun for students. As Luise explains, "From bears to bugs and trees to turtles, I like writing about nature to help people understand the weird and wonderful world we live in."

Story Questions & Activities

1. What kind of work does Sylvia Earle do?
2. How does scuba gear help Sylvia do her work?
3. How is Sylvia Earle's work important to scientists?
4. What is the main idea of this selection?
5. Imagine that Sylvia had a chance to study Scruffy and the wolf pack. Do you think she could use her science skills to study life on land? Why or why not?

Write a How-to Guide

Sylvia is always trying to find out how to go deeper into the ocean. That's why she has learned how to use a "Jim Suit" and a one-person sub. Write a how-to guide to explain a sport, such as swimming, that you know how to do. Give step-by-step instructions. Use a diagram, chart, or pictures to show the steps.

Make a Mobile

Most of what we know about the ocean comes from studying things we have taken out of it. Plan a mobile of underwater animals. Use colored clay, paper, beads, feathers, and other art supplies. Attach your sea creatures to a hanger. Use yarn or string. Then hang up your mobile. These colorful ocean creatures will float in the air as if they were in the ocean.

Draw a Poster

What makes some fish so unusual? Does the catfish really walk? How did the porcupine fish get its name? Take a trip to an aquarium or a pet shop. Find out some interesting information about fish. Then make a poster of "fish" facts. Include your own artwork.

Find Out More

In the selection, Sylvia wears a "Jim Suit" that allows her to walk on the ocean floor. Like other scuba gear, a Jim Suit lets divers breathe under water. Look in an encyclopedia or visit a scuba shop, if there is one in your area. Give a report on how to scuba dive.

Read a Time Line

Sylvia Earle has led an exciting life as an underwater explorer. You can learn about some important events in her life by reading this time line. A **time line** shows related events in the order they happened.

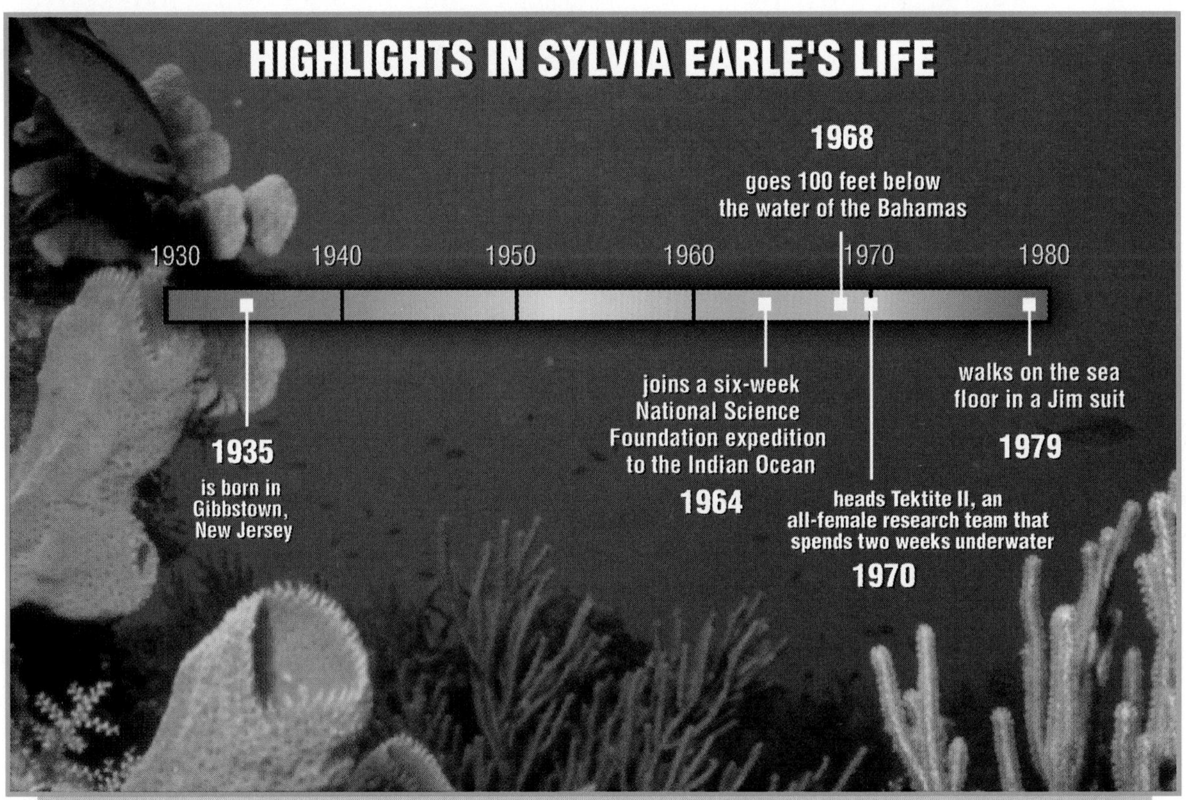

Use the time line to answer these questions.

1. In what direction should you read this time line?
2. What did Sylvia Earle do in 1968?
3. When did Sylvia Earle go on an expedition to the Indian Ocean?
4. How old was Sylvia Earle when she headed Tektite II?
5. How does a time line help you to understand the events in Sylvia Earle's life?

TEST POWER

Test Tip
Look for clues to the meaning of the underlined word.

DIRECTIONS
Read the sample story. Then read each question about the story.

SAMPLE

Little Feather Learns

A great storm flooded the land and ruined the corn the Plains people planted. They were worried. Without an <u>adequate</u> supply of corn, they would not be able to survive the winter ahead.

The Mountain people had excess corn that they said they would share. The Plains people would need to send someone to get it.

When the leaders chose Little Feather, he was fearful. But the leaders taught him all of the skills required for a successful journey. Little Feather set forth toward the mountains and returned with plenty of corn. He had met the challenge and would never doubt himself again.

1 In this passage, the word <u>adequate</u> means—

A old

B enough

C rotten

D too much

2 The main idea of the third paragraph is—

F Little Feather gains confidence

G growing corn is a hard thing to do

H a trip to the mountains is fun

J storms can ruin a crop

Stories in Art

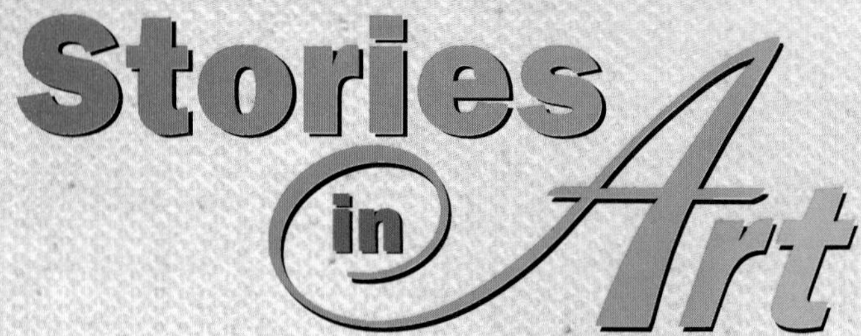

Like the Stories in Art before this one, this artwork uses pieces of broken glass. Yet the steps that went into making this sculpture were very different.

Look at this sculpture. Have you ever seen a fish like this? What do you think the artist did first to make this strange sculpture? What did he do next? How did he join together the pieces of broken glass? What do you think he did last?

Think of a strange animal that you would like to make. What materials would you use? What would you do first? Next? After that? Last? Explain the steps you would take to make your imaginary animal.

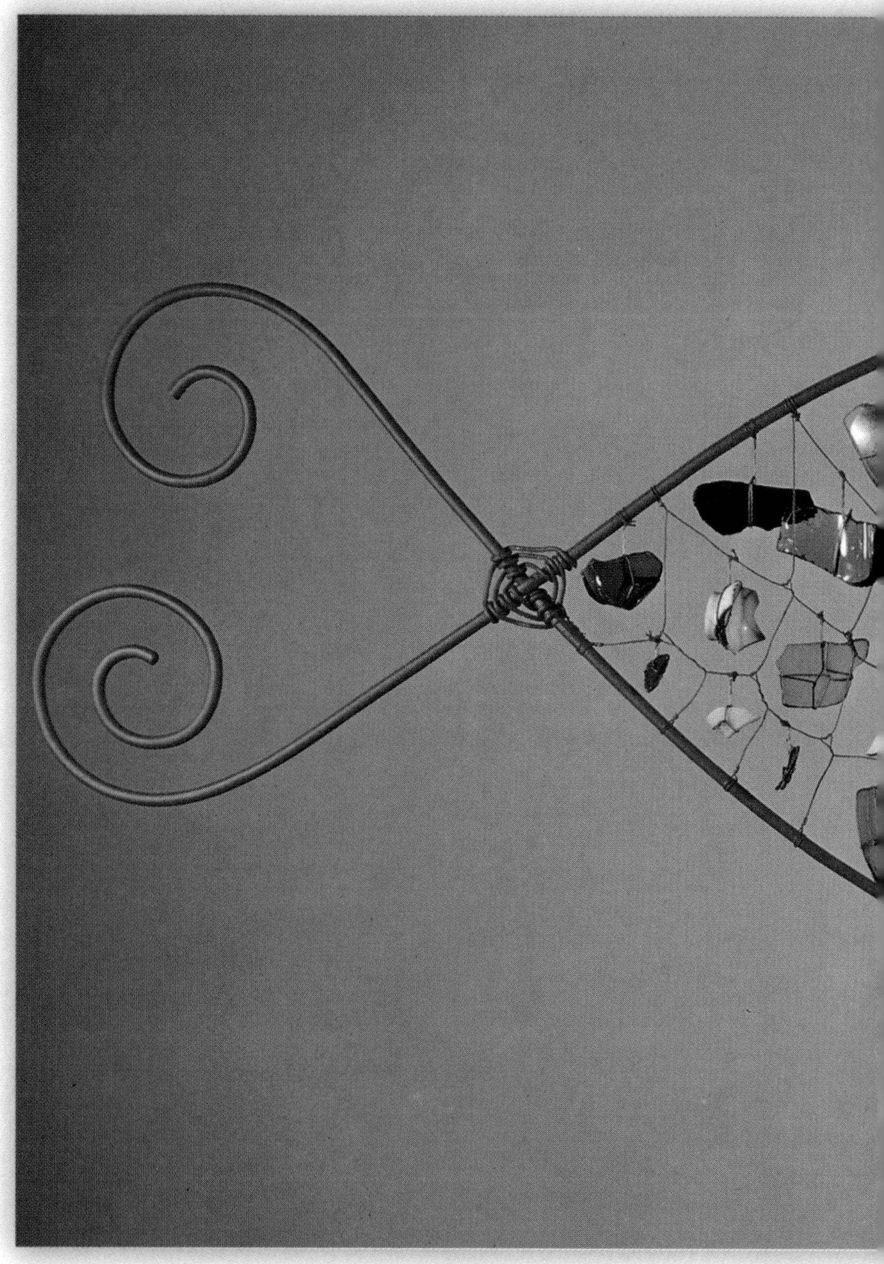

Fish **by Alexander Calder**
Private Collection

MEET
JOANNA COLE

As a child, Joanna Cole never imagined she would write books for a living. "I didn't know that a housepainter's daughter could become a writer," she says in her autobiography. Yet Cole is now the author of many books, including the popular *Magic School Bus* series.

Today, Cole writes mostly science books, which are anything but a list of humdrum facts. In the chapters from *On the Bus with Joanna Cole* printed here, Cole explains that the way she writes her books now is a lot like the way she wrote reports when she was in school.

On the Bus with

JOANNA COLE

A CREATIVE AUTOBIOGRAPHY

By JOANNA COLE With WENDY SAUL

Don't Worry. We Have

Plenty Back at the Lab.

INFORMATION—HOW TO FIND IT

In preparing to write a science book, I always read much more than one would think I needed to. I read as many books as I can find on the subject. I look in libraries and bookstores. I ask for help from librarians. I dip into the computer at the library. I try to find articles in scientific magazines, and I search for videos about my subject. Sometimes, but not always, I read children's books to see how other authors have handled the subject.

Basically, I'm a reader. If I have read two books and three articles on coral reefs, and then I watch a TV special about them, chances are I will already know almost everything on the show. I believe in reading!

As I read, I absorb an enormous amount of information. I take some notes, but I'm not very traditional. I don't keep files of carefully coded index cards, for instance. But that isn't to say I'm not well organized. Early in my reading, I abandon the rough outline I made previously and make a blank dummy out of typing paper. I number the pages and write some words in pencil on each page—for instance, in the *Dinosaur* dummy, one page was marked "In the classroom—it's visitors day" and another was "Time machine," another, "Dinosaur dig—which bones are which?" and still another, "Sauropods—special stomach." Then as I read, I write down on sticky notes any special information I don't want to forget and attach the notes on the appropriate dummy pages.

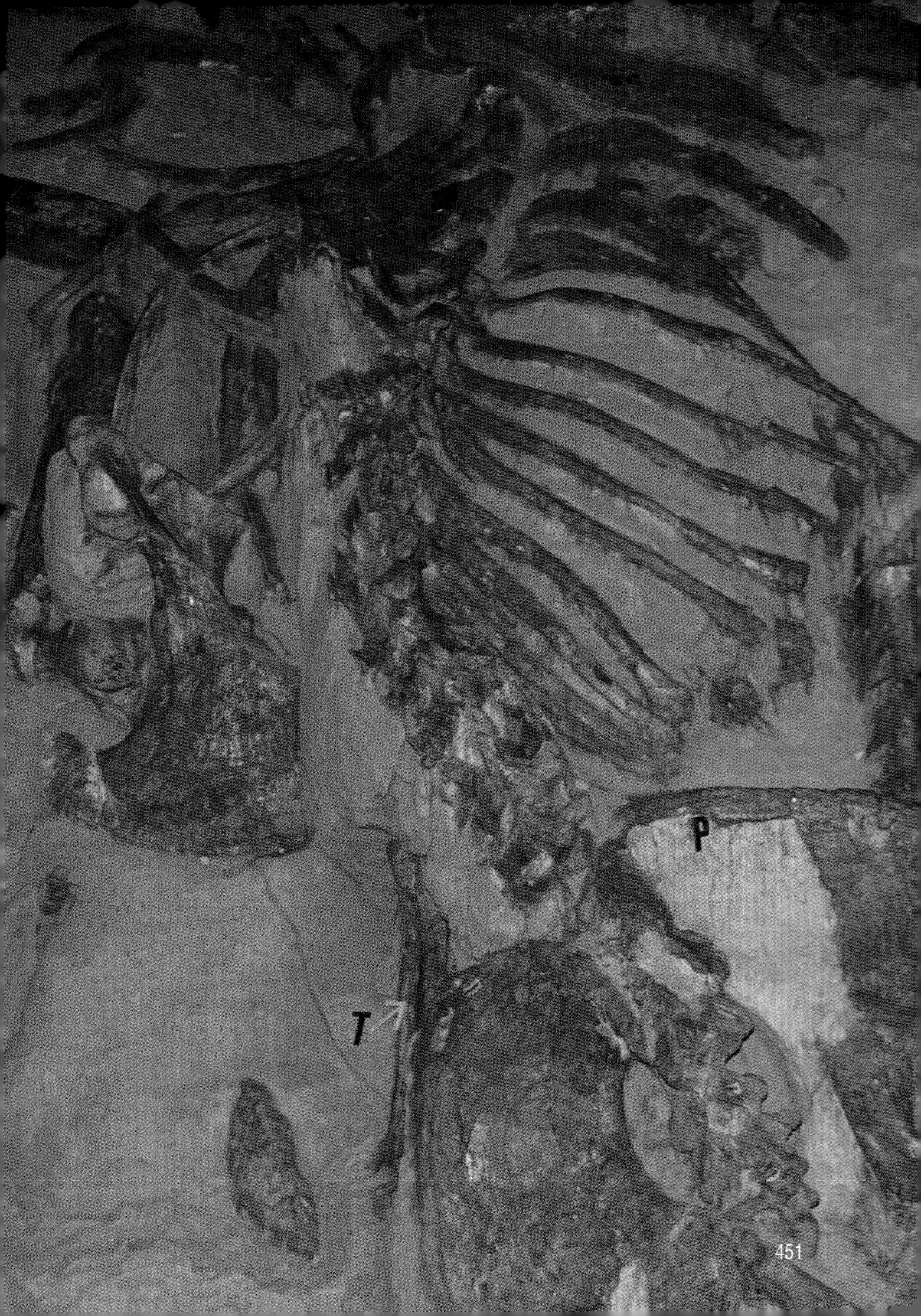
P
T

Here are some "outtakes" from the *Magic School Bus* book on honey bees. Some of these reports and word balloons never made it into the final book.

Later I begin to work on the computer, writing the actual book. For a *Magic School Bus* book, I write the text, the word balloons, and the school reports in different files. As I go along, I print them out, cut them up, and tape them into the dummy.

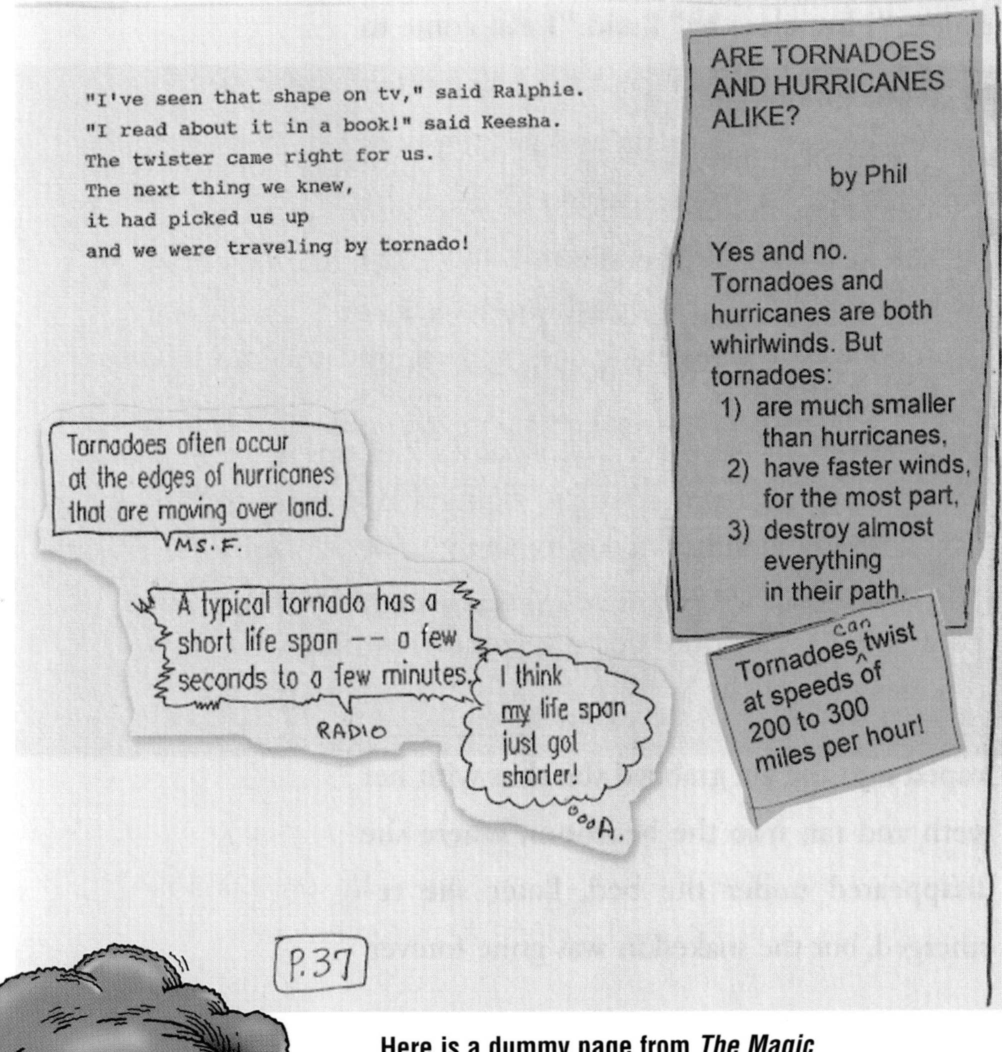
"I've seen that shape on tv," said Ralphie.
"I read about it in a book!" said Keesha.
The twister came right for us.
The next thing we knew,
it had picked us up
and we were traveling by tornado!

ARE TORNADOES AND HURRICANES ALIKE?

by Phil

Yes and no. Tornadoes and hurricanes are both whirlwinds. But tornadoes:
1) are much smaller than hurricanes,
2) have faster winds, for the most part,
3) destroy almost everything in their path.

Tornadoes often occur at the edges of hurricanes that are moving over land.
MS. F.

A typical tornado has a short life span -- a few seconds to a few minutes.
RADIO

I think my life span just got shorter!
A.

Tornadoes can twist at speeds of 200 to 300 miles per hour!

P.37

Here is a dummy page from *The Magic School Bus Inside a Hurricane.*

Gradually, the blank dummy gets filled up and becomes a complete manuscript of the book. In the process, the original notes I made get covered up, so at the end of the writing, I can't really find them anymore.

Part of my research is finding an expert on my subject. For instance, in 1980, when I was writing *A Snake's Body*, I needed to talk to a snake scientist. I had some specific questions to ask, and I wanted someone to read what I had written and tell me if I'd got it right.

I lived in New York City, down the street from the Museum of Natural History. I called the museum and spoke to a friendly snake expert. "I live close by," I said. "I can come to see you at the museum." But the scientist felt like getting some fresh air, and he suggested that he walk over to my apartment. When he arrived, I showed him my dummy and asked him my questions, while Taffy, my Yorkshire terrier, slept on the floor next to my chair. Finally, the snake expert said, "The snakes in our lab shed their skins frequently, and I brought along a snakeskin just to show what they look like." He pulled out a transparent skin from his bag and reached over to give it to me. Instantly, Taffy's eyes sprang open, she leaped into the air, grabbed the skin with her teeth and ran into the bedroom, where she disappeared under the bed. Later she reemerged, but the snakeskin was gone forever. "Don't worry," said the scientist, "we have plenty of them back at the lab."

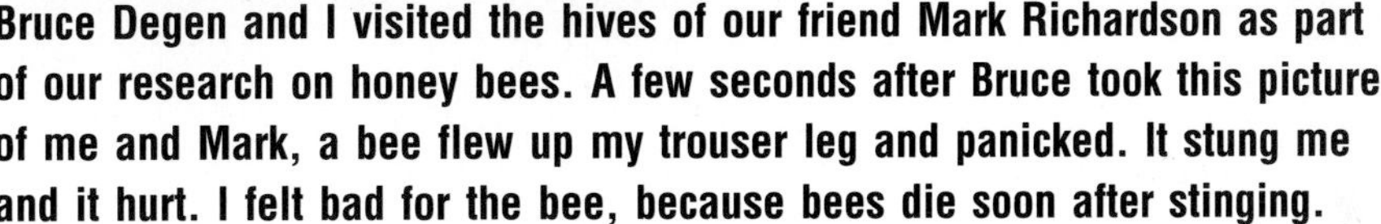

Bruce Degen and I visited the hives of our friend Mark Richardson as part of our research on honey bees. A few seconds after Bruce took this picture of me and Mark, a bee flew up my trouser leg and panicked. It stung me and it hurt. I felt bad for the bee, because bees die soon after stinging.

I know how much I owe the experts who help me and the scientists who find out all the interesting information I use in my writing. Without scientists, I as a writer would have nothing to report, and all of us as a culture would be significantly poorer. I know that I am not a scientist; I am a science writer, which is quite different. My job is to try to understand scientists' complex ideas and to communicate them in a way that makes sense to my readers.

Why Are Leaves Green?

WRITING ABOUT THE HOWS AND WHYS

For a science writer, it doesn't matter what the topic is, as long as it interests you. Because science isn't about *what*, it's about *how* and *why*. Let's say that you are waiting for the school bus, and you notice the leaves on the trees around you. You remember you have a school report due soon. Maybe it could be about leaves.

How would I, Joanna, begin such a report? First, here's what I wouldn't do. I wouldn't decide right there at the bus stop what the report would say. I wouldn't go to the encyclopedia as soon as I got to school and start copying down information. I wouldn't make an outline. Some other writers might do these things successfully. But not me. First, I would read.

I would read in a very relaxing way. At the library, I would find encyclopedia articles on trees and on plants, and I'd see if there was a separate article on leaves. If possible, I would photocopy these and take them with me. I would ask the librarian to help me find a few good books on plants with chapters on leaves. If there were a whole book on leaves, all the better.

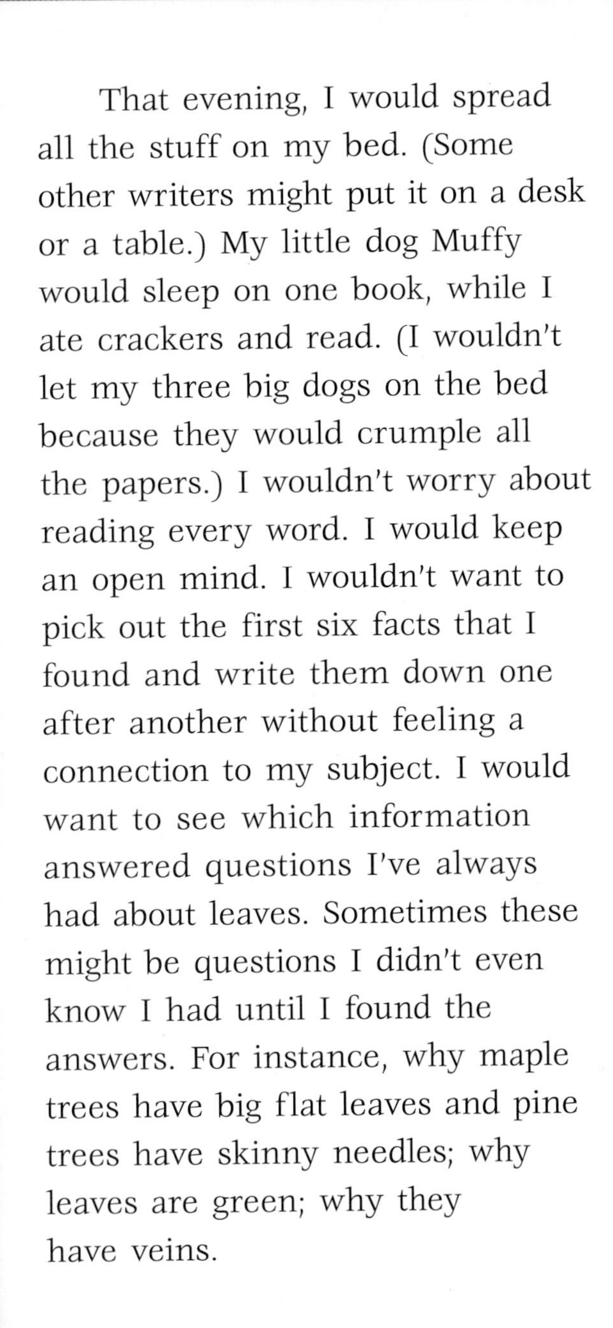

That evening, I would spread all the stuff on my bed. (Some other writers might put it on a desk or a table.) My little dog Muffy would sleep on one book, while I ate crackers and read. (I wouldn't let my three big dogs on the bed because they would crumple all the papers.) I wouldn't worry about reading every word. I would keep an open mind. I wouldn't want to pick out the first six facts that I found and write them down one after another without feeling a connection to my subject. I would want to see which information answered questions I've always had about leaves. Sometimes these might be questions I didn't even know I had until I found the answers. For instance, why maple trees have big flat leaves and pine trees have skinny needles; why leaves are green; why they have veins.

I notice as I read that leaves are not there just to look pretty. In nature almost everything has a function, a reason for being that makes sense. Leaves have work to do. They are green because they have a green chemical called chlorophyll that is used to change light energy into food. Maple trees and other trees that are bare in winter have big, flat leaves with a large surface area to catch more sunlight to manufacture more food in the summer to make up for all those winter months when the tree doesn't have leaves. Evergreens usually have small, waxy-coated needles to conserve water during the long, dry winter, when water is often frozen and not available to plants. And because needles stay on in winter, evergreens can do some extra food-making on warm, sunny winter days, making up for what they miss on account of their small size.

Leaves have veins that carry water up from the tree's roots because to make food, leaves need water, as well as chlorophyll, sunlight, and carbon dioxide from the air. Finally, an idea for my report starts taking shape. How about a report called "Leaves Are Food Makers"?

So now I will take notes about leaves as food makers. I won't worry about all the other facts about leaves. I will use facts to *explain* how leaves work to make food. So the report won't be just a stack of facts. It's sort of like a story, and it's sort of like an argument.

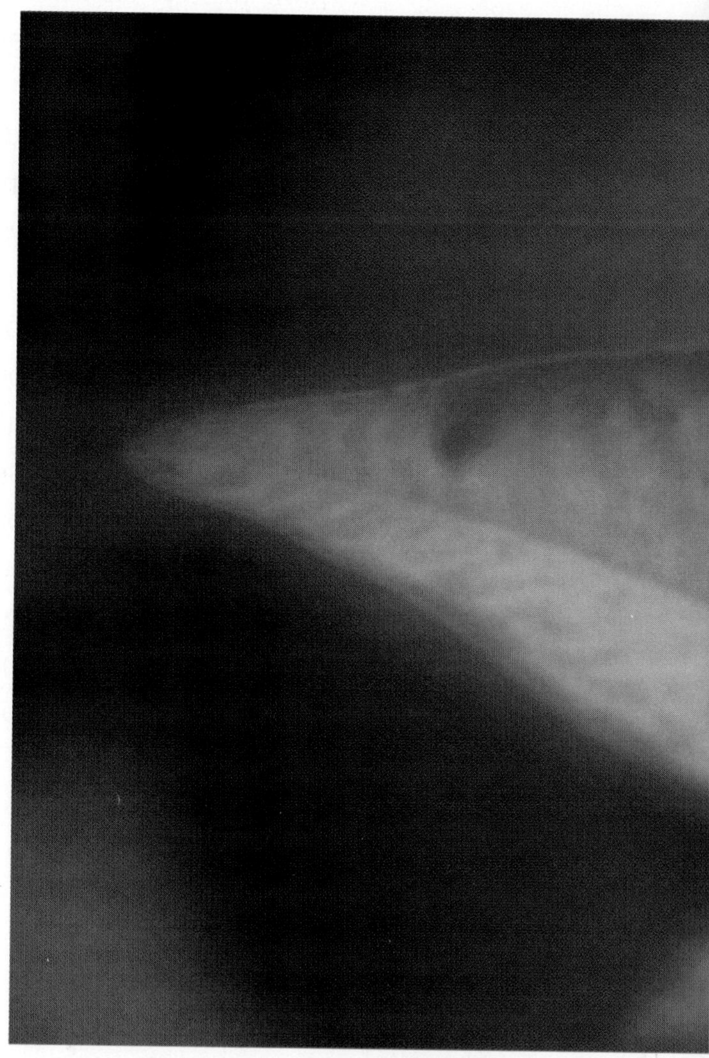

It has a beginning, a middle, and an end, starting with the sun shining on the leaf and ending with the veins carrying the food away to other parts of the tree and water vapor and oxygen exiting the leaves through pores.

This is the way I wrote school reports when I was young, and this is the way I write my science books today.

Story Questions & Activities

1. What is the first thing Joanna Cole does before writing a science book?
2. What steps would Joanna take to write a book about bees?
3. What makes Joanna Cole such a good science writer? Explain.
4. What is the main idea of this selection?
5. Imagine that Joanna Cole could interview Sylvia Earle in "Meet an Underwater Explorer." What is the first question Joanna might ask? How do you think Sylvia Earle would answer it?

Write a How-to Essay

Could you teach someone how to make a peanut butter-and-jelly sandwich? Choose something you know how to do well. Write step-by-step instructions for a person who would be trying it for the first time. Be sure that your essay has a beginning, a middle, and an end. Add a diagram or pictures with captions showing the steps.

Show the Steps

Draw step-by-step pictures with captions of how Joanna Cole would plan to write a book about pine cones. Show her trip to the library and the books she would read. Show the people she would interview and the places she would visit. Number your drawings in order.

Role-play an Interview

Being a science writer takes a lot of research. With a partner, act out an interview with a science writer. Together, make a list of questions you could ask. Then role-play the interview.

Find Out More

Joanna often uses questions to get ideas for her writing. To answer why bees make honey, she may read books and talk to experts. Answer one question you have about science by reading a book or by watching a television program on the subject.

Follow Directions

In some ways, learning how to be a writer is like building a house. For both, you have to start from the bottom and build your way up. You also need to follow directions. Suppose that you really wanted to build a house. What would you do first? Second? Third? Look at the numbered steps below.

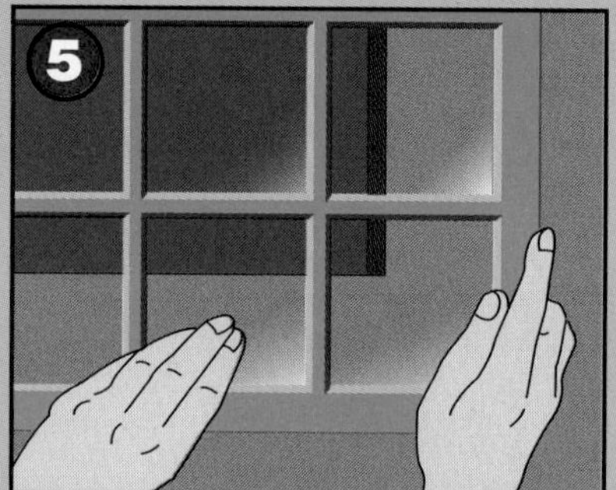

Follow the directions to answer these questions.

1. What is the first thing you would do to build a house?
2. What is the second step?
3. Between which two steps would you put up the walls and the roof?
4. What is the last thing you would do?
5. How would you describe each of the steps in the pictures? Explain on a separate sheet of paper.

TEST POWER

Test Tip

For a main idea question, eliminate answers that are too detailed.

DIRECTIONS

Read the sample story. Then read each question about the story.

SAMPLE

Weather Satellites

A satellite is a machine that scientists put into space. Satellites orbit the Earth, circling the Earth just as the moon does. Some satellites take pictures of the Earth and send the pictures back to scientists on Earth. The scientists use the pictures to tell what the weather is doing.

There are two types of weather satellites. One is a GOES satellite. It travels around the Earth at the same speed that the Earth turns, so it's always over the same spot. The other is a POSE satellite. It moves from north to south around the Earth and is located at different points each day.

1 The word orbit in this passage means—

A travel around something

B shoot into space

C provide pictures

D predict the weather

2 What is the main idea of the second paragraph?

F Satellites are easy to make.

G Satellites provide useful information.

H Scientists live in the satellites.

J There are two kinds of weather satellites.

Art begins with the things artists see and remember. But sometimes artists have to rely on their imagination.

Look at the dinosaurs in this picture. Are they exactly alike? Which two are similar but not identical? What are the differences? Has the artist drawn their size about right? How do you know?

Look at the painting again. What is happening in this scene? What is the artist trying to say about these early creatures? How do they compare with the animals today?

Life Around Jurassic Shores
English School (Twentieth Century)

TIME FOR KIDS

SPECIAL REPORT

This crablike creature, *Anomalocaris,* lived more than 500 million years ago.

EARTH'S FIRST CREATURES

The Earliest Animals

Why did a weird crop of creatures appear more than 500 million years ago?

If you could travel 600 million years back in time, you would not see a single animal on Earth. In fact, you would be the only creature bigger than the head of a pin. Earth had been around for more than 4 billion years by that time. But only the simplest, smallest kinds of life had made it their home.

Wiwaxia **defended itself with sharp spines.**

Some scientists believe that ancient relatives of nearly every species that has ever crawled, flown, or walked showed up between 543 million and 510 million years ago. This time is called the Cambrian Period. Earth's animal population grew so suddenly that scientists call it the "Cambrian explosion."

It's hard to believe that the Cambrian creatures are the ancestors of today's animals. *Anomalocaris* had spiny arms to catch small animals. It would then crush them with its jaw. Scientists say this creature might be related to today's crabs and spiders.

Sharp spines helped *Wiwaxia* take care of itself. *Opabinia* was a five-eyed creature with a nose like a hose.

Ottoia **grew up to six inches. It hid in the sea floor and sucked up food with its snout.**

COVER: JOHN SIBBICK; THIS PAGE: KAM MAK/NATIONAL GEOGRAPHIC IMAGE COLLECTION

WHERE DID THEY COME FROM?

Where did these weird wonders come from? Did a change in Earth's climate make it possible for them to appear suddenly? To find the answers, scientists turned to the time just before the Cambrian Period. It was a time that lasted about 20 million years.

Not much is known about this earlier time. But in the last few years, scientists have discovered fossils from this period. The fossils were dug up in ancient rocks in Africa and Siberia. They help explain how the earliest ancestors of today's animals may have come to be.

The fossils show that animals just before the Cambrian Period were bigger than earlier, almost invisible animals.

Hallucigenia **puzzled scientists, who thought its spikes were legs until they turned it right side up!**

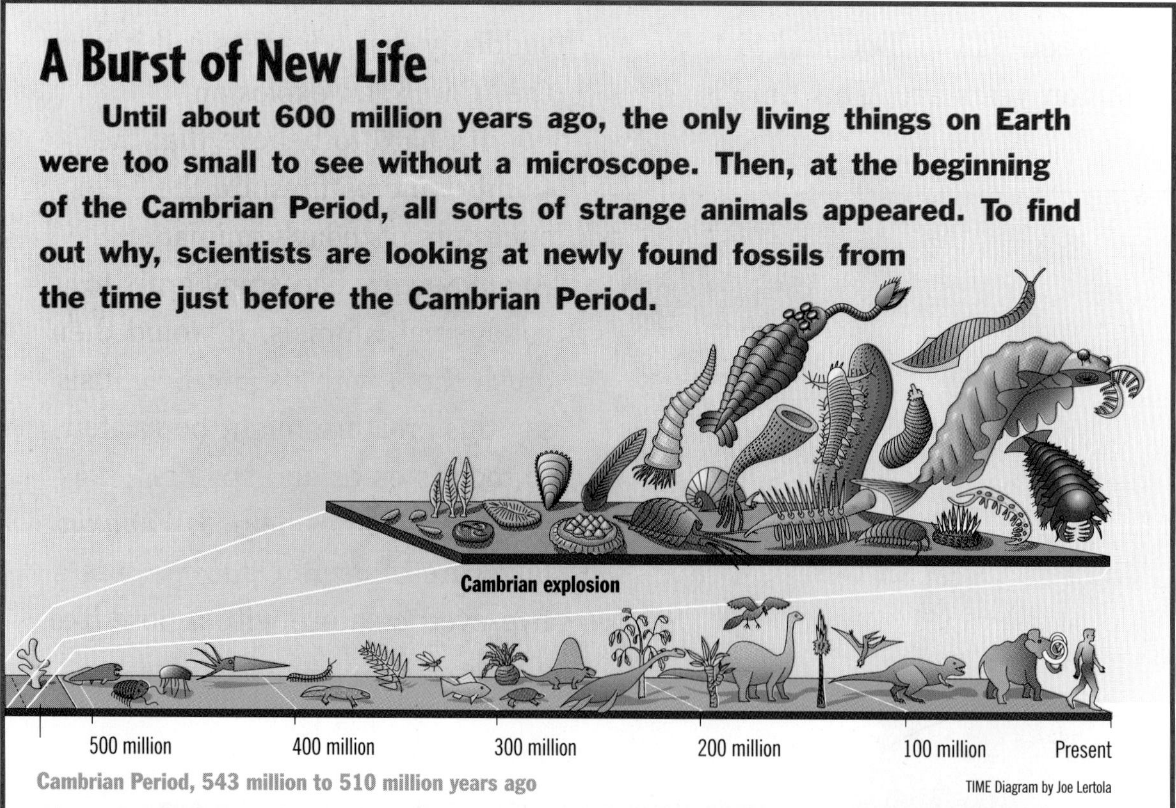

Some looked like worms. Some were three feet across. Others had shells. They all floated or crawled in the sea. And most of the animals had more developed body systems than earlier creatures.

Some scientists think that these body changes were important steps leading to the Cambrian animals. Others think ice ages, when the weather turned cold, made it possible for the strange Cambrian animals to develop. Perhaps it was a natural disaster, such as a huge earthquake or a giant meteor crashing to Earth, that somehow changed the environment. Still others think changes in Earth's atmosphere led to the Cambrian creatures.

Scientists still aren't sure why the Cambrian animals came to be. One thing they are sure of is that the Cambrian animals came on the scene very quickly. New ways of measuring fossils show that the animal explosion happened within a period of 5 million to 10 million years. And in the history of the planet, that's practically no time at all!

This is one artist's idea of what some Cambrian creatures may have looked like.

FIND OUT MORE

Visit our website:

www.mhschool.com/reading

Story Questions & Activities

1. When did animals first appear?
2. Why is time important in this article?
3. How are Earth's first creatures different from today's animals? Explain.
4. What is the main idea of this selection?
5. Compare "Earth's First Creatures" with a book you have read about dinosaurs or other animals that no longer exist, or with a movie such as *Jurassic Park*. Which has more facts—this article or the book or movie? Explain.

Write a Plan

This selection says that all these early animals floated or crawled in the sea. Suppose that you wanted to start your own community aquarium. Where would you begin? How would you choose a place for your fish and other ocean animals? Write your plan. Include the steps you would take to start your aquarium.

Measure a Time Line

Figure out how to make a time line based on the information in the selection. How would you represent events that happened 500 million years ago? How would you show those years in relation to the present? Describe your scale in centimeters or inches.

Draw a Picture

Scientists believe that the *Anomalocaris*, with its spiny arms and strong jaw, may be a cousin to today's crabs and spiders. Choose another early animal and draw a picture of it. Then draw a picture of an animal or an insect in the world today that might be its relative. Compare the two animals.

Find Out More

Discover more information about an animal that lived millions of years ago. This animal could be a dinosaur, a woolly mammoth, or a saber-toothed tiger. Start by looking in an encyclopedia or a science book. Find out when and where this animal lived, what its habits were, and what happened to it. Share your information with your classmates.

Read a Chart

This chart describes five odd animals that first appeared between 500 and 600 million years ago, during the Cambrian Period. **Charts** organize information. They can help you compare similar objects to see how they are alike and how they are different.

Animals of the Cambrian Period

- **Anomalocaris** crablike; spiny arms to catch small animals; may be related to crabs and spiders
- **Ottoia** up to six inches long; hid in the sea floor; sucked up food with its snout
- **Wiwaxia** had sharp spines to defend itself
- **Opabinia** had five eyes and a nose like a hose
- **Hallucigenia** had spikes that looked like legs

Use the chart to answer these questions.

1. How many eyes did *Opabinia* have?
2. Which animal may be related to today's spiders?
3. How did *Anomalocaris* and *Ottoia* get their food?
4. How did *Ottoia* and *Wiwaxia* keep themselves safe?
5. How did this chart help you understand information from the article?

TEST POWER

Test Tip

Look in the passage for clues to answer the question.

DIRECTIONS

Read the sample story. Then read each question about the story.

SAMPLE

Paddling a Canoe

José was not excited about the canoe trip. He hadn't been in a canoe before. He asked his friend Karen if she would show him how to use the paddle.

"You can use different strokes to paddle the canoe in different directions," Karen said. She handed him a paddle and helped him into the canoe. "When you paddle on the right side of the canoe, the canoe moves to the left; when you paddle on the left, the canoe moves to the right," she explained.

José paddled on the right, and the front of the canoe edged through the water and <u>veered</u> left. "This is great!" he cried.

1 The word <u>veered</u> in this story means—

A tried

B smiled

C paddled

D turned

2 The author gives you reason to believe that—

F Karen was more skilled at canoeing than José

G Karen was upset that José did not know how to paddle the canoe

H José could do tricks with the paddle

J José's teacher told him to paddle the canoe

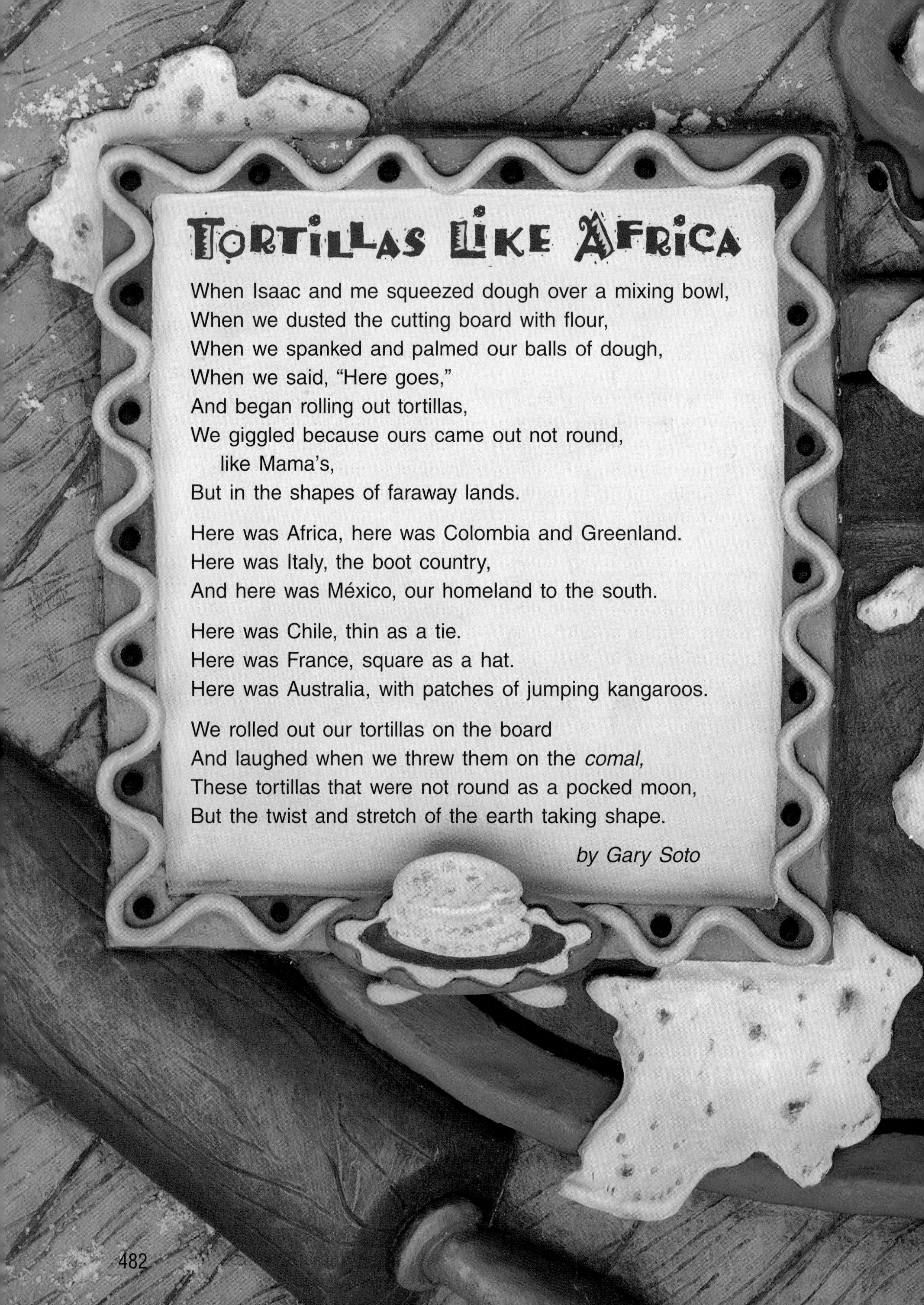

Tortillas Like Africa

When Isaac and me squeezed dough over a mixing bowl,
When we dusted the cutting board with flour,
When we spanked and palmed our balls of dough,
When we said, "Here goes,"
And began rolling out tortillas,
We giggled because ours came out not round,
    like Mama's,
But in the shapes of faraway lands.

Here was Africa, here was Colombia and Greenland.
Here was Italy, the boot country,
And here was México, our homeland to the south.

Here was Chile, thin as a tie.
Here was France, square as a hat.
Here was Australia, with patches of jumping kangaroos.

We rolled out our tortillas on the board
And laughed when we threw them on the *comal,*
These tortillas that were not round as a pocked moon,
But the twist and stretch of the earth taking shape.

by Gary Soto

UNIT 5

MAKE a PLAN

HOW TO TELL THE TOP OF A HILL

The top of a hill
Is not until
The bottom is below.
And you have to stop
When you reach the top
For there's no more UP to go.

To make it plain
Let me explain:
The one *most* reason why
You have to stop
When you reach the top—is:
The next step up is sky.

by John Ciardi

Stories in Art

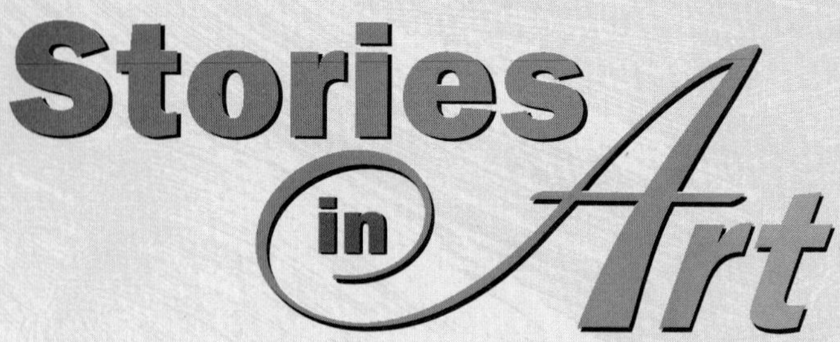

When you look at this painting you can almost tell what will happen next. That's because the artist has created a feeling of tension or fear.

Study the painting. What animals do you see? Which animal is stalking its prey? Do the other animals seem afraid? How do you know?

Look at the painting again. Whose footprints do you see? What do you think will happen next? After that? Finally? If the painting suddenly came to life, would you hear movement or silence? Why?

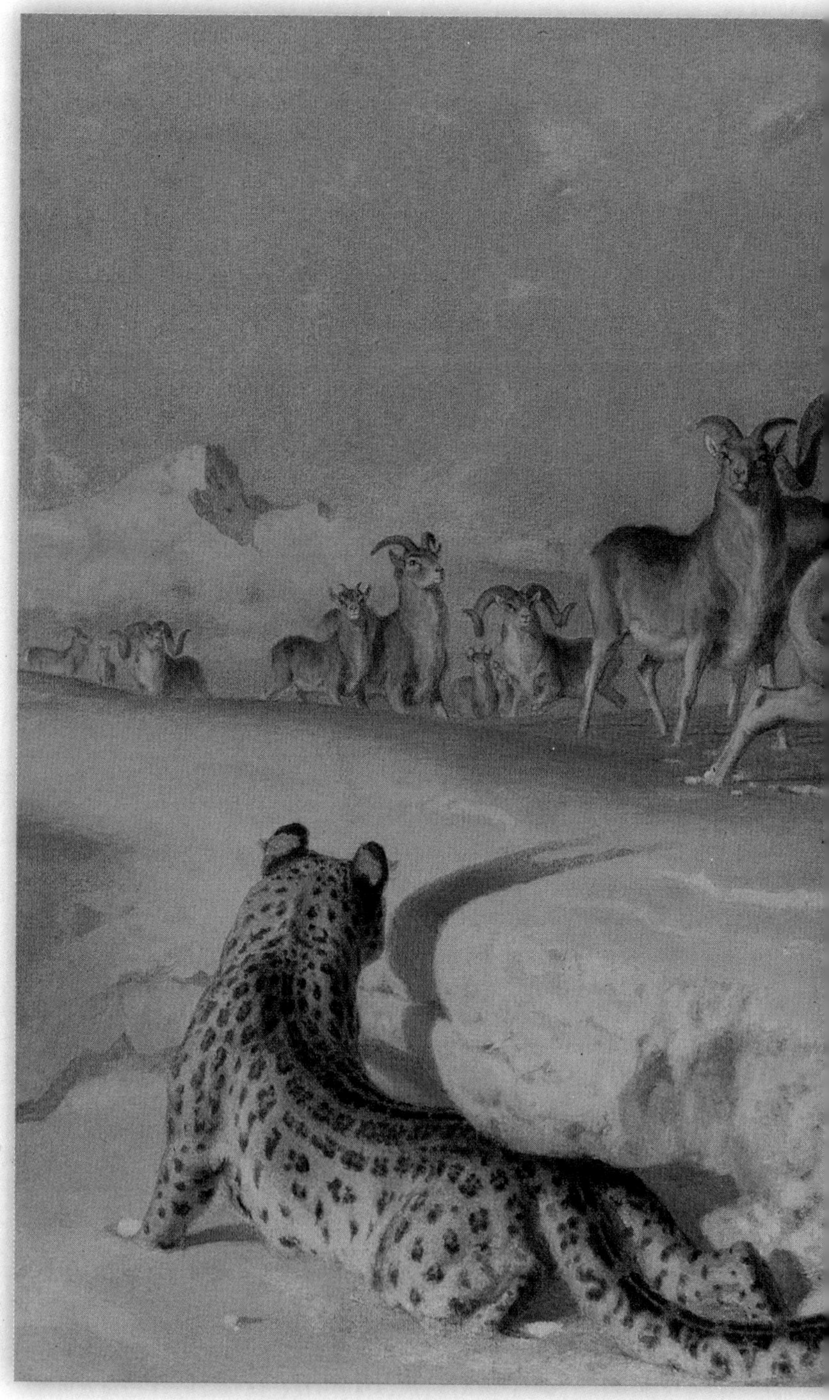

A Snow Leopard Stalking Ovis Polii
by Joseph Wolf, 1890

MEET KEVIN HAWKES

Kevin Hawkes studied illustration in Utah and then worked in a bookstore in Boston, Massachusetts. His success as an illustrator began when his first book, *Then the Troll Heard the Squeak*, was published in 1991. Since then, he has written and illustrated many successful books.

Hawkes creates characters who are fun, but sometimes a little bit scary. "My artwork often has a darker, European look to it, perhaps the result of my stay as a child in Europe," says Hawkes. The playful side of his work and his special sense of humor can be seen in the illustrations for *The Fox and the Guinea Pig*.

MEET MARY ANN NEWMAN

When she was a child, Mary Ann Newman visited Cuba with her parents and fell in love with the colors and smells of Havana. She also fell in love with the sound of the Spanish language. She has spent her life since then studying and working with the Spanish and Catalan languages. By teaching and translating, she gets to share with English speakers the stories she loves in Spanish.

Newman has lived in Chile, Mexico, and Spain. She has been given many honors—by foundations in both the United States and Spain—for her study and translation of Spanish. Although she lives in New York City, Newman considers Barcelona, Spain, to be her second home.

The Fox and the Guinea Pig

Folk Tale

Illustrated by Kevin Hawkes
Translated by Mary Ann Newman

Returning from the market one day, Don Emicho was very surprised to find his alfalfa patch in a terrible mess. His little plants were all dug up, strewn about, and nibbled at.

"How strange," he said, deep in thought. "Who could have done this?"

He had to do something before the intruder ate up and destroyed his entire green field of alfalfa. Then he had an idea.

"I know, I know," he smiled, and he started making a trap out of sticks, twigs, and thorns.

Four days went by, and the intruder didn't return. Don Emicho said to himself:

"Maybe my trap scares him," and he started making a smaller trap. Then he went to bed.

He was dreaming of dancing in the town fair when the sound of screeching awakened him.

He got right out of bed. He ran to his alfalfa patch and saw a guinea pig in his trap. It was just about to escape! But Don Emicho dove headlong and grabbed the guinea pig.

"So, it was you who destroyed my green alfalfa patch, was it?" he said as he tied him to a tree, thinking about a meal of stewed guinea pig with potatoes, peanuts, and hot peppers.

He licked his lips with delight! And the guinea pig couldn't move a muscle.

"When the sun comes up, I'll be back to cook you," Don Emicho warned him, and he went back to bed since it was still dark out.

The guinea pig was quite worried. What could he do to get away? Just then a fox appeared.

"My friend! What happened?" he said.

"Nothing, my friend," the guinea pig smiled. "Don Emicho has three beautiful daughters and he wants me to marry the eldest, Florinda, you know."

"And that's why you're all tied up?" asked the fox in amazement.

"For that very reason," the guinea pig went on. "Don Emicho thinks that if I marry Florinda, I'll learn to enjoy eating chicken. They eat nothing but fowl. Besides, I don't want to get married."

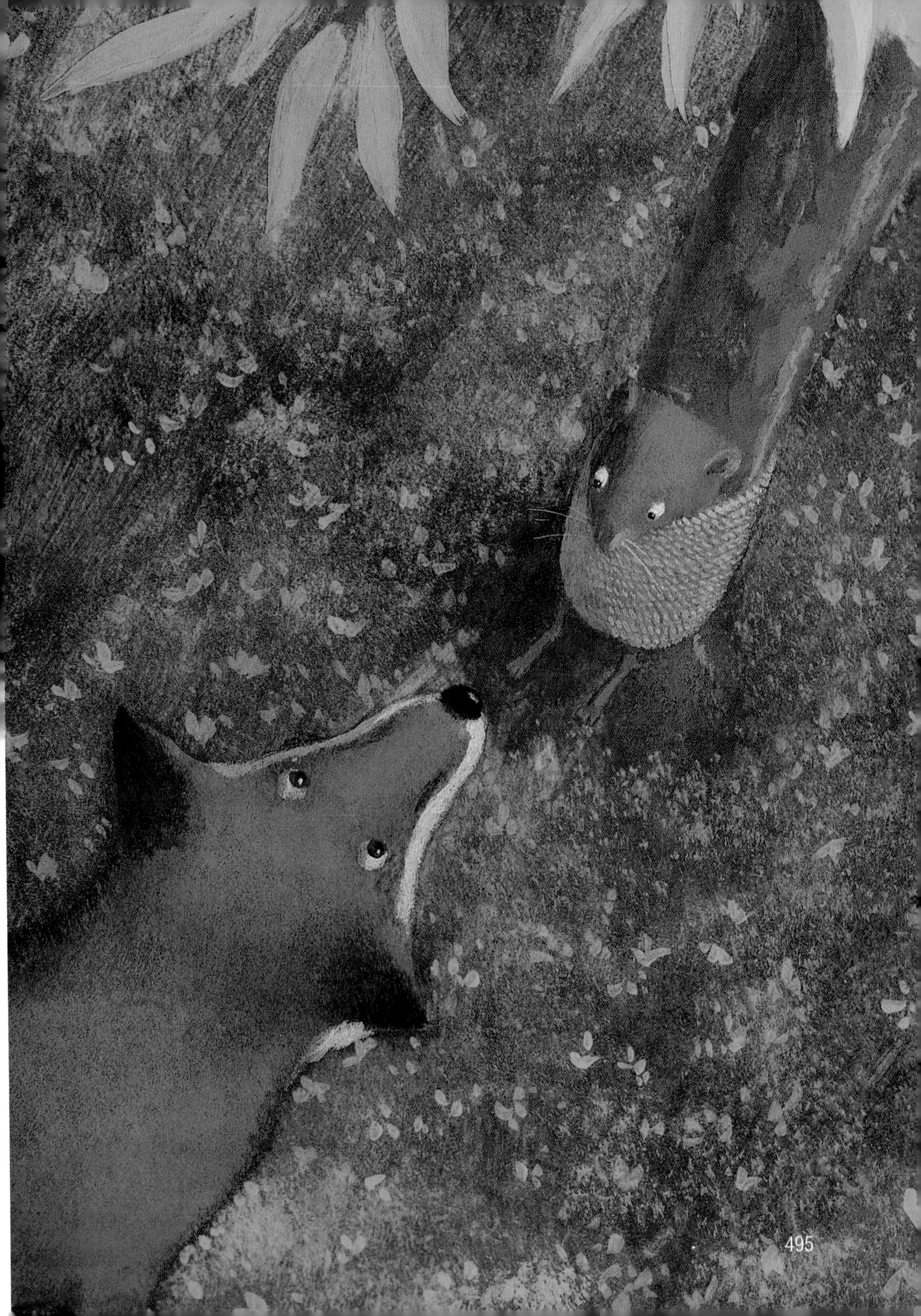

"I love chicken," said the fox enthusiastically.

"Hmm," said the guinea pig. "Would you like to trade places with me? Would you like to marry Florinda and eat chicken every day?"

The fox happily untied the guinea pig and took his place. The guinea pig tied him up as tightly as he could, and said a very serious goodbye.

When Don Emicho went out to cook the guinea pig, he almost keeled over with surprise to find the fox all tied up and with a smile on his face.

"You're going to pay for this!" he said angrily. "Last night you were a guinea pig and today you've turned yourself into a fox!" Picking up a stick, he started to hit the fox.

"I'll gladly marry Florinda, I will!" the fox cried out, braving the blows of the stick.

And through his tears he told Don Emicho the story the guinea pig had told him.

Don Emicho's belly danced with laughter when he heard how the guinea pig had tricked the fox.

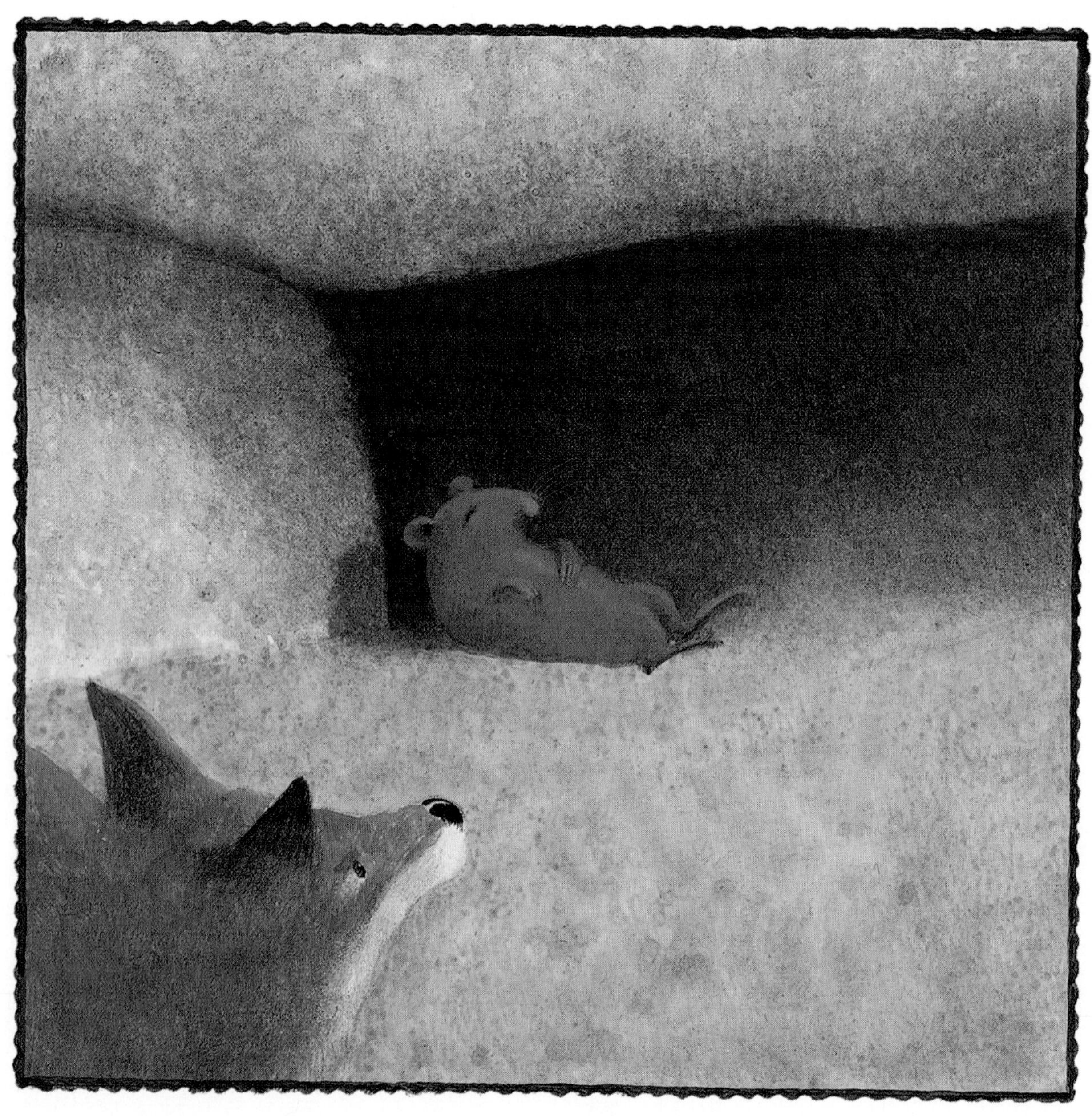

Time went by. The fox looked all over for the guinea pig, until one day he found him sleeping like a log.

"Now you're going to pay," the fox murmured.

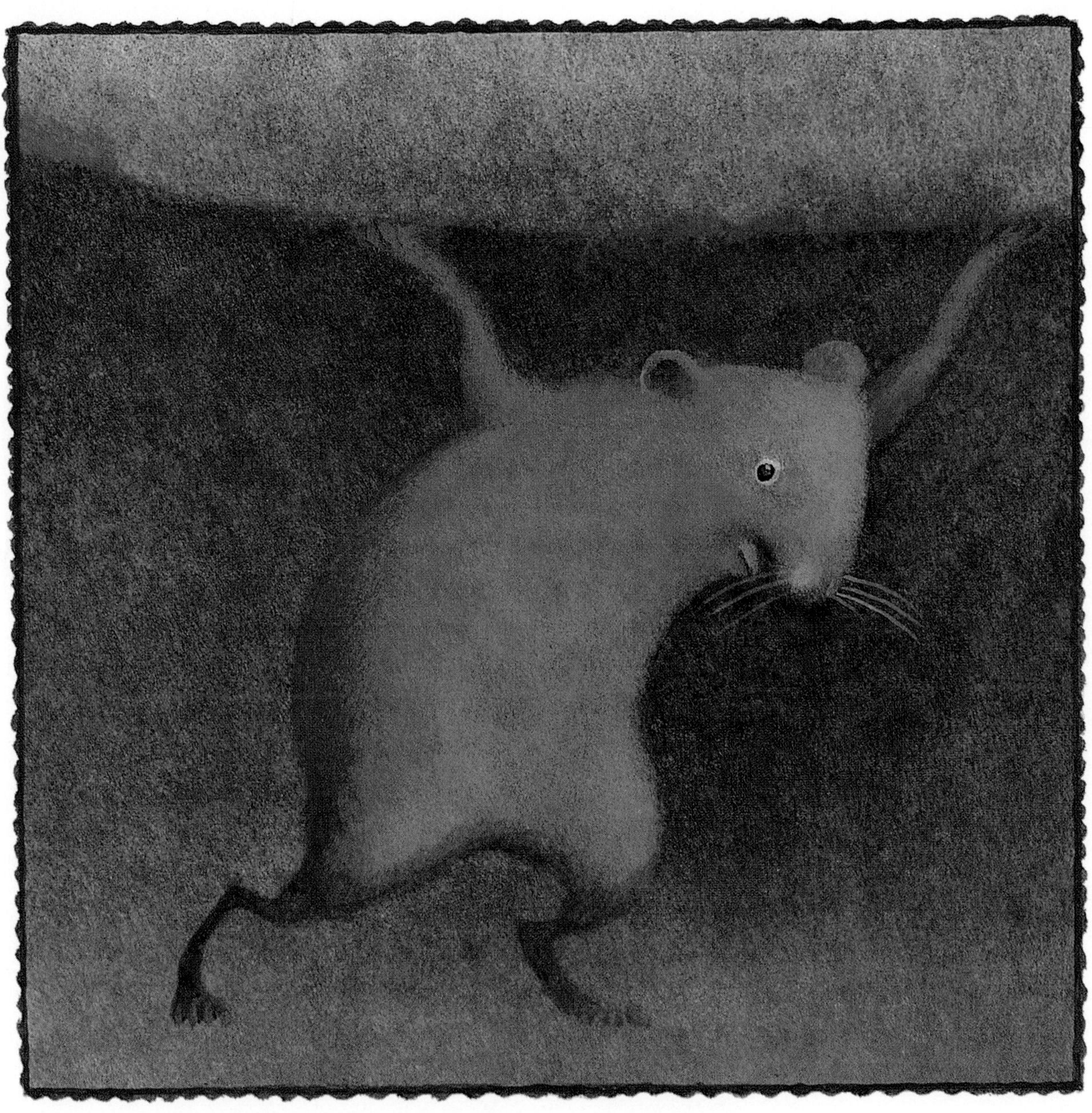

When the guinea pig realized he'd been spotted, he stood up on his little hind legs under a great rock and said to the fox:

"My friend, the world is falling down, and we have to hold it up. I'm getting tired. Can't you see how tired I'm getting?"

The fox really believed that the world was falling down. Frightened, he closed his eyes and, without a second thought, started holding up the great rock.

"I'm going to go look for a stake. Don't let go of the rock now, I'll be back in a flash!" said the guinea pig, with a sigh of relief.

The fox waited more than an hour. He was sweating. And he didn't let go of the great rock for fear of being crushed to death by the mountain and the whole world. More than three hours went by. And nothing happened.

All tired out, the fox finally let go of the enormous rock. And nothing happened then, either.

When he realized how the guinea pig had tricked him, he began kicking and screaming with anger. But it wasn't long before he ran into the guinea pig again.

"This time he's not going to get away from me," he thought, looking all around him.

The guinea pig was resting, lulled to sleep by the brilliant midday sun. His white teeth showing, the fox moved toward him, very confidently and in no hurry at all.

When the guinea pig saw how angry the fox was, he started digging and digging, all the while shouting in a panic:

"Quickly, my friend, quickly! The end of the world is coming!"

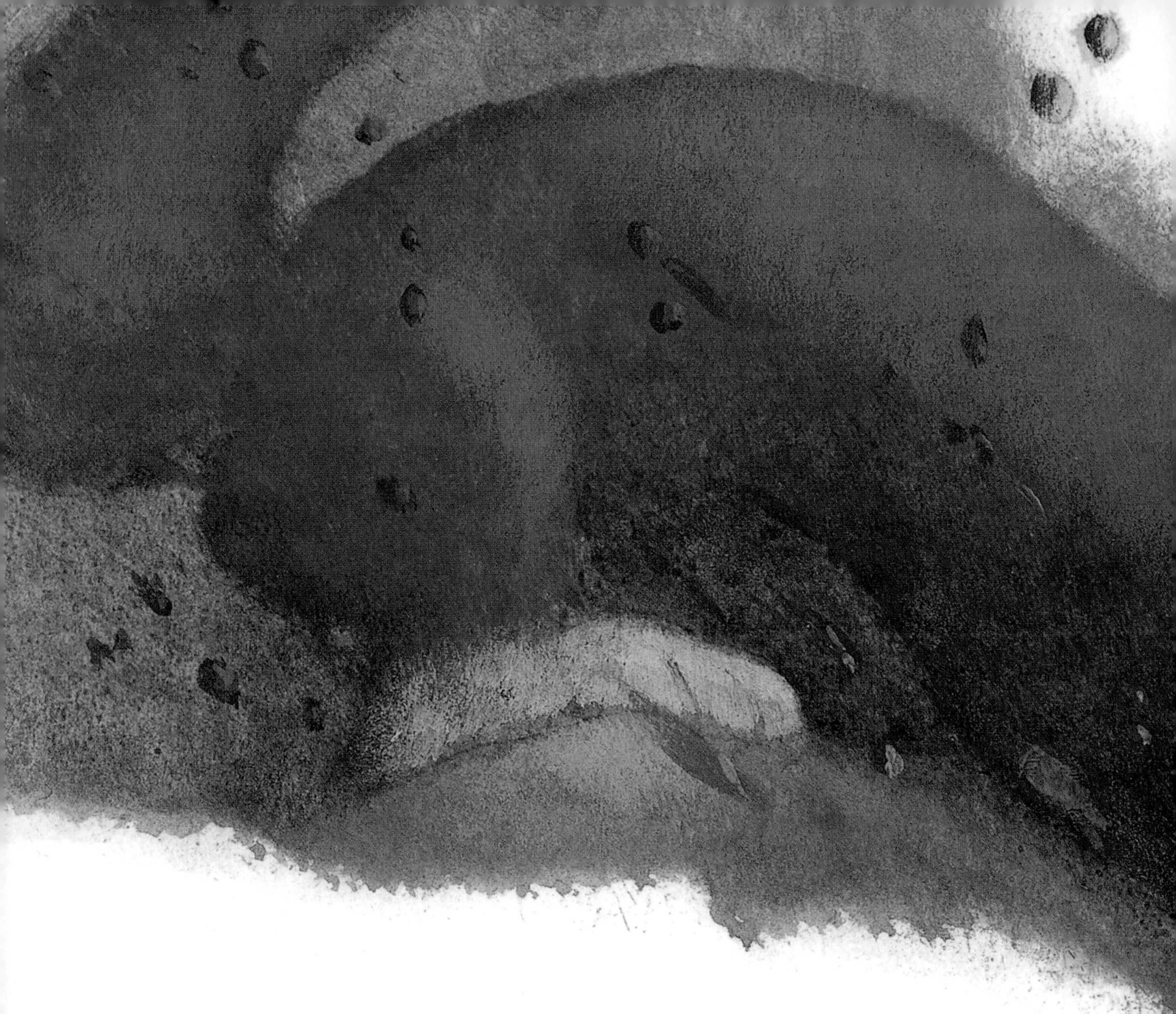

"The end of the world?" the fox stopped short.

"It's going to rain down fire!" And more and more perturbed, he went on digging.

"It's going to rain down fire?" The fox was beginning to be frightened.

"Yes, it is going to rain down flames! So forgive me, but this is no time for small talk!" And he pushed the fox away with his little paw.

The fox, more frightened than ever, started to dig right next to the guinea pig, saying:

"I'll help you, my friend, I'll help you."

When the hole was really deep, and the fox saw that the guinea pig was about to hop into it, he jumped in himself, begging the guinea pig:

"Let me go first! I don't want to die by fire! Bury me in the dirt, little brother. Bury me quickly, please!"

The fox was so frightened that all by himself he imagined that the first lightning bolts and thunderclaps were on their way, and that very soon fire would rain down from the sky. The truth be told, he was a very nervous fox.

"All right," said the guinea pig, burying him under dirt and stones. "I'm going to bury you so that you can be saved, but promise me you'll never forget my friendship and sacrifice."

"I promise! I promise!" the fox thanked him, with just his muzzle sticking up out of the ground.

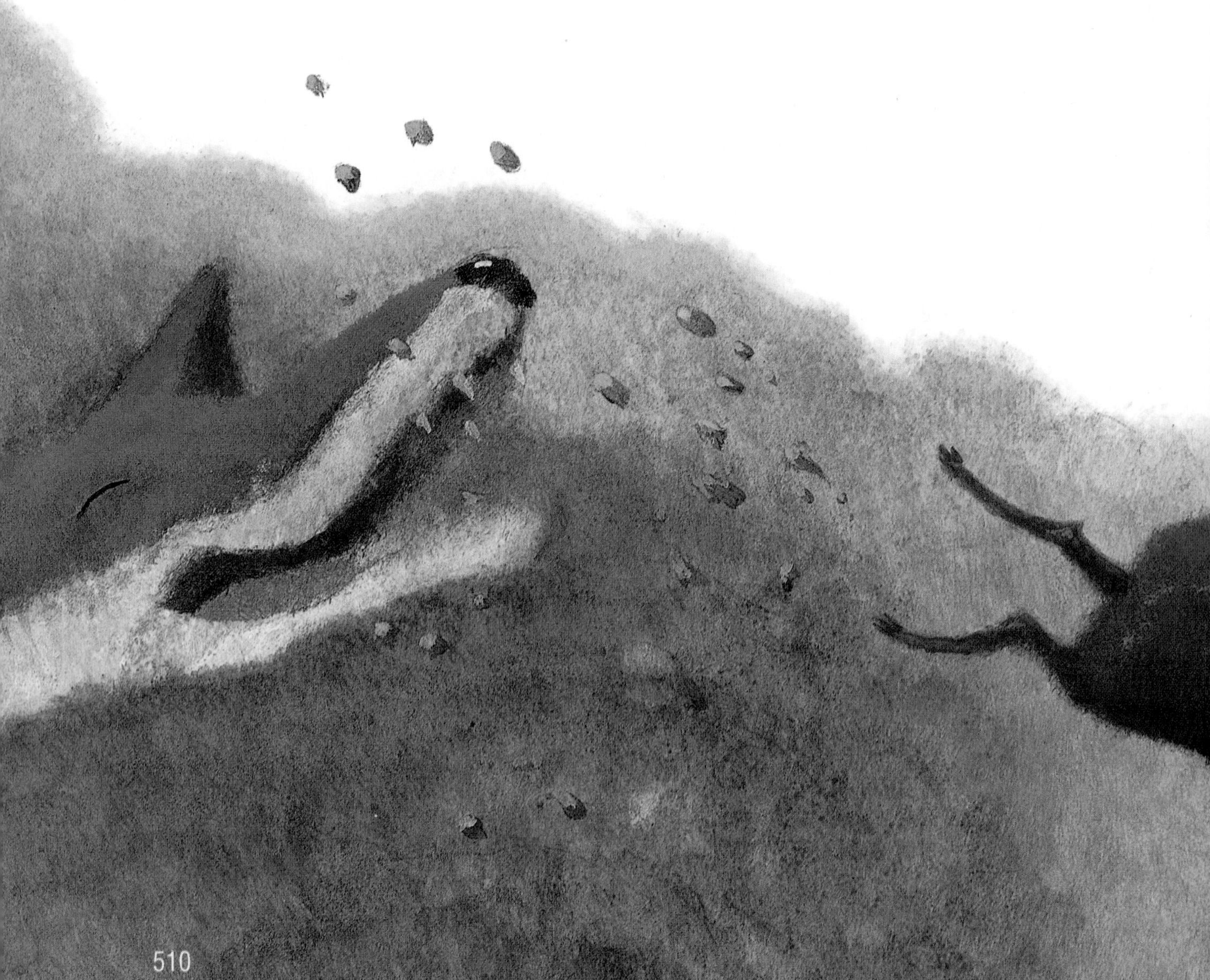

And that was how the clever
guinea pig got free of the fox forever.

Story Questions & Activities

1. What does the guinea pig do to trick the fox the first time?
2. How does the guinea pig continue to trick the fox?
3. Many folk tales use animal characters to teach a lesson. What lesson do the fox and the guinea pig teach in this folk tale?
4. What is this story mostly about?
5. Imagine that the fox became part of the picture on pages 486–487. What do you think he would say about the footprints in the snow?

Write a Folk Tale

Foxes are supposed to be clever. But the guinea pig in this story "outfoxes" the fox! Think of another story or folk tale you know in which one animal tricks another. Write that story—or make up your own. Be sure that your story has a beginning, a middle, and an end.

Make a Plan

Imagine that you are Don Emicho and you must come up with a plan to stop something from eating your alfalfa crop. If it is an animal, will you build a cage? If it is an army of ants, will you buy an anteater? Consider five possibilities, and come up with a plan for each.

Pantomime a Story

What happens when you tell a story without using words? Work with a group of classmates to pantomime the characters and events in a story that your classmates would know. Have another group guess the name of your story.

Find Out More

People have always told stories. In fact, the person who told the best stories became the storyteller for the community. Find out more about this storytelling tradition by looking in an encyclopedia under "storytelling" or "folklore." Write down three facts you learn and share them with the class.

Read Advertisements

The guinea pig in this story would probably be good at writing advertisements. He gets the fox to trade places with him and even to believe that the world is falling down. In a similar way, an **advertisement** uses just a few words to persuade people to do or buy something. Although ads should be truthful, they often stretch the truth. It always pays to read an advertisement carefully. This will help you to see if the item is what it says it is—and if it is something that you want.

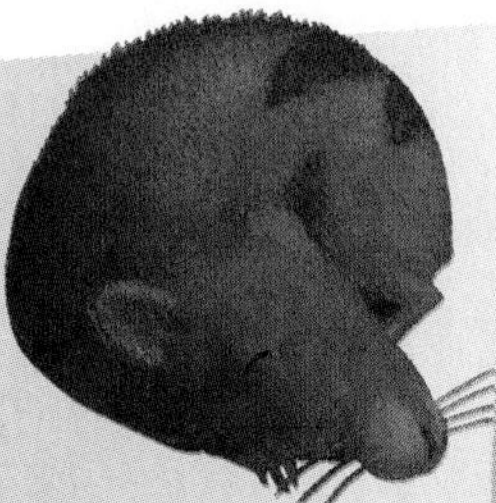

Adorable, friendly guinea pigs. Clean, easy to care for. Excellent pets.

Reasonable price.
Call 555-1777.

Disaster Insurance

Smart people are preparing for any disasters by buying insurance now! This insurance costs only pennies a day. It always pays to be prepared. Just fill out the form below and send your money to G. Pig Insurance Company, P.O. Box 000. Act today before time runs out!

Use the advertisements to answer these questions.

1. What is each advertisement selling?
2. How does each ad try to get you to buy the item?
3. What does each advertisement *not* tell you?
4. Based on the ad, would you buy a guinea pig? Insurance?
5. Why is it important to read advertisements carefully?

TEST POWER

Test Tip

Take your time as you do your work.

DIRECTIONS

Read the sample story. Then read each question about the story.

SAMPLE

The Sandwich Shop Contest

Rebecca ran down to the sandwich shop. She sat at her usual seat by the window. She was extremely excited. The owner of the sandwich shop, Mr. Dobbs, was holding a talent show. Rebecca's sister, Sarah, was going to sing and play her guitar. Rebecca hoped that Sarah would win!

Mr. Dobbs spoke into the microphone at the front of the room. "Let's all give a big round of applause for our first contestant, Sarah Gifford!" he said in a booming voice.

Everyone cheered as Sarah took the microphone. Rebecca sat <u>anxiously</u> in her seat—she couldn't wait to hear her sister sing and play!

1 The word <u>anxiously</u> in this story means—

A easily

B smoothly

C impatiently

D uneasily

2 Which of the following is a FACT from the passage?

F Rebecca played the guitar.

G Sarah was very shy.

H Sarah was going to sing.

J This was Mr. Dobbs's first talent show.

Stories in Art

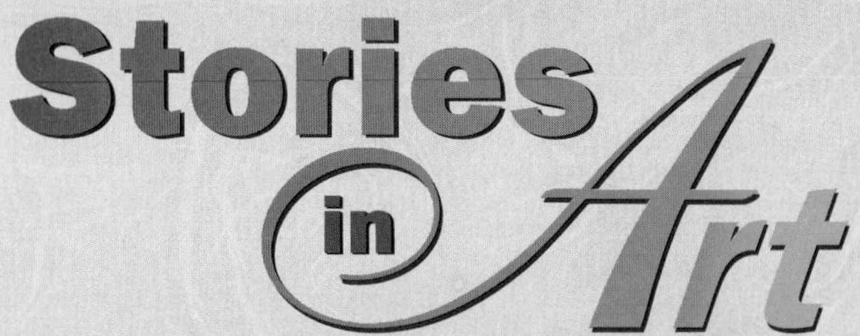

Art is a special way of sharing important ideas and feelings. Through art, artists can express something they feel strongly about. They can also show the life of the people around them.

Look at this street mural. What can you tell about it? How does it show something important to the community? What does it say about this park and these people?

Look at the painting again. What sweeps your eye around the picture? If you had to explain this wall mural to a friend, which important details would you mention? Which details seem less important? Why?

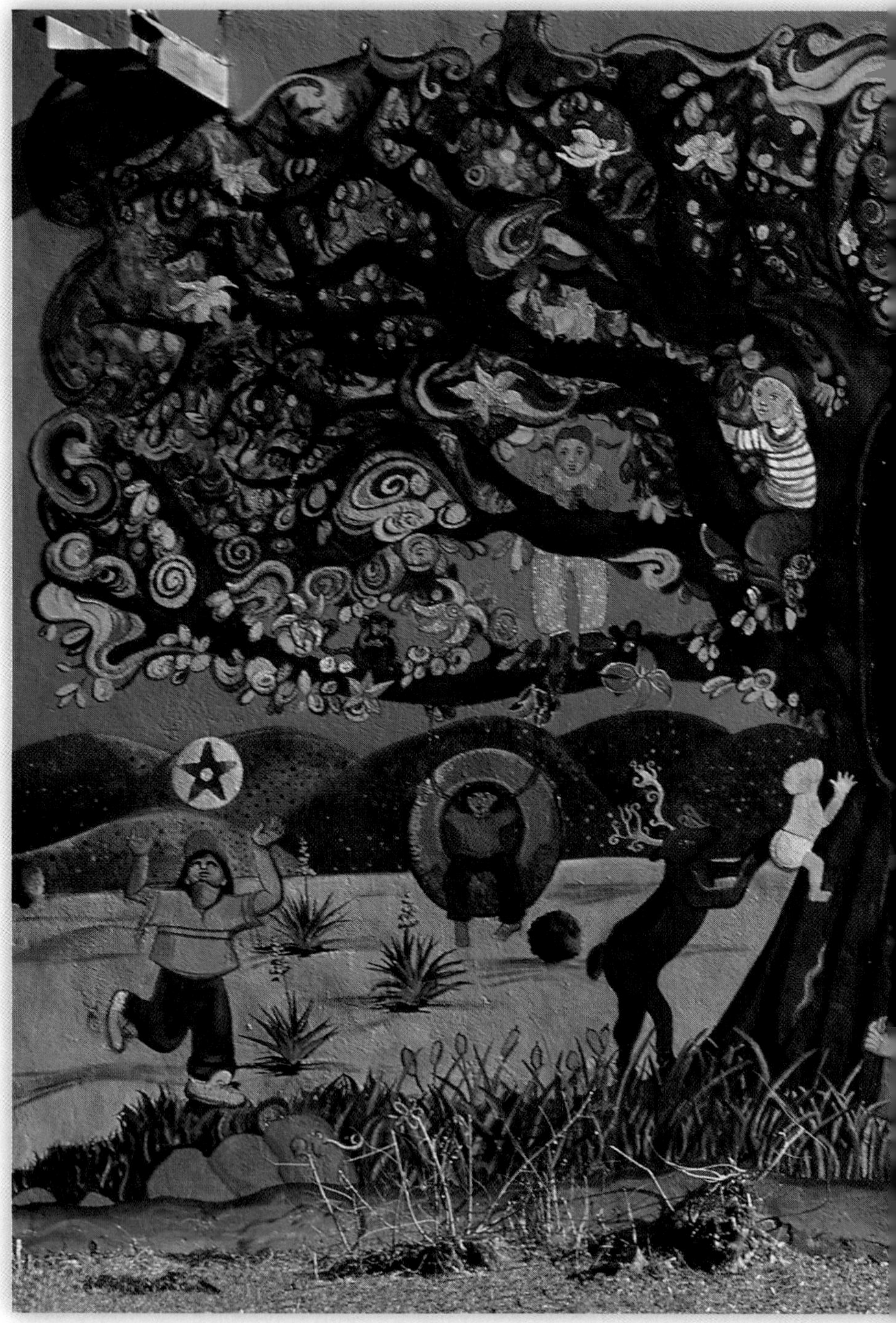

Community Mural
Santa Fe, New Mexico

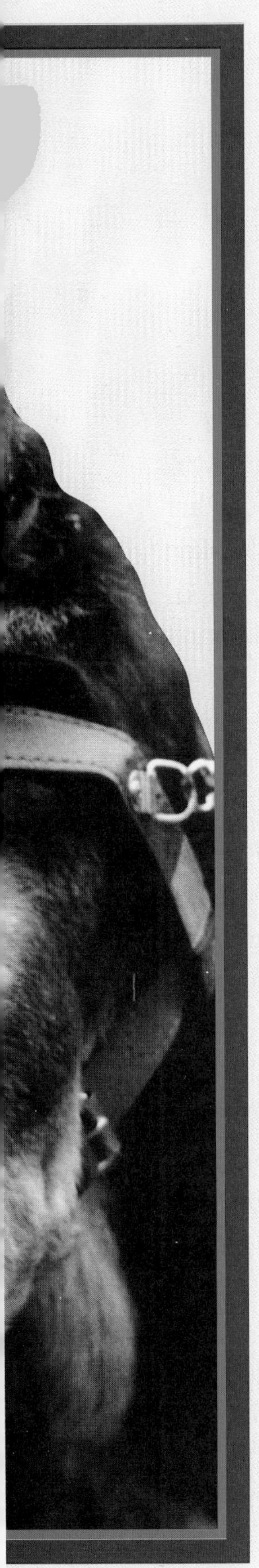

MOM'S BEST FRIEND

by Sally Hobart Alexander
photographs by George Ancona

The best thing about having a mom who's blind is getting a special dog like Marit, Mom's dog guide. At least that's what my brother, Joel, and I used to think. Then, four months ago, Marit died. And it became the worst thing.

Marit had been with us since before I was born. Her death left a big hole in our family. I kept thinking I heard her whimpering for a Frisbee game. Any time I left pizza on the counter, I would race back to the rescue. But there was no sneaky dog about to steal it.

For my birthday Joel gave me a rabbit that I named Methuselah. Although it helped to have a soft bunny, I still wanted Marit.

Mom missed her even more. She didn't lose just a sweet, furry pet. She lost her favorite way of traveling, too. She had to use her cane again, and crept along the sidewalk like a snail. Once, when she crossed the street, she missed the opposite curb and kept walking toward the traffic. I had to holler to get her onto the sidewalk.

After that, I worried about her running errands by herself. I asked her to "go sighted guide," holding Dad's, Joel's, or my arm. Sometimes she did. But mostly she used the cane. She didn't want to depend on us—or on anybody.

A lot of blind people do fine with a cane. It's like a real long arm to help them feel what's around: walkways, hedges, mailboxes.

With a dog guide, blind people use their hearing more than touch. Mom has trained her ears. It's amazing: she can tell when something, like a movie marquee, is above her head, and when she passes a lamppost. She knows from the change in the sound of her footsteps.

In spite of Mom's special hearing, I worried. I was relieved when she decided to go back to The Seeing Eye for a new dog guide.

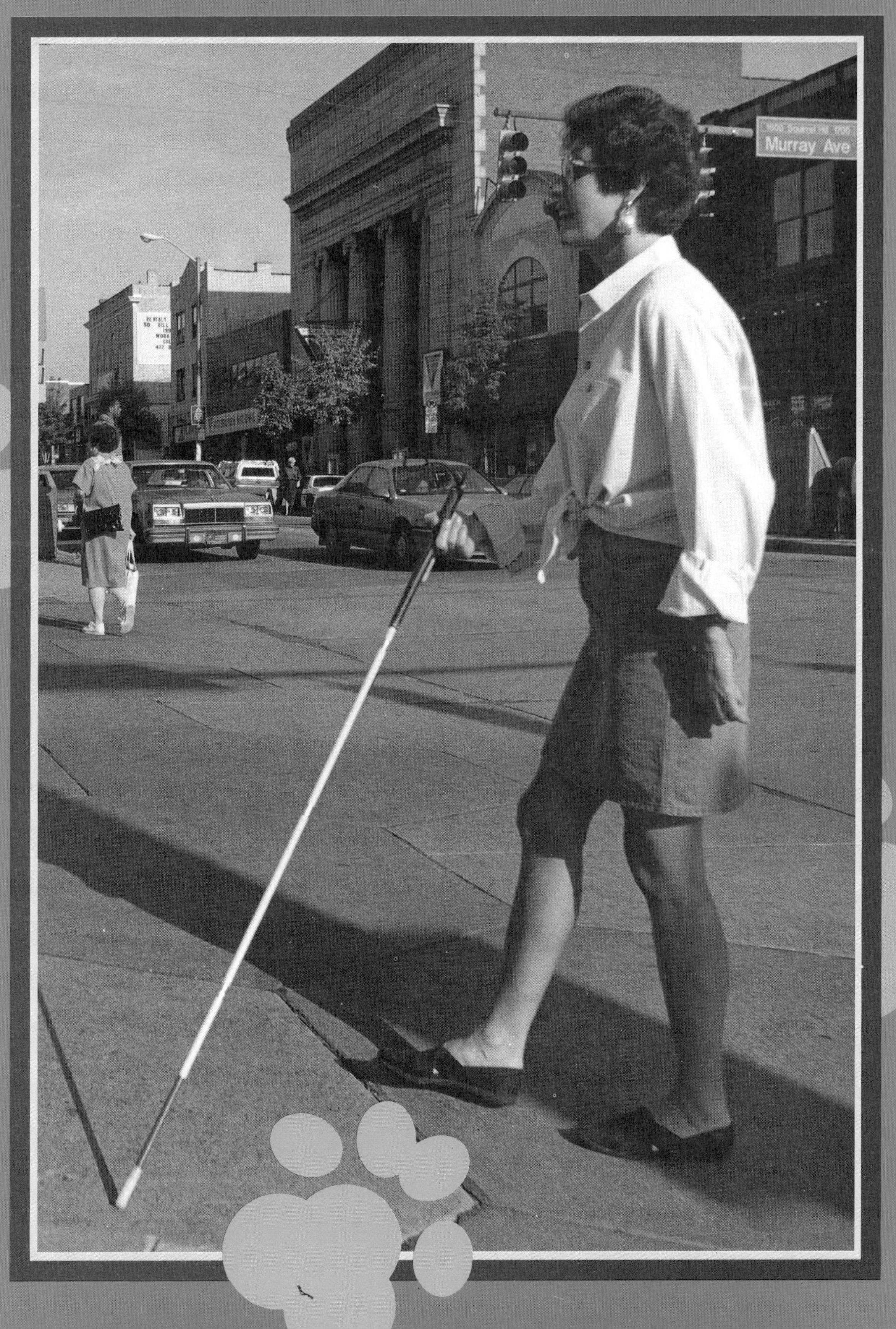
Murray Ave

Before Mom left, I told her I wouldn't be able to love the new dog as much as Marit. Mom hugged me and said, "The night before you were born, I wondered how I could love a second child as much as your brother. Then you came, and like magic, I was just as crazy about you."

The Seeing Eye, in Morristown, New Jersey, was the first dog guide school in the United States. (Now there are nine others.) It trains German shepherds and Labrador and golden retrievers for three months. Then, for about a month, it teaches blind people to use the dogs.

When Mom arrived at The Seeing Eye, she was met by her instructor, Pete Jackson.

I missed Mom as much as I missed Marit, but at least Mom called every night. She also wrote letters and sent pictures.

Mom's first day was a cinch. She'd gone to Seeing Eye twelve years before to get Marit, and still remembered her way around. Usually when she's in a new place, she has to move from room to room with her cane, memorizing the layout.

In the morning Mom walked with Pete Jackson so that he could check her pace. He wanted to choose the dog that would suit her best. Then she was free to play the piano, exercise . . . and worry. Would she get along with the new dog? Would they work well together?

The next day she got Ursula. What a strange name! The staff at Seeing Eye's breeding station had named Ursula when she was born. (Ursula's brothers and sisters were also given names starting with *U*.) Dog guides need a name right away so that Seeing Eye can keep track of the four hundred or so pups born each year. At two months of age, the pups go to Seeing Eye puppy-raising families to learn how to live with people. At fifteen months, they are mature enough to return to Seeing Eye for the three-month training program.

Dad said that Ursula means "bear." But in the pictures Mom sent, Ursula looked too pip-squeaky to be called bear. Mom explained that Seeing Eye is now breeding some smaller dogs. They are easier to handle and fit better on buses and in cars.

My friends thought dog guides were little machines that zoomed blind people around. Until Mom went away, even I didn't understand all the things these dogs were taught.

But on Mom's first lesson in Morristown, Ursula seemed to forget her training. She veered on a street crossing and brushed Mom into a bush. Mom had to make her correct herself by backing up and walking around the bush. Then Mom praised her.

After ten practice runs with Pete, Mom and Ursula soloed. Ursula didn't stop at a curb, so Mom had to scold her and snap her leash, calling, "Pfui." Later Ursula crashed Mom into a low-hanging branch. "Ursula will have to start thinking tall," Mom said that night, "or I'll have to carry hedge clippers in my purse."

Even though Ursula had walked in Morristown a lot with Pete, she was nervous when Mom's hand was on the harness. Mom talked and walked differently. And Mom was nervous, too. Ursula moved so much faster than old Marit had, and Mom didn't trust her.

Every day Mom and Ursula made two trips. Every week they mastered new routes. Each route got longer and more complicated, and Mom had less time to learn it. Every night Mom gave Ursula obedience training: "Come. Sit. Down. Rest. Fetch." I thought she should try obedience training on Joel.

While Mom worked hard, Dad, Joel, and I went on with our normal lives—school, homework, soccer, piano, spending time with friends. We divided Mom's chores: Dad did the cooking, Joel, the vacuuming and laundry, and I did the dishes, dusting, weeding. The first two weeks were easy.

In a phone call Mom said that things were getting easier for her, too. "Remember how tough curb ramps have been for me?" she asked. "They feel like any other slope in the sidewalk, so I can't always tell that I've reached the street. Well, Ursula stopped perfectly at every ramp. And she guided me around, not under, a ladder and right past a huge parking lot without angling into it. But best of all, she actually saved my life. A jackhammer was making so much noise that I couldn't hear whether the light was green or red. When I told Ursula, 'Forward!' she refused to move and kept me from stepping in front of a car. (Of course, Pete would have saved me if Ursula hadn't.)"

Mom barely asked about us. It was all Ursula, Ursula, Ursula! She seemed to be forgetting Marit, too. When a letter came a few days later, I was sure she didn't miss anyone.

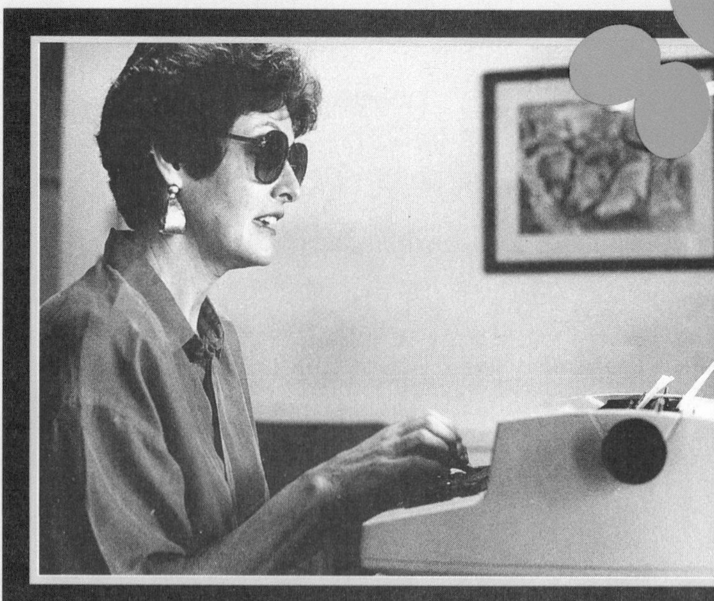

Dear Bob, Joel, and Leslie,

Today Ursula and I faced several disasters! She tried hard to ignore a boxer dog who wanted to play. A few minutes later, a great Dane lunged out from nowhere, jumped all over her, and loped off. Ursula's instinct is to chase dogs, but she didn't move a paw after that one. As if the dogs weren't enough trouble, fire engine sirens went off. Ursula just strolled down the sidewalk.

Mostly, life is smooth here. Seeing Eye is a vacation—no cooking, no cleaning, lots of time to talk to new friends, like Dr. Holle, the veterinarian. And since I don't have many blind friends, it's a treat to be with my roommate and the twenty other students. We laugh about the same things, like the great enemy of the blind—trash collection day! Every twenty feet there's a garbage can reeking of pizza, hoagies, old cheese. Usually Ursula snakes me around these smelly obstacles. But sometimes the temptation to her nose wins out, and I have to correct her, all the while holding my own nose.

Some trainees really inspire me, like Julie Hensley, who became blind from diabetes at twenty-two. Even though she's been blind for twelve years, she still teaches horses to do stunts. She judges her location from a radio playing music in the center of the pen, and gallops around as fast as she ever did when she could see.

Bob Pacheco used to race motorcycles and hunt. Then, two years ago, when he was twenty-nine, he developed optic atrophy and became blind two months later. He took up fishing, swimming, even trapping. But something was missing. He couldn't get around quickly enough. After the first trip with his dog guide, he was overjoyed. "Sally!" He grabbed my hand. "I don't feel blind any more."

The dogs are wonderful, and the people here are very special. So are you.

Love,
Mom

Well, life at home wasn't very wonderful or special. Dad ran out of the casseroles Mom had frozen ahead of time, and although his meals were okay, I missed Mom's cooking. Worse, the dishes kept piling up. I never knew Joel ate so much.

Then things got really bad. While Dad was teaching his American literature night class, Joel and I faced a disaster Mom and Ursula couldn't have dreamed of: the toilet bowl overflowed! We wiped the floor with towels. As Joel took the towels down to the washing machine, he found water dripping through the ceiling—all over the dining room table, all over the carpet. He ran for more towels, and I ran for the furniture polish and rug shampoo. When Dad got home, everything looked perfect. But I wrote a braille letter.

Dear Mom,

Come home soon. The house misses you.

Love,

Exhausted in Pittsburgh

Mom wrote back.

Dear Exhausted,

Hang on. We'll be home to "hound" you Thursday. Be prepared. When you see me, I will have grown four more feet.

Mom

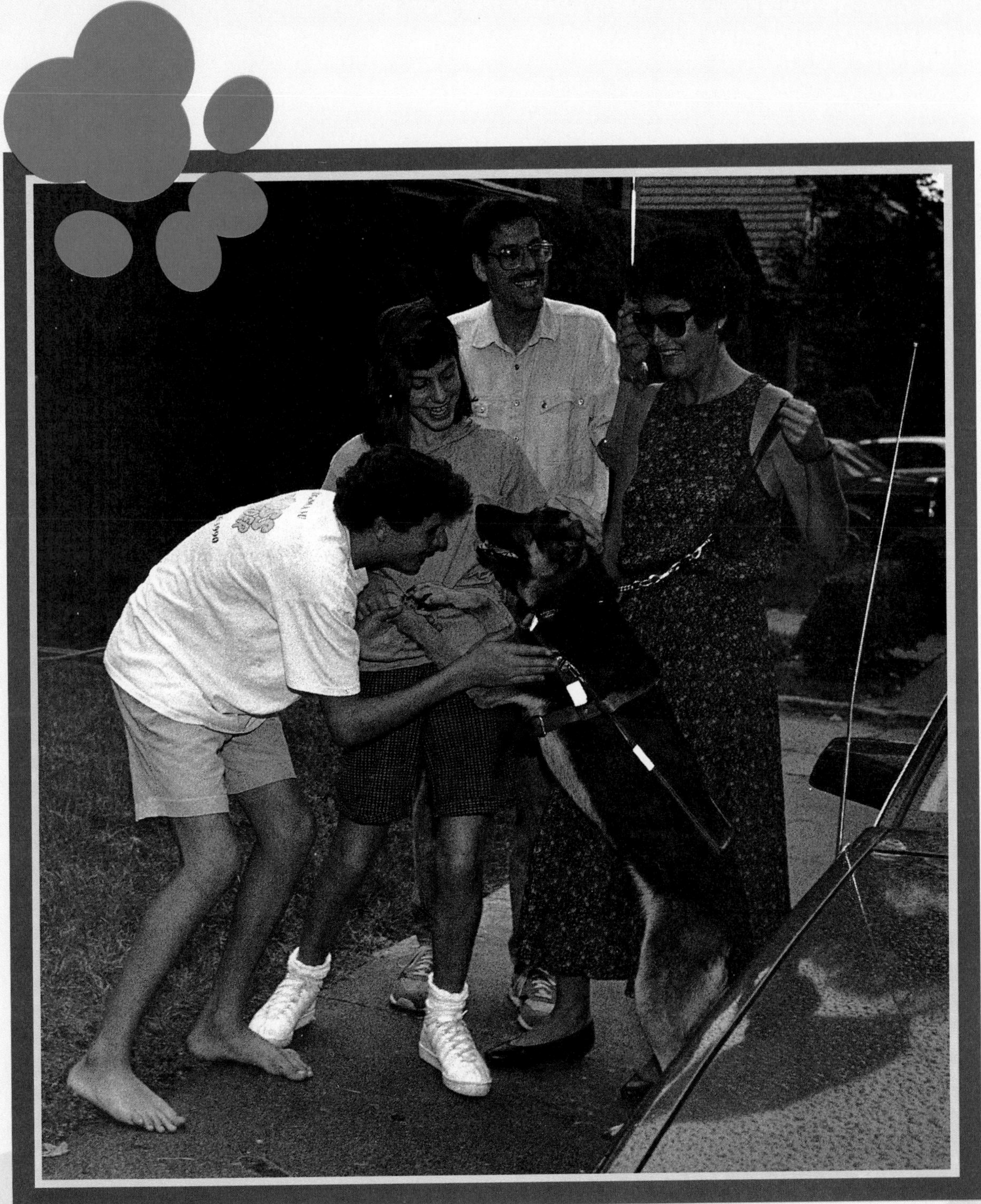

I couldn't laugh. I was too tired and worried. What if I couldn't love Ursula? Marit was the best dog ever.

Soon they arrived. Ursula yanked at her leash and sprang up on me. She pawed my shoulders, stomach, and arms just the way Marit used to, nearly knocking me over. She leaped onto Joel, licking him all over. As she bounded up onto me again, I realized Mom was right. Like magic, I was crazy about this shrimpy new dog.

But by the end of the day, I had a new worry. Was *Ursula* going to love *me?* She seemed friendly enough, but keyed up, even lost in our house.

Mom explained that Ursula had already given her heart away three times: first to her mother, then to the Seeing Eye puppy-raising family, and finally to Pete. Mom said we had to be patient.

"Remember how Marit loved you, Leslie? When you were little, she let you stand on her back to see out the window. Ursula will be just as nuts about you. Love is the whole reason this dog guide business works."

So I tried to be patient and watched Mom work hard. First she showed one route in our neighborhood to Ursula and walked it over and over. Then she taught her a new route, repeated that, and reviewed the old one. Every day she took Ursula on two trips, walking two or three miles. She fed her, groomed her, gave her obedience training. Twice a week Mom cleaned Ursula's ears and brushed her teeth.

"I'm as busy as I was when you and Joel were little!" she said.

Mom and Ursula played for forty-five minutes each day. Joel, Dad, and I were only allowed to watch. Ursula needed to form her biggest attachment to Mom.

Mom made Ursula her shadow. When she showered or slept, Ursula was right there.

Still, Ursula didn't eat well—only half the amount she'd been eating at Seeing Eye. And she tested Mom, pulling her into branches, stepping off curbs. Once she tried to take a shortcut home. Another time, because she was nervous, she crossed a new street diagonally.

Crossing streets is tricky. Ursula doesn't know when the light is green. Mom knows. If she hears the cars moving beside her in the direction in which she's walking, the light is green. If they're moving right and left in front of her, it's red.

I worried about Ursula's mistakes, but Mom said they were normal. She kept in touch with her classmates and knew that their dog guides were goofing, too. One kept eating grass, grazing like a cow. Another chased squirrels, pigeons, and cats. Still another always stopped in the middle of the street, ten feet from

the curb. Once in a while her friends got lost, just like Mom, and had to ask for help.

Mom said it takes four to six months for the dogs to settle down. But no matter how long she and Ursula are teamed up together, Ursula will need some correcting. For instance, Ursula might act so cute that a passerby will reach out to pet her. Then Mom will have to scold Ursula and ask the person not to pet a dog guide. If people give Ursula attention while she's working, she forgets to do her job.

After a month at home, Ursula emptied her food bowl every time. She knew all the routes, and Mom could zip around as easily as she had with Marit.

"Now it's time to start the loneliness training," Mom said. She left Ursula alone in the house, at first for a short time while she went jogging with Dad. Ursula will never be able to take Mom jogging because she can't guide at high speeds.

Each week Mom increased the amount of time Ursula was alone. I felt sorry for our pooch, but she did well: no barking, no chewing on furniture.

Then Mom said Joel and I could introduce Ursula to our friends, one at a time. They could pet her when she was out of harness.

Every morning Ursula woke Joel and me. Every night she sneaked into my bed for a snooze.

Finally Mom allowed Joel and me to play with Ursula, and I knew: shrimpy little Ursula had fallen for us, and we were even crazier about her.

But we haven't forgotten Marit. Joel says that Ursula is the best dog alive. And I always say she's the best dog in this world.

Meet
Sally Hobart Alexander

Sally Hobart Alexander loved stories as a child. She and her friends would often put on plays and write stories for their classmates.

Alexander's sight problems began as an adult, but she didn't let them keep her from writing. Instead, she published her first two books, *Mom Can't See Me* and *Sarah's Surprise.* Now, several books later, Sally Hobart Alexander's message is simple: "If I can do it, you can, too!"

Meet
George Ancona

Curiosity drives George Ancona's work. He says, "I love to find myself in strange places, meeting people, getting to know them and learning about them. This helps me to learn about myself."

He felt lucky to have spent time with Sally Hobart Alexander and her family. He describes them as "wonderful" and "warm."

Ancona says he often remains friends with the people he photographs. With nearly 80 books to his credit, that's a lot of friends!

Story Questions & Activities

1. What kind of training does a dog guide need?
2. What important information about dog guides is given in this true story?
3. What makes Ursula "Mom's best friend"?
4. What is the main idea of this selection?
5. Compare Ursula's job to Scruffy's. What do their jobs have in common? How are they different?

Write a Story

Ursula is a dog guide. Other dogs help people, too. Write a story about a dog that becomes a person's "best friend." Use "I" to tell the story. Create an interesting beginning and a strong ending. Describe how your dog character looks and sounds.

Draw a Map

Draw a simple map of your neighborhood. Include your home, school, library, park, and post office. Place an "X" on all the obstacles, or anything that might get in the way, for a blind person. Then plot the way from the post office to your house, for example. How would you describe this route to someone who is blind? What dangers would you point out?

Listen to Music

What happens when people lose their sight? They usually develop a keen sense of hearing. Listen to a favorite piece of music. Keep your eyes closed as you listen. Do you hear anything new in the music? Can you identify the different instruments? Write down how it felt to really listen.

Find Out More

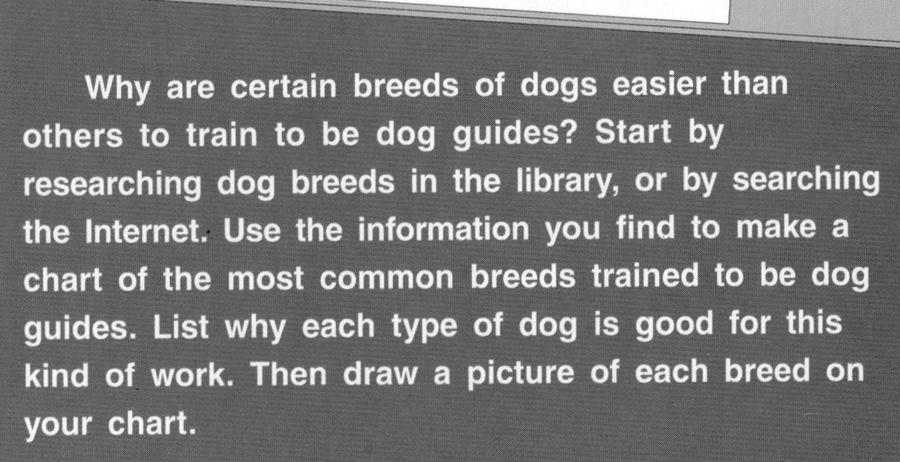

Why are certain breeds of dogs easier than others to train to be dog guides? Start by researching dog breeds in the library, or by searching the Internet. Use the information you find to make a chart of the most common breeds trained to be dog guides. List why each type of dog is good for this kind of work. Then draw a picture of each breed on your chart.

Read a Newspaper

Every day you can read true stories like "Mom's Best Friend." Just look in the newspaper. Like radio, television, and computers, **newspapers** give you important information about current events. These events may be happening in your city or town, in the nation, or in the world.

You know that newspapers have many news articles. A **news article** begins with a headline. The **headline** uses words in large type across the top of the article to catch your attention. Usually, a news article also has a dateline. The **dateline** is below the headline and tells when and where the news article was written.

Every news article answers the questions *Who? What? When?* and *Where? Who* and *what* is the story about? *When* and *where* did it happen? Read this news article. See how it answers these questions.

The Pittsburgh News

Pittsburgh — Wednesday, August 9

Dog guide saves woman

Pittsburgh, August 7– On Saturday a dog guide named Ursula saved the life of its owner. The dog's owner, Sally Hobart Alexander, whose sight problems began ten years ago, said that she owes her life to Ursula, a German shepherd. Trained at the Seeing Eye in Morristown, New Jersey, Ursula has been with Mrs. Alexander for the past two months. "We've had a lot of near-misses," Ursula's owner says, "but none as close as on Saturday." While trying to cross the street at North and Main, Mrs. Alexander was almost hit by a car. "I thought it was safe to cross," said Mrs. Alexander, "so I gave the 'Forward!' command. But Ursula wouldn't move. She really stopped me from stepping in front of that car."

Use the news article to answer these questions.

1. What is the name of the newspaper?
2. Does the headline get your attention? How?
3. What information does the dateline give?
4. How does the news article answer the questions *Who? What? When?* and *Where?*
5. Compare this news article with the selection "Mom's Best Friend." List the ways they are the same. What are the differences?

TEST POWER

Test Tip

Always read the answer choices carefully.

DIRECTIONS

Read the sample story. Then read each question about the story.

SAMPLE

Tell-Your-Funniest-Joke Day

Today was Jesse's big day. His parents had always told him he was funny, but he never really believed them. His dad had insisted that he was the funniest kid he had ever met. But today, after recess, each of the kids in class would get up and tell his or her favorite joke. Today was the day that Jesse would find out if he really was funny.

He was petrified! No one but his dad had ever told him he was funny. And he'd never told any jokes in front of so many people, much less his teacher.

"I'll just imagine that everyone in the audience is my dad," he assured himself.

1 What will Jesse probably do next?

A Tell his favorite joke

B Hide in the bathroom

C Go to the cafeteria

D Draw a picture

2 The word insisted in this story means—

F joked

G claimed

H worked

J laughed

Stories in Art

Thinking can help you in art, just as it can in games. But in art, questions often have more than one right answer.

What can you tell about the painting? How has the artist used bright colors to help you focus on the game? Look at the checkerboard. Can you predict who will win? How will the winner feel? How might the loser react?

Imagine that you are going to challenge the winner. Who do you think will win? Why? Now make up some questions about the painting to ask your classmates.

The Painter's Family
by Henri Matisse, 1911
Hermitage Museum, St. Petersburg, Russia

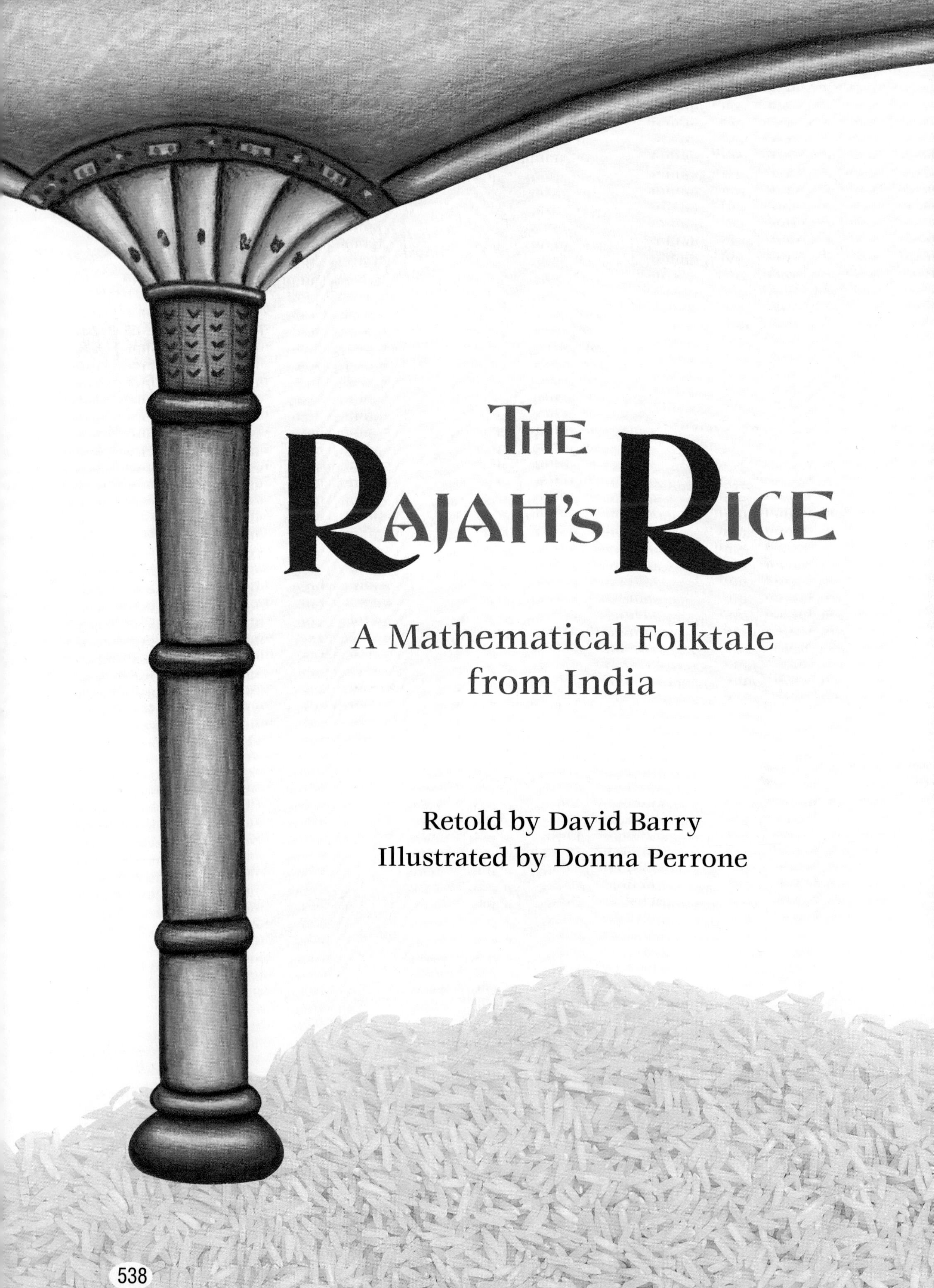

The Rajah's Rice

A Mathematical Folktale from India

Retold by David Barry

Illustrated by Donna Perrone

Once upon a time a long time ago, a girl named Chandra lived in a small village in India. Chandra loved elephants. She also loved numbers. So of course she loved all numbers to do with elephants: two tusks to polish on each elephant, eighteen toenails to clean, a hundred scrubs on a side at each bath. Chandra had many chances to think about elephant numbers because she had a special job: She was the bather of the Rajah's elephants.

Chandra liked other numbers, too. As she walked past rice paddies, muddy after the harvest, she counted the snowy egrets that flew above her.

She passed through the marketplace at the edge of the village and stopped to help the spice peddler count change.

When she joined her friends where they stood watching the Rajah's elephants parade through the town square, she remembered every elephant number she knew. Then she started thinking about rice.

It was rent collection day, and bags bulging with rice hung from the sides of the elephants.

No wonder the people looked sad. The Rajah had taken so much rice for himself that the whole village would be hungry.

But this was the way it had always been. For thousands of years, the villagers had farmed the Rajah's land. For thousands of years, he had come with his elephants to take most of the rice harvest.

The whole thing made Chandra angry, but what could she do?

On the elephants' next bath day, Chandra packed up her equipment and walked over the fields to the palace. She was about to enter the gates when the guard stopped her.

"You cannot come in this morning, Elephant Bather. The elephants have taken sick."

Chandra peered through the bamboo gate into the elephant yard. There she could see her elephants lying on the ground as still as felled trees. No amount of calling, singing, or cooing made them so much as raise their heads.

Over the days that followed Chandra sat watch over her precious elephants. She was not allowed inside, so she waited at the gate, watching medical men from all across the land come to cure the elephants.

The first doctor sat on cushions in the courtyard and feasted: he ate eight meat pastries, ten

chickpea dumplings, and twelve sand lobsters served on banana leaves at each meal. While he ate, the elephants got sicker.

Another doctor spent all day and most of the night in the elephant yard chanting and burning incense. The elephants got even sicker.

Seven more doctors came and went, but the elephants got still sicker.

One morning, the Rajah returned from a walk in the gardens to find Chandra at the gate, staring in at the elephants. "What are you doing here, Elephant Bather?" he asked.

"I worry about the elephants," she said. "I love them all and know them well. Maybe I can help them."

The Rajah thought for a moment. "Go ahead and try," he said. "I need those elephants. Without them, I will not be able to carry the rice to market on market day. If you can save them, you may choose your own reward."

The guard opened the gates, and Chandra and the Rajah walked in silence to the elephant yard. Chandra approached Misha, the Rajah's favorite elephant. She studied his

feet: the nails, the pads, the cuticles. She studied his tusks and the eight molars deep inside his mouth. She studied the lips, the tongue and the throat. She looked deep into his eyes.

When Chandra got to the first ear, she discovered a painful-looking infection inside the ear canal. The other ear was the same. So were the ears of the other elephants. Chandra cleaned their ears, sang the elephants a soothing song, and went home.

At dawn the next day, when Chandra returned, the elephants were walking unsteadily around their yard. They greeted her with joyful trumpeting.

The Rajah was overjoyed. He declared a festival day and invited everyone in the land to the palace.

The Rajah led Chandra to the ceremony room. Piled on a long table, next to the Rajah's chessboard, was a glittering array of gold necklaces, brilliant sapphires and rubies, diamond brooches, bags of gold rupees, and other treasures.

The guests began to arrive, and soon the ceremony room was crowded with villagers.

"Name your reward, Elephant Bather," said the Rajah.

Chandra looked at the beautiful jewels on the table before her. She thought about her elephants and the hundreds of sacks of rice they carried away from the village each year. And then she noticed the chessboard.

"The villagers are hungry, Rajah," she began. "All I ask for is rice. If Your Majesty pleases, place two grains of rice on the first square of this chessboard. Place four grains on the second square, eight on the next, and so on, doubling each pile of rice till the last square."

The villagers shook their heads sadly at Chandra's choice.

The Rajah was secretly delighted. A few piles of rice would certainly be far cheaper than his precious jewelry. "Honor her request," he boomed to his servants.

Two servants brought out a small bowl of rice and carefully placed two grains of rice on the first square of the board. They placed four grains on the second square. Then eight on the third square, sixteen on the fourth square, thirty-two on the fifth square, sixty-four on the sixth square, 128 on the seventh square, and finally 256 grains of rice on the eighth square at the end of the row.

Several servants snickered at Chandra's foolishness, for although the 256 grains filled the eighth square completely, they amounted to only a single teaspoon of rice.

At the first square of the second row, the servants stood awkwardly, not knowing how to count out the rice. The next number was 512, but that was too high to count quickly, and besides, it was too many grains of rice to fit on one square of the chessboard.

Chandra started to explain, "Since you had one teaspoon of rice at the end of the first row, why not just put two teaspoons—"

But the Rajah cut in. "Just keep doubling the rice," he ordered. "You don't need to count every grain."

So the servants put two teaspoons of rice into a bowl for the first square of the second row. For the second square, they put four teaspoons of rice in the bowl. Then eight teaspoons of rice for the third square, and so continued, doubling the number of teaspoons each square.

The eighth square on the second row needed 256 teaspoons of rice, which by itself filled another bowl.

On the third row, the servants started to count by teaspoons again, but the Rajah cut in. Showing off his knowledge of mathematics, he said, "If the sixteenth square takes one bowl of rice, then the seventeenth square takes two bowls of rice. You don't need to count by teaspoons anymore."

So the servants counted by bowls. Two bowlfuls for the first square, then four, then eight, then sixteen, and so on. The rice for the last square of the third row completely filled a large wheelbarrow.

Chandra's neighbors smiled at her. "Very nice," one of them said. "This would feed my family for a whole year."

As the servants worked through the fourth row, wheelbarrow by wheelbarrow, the Rajah paced back and forth, his eyes wide in amazement. His servants gathered around him. "Shall we bring rice from your royal storehouses?" they asked.

"Of course," was the reply. "A Rajah never breaks a promise." The servants took the elephants and headed out to the first storehouse to get more rice.

By late afternoon, the Rajah had collapsed onto his couch. As his attendants fanned him with palm fronds, the servants started on the fifth row of the chessboard, and soon they were emptying entire storehouses into the courtyard.

Within several squares, rice poured from the windows of the palace and into the gardens beyond. By the middle of the fifth row, all of the Rajah's storehouses were empty.

He had run out of rice.

The Rajah struggled to his feet and ordered the rice to be loaded onto the elephants and taken to the village. Then he approached Chandra.

"Elephant Bather," he said to her, "I am out of rice and cannot fill the chessboard. Tell me what I can give you to be released from my vow."

"You can give the people of the village the land they farm, and take only as much rice as you need for yourself," answered Chandra.

The Rajah gazed at the mountains of rice that filled his palace and gardens, then out beyond the gardens to the fields the villagers farmed, stretching as far as he could see. Then he looked back at Chandra, the elephant bather.

"It is done," he said.

That night the Rajah arrived in the village as Chandra and the other villagers prepared a celebration feast.

"Would you be so kind as to join me for a short walk, Chandra?" he asked. "I have a question for you."

As they strolled toward the village square, the Rajah spoke. "I am a very rich man, and it took all of the rice I owned to fill little more than one-half of the chessboard. How much rice would it have taken to fill the whole board?" he asked.

"If you had kept doubling the rice to the last square of the chessboard, all of India would be knee deep in rice," said Chandra, and smiled.

NOTE ON THE MATH

Powers of two, as mathematicians call doubling, are very powerful indeed. Taking the number 2 and doubling it 64 times (the number of squares on a chessboard) results in the number 18,446,744,073,709,551,616, enough grains of rice to fill the great volcano, Mt. Kilimanjaro.

Here is a chart that should give you a feel for how fast something will grow when you double it over and over.

Start with grains of rice.

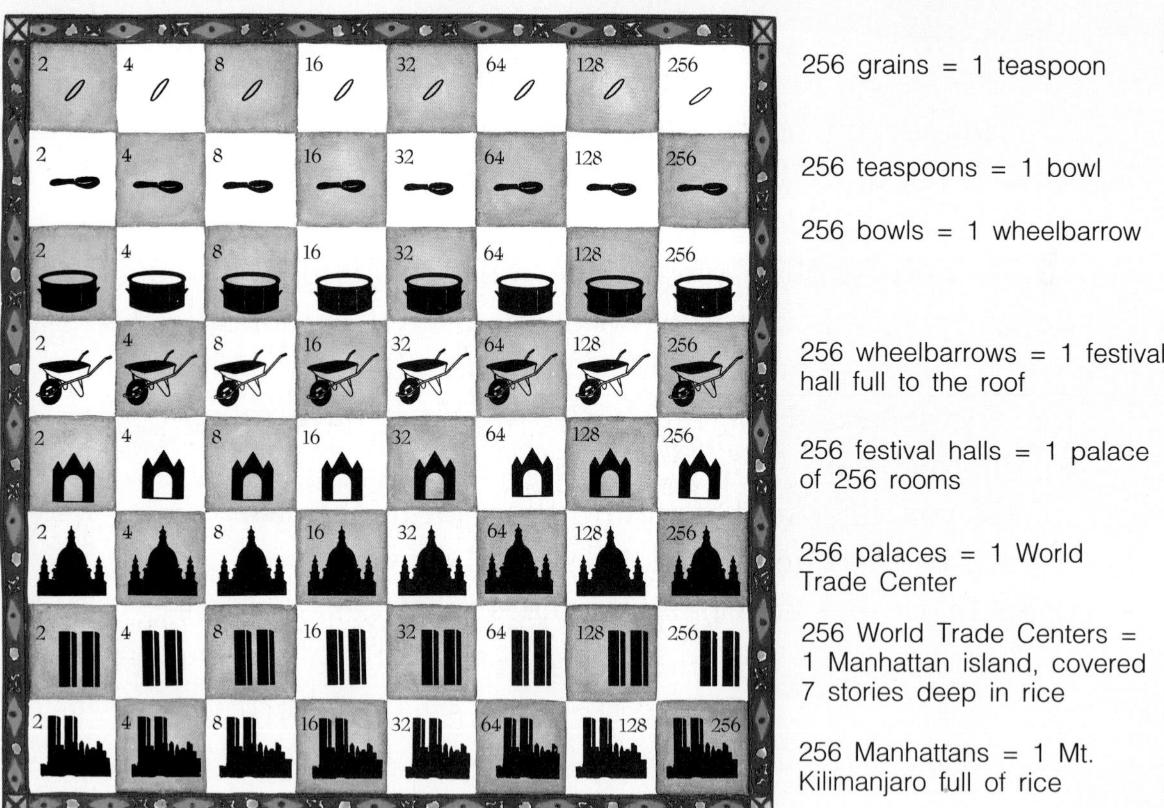

256 grains = 1 teaspoon

256 teaspoons = 1 bowl

256 bowls = 1 wheelbarrow

256 wheelbarrows = 1 festival hall full to the roof

256 festival halls = 1 palace of 256 rooms

256 palaces = 1 World Trade Center

256 World Trade Centers = 1 Manhattan island, covered 7 stories deep in rice

256 Manhattans = 1 Mt. Kilimanjaro full of rice

Add all 64 squares together and you get India, covered knee deep in rice.

Meet DAVID BARRY

Next to words, David Barry says he likes nothing better than numbers. That is why he has always liked the math concepts in the tale of *The Rajah's Rice.*

Like Chandra, Barry understands the power of math. He explains, "It is a good starting point. If you're good in math, you can go anywhere, do anything."

Meet DONNA PERRONE

Donna Perrone loves art from around the world. She travels to places she reads about in art books. Then she uses photographs she takes to recreate those places.

For *The Rajah's Rice,* she studied the use of detail in Indian art. You can see this detail in the lively market scene. This scene is Perrone's favorite.

Story Questions & Activities

1. What two things does Chandra love?
2. How is math important to the story?
3. Do you think the Rajah will keep his promise at the end of the story? Why or why not?
4. What are the most important parts of this story?
5. Compare "The Rajah's Rice" with "The Fox and the Guinea Pig." How do both stories use tricks to fool a character? Did you figure out the ending for each? Explain.

Write a Dialogue

The dialogue between Chandra and the Rajah makes the characters come alive. Write a dialogue between yourself and an older person. Present a problem. It can be from real life. Work together in the dialogue to find a solution.

Make a Calendar

Suppose that you have a chance to visit India for one week. What places would you like to see there? Make a calendar with room to write in it. Draw a full-page picture of a famous sight in India, such as the Taj Mahal. Then choose the month you would like to travel. Write in the days and the dates. For seven of those days, jot down the things you would like to see and do on your trip to India.

Create Penny Squares

What would happen if you put pennies instead of rice on the squares of the chessboard? On the first square you would put two pennies. On the second square you would put four cents. How much money would you put on the third square? On the fourth? On the ninth? On which square would you put $10.24?

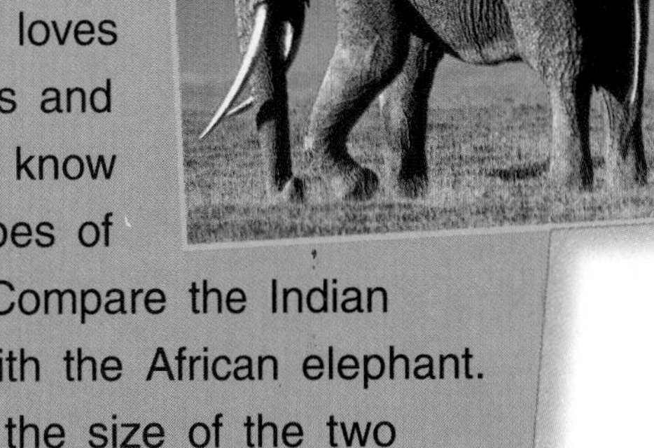

Find Out More

Chandra has two loves in the story: elephants and numbers. But do you know that there are two types of elephants? Compare the Indian elephant with the African elephant. Compare the size of the two elephants' ears and tusks. Draw a graph, chart, or picture to show the differences.

Follow a Recipe

Rice is an important food in India. The Indian people prepare rice in many different ways. They add spices to it or serve it with sauces or stews. One way of preparing rice in India is with curry. Curry is a special combination of spices.

RICE CURRY

Ingredients

3 cups hot cooked rice
(use instant or quick-cooking rice)
1 tablespoon chopped onion
2 tablespoons margarine or butter
1 teaspoon curry powder
1/4 teaspoon salt
1/4 teaspoon pepper
1/4 cup thinly sliced almonds
1/4 cup chopped olives

Directions

Prepare rice according to package directions, about 20 minutes for quick rice; keep warm. In a skillet, cook the onion with the margarine or butter over medium heat. Stir constantly, until the onion is cooked, but not brown, about three minutes. Add curry powder, salt, and pepper and stir until blended. Add the pre-cooked rice. Stir to coat the rice with the curry sauce. Top with almonds and olives. Serve immediately. Makes 6 side dishes or 3 main-dish servings.

Use the recipe above to answer these questions.

1. What do you have to do first, before you make the curry?
2. How long do you cook the onion?
3. When do you add the almonds and olives?
4. How much rice would you need to make rice curry as a main course for six people?
5. Why is it important to follow a recipe carefully?

TEST POWER

Test Tip

Look in the passage for clues about how the character feels.

DIRECTIONS

Read the sample story. Then read each question about the story.

SAMPLE

The Town Race

Mindy could hardly wait for this year's Town Race. During the Town Race, runners would run to six places in town. When the whistle blew, participants would first run to the library where they would find a slip of paper that directed them to the next site. Runners never knew which site was next until they read the piece of paper. At the next site, the runners would find another slip of paper. The runners continued until they had visited all six sites. The runner with the fastest time would be the winner!

Mindy was sure she could win this year. She loved to run!

1 In this passage, the word participants means people who—

A have done something before

B are involved in the event

C are not interested

D are laughing at someone

2 How did Mindy feel about running in the race?

F Excited

G Angry

H Lazy

J Bored

Stories in Art

Every picture tells a story. In a collage, an artist uses cut or torn paper shapes to tell a story in a new way.

Look at this collage. What can you tell about it? What different shapes do you notice? Now use the shapes to move your eyes around the artwork. How does the artist arrange the shapes to show a whole picture?

Look at the collage again. Describe what is happening in the scene. What do you think happened before the performance? Did the band practice? Will they pack up their instruments when they finish playing? Explain your answers.

Masters of Midnight
by Phoebe Beasley

Yeh-Shen
A Cinderella Story from China

This story is older than the Cinderella story as most people know it. It predates all European versions of the story by at least 800 years.

retold by Ai-Ling Louie
illustrated by
Ed Young

In the dim past, even before the Ch'in and the Han dynasties, there lived a cave chief of southern China by the name of Wu. As was the custom in those days, Chief Wu had taken two wives. Each wife in her turn had presented Wu with a baby daughter. But one of the wives sickened and died, and not too many days after that Chief Wu took to his bed and died too.

Yeh-Shen, the little orphan, grew to girlhood in her stepmother's home. She was a bright child and lovely too, with skin as smooth as ivory and dark pools for eyes. Her stepmother was jealous of all this beauty and goodness, for her own daughter was not pretty at all. So in her displeasure, she gave poor Yeh-Shen the heaviest and most unpleasant chores.

The only friend that Yeh-Shen had to her name was a fish she had caught and raised. It was a beautiful fish with golden eyes, and every day it would come out of the water and rest its head on the bank of the pond, waiting for Yeh-Shen to feed it. Stepmother gave Yeh-Shen little enough food for

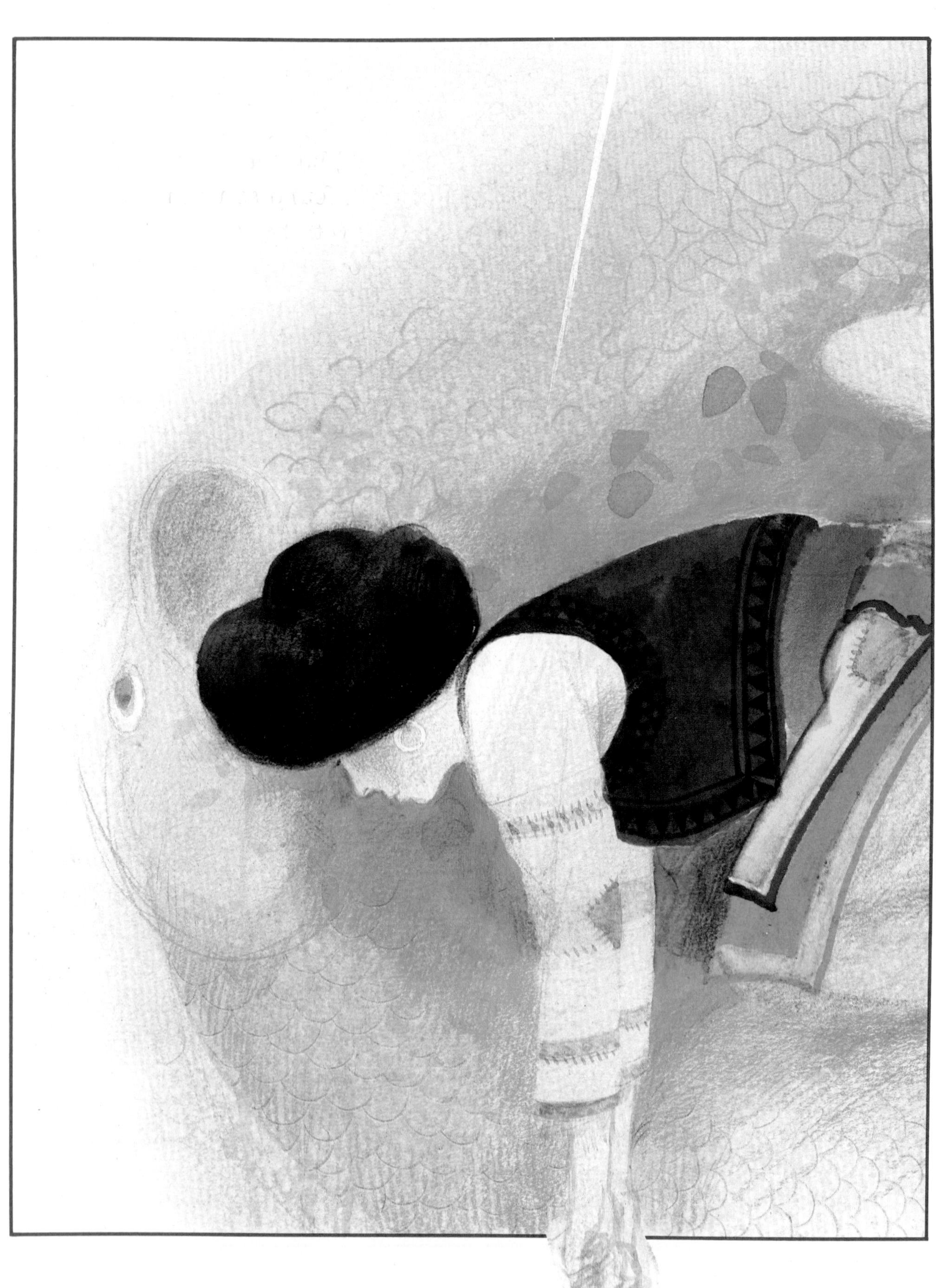

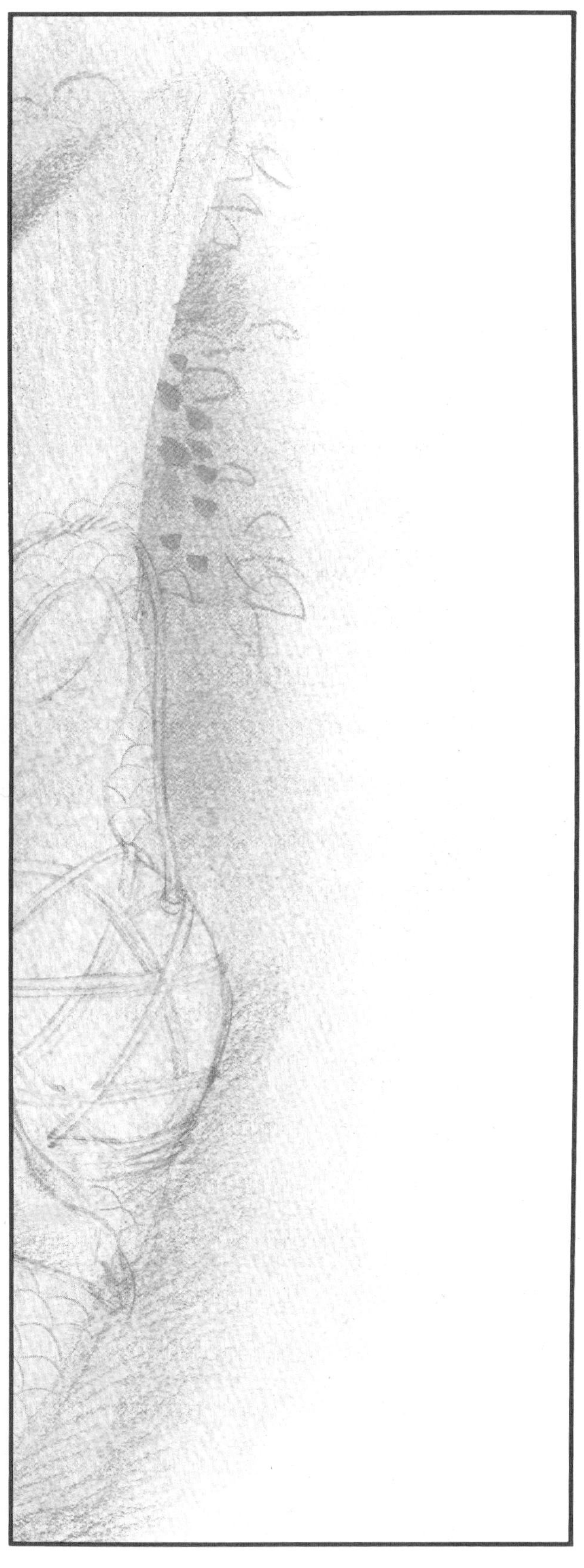

herself, but the orphan child always found something to share with her fish, which grew to enormous size.

Somehow the stepmother heard of this. She was terribly angry to discover that Yeh-Shen had kept a secret from her. She hurried down to the pond, but she was unable to see the fish, for Yeh-Shen's pet wisely hid itself. The stepmother, however, was a crafty woman, and she soon thought of a plan. She walked home and called out, "Yeh-Shen, go and collect some firewood. But wait! The neighbors might see you. Leave your filthy coat here!" The minute the girl was out of sight, her stepmother slipped on the coat herself and went down again to the pond. This time the big fish saw Yeh-Shen's familiar jacket and heaved itself onto the bank, expecting to be fed. But the stepmother, having hidden a dagger in her sleeve, stabbed the fish, wrapped it in her garments, and took it home to cook for dinner.

When Yeh-Shen came to the pond that evening, she found her pet had disappeared. Overcome with grief, the girl collapsed on the ground and dropped her tears into the still waters of the pond.

"Ah, poor child!" a voice said.

Yeh-Shen sat up to find a very old man looking down at her. He wore the coarsest of clothes, and his hair flowed down over his shoulders.

"Kind uncle, who may you be?" Yeh-Shen asked.

"That is not important, my child. All you must know is that I have been sent to tell you of the wondrous powers of your fish."

"My fish, but sir . . ." The girl's eyes filled with tears, and she could not go on.

The old man sighed and said, "Yes, my child, your fish is no longer alive, and I must tell you that your stepmother is once more the cause of your sorrow." Yeh-Shen gasped in horror, but the old man went on. "Let us not dwell on things that are past," he said, "for I have come bringing you a gift. Now you must listen carefully to this: The bones of your fish are filled with a powerful spirit. Whenever you are in serious need, you must kneel before them and let them know your heart's desire. But do not waste their gifts."

Yeh-Shen wanted to ask the old sage many more questions, but he rose to the sky before she could utter another word. With heavy heart, Yeh-Shen made her way to the dung heap to gather the remains of her friend.

Time went by, and Yeh-Shen, who was often left alone, took comfort in speaking to the bones of her fish. When she was hungry, which happened quite often, Yeh-Shen asked the bones for food. In this way, Yeh-Shen managed to live from day to day, but

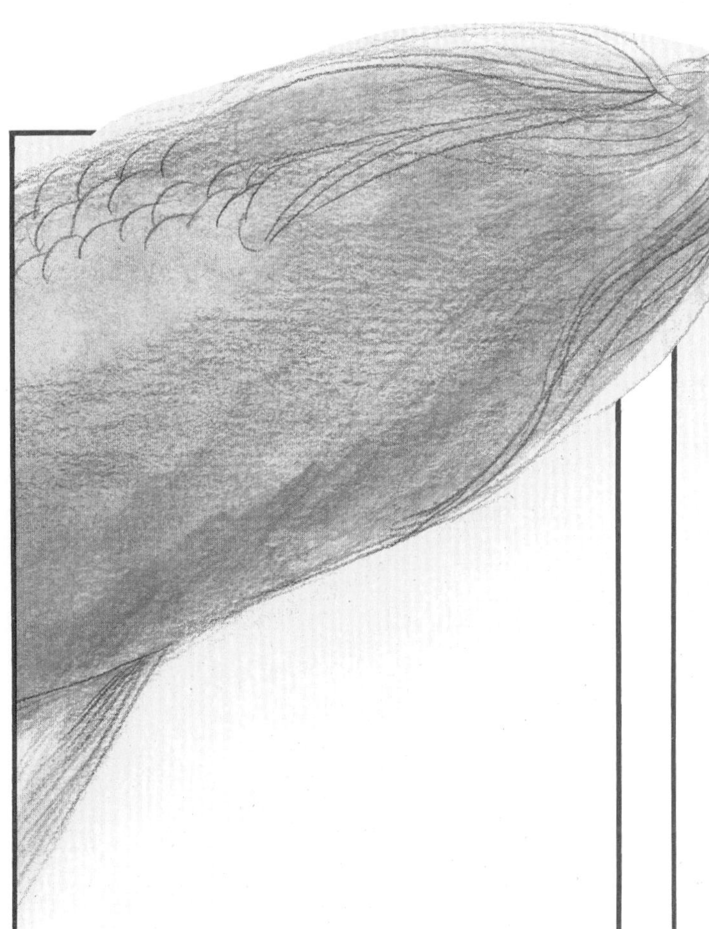

she lived in dread that her stepmother would discover her secret and take even that away from her.

So the time passed and spring came. Festival time was approaching: It was the busiest time of the year. Such cooking and cleaning and sewing there was to be done! Yeh-Shen had hardly a moment's rest. At the spring festival young men and young women from the village hoped to meet and to choose whom they would marry. How Yeh-Shen longed to go! But her stepmother had other plans. She hoped to find a husband for her own daughter and did not want any man to see the beauteous Yeh-Shen first. When finally the holiday arrived, the stepmother and her daughter dressed themselves in their finery and filled their baskets with sweetmeats. "You must remain at home now, and watch to see that no one steals fruit from our trees," her stepmother told Yeh-Shen, and then she departed for the banquet with her own daughter.

As soon as she was alone, Yeh-Shen went to speak to the bones of her fish. "Oh, dear friend," she said, kneeling before the precious bones, "I long to go to the festival, but I cannot show myself in these rags. Is there somewhere I could borrow clothes fit to wear to the feast?" At once she found herself dressed in a gown of azure blue, with a cloak of kingfisher feathers draped around her shoulders. Best of all, on her tiny feet were the most beautiful slippers she had ever seen. They were

woven of golden threads, in a pattern like the scales of a fish, and the glistening soles were made of solid gold. There was magic in the shoes, for they should have been quite heavy, yet when Yeh-Shen walked, her feet felt as light as air.

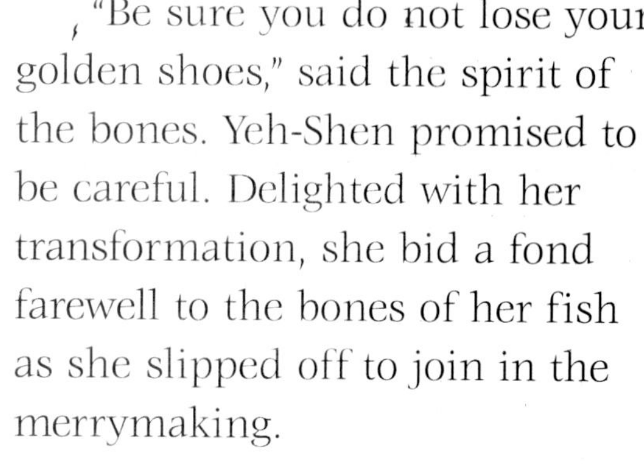

"Be sure you do not lose your golden shoes," said the spirit of the bones. Yeh-Shen promised to be careful. Delighted with her transformation, she bid a fond farewell to the bones of her fish as she slipped off to join in the merrymaking.

That day Yeh-Shen turned many a head as she appeared at the feast. All around her people whispered, "Look at that beautiful girl! Who can she be?"

But above this, Stepsister was heard to say, "Mother, does she not resemble our Yeh-Shen?"

Upon hearing this, Yeh-Shen jumped up and ran off before her stepsister could look closely at her. She raced down the mountainside, and in doing so, she lost one of her golden slippers. No sooner had the shoe fallen from her foot than all her fine clothes turned back to rags.

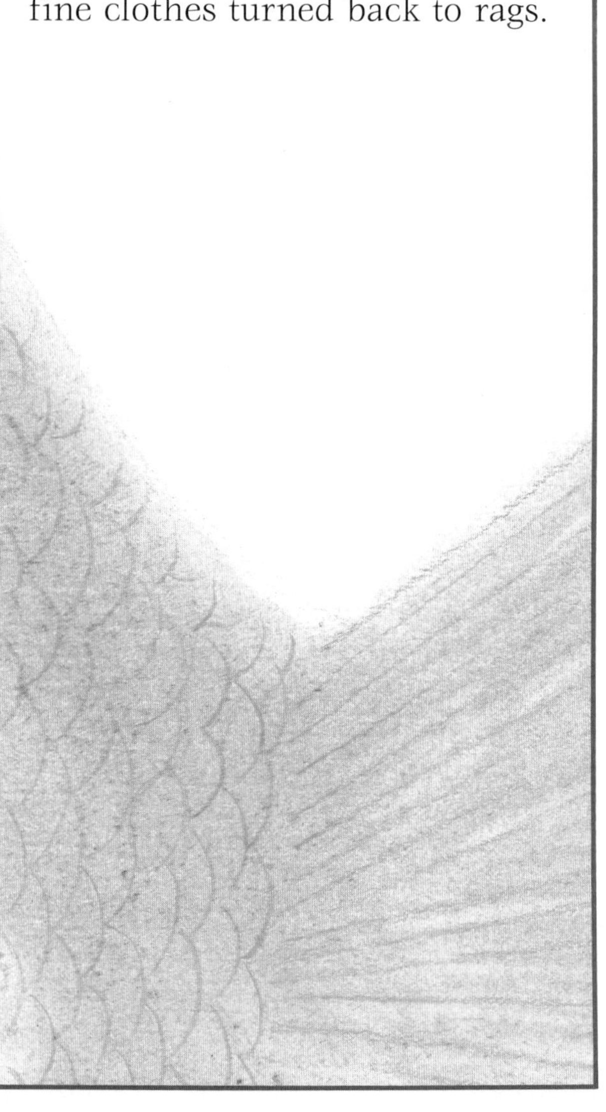

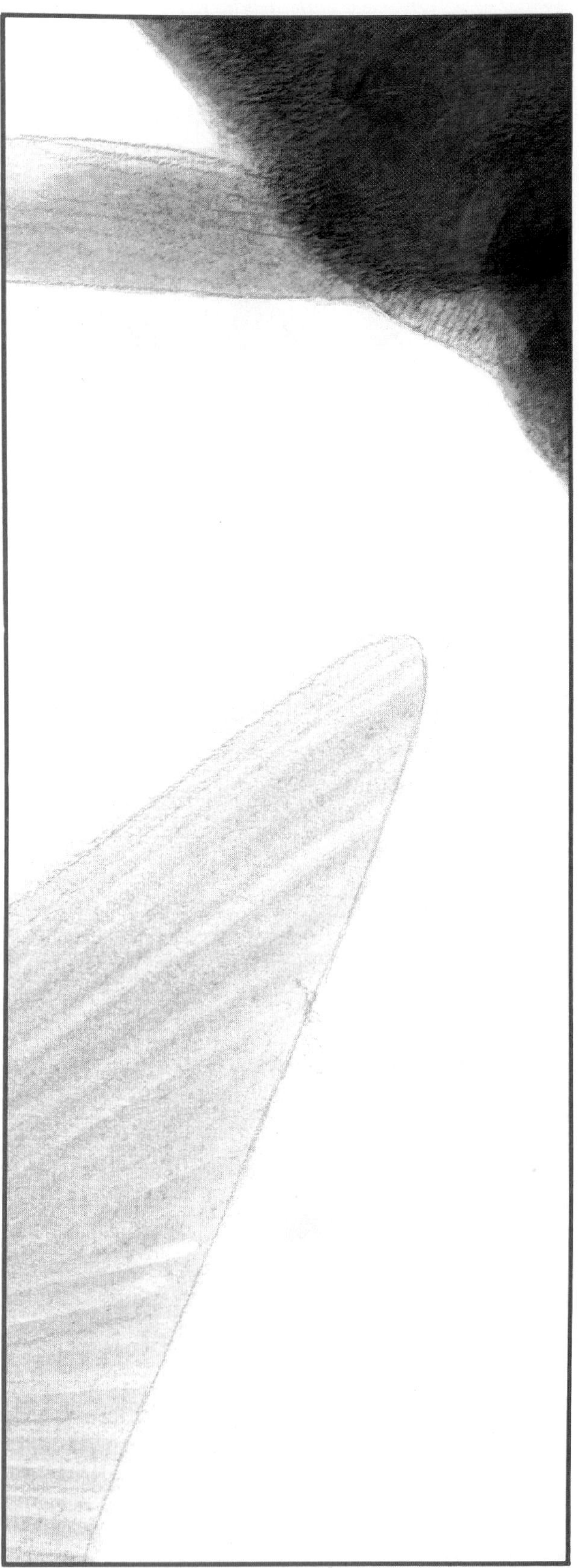

Only one thing remained—a tiny golden shoe. Yeh-Shen hurried to the bones of her fish and returned the slipper, promising to find its mate. But now the bones were silent. Sadly Yeh-Shen realized that she had lost her only friend. She hid the little shoe in her bedstraw, and went outside to cry. Leaning against a fruit tree, she sobbed and sobbed until she fell asleep.

The stepmother left the gathering to check on Yeh-Shen, but when she returned home she found the girl sound asleep, with her arms wrapped around a fruit tree. So thinking no more of her, the stepmother rejoined the party. Meantime, a villager had found the shoe. Recognizing its worth, he sold it to a merchant, who presented it in turn to the king of the island kingdom of T'o Han.

The king was more than happy to accept the slipper as a gift. He was entranced by the tiny thing, which was shaped of the most precious of metals, yet which made no sound when touched to stone. The more he marveled at its beauty, the more determined he became to find the woman to whom the shoe

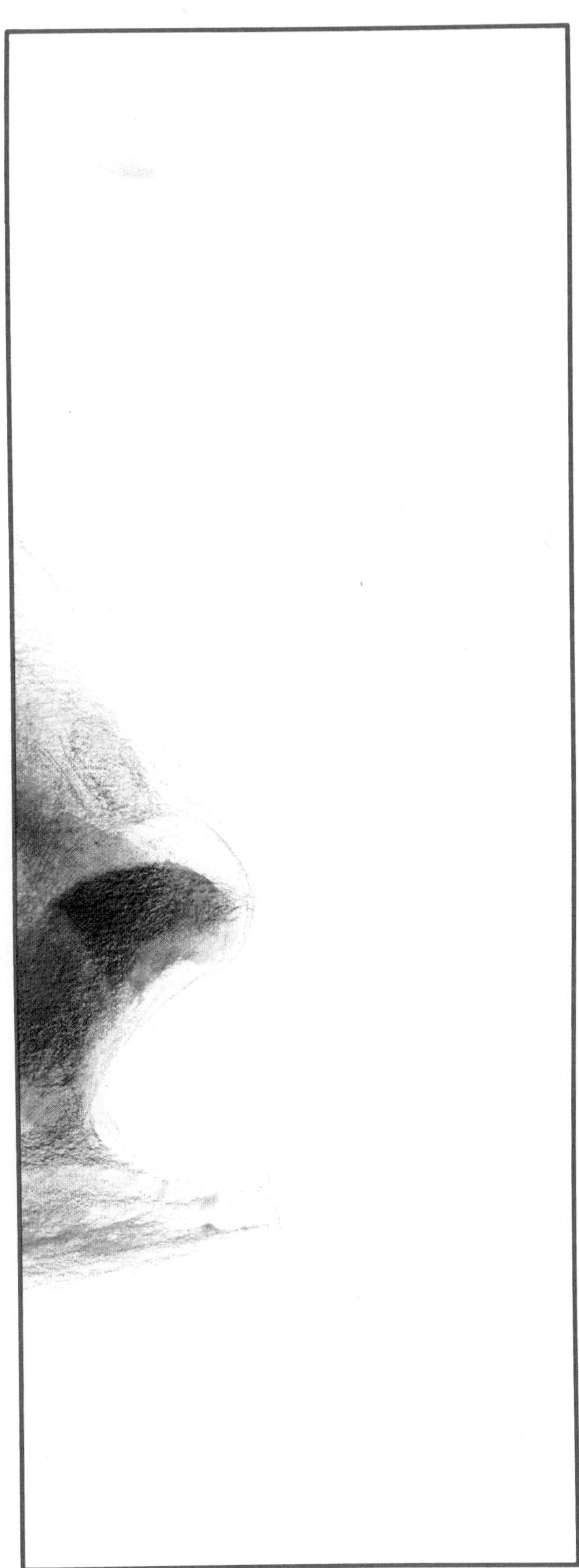

belonged. A search was begun among the ladies of his own kingdom, but all who tried on the sandal found it impossibly small. Undaunted, the king ordered the search widened to include the cave women from the countryside where the slipper had been found. Since he realized it would take many years for every woman to come to his island and test her foot in the slipper, the king thought of a way to get the right woman to come forward. He ordered the sandal placed in a pavilion by the side of the road near where

it had been found, and his herald announced that the shoe was to be returned to its original owner. Then from a nearby hiding place, the king and his men settled down to watch and wait for a woman with tiny feet to come and claim her slipper.

All that day the pavilion was crowded with cave women who had come to test a foot in the shoe. Yeh-Shen's stepmother and stepsister were among them, but not Yeh-Shen—they had told her to stay home. By day's end, although many women had eagerly tried to put on the slipper, it still had not been worn. Wearily, the king continued his vigil into the night.

It wasn't until the blackest part of night, while the moon hid behind a cloud, that Yeh-Shen dared to show her face at the pavilion, and even then she tiptoed timidly across the wide floor. Sinking down to her knees, the girl in rags examined the tiny shoe. Only when she was sure that this was the missing mate to her own golden slipper did she dare pick it up.

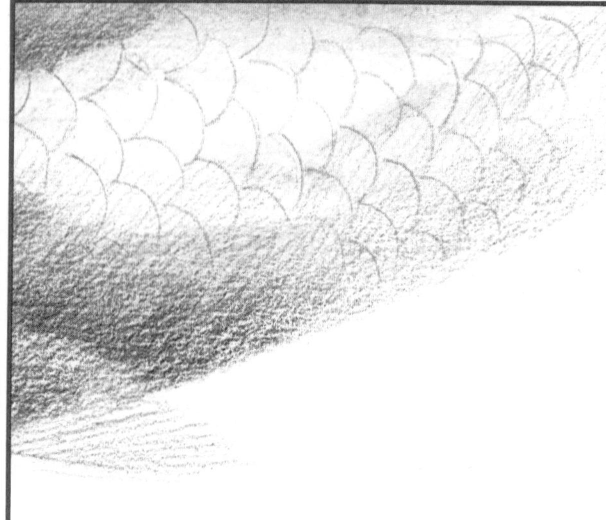

At last she could return both little shoes to the fish bones. Surely then her beloved spirit would speak to her again.

Now the king's first thought, on seeing Yeh-Shen take the precious slipper, was to throw the girl into prison as a thief. But when she turned to leave, he caught a glimpse of her face. At once the king was struck by the sweet harmony of her features, which seemed so out of keeping with the rags she wore. It was then that he took a closer look and noticed that she walked upon the tiniest feet he had ever seen.

With a wave of his hand, the king signaled that this tattered creature was to be allowed to depart with the golden slipper. Quietly, the king's men slipped off and followed her home.

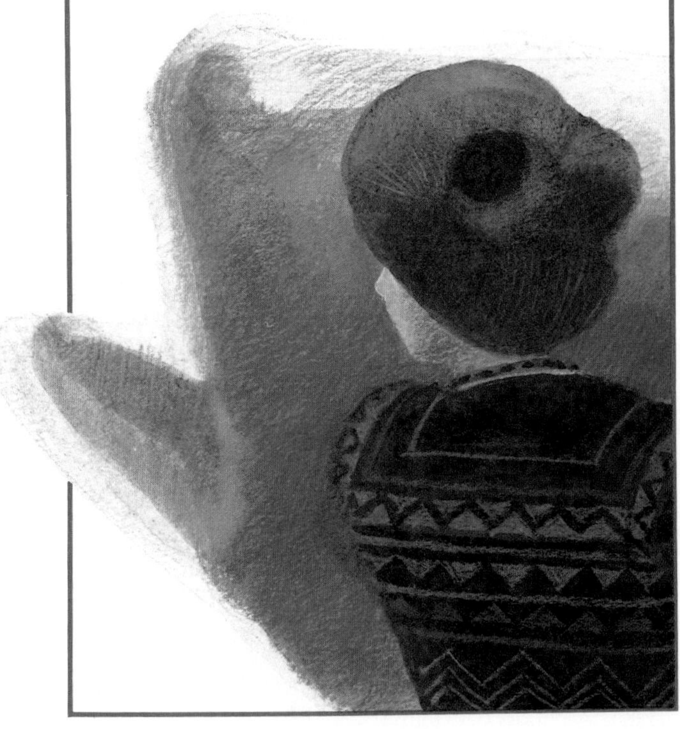

All this time, Yeh-Shen was unaware of the excitement she had caused. She had made her way home and was about to hide both sandals in her bedding when there was a pounding at the door. Yeh-Shen went to see who it was—and found a king at her doorstep. She was very frightened at first, but the king spoke to her in a kind voice and asked her to try the golden slippers on her feet. The maiden did as she was told, and as she stood in her golden shoes, her rags were transformed once more into the feathered cloak and beautiful azure gown.

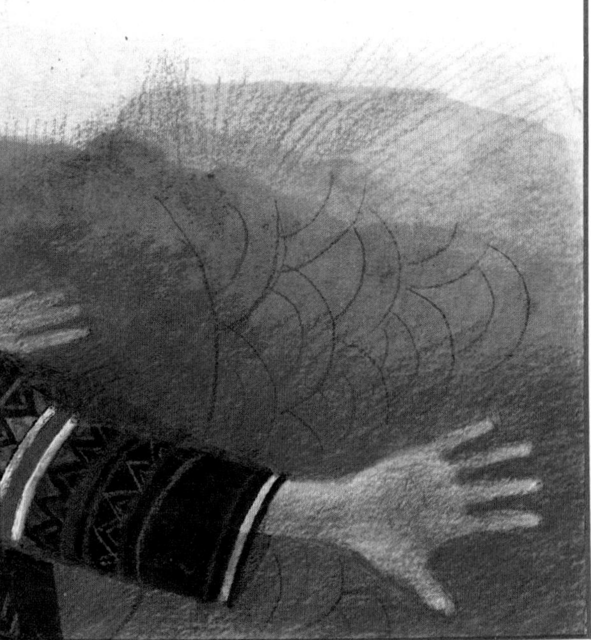

Her loveliness made her seem a heavenly being, and the king suddenly knew in his heart that he had found his true love.

Not long after this, Yeh-Shen was married to the king. But fate was not so gentle with her stepmother and stepsister. Since they had been unkind to his beloved, the king would not permit Yeh-Shen to bring them to his palace. They remained in their cave home, where one day, it is said, they were crushed to death in a shower of flying stones.

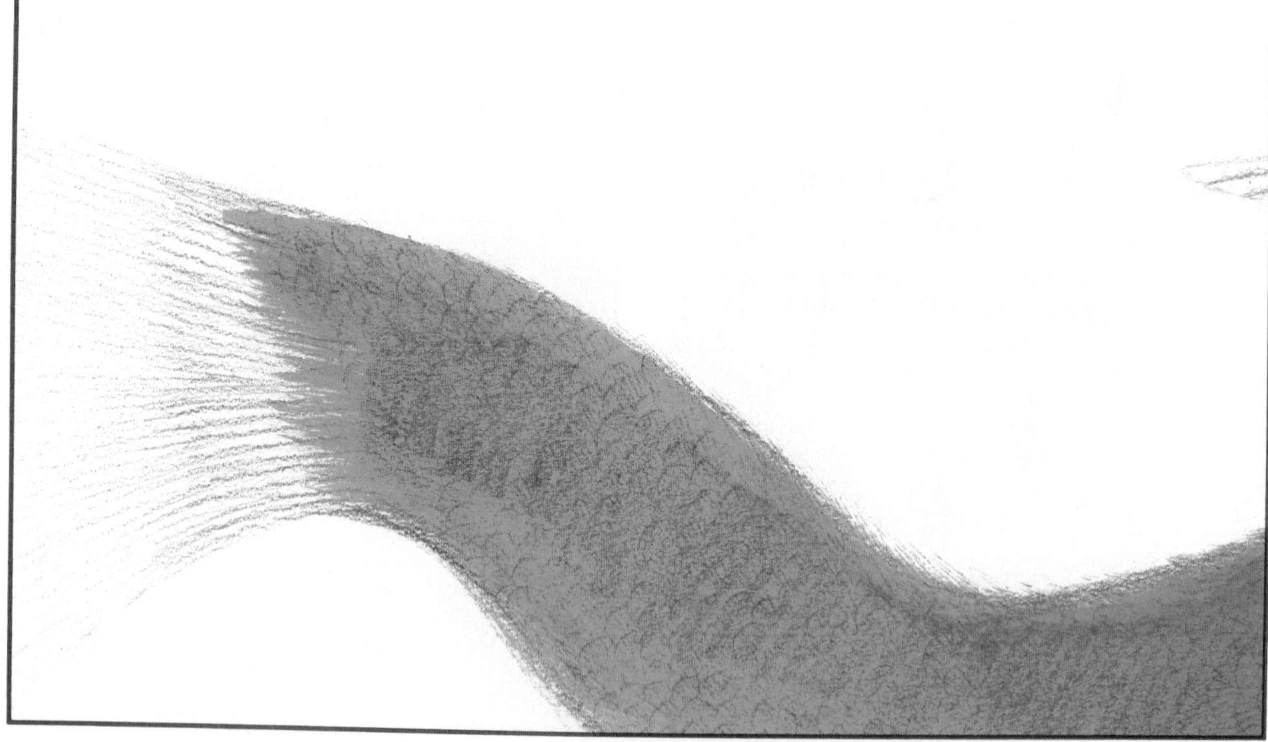

Meet Ed Young

In Shanghai, China, where Ed Young grew up, his father would entertain the family by reading and spinning endless tales. Young still remembers some of the scenes he imagined as he listened. He made his own drawings, too. "I drew everything that happened to cross my mind: airplanes, people, a tall ship. . . . I have always been happiest doing my own thing."

In some of his books, Young combines his love of storytelling and drawing. One of his best-known books, *Lon Po Po,* is his retelling of a Chinese Little Red-Riding Hood story, for which he won the Caldecott Medal. For both *Lon Po Po* and *Yeh-Shen,* Young set his art in colorful panels like those of Chinese folding screens. He also created hidden images. In *Lon Po Po,* the wolf's image is cleverly hidden in some drawings. Looking closely at the drawings in *Yeh-Shen,* you will see Yeh-Shen's fish hidden in the panels.

Meet Ai-Ling Louie

Books have always been a part of Ai-Ling Louie's life. "When I was a girl, it seemed I always had my nose in a book," she says. Ai-Ling Louie's career as a teacher brought out her desire to write. "I used to love to write stories to tell the children."

Louie wrote down *Yeh-Shen: A Cinderella Story from China* for one of her classes. She learned the story from her mother, who first heard it as a child in China.

Story Questions & Activities

1. What do the bones of the fish give Yeh-Shen so she can go to the festival?
2. How is the slipper important to the story?
3. What makes this story a "Cinderella story"?
4. What are the important events in this fairy tale? Give them in order.
5. Compare the story of "Yeh-Shen" with "Cinderella." How are the characters and events alike?

Write a Sequel

Fairy-tale writers don't tell you everything at the end of the story. They usually just say "And they lived happily ever after." Write a sequel, or a follow-up story, to "Yeh-Shen." You can begin with Yeh-Shen's wedding to the king. Then tell what happens.

Tell a Cinderella Story

Read one of the many stories of Cinderella. This could be a Cinderella story that you know, or it could be a story that you would like to read for the first time. Examples of Cinderella stories are "The Brocaded Slipper," from Vietnam or "The Egyptian Cinderella." Read the story a few times. Then practice telling it. When you feel that you know the story well, tell it to a group of your classmates.

Draw the Cover

What would you do if you were asked to draw a new cover for "Yeh-Shen"? Choose what you think is the most important scene in the story. Then paint or draw it for the cover.

Find Out More

"Yeh-Shen" is a Cinderella story from China. Where is China? What is that country like? Start by looking up China in an encyclopedia or on the Internet. Then find a topic that interests you. It could be the Great Wall of China, the travels of Marco Polo, Chinese writing or cooking, or something else. Share what you learn with your classmates.

Read E-mail

If Yeh-Shen had **E-mail** at the palace, she could have written to the magic fish. E-mail, or electronic mail, lets you send messages instantly by computer. By clicking on small pictures, called **icons**, you can reply to an E-mail, forward it to other people, and print it out.

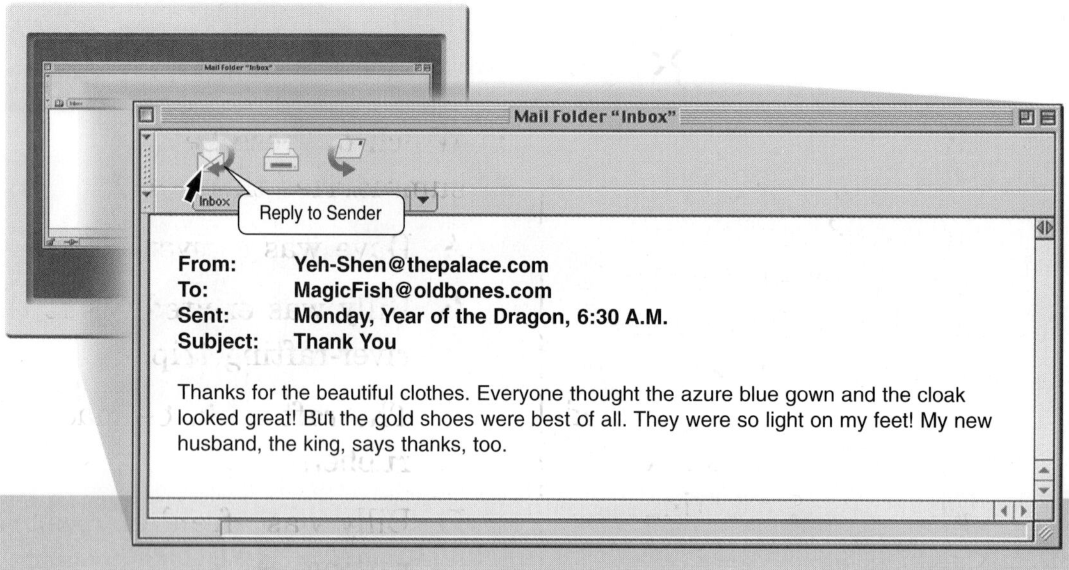

Use the E-mail to answer these questions.

1. Who sent this message?
2. How many icons are shown on the screen?
3. When was the message sent? When do you think it was received?
4. Yeh-Shen didn't sign her E-mail. Why not?
5. Compare E-mail to regular mail. What are some advantages and disadvantages?

TEST POWER

Test Tip

The summary tells what the passage is mostly about.

DIRECTIONS

Read the sample story. Then read each question about the story.

SAMPLE

River Raft

Today Billy was going on a river-rafting trip. Parts of the river were considered the most <u>treacherous</u> stretches of water in the United States. Its currents and underwater snags were only some of the dangerous aspects of the water. But Billy was not afraid. He was going rafting with his friend Dave and Dave's father. Dave's father was a river guide in Wyoming. He knew more about rivers and rafting than anyone else Billy knew.

They put on their life vests and climbed aboard the raft. With one push, away they went. Billy was sure that it was going to be fun.

1 Which of these best summarizes the story?

A Dave was a river guide.

B Billy was excited about the river-rafting trip.

C The raft could be made of rubber.

D Billy was afraid of river rafting.

2 In this story, the word <u>treacherous</u> means—

F dirty

G far away

H dangerous

J calm

Stories in Art

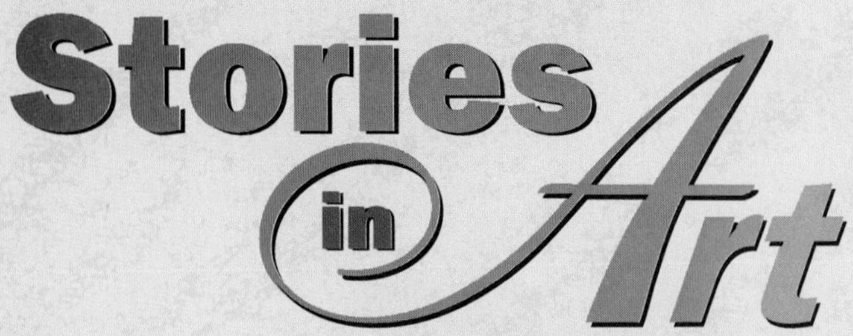

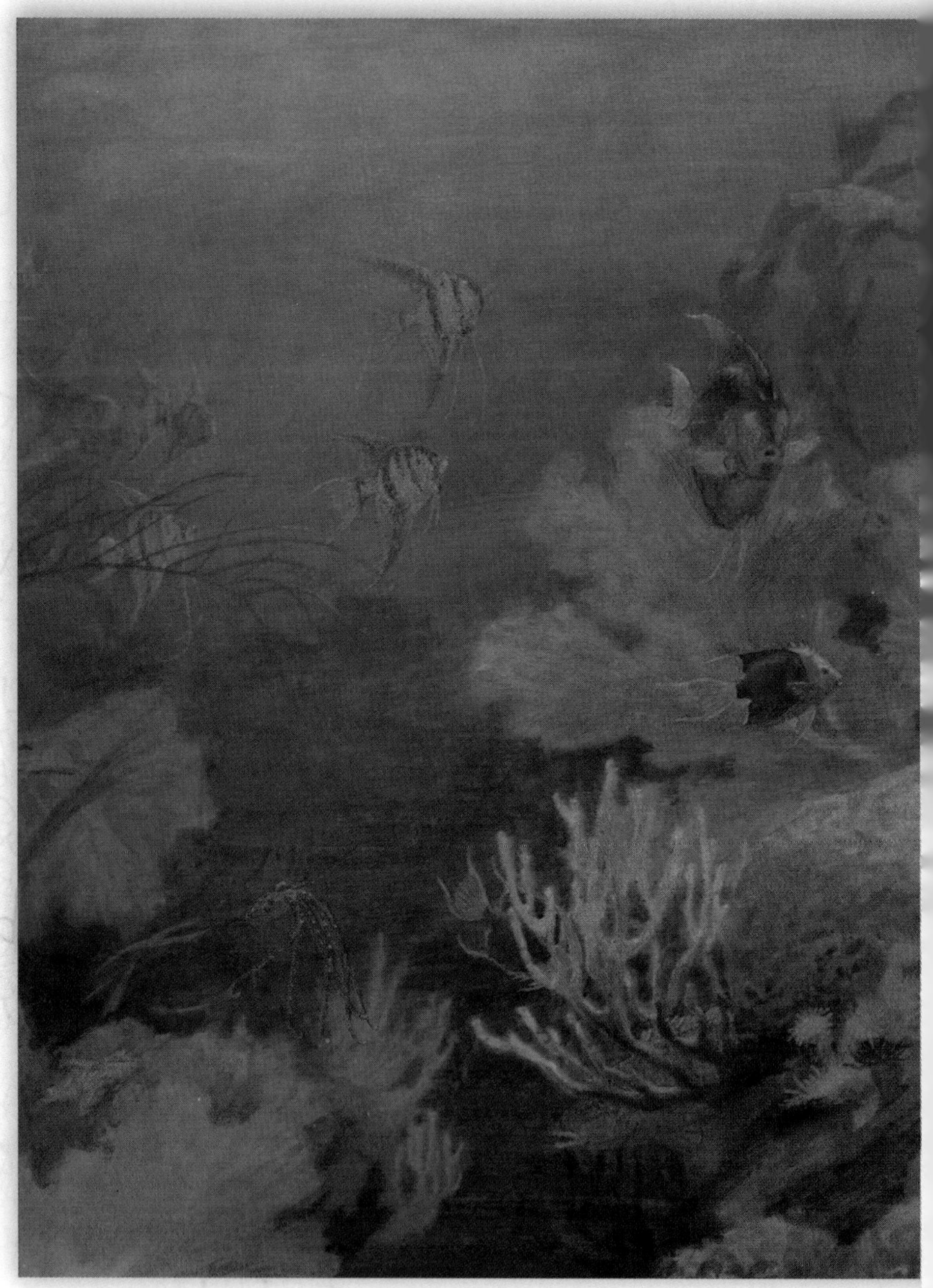

Art can be made from almost anything. Before an artist begins a painting, he or she decides which materials to use and which information is important to show.

Look at the sketch of a coral reef. The artist made it before creating a diorama. What details do you notice? How does the sketch help the artist decide which information to show? How does it help him leave out unimportant details?

Look at the painting again. What does it tell you about a coral reef? What do you think are the important details in the picture?

Proposed Diorama of the Undersea Gardens, Bermuda
by Samuel Ernest Whatley
The Maas Gallery, London

TIME FOR KIDS

SPECIAL REPORT

CAN WE RESCUE THE REEFS?

This tiger grouper in the Caribbean Sea is one of thousands of creatures that live in coral reefs.

Getting to Know Reefs

Understanding coral reefs may be the key to saving them

Coral reefs in the Caribbean and around the world are in danger of dying. Up to 60 percent may be destroyed in the next 45 years if the reefs are not protected. There are many reasons why about 10 percent of the world's reefs have been killed, including pollution, overfishing, and careless divers.

"You can never point to just one thing and say it's *this* that's killing the reefs," says Clive Wilkinson, a biologist at the Australian Institute of Marine Science. "It's almost everything."

Scientists and nature lovers want everyone to understand the importance of protecting Earth's precious reefs. If people understand the problem, they may be able to do something about it.

BUILDING A REEF

Coral reefs are built out of colonies of see-through animals. These animals are called corals. Corals are cousins of jellyfish. Corals even sting as jellyfish do. The animals develop a hard outer shell.

Can you tell how whip coral (above) and brain coral (right) got their names?

They stick together to build their colonies in beautiful shapes.

Corals can look like tall towers, bundles of brains, or even big bunches of noodles. Only the outermost corals are alive. All the corals together make up a reef. Reefs can be hundreds of miles long. Some are 7,000 years old.

Reefs come in many colors. Their brilliant colors come from tiny plants that live inside each coral. These plants turn sunlight into food, just as plants on land do. Corals need the plants to live. Plants are their food supply.

REEFS HAVE WORK TO DO!

Reefs help fish and humans in many ways. They protect shorelines against storms and provide safe harbor for ships. They offer food and hiding places for small fish. Bigger fish use the reefs to hunt for smaller animals.

The white part of the coral is dead.

An angelfish swims by a tower of pillar coral in the Caribbean.

"Reefs are tough," says Clive Wilkinson. "You can hammer them with cyclones, and they'll bounce right back." But reefs can't bounce back from the damage caused by humans.

Too much fishing around a reef can upset its balance. Without fish to eat seaweed, a reef can become overgrown with the plants. The reefs around Jamaica have been smothered by seaweed for years. In the Philippines, fishing has caused almost all of the country's reefs to die or be seriously damaged.

FIND OUT MORE

Visit our website:

www.mhschool.com/reading

PEOPLE ON LAND CAN HARM REEFS

Believe it or not, chopping down trees can harm faraway coral reefs. Soil that used to cling to tree roots is loosened. It slides into rivers by the ton and washes out to sea. The soil blocks sunlight from reaching the corals. So they die.

Coral reefs cannot live in water that is too warm. Scientists worry that warming temperatures around the world will also hurt the reefs.

What can be done to save the reefs? Educating the people who live near the reefs will help, says Clive Wilkinson. Some people, he says, don't understand how their actions can cause damage below sea level. People need to understand how delicate coral reefs are. Then they'll appreciate them, he believes. And if that happens, maybe, just maybe, coral reefs will be around forever.

Some 5,000 kinds of fish live in coral reefs.

DAVID FLEETHAM/FPG; OPPOSITE PAGE: TOP: STEPHEN FRINK/CORBIS; BOTTOM: MARTY SNYDERMAN

DID YOU KNOW?

REEF FACTS

- **The Great Barrier Reef in Australia is 1,250 miles long.**
- **Coral reefs cover less than one percent of the ocean floor, but they contain about 25 percent of the ocean's species.**
- **There are about 2,500 different kinds of coral.**
- **Sixty percent of the world's coral reefs are found in the Indian Ocean and the Red Sea.**

Based on an article in *TIME FOR KIDS.*

Story Questions & Activities

1. What is a coral reef?
2. How are people destroying the coral reefs?
3. What makes coral reefs worth saving?
4. What are the most important facts in this selection?
5. Imagine that Sylvia Earle in "Meet an Underwater Explorer" was writing about the coral reefs. What do you think she would say?

Write a Fantasy

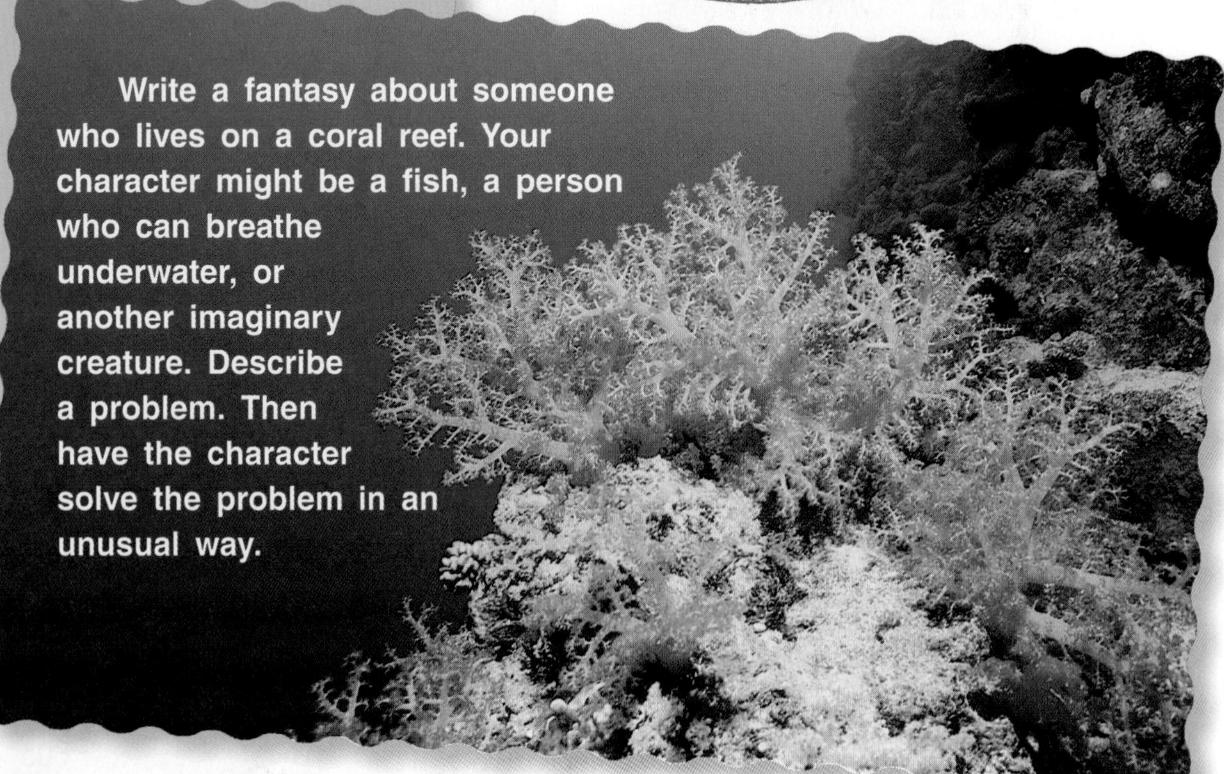

Write a fantasy about someone who lives on a coral reef. Your character might be a fish, a person who can breathe underwater, or another imaginary creature. Describe a problem. Then have the character solve the problem in an unusual way.

Create a Collage

Coral reefs come in many shapes, sizes, and colors. Get together with a group of classmates to plan a collage of a coral reef. Cut colorful shapes out of construction paper, or use objects found in nature. Arrange and then paste the objects on an ocean-blue background. Draw fish, giant clams, sea turtles, starfish, birds, and plants. Place them above or around the coral. Then title your "undersea garden," and sign it.

Paint the Colors of a Coral Reef

What happens when billions of coral attach themselves to a coral reef? Show what happens in a colorful painting. Use blue, green, purple, red, pink, and yellow paint. Make splotches of color. Then ask your family or friends to guess the subject of your painting.

Find Out More

Did you know that the Great Barrier Reef in Australia is the largest group of coral reefs in the world? Yet it is facing many problems. Look in an encyclopedia under "Great Barrier Reef." Find out about the crown-of-thorns starfish that are hurting the reef. Also discover what people have done to stop oil drilling in the area. Share important information with a partner.

Use a Telephone Directory

Would you like to scuba dive among beautiful coral reefs? You may need some instruction and equipment. Both can be found through the **yellow pages** of a **telephone directory.** Telephone directories list names, addresses, and phone numbers. The yellow pages list information about local businesses.

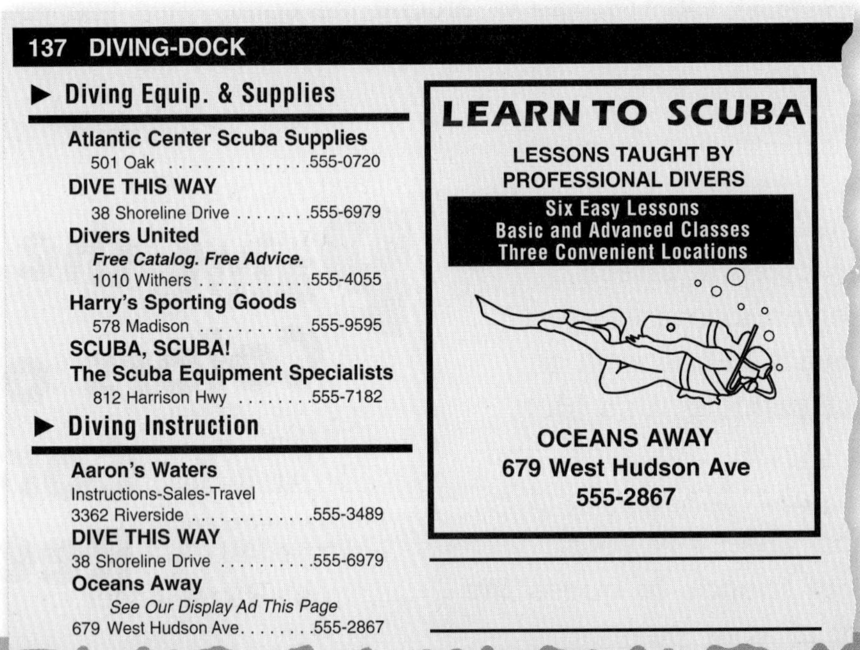

137 DIVING-DOCK

▶ Diving Equip. & Supplies

Atlantic Center Scuba Supplies
501 Oak 555-0720
DIVE THIS WAY
38 Shoreline Drive 555-6979
Divers United
Free Catalog. Free Advice.
1010 Withers 555-4055
Harry's Sporting Goods
578 Madison 555-9595
SCUBA, SCUBA!
The Scuba Equipment Specialists
812 Harrison Hwy 555-7182

▶ Diving Instruction

Aaron's Waters
Instructions-Sales-Travel
3362 Riverside 555-3489
DIVE THIS WAY
38 Shoreline Drive 555-6979
Oceans Away
See Our Display Ad This Page
679 West Hudson Ave........ .555-2867

LEARN TO SCUBA
LESSONS TAUGHT BY PROFESSIONAL DIVERS
Six Easy Lessons
Basic and Advanced Classes
Three Convenient Locations
OCEANS AWAY
679 West Hudson Ave
555-2867

Use the telephone directory to answer these questions.

1. What is the address and telephone number for Divers United?
2. Would you find a listing for Dog Walkers on this page? Explain why or why not.
3. Which business sells both equipment and lessons?
4. Which business has three locations?
5. When is it helpful to use the yellow pages?

TEST POWER

Test Tip

Read each answer choice slowly and carefully.

DIRECTIONS

Read the sample story. Then read each question about the story.

SAMPLE

The Rag-Doll Clown Show

After talking to her parents to make sure it was okay, Renée led her little brother to the bookstore to see a poster in the window. Renée knew how excited her brother would be to see this show.

Jester Theatre presents

The Famous Rag-Doll Clown Show

Saturday, May 2, and Sunday, May 3, at 3 P.M.
Prices: 13 and older, $3.00
ages 4-12, $1.00
under age 4, FREE!

The performance will be held at the outdoor stage area at the municipal swimming pool. Get your tickets by phone or at this store!

1 Where was the Rag-Doll Clown Show to be held?

A At the outdoor stage area

B In the bookstore

C At school

D At Renée's house

2 According to the poster, what could Renée order by phone?

F Posters

G A rag-doll

H A clown

J Tickets

The Garden We Planted Together

From all over the world
together they came,
to make a garden
with shovels and spades.

Disagreement crept in—
which flowers to grow?
So they sat in a circle
and agreed row by row.

They wrote down their rules
in a big, mighty book
and promised to keep them
by hook and by crook.

With the book to guide them,
they grew beautiful flowers,
each of them equal,
none higher, none lower.

When some flowers grow weak
or ready to die,
the children get together,
new solutions to try.

They share water and seeds,
all must have enough,
the book just demands it
when the going gets tough.

The garden remains a symbol to all,
its flowers are fifty years old this fall.
The book is known as a charter of
peace—
its rules are still valid, so read if you
please.

Anuruddha Bose, age 11, India

UNIT 6

Sorting It Out

Your World

Your world is as big as you make it.
I know, for I used to abide
In the narrowest nest in a corner,
My wings pressing close to my side.

But I sighted the distant horizon
Where the sky line encircled the sea
And I throbbed with a burning desire
To travel this immensity.

I battered the cordons around me
And cradled my wings on the breeze
Then soared to the uttermost reaches
With rapture, with power, with ease!

by Georgia Douglas Johnson

Stories in Art

Artists communicate through their art. Their paintings may express their feelings about people and places, family and friendship.

Look at this painting. What do you see? What can you tell about the two young women? How do you know they are friends? How does the artist show you they are "in step" with each other?

Close your eyes. What do you think has caused the women to take a walk by the water? What effect does the day have on them? What effect does the painting have on you? Explain.

***Daughters of the South*, 1993**
Jonathan Green
Oil on canvas 71" x 72"
Collection of Julia J. Norrell

TEAM

by Peter Golenbock

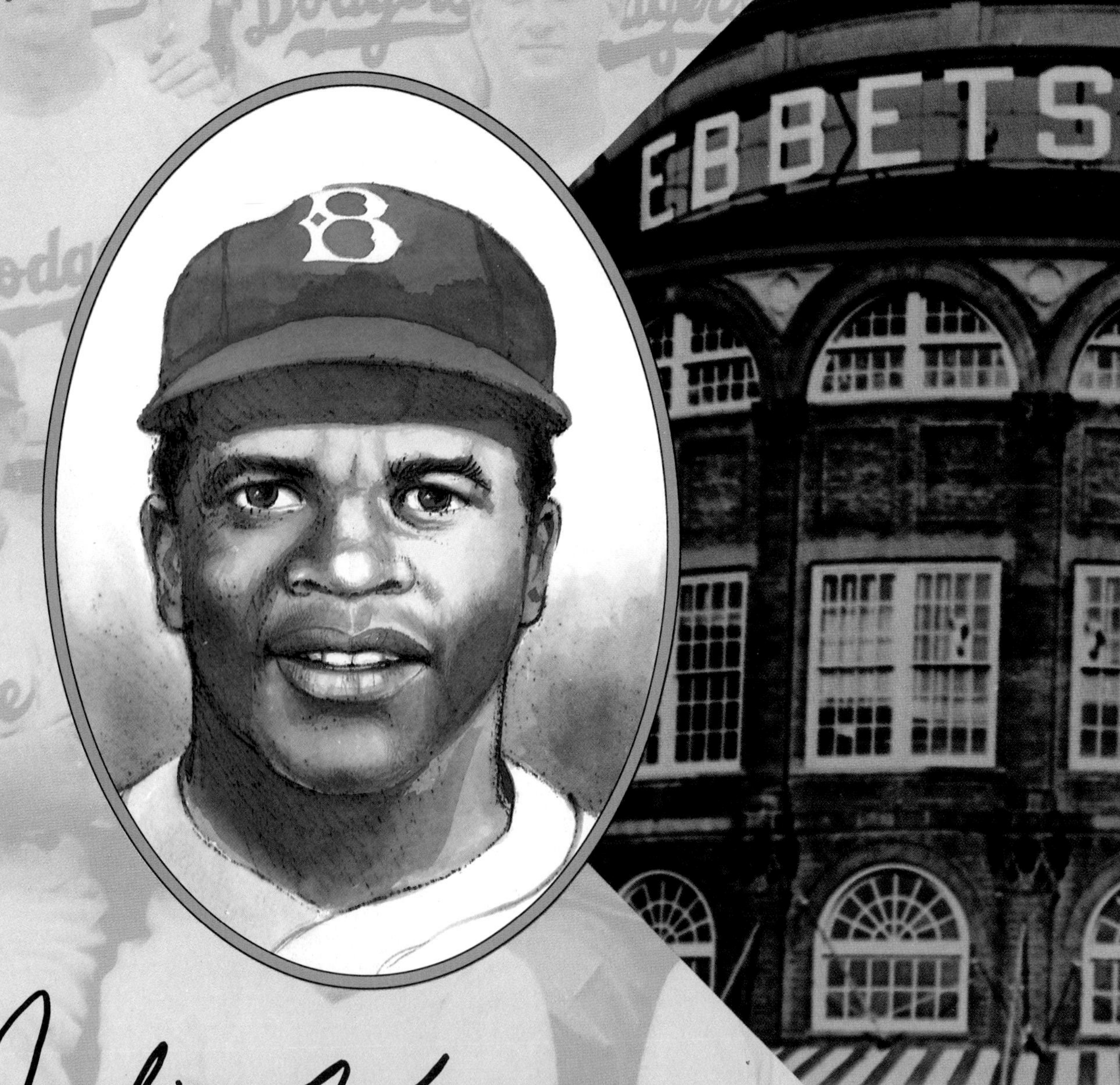

MATES

illustrated by Paul Bacon

"Pee Wee" Reese

Jackie Robinson was more than just my teammate. He had a tremendous amount of talent, ability, and dedication. Jackie set a standard for future generations of ball players. He was a winner.

Jackie Robinson was also a man.

PEE WEE REESE
October 31, 1989

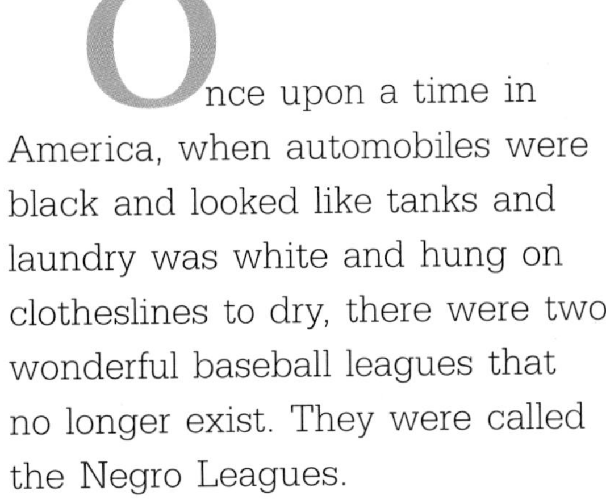

Once upon a time in America, when automobiles were black and looked like tanks and laundry was white and hung on clotheslines to dry, there were two wonderful baseball leagues that no longer exist. They were called the Negro Leagues.

The Negro Leagues had extraordinary players, and adoring fans came to see them wherever they played. They were heroes, but players in the Negro Leagues didn't make much money and their lives on the road were hard.

Laws against segregation didn't exist in the 1940s. In many places in this country, black people were not allowed to go to the same schools and churches as white people. They couldn't sit in the front of a bus or trolley car. They couldn't drink from the same drinking fountains that white people drank from.

Back then, many hotels didn't rent rooms to black people, so the Negro League players slept in their cars. Many towns had no restaurants that would serve them, so they often had to eat meals that they could buy and carry with them.

Life was very different for the players in the Major Leagues. They were the leagues for white players. Compared to the Negro League players, white players were very well paid. They stayed in good hotels and ate in fine restaurants. Their pictures were put on baseball cards and the best players became famous all over the world.

Many Americans knew that racial prejudice was wrong, but few dared to challenge openly the way things were. And many people were apathetic about racial problems. Some feared that it could be dangerous to object. Vigilante groups, like the Ku Klux Klan, reacted violently against those who tried to change the way blacks were treated.

The general manager of the Brooklyn Dodgers baseball team was a man by the name of Branch Rickey. He was not afraid of change. He wanted to treat the Dodger fans to the best players he could find, regardless of the color of their skin. He thought segregation was unfair and wanted to give everyone, regardless of race or creed, an opportunity to compete equally on ballfields across America.

To do this, the Dodgers needed one special man.

Branch Rickey launched a search for him. He was looking for a star player in the Negro Leagues who would be able to compete successfully despite threats on his life or attempts to injure him. He would have to possess the self-control not to fight back when opposing players tried to intimidate or hurt him. If this man disgraced himself on the field, Rickey knew, his opponents would use it as an excuse to keep blacks out of Major League baseball for many more years.

Rickey thought Jackie Robinson might be just the man.

BRANCH RICKEY

Dodgers
Dodgers
42
5
11
Dodgers

Jackie rode the train to Brooklyn to meet Mr. Rickey. When Mr. Rickey told him, "I want a man with the courage not to fight back," Jackie Robinson replied, "If you take this gamble, I will do my best to perform." They shook hands. Branch Rickey and Jackie Robinson were starting on what would be known in history as "the great experiment."

At spring training with the Dodgers, Jackie was mobbed by blacks, young and old, as if he were a savior. He was the first black player to try out for a Major League team. If he succeeded, they knew, others would follow.

Initially, life with the Dodgers was for Jackie a series of humiliations. The players on his team who came from the South, men who had been taught to avoid black people since childhood, moved to another table whenever he sat down next to them. Many opposing players were cruel to him, calling him nasty names from their dugouts. A few tried to hurt him with their spiked shoes. Pitchers aimed at his head. And he received threats on his life, both from individuals and from organizations like the Ku Klux Klan.

Despite all the difficulties, Jackie Robinson didn't give up. He made the Brooklyn Dodgers team.

But making the Dodgers was only the beginning. Jackie had to face abuse and hostility throughout the season, from April through September. His worst pain was inside. Often he felt very alone. On the road he had to live by himself, because only the white players were allowed in the hotels in towns where the team played.

The whole time Pee Wee Reese, the Dodger shortstop, was growing up in Louisville, Kentucky, he had rarely even seen a black person, unless it was in the back of a bus. Most of his friends and relatives hated the idea of his playing on the same field as a black man. In addition, Pee Wee Reese had more to lose than the other players when Jackie joined the team.

Jackie had been a shortstop, and everyone thought that Jackie would take Pee Wee's job. Lesser men might have felt anger toward Jackie, but Pee Wee was different. He told himself, "If he's good enough to take my job, he deserves it."

When his Southern teammates circulated a petition to throw Jackie off the team and asked him to sign it, Pee Wee responded, "I don't care if this man is black, blue, or striped"—and refused to sign. "He can play and he can help us win," he told the others. "That's what counts."

Very early in the season, the Dodgers traveled west to Ohio to play the Cincinnati Reds. Cincinnati is near Pee Wee's hometown of Louisville.

The Reds played in a small ballpark where the fans sat close to the field. The players could almost feel the breath of the fans on the backs of their necks. Many who came that day screamed terrible, hateful things at Jackie when the Dodgers were on the field.

More than anything else, Pee Wee Reese believed in doing what was right. When he heard the fans yelling at Jackie, Pee Wee decided to take a stand.

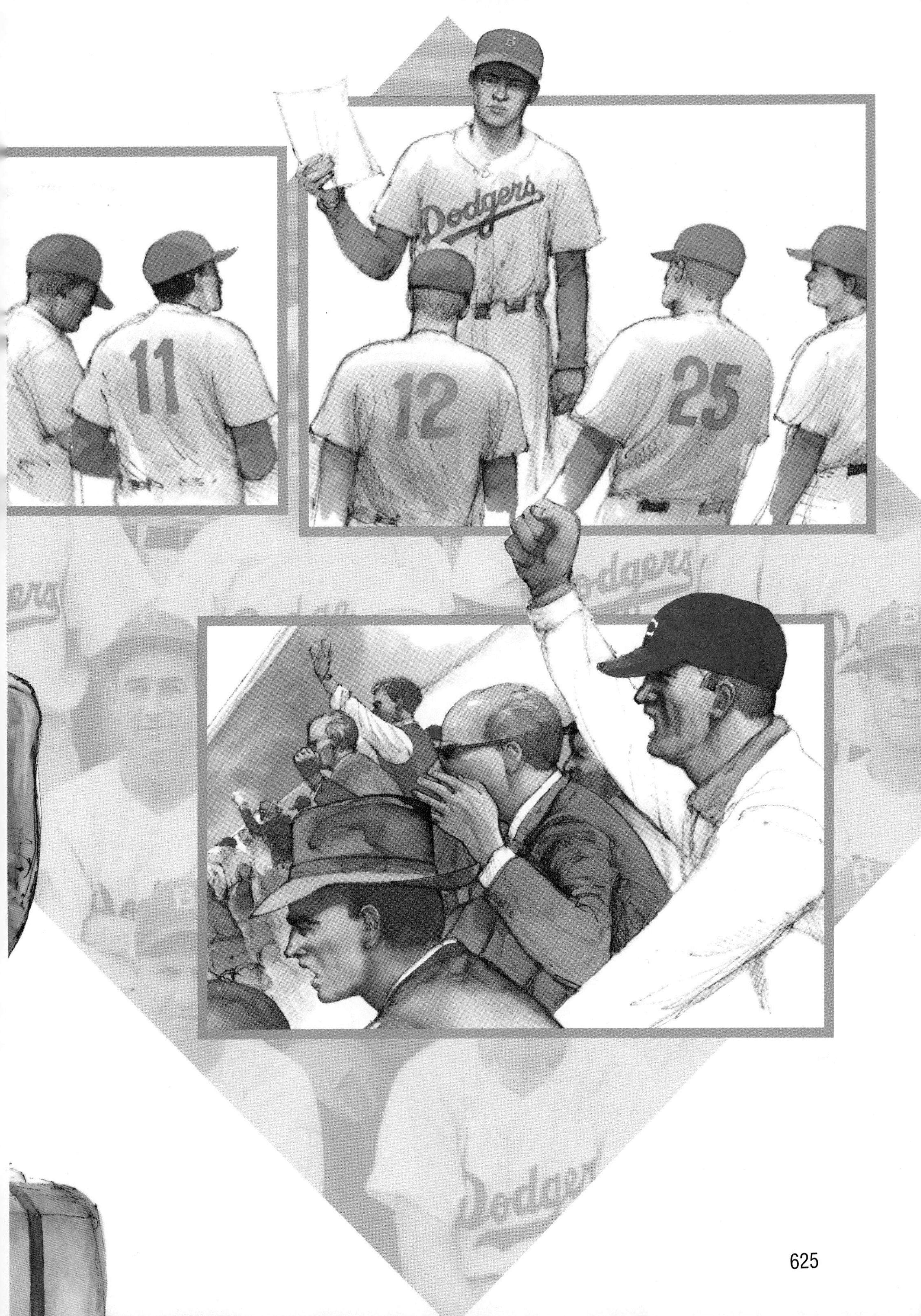
Dodgers
11
12
25
Dodgers

With his head high, Pee Wee walked directly from his shortstop position to where Jackie was playing first base. The taunts and shouting of the fans were ringing in Pee Wee's ears. It saddened him, because he knew it could have been his friends and neighbors. Pee Wee's legs felt heavy, but he knew what he had to do.

As he walked toward Jackie wearing the gray Dodger uniform, he looked into his teammate's bold, pained eyes. The first baseman had done nothing to provoke the hostility except that he sought to be treated as an equal. Jackie was grim with anger. Pee Wee smiled broadly as he reached Jackie. Jackie smiled back.

Stopping beside Jackie, Pee Wee put his arm around Jackie's shoulders. An audible gasp rose up from the crowd when they saw what Pee Wee had done. Then there was silence.

Outlined on a sea of green grass stood these two great athletes, one black, one white, both wearing the same team uniform.

"I am standing by him," Pee Wee Reese said to the world. "This man is my teammate."

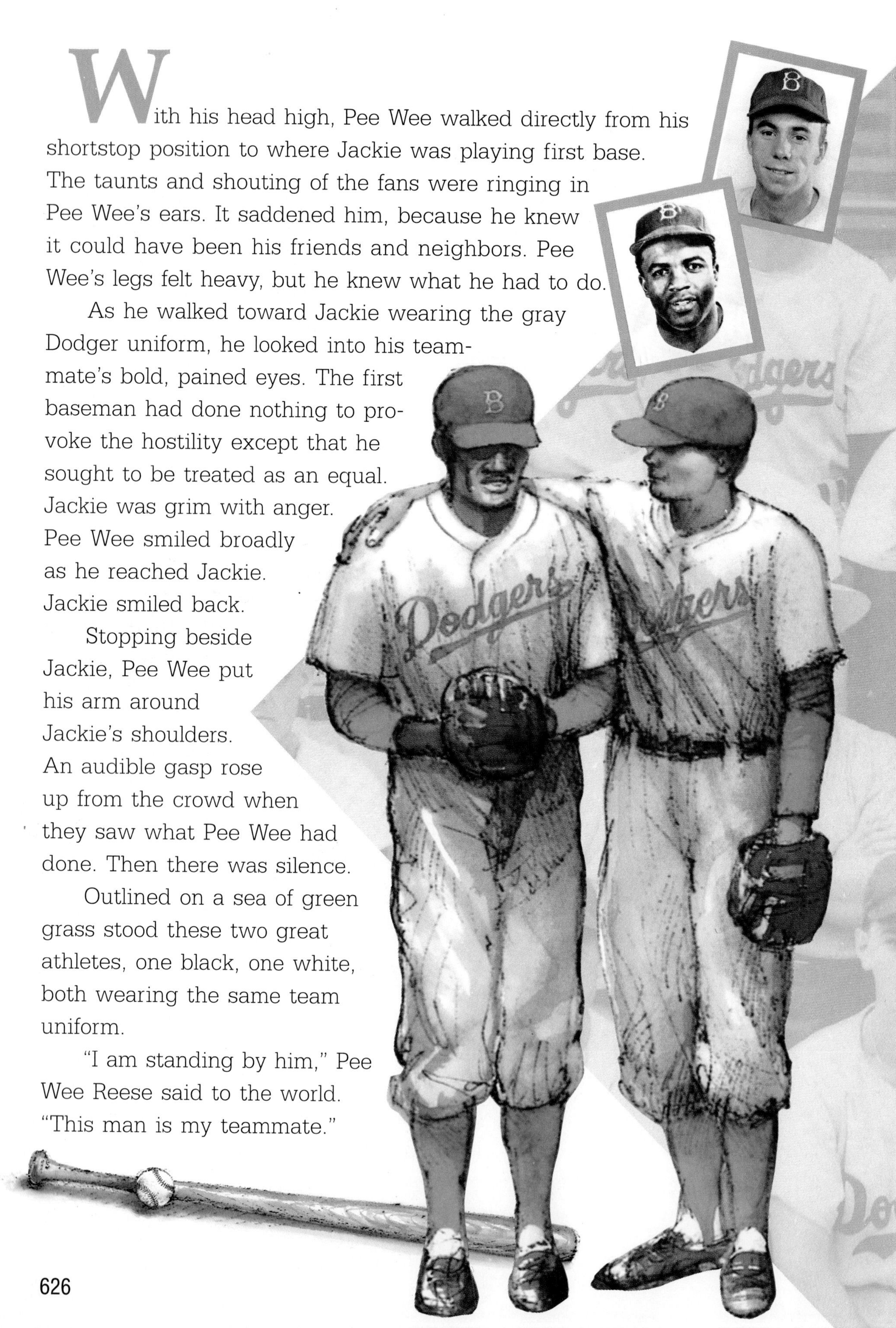

MEET *Peter Golenbock*

When Peter Golenbock was thirteen, he met one of his heroes. After a World Series game between the Dodgers and the Yankees, he was introduced to Jackie Robinson. Meeting the great baseball player was quite an experience. "I was in awe of him," Golenbock remembers. "Robinson was huge. When I shook his hand, mine disappeared in his."

Years later, Golenbock became a sportswriter and learned more about Robinson. Rex Barney, who had pitched for the Dodgers when Robinson was a player, told the writer a true story about two teammates—Jackie Robinson and Pee Wee Reese, the Dodgers' shortstop. Peter Golenbock never forgot that story.

When he was asked to write about baseball for young people, he thought about Jackie Robinson. He remembered Robinson's courage—as an athlete and as the first African-American player in the major leagues. He also remembered the story that Rex Barney had told him.

In Teammates, *Peter Golenbock wrote about baseball and how Robinson changed it. It is a story you, like the author, may never forget.*

Story Questions & Activities

1. What were the names of the baseball leagues for African American and white players before the 1940s?

2. Why did Branch Rickey decide to hire Jackie Robinson?

3. What effect did Branch Rickey's decision to hire Jackie Robinson have on the game of baseball?

4. What is the main idea of this true story?

5. Imagine that Jackie Robinson became part of the painting on pages 614–615. What do you think he would say to the women about the real meaning of teammates? Do you think they would agree with him? Explain.

Write an Essay

Jackie Robinson played for the Brooklyn Dodgers. Write an essay about this team. Choose one year to write about. If possible, interview older people who remember the team. Ask them about famous players and games.

Create a Collage

Jackie Robinson was the first African American player in the Major Leagues. Plan a collage of other "firsts." Include people who were first, such as Amelia Earhart, who was the first woman to fly a plane across the Atlantic Ocean. Find pictures of these famous people. Then arrange them to make a collage. Be prepared to explain who each person was and what he or she did to be first.

Use Baseball Math

Use the Internet or a baseball almanac to solve these baseball math problems.

- How many years did Jackie Robinson play in the Major Leagues?
- How many home runs did he hit during his first five years as a Dodger?
- In his first eight years in the majors, how many bases did he steal?

Think of other baseball math problems. Try to stump your friends.

Find Out More

Jackie Robinson was the first African American to play in the National League. But who was the first African American to play in the American League? Which Negro League stars followed these two players into the Major Leagues? Find out the answers in a baseball encyclopedia or a baseball almanac. Then tell a friend what you learned.

Use the Card Catalog: Subject Card

Where would you look if you wanted to find a book about the Negro Leagues? The **card catalog** in the library is a good place to start. Each book in the library has an **author card**, a **title card**, and a **subject card**. Some libraries have card catalogs that are alphabetically arranged in drawers. Other libraries let you search the card catalog by computer. For a book about baseball, you would look at a subject card. The **call number** at the top of the card tells you where to find the book on the library shelf.

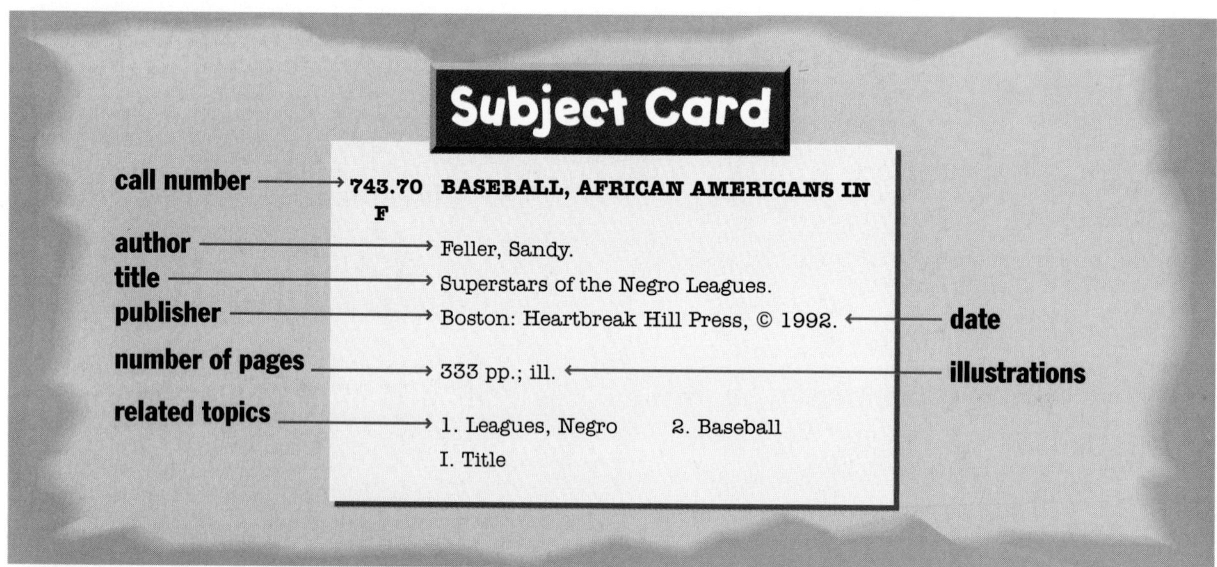

Use the subject card to answer these questions.

1. What is the subject of the book?
2. What is the title?
3. Who is the author?
4. How many pages does the book have?
5. How would you use the call number at the top of the card?

TEST POWER

Test Tip

An OPINION is based on someone's feelings.

DIRECTIONS

Read the sample story. Then read each question about the story.

SAMPLE

Time for New Trees

"Dad, must all the trees be cut down?" Barbara asked.

Barbara's father had just finished explaining why the trees would be cut down that day. They were all elm trees, and they all had Dutch elm disease. The disease would spread to all the other elm trees in the city if the infected trees were not removed right away.

"Unfortunately, there is nothing that can be done to save them," her father said.

"Maybe we'll feel better if we plant some new trees," Barbara suggested brightly. "How about if we go over to the university and ask for some recommendations from the tree specialist?"

1 Why were the elm trees being cut down?

A They put in a sidewalk.

B The trees had a disease.

C They planted new trees.

D Barbara likes trees.

2 Which is an OPINION in this passage?

F Barbara will feel better if they plant new trees.

G Barbara and her father will visit the university.

H The infected trees will make the other trees sick.

J The trees are elm trees.

Imagination is as important to an artist as it is to a writer. Both use their imagination to get ideas.

Look at the painting. What does it remind you of? Is this a picture of a royal person? Does she live in a palace? How do you know? What can you tell about the bird? Is it sick? If so, how might the woman help it to get well?

Look at the painting again. Notice the writing in the borders. Imagine that you could read these words. Do you think they would tell you the story shown in the painting? Why or why not?

Lady Feeding a Bird
Early Seventeenth Century, Deccan
Bijapur, India, Chester Beatty Library, Dublin

Meet
Alma Flor Ada

By the time she was in fourth grade, Alma Flor Ada knew that she would be a writer someday. She says, "I couldn't accept the fact that we had to read such boring textbooks while my wonderful storybooks awaited at home." As a result, she decided to devote her life to making schoolbooks that would be fun. "Since then," she says, she has been "having a lot of fun doing just that!"

Ada was born in Cuba, but she has also lived in Spain and Peru. Today, she makes her home in San Francisco, California. She admits that her four children inspire her writing. They help in other ways, too. One of her greatest joys is that her daughter has translated many of her books, some into English and some into Spanish. For Ada, knowing two languages has made her world richer. She is happy that it has also enriched her daughter's life. In fact, Ada believes that all students should be given the chance to learn two or more languages.

Meet
Leonid Gore

Leonid Gore is proud of his illustrations in *The Malachite Palace*. Although the work was a challenge, it wasn't much different from the work he had done on more than fifty children's books in his native country. Born and raised in the former Soviet Union, Gore moved to the United States in 1990. Over the years, he has developed a light and delicate style of painting. This style is perfect for the fairy-tale feeling in *The Malachite Palace*.

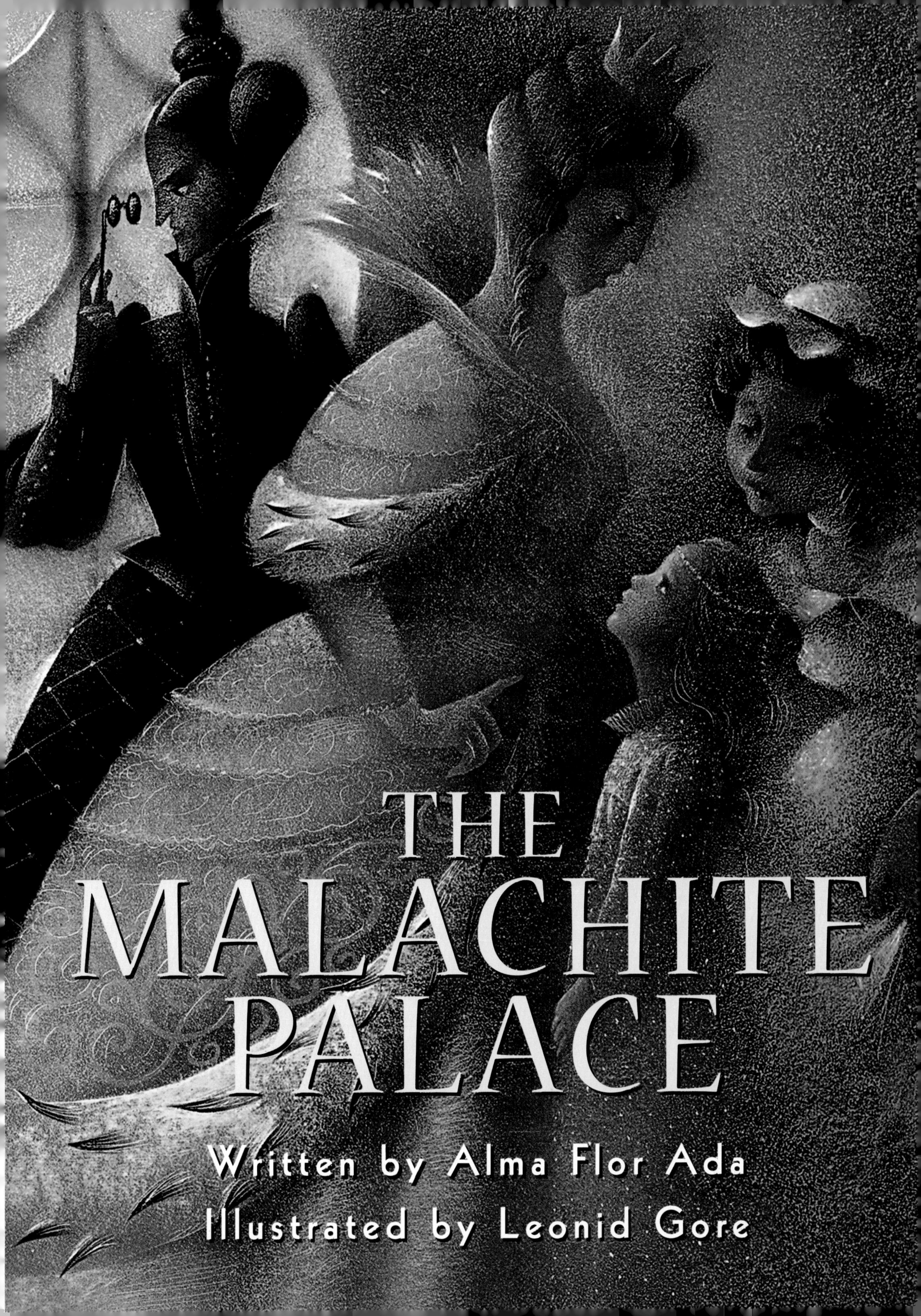

THE MALACHITE PALACE

Written by Alma Flor Ada

Illustrated by Leonid Gore

There once was a princess who lived in a malachite palace. She had everything she could possibly want. Everything, that is, except for a friend.

On the other side of ornate iron gates, many children laughed and played in the fields beyond the palace. But neither the lady-in-waiting, all dressed in white, nor the governess, all dressed in black—and much less the queen, all dressed in gold—would have thought, even for a moment, that the princess could be allowed to play with the other children.

"Those children are rude!"

"Those children are ignorant!"

"Those children are common!" they would say, as if in a chorus.

And so the princess always kept the windows of her room in the malachite palace tightly closed so that the voices of the children playing in the open fields would not reach her. Perhaps she had come to believe what her elders said about those children; or perhaps she just didn't want to be reminded of how happy the children sounded as they scampered about.

One windy morning in early spring, the princess heard a *tap, tap, tap* at her window. She looked and saw a cherry branch, heavy with blossoms. When she opened the window to reach the flowers, a little bird flew into the room.

It was a tiny yellow bird, with bright black eyes. And when he opened his beak to sing, a light and joyful music filled the palace.

"Quickly, quickly!" cried the princess as she closed the window. "Come catch him, come catch him!"

The lady-in-waiting appeared immediately with a towel in hand, while the governess hastily took off her black shawl. Between the two of them, they soon captured the tiny bird and locked him in a silver cage.

"What a rare and precious bird!" said the queen. "It's very fitting that he chose to come to my princess."

"How cultured," said the governess.

"How elegant," said the lady-in-waiting.

The princess wanted very much to hear the bird sing again. But many days went by, and the tiny bird did not let forth even a small warble.

"I'm sure that he knows how to sing," said the princess. "The day we caught him, he sang beautifully."

"Let's bring him chocolate," said the lady-in-waiting.

"Or caviar," suggested the governess.

"Let's gild his silver cage," ordered the queen. "He will certainly sing for us once he has a golden cage."

But in spite of all their efforts, the little bird remained silent.

Maybe he needs some air, thought the princess. *Perhaps he misses the fragrance of the flowers. . . .* So she opened the window and placed the birdcage on her balcony. When she did this, the bird began to sing once more. But his song was sad and feeble, unlike the joyful song he had brought with him when he first arrived.

Since the window was now kept open, the little princess could once again hear the sounds of the children playing in the fields. And she noticed that each time the children laughed, the bird would perk up a little, and his song became brighter. Sometimes when the bird sang, the children would peek into the palace gardens through the iron fence.

"How unseemly!" said the lady-in-waiting.

"How ill-mannered!" complained the governess.

"I'll put a stop to it!" announced the queen. And she ordered vines planted inside the iron fence. Soon the vines grew thick and tall, and the children's faces could no longer be seen, nor their laughter heard, from inside the palace.

When summer came, the vines grew even thicker. In the fall, the leaves changed color, and the palace seemed to be surrounded by walls of fire. Meanwhile, the tiny bird's song was becoming sadder and quieter every day. Finally, it stopped altogether.

The princess tried everything she could think of to cheer him up. She told the bird the story of how his beautiful cage, a gift from a faraway emperor, had arrived at the palace balanced atop a tower of presents all carried by a white elephant. She hummed her favorite lullaby, and offered him dry dates and figs. But the bird remained silent.

As the days grew colder, the princess moved the cage with the silent bird indoors. One morning, after all the leaves from the vines had fallen, the princess opened the door to the balcony. *Maybe if the bird sees the sky and fields again, he'll want to sing once more,* she thought. As she stood with the cage on the balcony, she heard the voices of the children playing outside the gates. They shouted and laughed as they slid over the snow with their sleds, and built a large snowman with a full, round face.

The princess listened to the children's voices, longing to join them. Then without knowing quite why, she opened the door to the cage and let the tiny yellow bird fly away.

For many days, the princess looked and looked at the empty cage, and listened to the sounds of the children as they played in the snow.

One morning, she woke up and saw frost covering the window. The princess called out for a lackey: "Quickly, quickly, I need some tools!"

And then the little princess, who had never before held a needle, a thimble, nor even a pair of scissors in her hands, began to work with the tools. Clumsily at first, and then more confidently, she managed to unhinge the delicate door of the cage. Next, she unfastened some of the bars from the other side. Now the cage resembled an open archway.

Then the princess said:

"Quickly, quickly, I want sunflower seeds, and millet, and nuts!"

And she filled the open cage with food, and placed it on the balcony.

That afternoon, as the setting sun turned the snow into a crimson blanket, the princess saw many hungry birds pecking at the seeds. In the midst of the bright red cardinals, the feisty blue jays, the brown-and-white chickadees, and the soft gray sparrows stood the tiny yellow bird.

"You've come back!" she cried. "And you've brought your friends."

The yellow bird took a sunflower seed in his beak and flew back over the iron fence.

The princess watched him fly away. The laughter of the children playing outside seemed more joyful than ever. She ran to the palace fence and opened the ornate gates.

And when the lady-in-waiting, in her starched white coif, the governess, in her black silk dress, and the queen, in her gold evening gown, said:

"You can't play with those children. They are rude!"

"And ignorant!"

"And common!"

The little princess answered:

"That's not true! That's not true! That's not true!"

Then she ran into the fields beyond the iron gates. There her laughter mingled with the laughter of the other children, while the yellow bird, perched on a leafless vine, sang louder and more sweetly than it ever had before.

Story Questions & Activities

1. Where does the princess live?
2. How is the princess's problem like the bird's?
3. How does the princess solve the bird's problem? How does she solve her own loneliness? What makes them both good solutions?
4. What is this fairy tale about?
5. Imagine that the princess is the woman in the painting on pages 632–633. How do you think she would feel about the bird in the picture?

Write a Nature Report

The princess put food out for hungry birds. Write a report about a bird that winters in your area. Tell where it nests, what it eats, and how it raises its young.

Create a Pet-care Book

Write a short book explaining how to care for a pet. First, select the pet. Then include tips on diet, health, exercise, grooming, and other important pet-care "musts." Include a pet-care cartoon, a photograph, or a drawing of the pet.

Design a Bird Cage

The bird in the story became sadder and sadder and even stopped singing. Design and draw a bird cage that you think would make a bird happy. Use a piece of construction paper or oaktag. Include the perch, water dish, feeder, bird toys, and other special features.

Find Out More

The word *malachite* is used only in the title and in the first line of the story. What is *malachite*? What does it look like? Where is it found? What is it used for? Start by looking in an encyclopedia. Use the answers to these questions and others to make a list of facts about malachite.

Use the Card Catalog: Author and Title Cards

A library **card catalog** helps you find books. The catalog includes title cards, author cards, and subject cards, all arranged alphabetically. **Author cards** help you find a book written by a certain author. **Title cards** help you find a book by the book's title. You can also find the card catalog on computer.

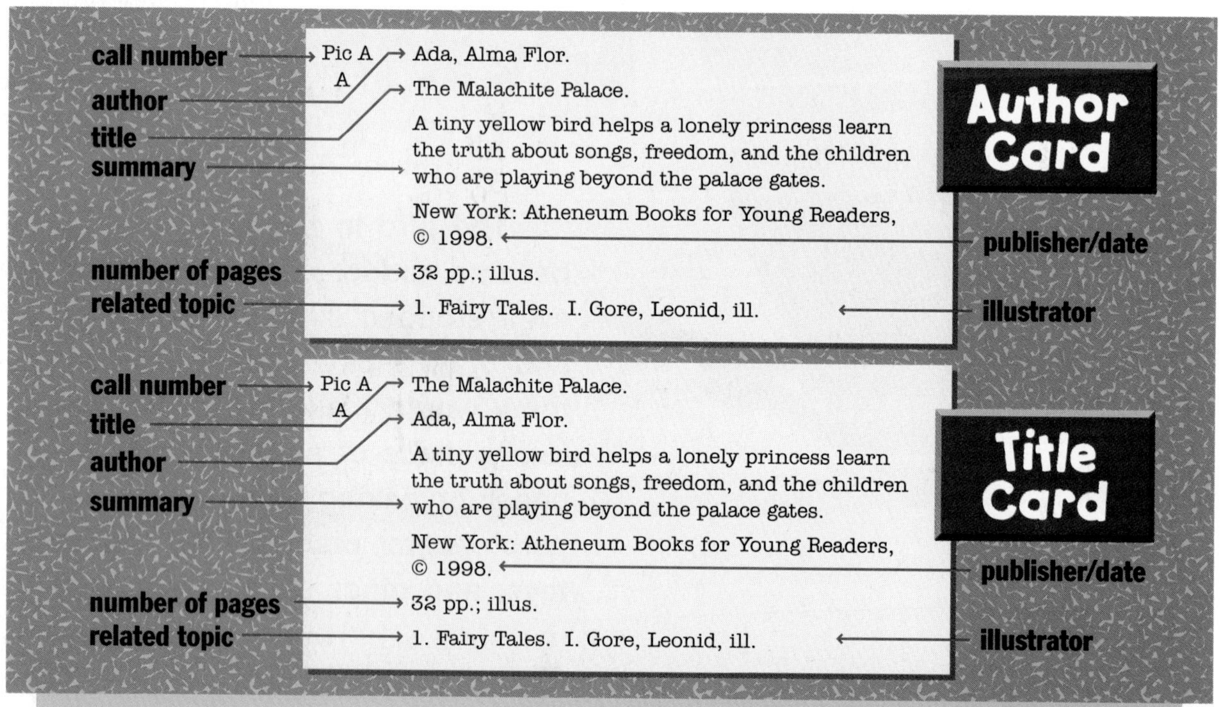

Use the cards above to answer these questions.

1. If you knew the book's author, which card would you use?
2. When would you use the title card?
3. Is *The Malachite Palace* a new book? Explain.
4. Does Alma Flor Ada's book have pictures? How do you know?
5. Why is it important to know how to use the card catalog?

TEST POWER

Test Tip

Read the directions first.

DIRECTIONS

Read the sample story. Then read each question about the story.

SAMPLE

Carlos Shovels Snow

Carlos stomped the snow off his boots. He was hot and frustrated. He came into the kitchen, tossed his hat onto the chair, and started removing his boots. His Aunt Teri finished pouring a cup of coffee and asked, "Is something bothering you?"

"I'm already exhausted from shoveling snow, and I just started half an hour ago! I was supposed to walk to the movies to meet Doug, but now I'll never arrive there in time."

"Well, put your boots back on and I'll drive you to town. You can finish shoveling after the movie," said Aunt Teri.

1 Why was Carlos frustrated at the beginning of the story?

- **A** He doesn't like his Aunt Teri.
- **B** He was going to be late for the movie.
- **C** He forgot to meet his friend Doug.
- **D** He did not want to see a movie.

2 The story takes place—

- **F** at school
- **G** in the driveway
- **H** in the kitchen
- **J** at the mall

This photograph shows a scene from an old silent film. Movies—old and new—often show characters making important decisions.

Look at this picture from the film *Modern Times*. What can you tell about the film? What is the character, played by Charlie Chaplin, deciding to do? Is he trying to help his coworker who is caught in the gears? Do you think Chaplin is trying to stop the machine? Explain your reasons. What might the filmmaker be saying about "man and machine" in the modern world?

Look at the picture again. How can you tell that this movie was made a long time ago? If you were to make this movie today, what machine would you use? Explain why.

Scene from
***Modern Times*, 1936**

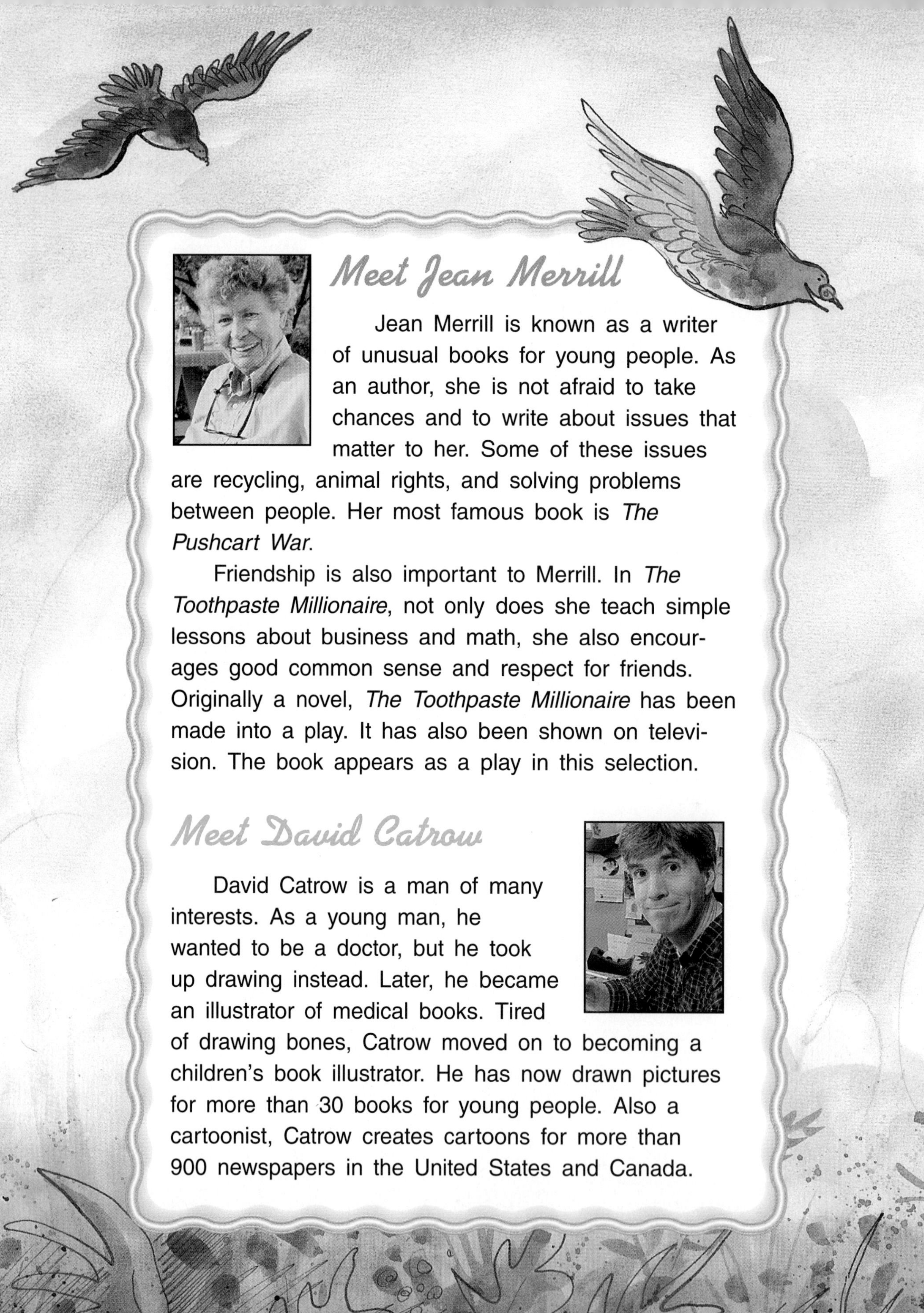

Meet Jean Merrill

Jean Merrill is known as a writer of unusual books for young people. As an author, she is not afraid to take chances and to write about issues that matter to her. Some of these issues are recycling, animal rights, and solving problems between people. Her most famous book is *The Pushcart War*.

Friendship is also important to Merrill. In *The Toothpaste Millionaire*, not only does she teach simple lessons about business and math, she also encourages good common sense and respect for friends. Originally a novel, *The Toothpaste Millionaire* has been made into a play. It has also been shown on television. The book appears as a play in this selection.

Meet David Catrow

David Catrow is a man of many interests. As a young man, he wanted to be a doctor, but he took up drawing instead. Later, he became an illustrator of medical books. Tired of drawing bones, Catrow moved on to becoming a children's book illustrator. He has now drawn pictures for more than 30 books for young people. Also a cartoonist, Catrow creates cartoons for more than 900 newspapers in the United States and Canada.

The Toothpaste Millionaire

Written by Jean Merrill

Dramatized by Susan Nanus

Illustrated by David Catrow

***R**ufus Mayflower was a young man with ideas who became a millionaire. He didn't set out to build a successful enterprise. He just had the initiative to put his ideas, himself, and his friends to work. Rufus became quite a celebrity. In this play, he is being interviewed by talk-show host Joe Smiley.*

CHARACTERS

Joe Smiley
Rufus Mayflower
Kate MacKinstrey
Mr. Conti
Clem
Josie
Lee Lu
James
Auctioneer
Customer #1
Customer #2
Customer #3
Hector
Josh
Sharon
Members of the Class
Mr. Perkell
Mr. Perkell's Secretary

A long bench is set up across the center of the stage. A large portable chalkboard is behind the bench. Downstage left is a long table with several bowls on it. Downstage right is a smaller table and two chairs. As the curtain opens, JOE SMILEY and RUFUS are seated at the small table.

JOE: Welcome to the Joe Smiley Show! Today we have a fantastic young guest who has used his fantastic young brain to become a millionaire! Meet Rufus Mayflower of East Cleveland, Ohio. ***(to Rufus)*** Welcome, Rufus!

RUFUS: Thank you, Mr. Smiley.

JOE: Now, Rufus, my first question is one that I know everyone wants to ask. How did you figure out how to make so much money?

RUFUS: Well, I wasn't trying to make money, just to make toothpaste.

JOE: All right, Rufus. What gave you that brilliant idea?

RUFUS: It all started when I was doing some shopping for my mother at the Cut-Rate Drugstore with my friend Kate.

(KATE comes out and stands in the middle of the stage. RUFUS joins her. KATE pantomimes pushing a shopping cart, while RUFUS pulls out a list.)

RUFUS: Now, let's see. I need toothpaste.

KATE: Here it is.

(She pretends to hand him a tube.)

RUFUS: One dollar and thirty-nine cents for a six-inch tube of toothpaste? That's crazy!

KATE: It's better than this other one for a dollar and eighty-nine cents.

RUFUS: That's even crazier! What can be in those tubes, anyway? Just some peppermint flavoring and some paste.

KATE: Maybe the paste is expensive to make.

RUFUS: Who knows? I never tried, but I bet it isn't hard. Put that tube back.

KATE: But Rufus, your mother said to get toothpaste. You can't help it if it's expensive.

RUFUS: I'll make her some. I bet I can make her a gallon for less than a dollar.

(KATE goes and sits on the bench. RUFUS returns to the small table to continue the interview with Joe Smiley.)

JOE: Fantastic! I suppose you stayed up day and night creating your secret formula.

RUFUS: No, I just used some stuff anybody can buy for a few cents and mix up in a few minutes. The main ingredient was plain old baking soda.

JOE: What happened next?

RUFUS: The next morning, Kate stopped by on the way to school.

(RUFUS goes over to the long table with the bowls. KATE joins him.)

KATE: What are you making?

RUFUS: I already made it.

(He hands KATE a spoonful.)

Don't eat it. Rub a little on your teeth.

(KATE tries some.)

KATE: What's in here?

RUFUS: A drop of peppermint oil. I've got enough for forty tubes of toothpaste here!

KATE: Wow! Wait until we tell the kids at school! Come on, Rufus.

(KATE and RUFUS hurry to the bench and sit down. CLEM, JOSIE, and LEE LU come out and join them. They face MR. CONTI, their math teacher, at the chalkboard.)

MR. CONTI: All right, class, take out your math books.

(RUFUS passes a note to CLEM, who hands it to JOSIE, who hands it to LEE LU, who hands it to KATE. KATE opens the note.)

MR. CONTI: Kate MacKinstrey, would you please bring me that note?

KATE: Well, it's not exactly a note, Mr. Conti.

MR. CONTI: I see. I suppose it's a math problem.

KATE: It looks like a math problem, Mr. Conti.

MR. CONTI: ***(reading)*** There are about 226 million people in the United States. Each one buys about ten tubes of toothpaste a year. That's two billion two-hundred-sixty million tubes of toothpaste a year! If an inventor made a new toothpaste, sold only *one* billion tubes, and made a one-cent profit on each tube, how much would he make? ***(looking up)*** Well, class, what would you do to figure it out?

CLEM: You'd have to take one billion times one cent or .01. That comes out to . . .

ALL: Ten million dollars!

JOSIE: Did you invent a toothpaste, Rufus?

CLEM: What's it called?

LEE LU: How much does it cost?

MR. CONTI: All right, class, quiet down.

(RUFUS gets up and goes back to sit at the small table with JOE SMILEY.)

RUFUS: I called it *Toothpaste.*

JOE: Not *Sparkle* or *Shine?*

RUFUS: No. Just plain *Toothpaste.* Kate and I packed it into sterilized baby jars, and we delivered them to customers on our bikes.

JOE: How much did you charge?

RUFUS: It cost me two cents to make, so I charged three cents unless I had to mail it somewhere out of town. Then I included postage. In a couple of months, I had so many customers that my math class had to help me out.

(RUFUS, KATE, CLEM, JOSIE, and LEE LU go over to the long table with the bowls. They pantomime filling the jars with toothpaste.)

CLEM: Rufus, what would you do if you had to pay us to do all this work?

JOSIE: We spend hours washing out baby jars and filling them with *Toothpaste*.

RUFUS: I don't have any profits to pay anybody yet. I've got to use the money I'm making to buy more stuff for *Toothpaste*. But I'll tell you what. I'll give you stock in my company.

CLEM: Stock? What good is that?

RUFUS: At the end of the year, every stockholder will get a share of the year's profits.

KATE: Like in that game you have called "Stock Market"?

RUFUS: Right. Anybody who puts in a hundred hours helping me make *Toothpaste* gets a stock certificate, which will entitle him or her to a share of the company's profits. I'll use the stock certificates from my game.

KATE: Well, I've already worked here more than two hundred hours.

RUFUS: So you are the first stockholder.

(RUFUS returns to JOE SMILEY to continue the interview.)

JOE: This is mind-boggling! What happened next?

RUFUS: The next part of the story belongs to Kate.

(KATE talks to LEE LU, CLEM, and JOSIE who are still working at the long table.)

KATE: You know, I wish we had real tubes instead of these baby jars.

LEE LU: It sure would look better.

KATE: I wonder if I can find any.

CLEM: I bet they'd be expensive even if you could.

KATE: I'm going to start looking around. ***(She looks at her watch.)*** Oh, oh, I have to get home for supper. See you tomorrow.

(KATE leaves the long table and goes back to the bench. Her brother, JAMES, comes out reading a newspaper and sits on the bench.)

KATE: Hi, James.

JAMES: Don't bother me, I'm reading.

KATE: Well, excuse me! I don't call that reading. It's just another list of companies going out of business.

JAMES: It can be very informative. Now, let's see . . . ***(reads)*** . . . Complete furnishings of ice cream parlor . . . Ferris wheel swings . . . 15 trailer trucks . . . 50 gross high-quality aluminum tubes . . .

KATE: Did you say *tubes*? Let me see. ***(She looks at the paper.)*** It doesn't give the price.

JAMES: Of course not. You have to go to the auction and bid on them.

KATE: An auction? Where?

JAMES: At Pulaski Brothers Warehouse. Somebody with a lot of tubes just went out of business.

(JAMES walks off. KATE goes behind the bench. Several CUSTOMERS come on stage and stand near KATE at the auction. The AUCTIONEER comes out and faces the CUSTOMERS and KATE.)

AUCTIONEER: Item Number 76: aluminum tubes, 50 gross. How much am I bid by the gross? Bidder takes the lot.

KATE: How much is a gross? I can't remember. Let's see 50 dozen is 600 and that's already a lot. ***(to AUCTIONEER)*** Excuse me, sir. Can I just bid on a couple of dozen?

AUCTIONEER: The bid is for the whole lot. Who'll bid five cents a gross?

CUSTOMER #1: Five cents!

KATE: Six cents!

AUCTIONEER: Six cents for the lady.

CUSTOMER #2: Seven cents!

KATE: Eight! We really need those tubes.

AUCTIONEER: Anyone for nine?

KATE: TEN!

CUSTOMER #1: I give up.

CUSTOMER #2: Me, too.

AUCTIONEER: Sold to the lady for ten cents a gross.

KATE: Oh, well, I guess we'll use up six hundred tubes.

CUSTOMER #3: Six hundred? You just bought seven thousand two hundred tubes.

KATE: Seven thousand two hundred!

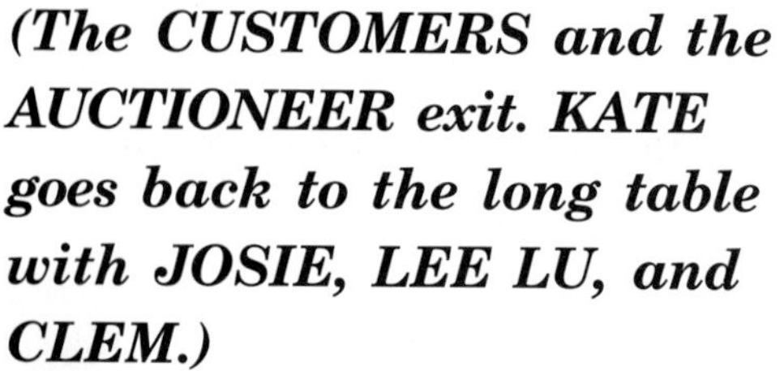

(The CUSTOMERS and the AUCTIONEER exit. KATE goes back to the long table with JOSIE, LEE LU, and CLEM.)

KATE: I forgot that a gross is a dozen dozen. Twelve times twelve times fifty is what I bought.

LEE LU: Isn't there some kind of machine for filling tubes?

CLEM: What about the place that all these tubes came from?

KATE: Let's see if there's a name on the box. ***(She pantomimes looking at a box and reads:)*** Happy Lips Lotion Company. I am going to the Happy Lips Lotion Company to check it out.

(HECTOR comes out on stage. He moves away the bench and brings the chalkboard downstage. He flips the chalkboard around to display a diagram of a complicated machine.)

(KATE comes up to HECTOR.)

HECTOR: Can I help you?

KATE: No thank you. I'm just looking.

HECTOR: Oh?

KATE: For a machine. I have a friend who needs a certain kind of machine for filling toothpaste tubes.

HECTOR: Did you say toothpaste tubes?

KATE: Like this.

(She pulls out a tube and shows it to him.)

HECTOR: Oh. Sure, that's the Number 5 aluminum round-end.

KATE: Are you in the toothpaste business?

HECTOR: No. I was a mechanic for the Happy Lips Lotion Company. Is *your* friend in the toothpaste business?

KATE: Yes. Is there a tube-filling machine still in there?

HECTOR: Is there! It's the most beautiful piece of machinery you ever saw.

(HECTOR shows KATE the machine on the chalkboard.)

HECTOR: The Happy Lips Lotion Company owed the owner of the building so much rent that they had to leave him this machine. The owner is paying me a small salary to keep an eye on the factory.

KATE: It looks like a wonderful machine.

HECTOR: Yes, ma'am. If your friend rented the place and hired me to look after the machinery, we could be in full production tomorrow. Have you got a lot of orders?

KATE: More than five thousand.

HECTOR: Do you think you can swing it? The rent's about three-hundred dollars a month.

KATE: The rent? Oh. I forgot about that. And how much would *you* want, Hector?

HECTOR: I was getting eight dollars an hour from Happy Lips. I guess that much would be fine.

KATE: Hmm. I think we better have a stockholders' meeting.

(The interview continues. RUFUS is talking with JOE SMILEY.)

RUFUS: So we all got together and discussed it. By now, we had a lot of other kids working with us, too.

(CLEM, JOSIE, and LEE LU remove the bowls from the table. They bring in chairs. KATE and RUFUS each sit at one end of the long table. CLEM, JOSIE, LEE LU, JOSH, SHARON, and other MEMBERS OF THE CLASS sit around the sides.)

RUFUS: Let's see, I'd say we need about $15,000.

LEE LU: Well, where do we get that? Just walk into a bank and ask for it?

RUFUS: Why not? Isn't that what other business people do? I'll just go down to Everybody's Friendly Bank and borrow the money!

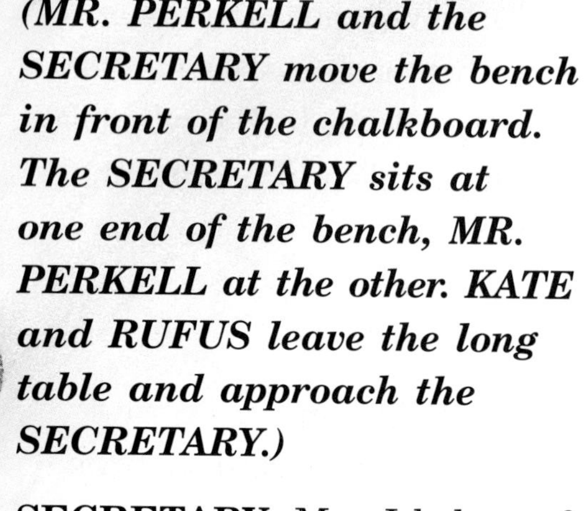

(MR. PERKELL and the SECRETARY move the bench in front of the chalkboard. The SECRETARY sits at one end of the bench, MR. PERKELL at the other. KATE and RUFUS leave the long table and approach the SECRETARY.)

SECRETARY: May I help you?

RUFUS: Yes, we'd like to see Mr. Perkell, the Vice President, please.

SECRETARY: I'm sorry, Mr. Perkell has an appointment at four o'clock.

RUFUS: I know. My name is Rufus Mayflower, and I'm Mr. Perkell's appointment.

SECRETARY: *You're* Mr. Mayflower?

MR. PERKELL: ***(comes to the SECRETARY'S end of the bench)*** Hello. What can I do for you?

RUFUS: You can lend us money for the business I'm starting. I have a product called *Toothpaste.*

MR. PERKELL: Ah, yes, I've heard of you. Just plain toothpaste, the kind that gets your teeth clean.

KATE: That's us! Can you lend us the money?

MR. PERKELL: I'm afraid not.

KATE: Why not? Your commercials say you lend money to everybody.

MR. PERKELL: Well, not exactly *everybody*.

RUFUS: In other words, not kids.

(MR. PERKELL and the SECRETARY walk off. RUFUS and KATE go back to the long table. HECTOR brings a chair and joins them.)

HECTOR: I can't believe it! Just because you're under age, they turn you down! We have the machine. We have the product. We can make it big!

RUFUS: I believe you, Hector. I believe you would even lend me the money, if you had it.

HECTOR: You bet I would!

RUFUS: Great! Hector, you can go to Mr. Perkell and ask him to lend you the money.

HECTOR: Me?

RUFUS: I'll hire you as manager of the toothpaste factory. The money you borrow will be used to pay your first year's salary, to pay the rent, and to buy more tubes. I'll also give you shares of stock in the company.

HECTOR: You mean I'd own part of the business? That would be beautiful!

(RUFUS goes back and sits with JOE SMILEY.)

JOE: Absolutely fantastic! And did you get the money?

RUFUS: We sure did. Then we had to find more customers. So we decided to advertise. My friend Lee Lu had a movie camera, so we all got together and decided to create the Absolutely Honest Commercial.

(CLEM and JOSIE and KATE move stage center. LEE LU is on his knees in front of them pantomiming shooting a movie camera.)

LEE LU: Okay, action!

CLEM: No fancy names.

JOSIE: No fancy promises.

KATE: All *Toothpaste* claims to do is clean your teeth.

CLEM: We make it as cheaply as possible so we don't have to charge you very much.

KATE: That's why *Toothpaste* comes in a plain cardboard box. All to keep the prices low.

JOSIE: We only make a one-cent profit on a tube, but we think it does the job as well as the more expensive kinds.

LEE LU: CUT!

(JOE SMILEY continues the interview with RUFUS.)

JOE: How big is this business now?

RUFUS: Let's put it this way. We had to order three more machines and hire ten people to work full time.

JOE: Fantastic! Well, Rufus, it looks like you really are a *Toothpaste* Millionaire. What's your next step? Do you have any new ideas up your sleeve?

RUFUS: ***(smiles)*** Not yet. But I'm not worried. All I have to do is walk into another store, or take a ride on my bike, or just keep my eyes and ears open and my brain working. Something will come to me.

JOE: Isn't he *fantastic?*

THE END

Story Questions & Activities

1. Why does Rufus decide to make his own toothpaste?
2. Why is Rufus's company so successful?
3. How do you know that Rufus is a good businessman? Explain.
4. What did you think of this play? Give reasons.
5. Imagine that Rufus had a chance to act in the movie shown on pages 664–665. Do you think he would want to play the "Charlie Chaplin" character in the picture? Why or why not?

Write a Business Report

What idea will Rufus think of next? Choose a product that might interest him. Investigate: find out how much the product costs and how it is made. Who buys this product and why? Write a report on what you discover. Include ideas for making a similar product better and cheaper.

Brush Up on Your Math

Rufus charged three cents for each tube of Toothpaste. How much would he have to charge if he wanted to double his profits? Triple them? If Rufus wanted to mark up Toothpaste by 100%, how much would he charge? By 1000%?

Take a Poll

Toothpaste comes in many different sizes, packages, flavors, and brands. Take a poll of 10 people. Ask them which brand of toothpaste they buy, and why. Report your findings in the form of a graph or a chart.

Find Out More

In the story, Rufus figures out that two billion two-hundred-sixty million tubes of toothpaste are sold in the United States each year. What makes people buy so much toothpaste? Why do people need to brush their teeth? Start by asking your dentist. Then look in an encyclopedia or a dentist's pamphlet. Create a poster of toothpaste facts.

Use an Online Library Catalog

Rufus has become a millionaire. He can learn more about money in the library. Most libraries have their catalog on computer. You can use the **online library catalog** to search for a book by title, author's name, or subject. The screens below show how to do an author search.

Welcome to the Online Public Access Catalog

SEARCH

Press A to search by AUTHOR'S NAME

Press B to search by TITLE

Press C to search by SUBJECT

Press A–C or a Command Key

AUTHOR SEARCH

Please type in the AUTHOR'S NAME that you are searching for below, and press the Return Key.

You must enter the author's last name first.

AUTHOR: Wesley, Jan

AUTHOR SCREEN

AUTHOR SEARCH: Wesley, Jan

Wesley, Jan–1944–A Child's History of Money

CALL NUMBER: 332W

AUTHOR: Wesley, Jan, 1944-

TITLE: A Child's History of Money/by Jan Wesley; illustrated by Ricky Smith; 99pp; ill. 23cm.

PUBLISHED: New York: Big Buck Books, © 2000
The story of money all over the world, from prehistoric times to the present.

LIBRARY HOLDINGS: at Mainview Branch.
ON SHELF

Use the online library catalog to answer these questions.

1. Who is the author of the book?
2. What is the book's title?
3. How would you enter the author's name?
4. How can you tell if this book is new or not?
5. How would you find a book in the library by using the Author Screen?

TEST POWER

Test Tip

Read all answer choices. Then pick the best one.

DIRECTIONS

Read the sample story. Then read each question about the story.

SAMPLE

The Toucan's Feathers

Even though Tanya was a toucan, she did not have colorful feathers like her parents.

For fun, Tanya would squawk and then hide among the other birds. The other animals couldn't tell who was making the awful sound.

"Who's making that hideous racket?" the animals asked.

One day, Tanya let out another tremendous *squawk*! She tried to hide, but the jungle animals saw her. Tanya's feathers had become brightly colored, like other toucans.

The jungle animals said to Tanya, "With those silly colored feathers you will stand out. Now we will know who makes the awful noise!"

1 In this passage, the word hideous means—

A loud

B horrible

C weird

D clever

2 Why did Tanya squawk?

F She did it for fun.

G She wanted everyone to see her.

H Many birds made noise.

J She wanted to talk to her friends.

Stories in Art

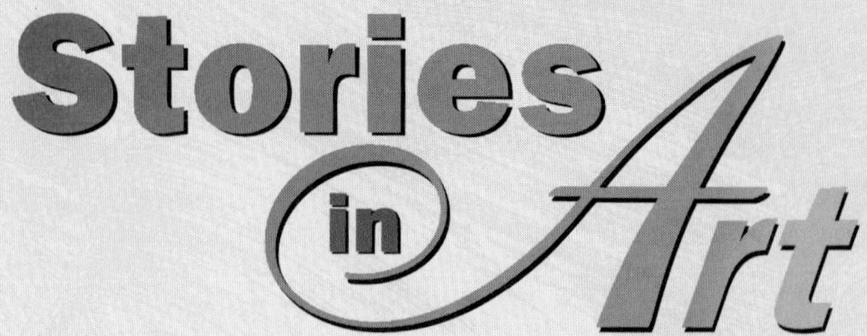

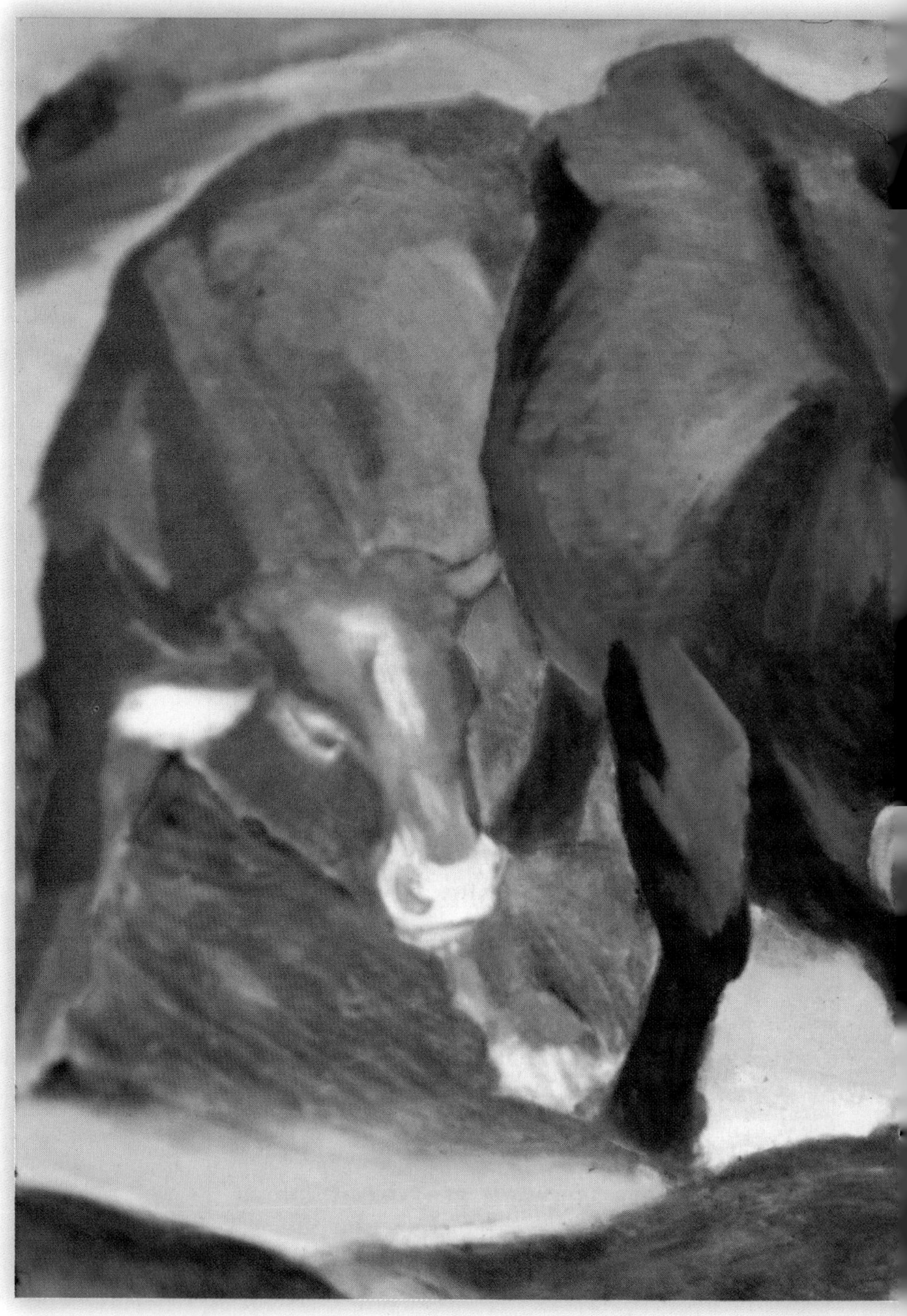

Sometimes artists create artwork so that people can see how things look like each other. Other times they use their art to show differences.

Look at this painting called *Fighting Cows*. Compare the two cows locking horns. How does the artist use line and form to make them seem similar? How does he use color to show their differences?

Look at the painting again. What parts look real? What parts look strange? Why does the artist want to show this ordinary scene in an unusual way?

Fighting Cows by Franz Marc

WHA
By Seymour Simon

LES

Sperm Whale

There are about ninety kinds of whales in the world. Scientists divide them into two main groups: toothed whales and baleen whales.

Toothed whales have teeth and feed mostly on fish and squid. They have only one blowhole and are closely related to dolphins and porpoises.

The **sperm whale** is the only giant among the toothed whales. It is the animal that comes to mind when most people think of a whale. A sperm whale has a huge, squarish head, small eyes, and a thin lower jaw. All the fist-sized teeth, about fifty of them, are in the lower jaw. The male grows to sixty feet long and weighs as much as fifty tons. The female is smaller, reaching only forty feet and weighing less than twenty tons.

A sperm whale's main food is squid, which it catches and swallows whole. A sperm whale is not a very fast swimmer, but it is a champion diver. It dives to depths of a mile in search of giant squid and can stay underwater for more than an hour.

There are smaller and less familiar kinds of toothed whales. The **narwhal** is a leopard-spotted whale about fifteen feet long. It is sometimes called the unicorn whale, because the male narwhal has a single tusk. The tusk is actually a ten-foot-long front left tooth that grows through the upper lip and sticks straight out. No one knows for sure how the narwhal uses its tusk. Narwhals live along the edge of the sea ice in the Arctic.

Narwhals

Perhaps the best known of the toothed whales is the killer whale, or **orca**. That's because there are killer whales that perform in marine parks around the country. A killer whale is actually the largest member of the dolphin family. A male can grow to over thirty feet and weigh nine tons.

Orcas are found in all of the world's oceans, from the poles to the tropics. They hunt for food in herds called pods. Orcas eat fish, squid, and penguins, as well as seals, sea lions, and other sea mammals, including even the largest whales. Yet they are usually gentle in captivity, and there is no record that an orca has ever caused a human death.

Orcas

Baleen whales differ from toothed whales. They have a two-part nostril or blowhole; and, instead of teeth, they have food-gathering baleen plates. Each whale has several hundred baleen plates, which hang down from the whale's upper jaw. The plates can be two to seven feet long and hang about one quarter of an inch apart. The inside edge of each plate is frayed and acts like a filter.

Baleen whales are the biggest whales of all, yet they feed on small fish and other very small sea animals, such as the shrimplike animals called krill. Krill, which are only as big as your little finger, occur in huge amounts in the Antarctic Ocean. In northern waters, baleen whales eat different kinds of small shrimplike animals.

Some baleen whales, such as the right whale, skim open-mouthed through the water. The frayed inner edges of the baleen trap the food animals while the water pours out through the gaps. In this way a right whale can filter thousands of gallons of seawater and swallow two tons of food each day.

The **right whale** was once very common in the North Atlantic Ocean. It was given its name by early whalers who regarded it as the "right whale" to catch, because it swam slowly, had lots of baleen and blubber, and floated when dead. So many right whales were killed that they are now quite rare.

Right whales may reach more than fifty feet and weigh more than seventy tons. They have large flippers and a long lower lip that covers and protects their baleen plates. Each right whale has its own pattern of strange bumps along its head called callosities. Scientists sometimes identify individual whales by the patterns of their callosities.

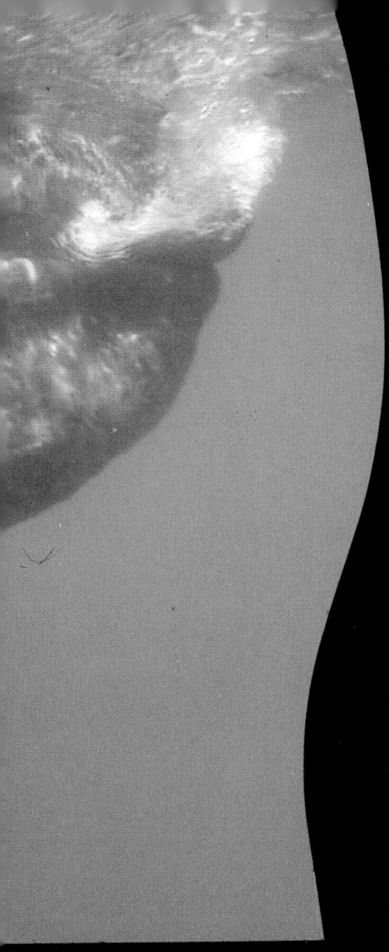

Gray Whales

The **gray whale** feeds differently from the way any other whale does. It swims on its side on the ocean bottom and pushes water out of its mouth between its baleen plates, stirring up sediment from the ocean floor. Then the whale draws back its tongue and sucks the sediment, and any living things around, into its mouth. As the whale rises to the surface, it rinses its mouth with fresh seawater and swallows the catch. This method of bottom feeding is sometimes called "grubbing."

Gray whales once swam, in both the North Atlantic and North Pacific oceans, in the shallow waters along the coasts. Now, because of whaling in the Atlantic, they live only in the North Pacific and Arctic seas.

In the summer, the gray whales feed in the cold waters of the Arctic. In the winter, they travel about ten thousand miles to Mexican waters. There, the females give birth in the warm, protected lagoons along the Baja California peninsula. The journey of the gray whales is the longest known yearly migration for any mammal.

Fin Whale

With its long, streamlined body, its pointed head, and its thin flukes, the **fin whale** has the right shape to be a fast and nimble swimmer—and it is. The long grooves on its throat allow the throat to expand while the whale is feeding. Whales that have these grooves, such as the fin, minke, humpback, and blue, are called rorquals, from the Norwegian word for groove or furrow.

Fin whales often work in pairs to round up and eat schools of fish. Fin whales are second only to blue whales in size. They can reach seventy to nearly ninety feet in length and weigh eighty tons.

The **blue whale** is bigger than the largest dinosaur that ever lived. The largest known dinosaur may have been 100 feet long and weighed 100 tons. But the biggest blue whales are over 110 feet long and weigh more than 150 tons. That's the weight of twenty-five full-grown elephants. The heart of a blue whale is the size of a small car.

A blue whale swims along the surface of the ocean up to a cloud of krill, opens its mouth wide, and sucks in fifty or more tons of water in one gulp. Then it opens its lips and strains out the krill through its baleen plates. In one day a blue whale eats more than four tons of krill, about forty *million* of these animals.

Blue whales have been hunted for many years. Even though they are now protected, only small numbers of blue whales are found in the Antarctic or anywhere else in the world.

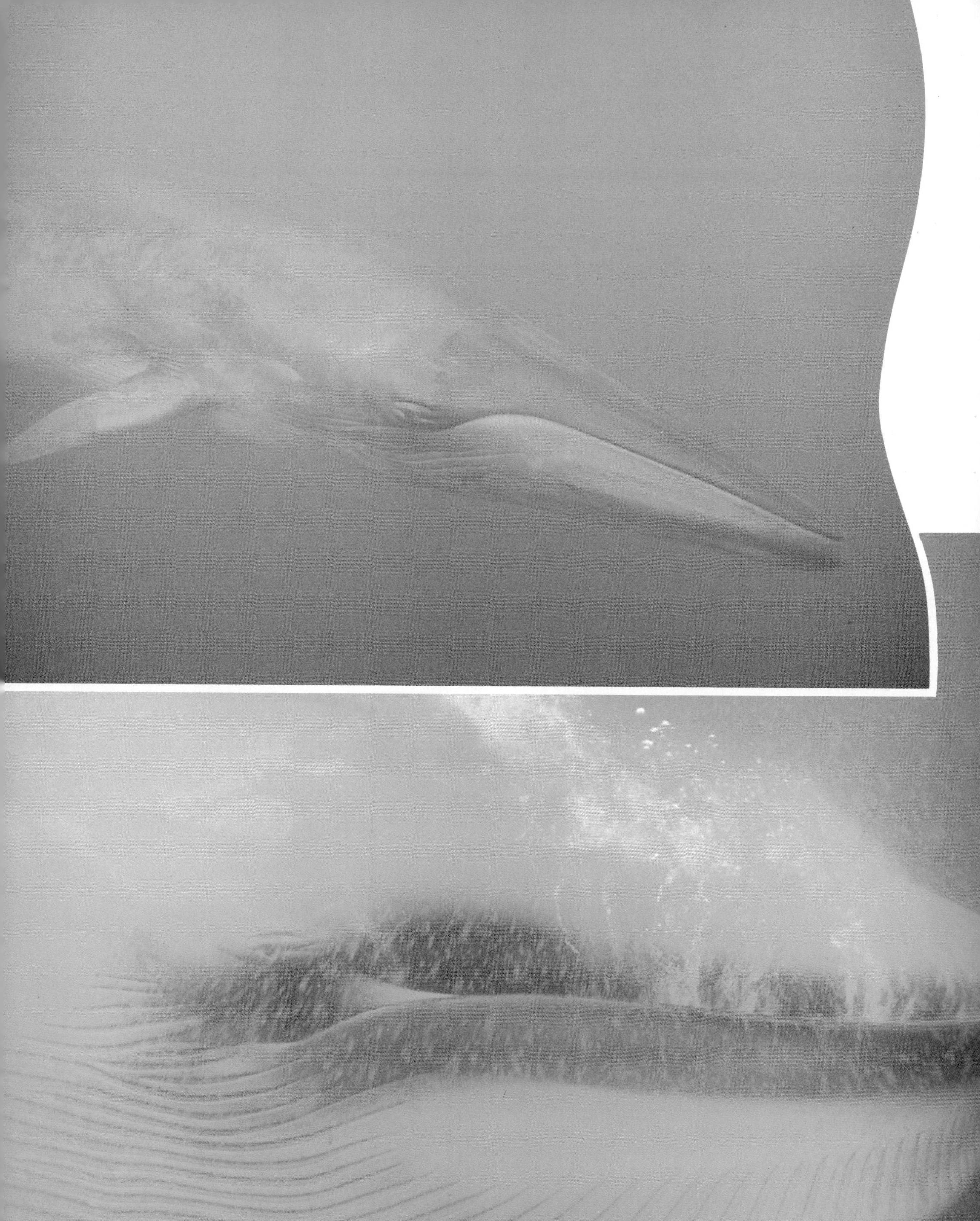

Humpback whales appear to be curious and seem to be accustomed to whale-watching boats. The whales show no hostility to the boats and are careful to avoid collisions.

Many whales make sounds, but the most famous are the songs of the humpbacks. They are sung only by the males. Some scientists think the songs may help to attract females or to keep other males from coming too close.

Whatever the reasons the whales have for singing them, the songs are strange and beautiful. Each one lasts as long as twenty or thirty minutes and is sung over and over again. The songs have patterns that repeat, but are different from one whale to another and from one year to the next. The song of a humpback can be heard from miles away.

Humpbacks feed in different ways. One way is called "bubble netting." A humpback sends out clouds of bubbles in a circle beneath a school of small fish or other food animals. When the fish are trapped by the bubbles, the whale lunges up inside the circle with its mouth open, swallowing huge amounts of water and food. A humpback's throat expands to make lots of room for the food and water. Sometimes several humpbacks feed together in the circle of bubbles.

In 1946, the International Whaling Commission (IWC) was set up to establish rules to limit whaling. Despite the rules, the numbers of whales steadily shrank. Some kinds of whales may be about to become extinct. Because of a worldwide movement to save the whales, the IWC banned all commercial whaling, beginning in 1985. But the governments of a few countries still allow their citizens to hunt whales.

Whales are one of the few wild animals that are commonly friendly to humans they encounter. Many people feel that we have an obligation to preserve these intelligent and special animals.

Will whales be allowed to remain to share the world with us? The choice is ours.

Meet Seymour Simon

From a very young age, Seymour Simon has been fascinated by whales. Simon's interest in the giant creatures has led him on whale watching expeditions from New York to Hawaii, and even to Alaska. "Whales are the greatest things going," he says.

The author of more than one hundred books, Simon has had more than forty of his books named as Outstanding Science Trade Books for Children. To Simon, a former teacher, science is a way of finding out about the world. Many of his books contain projects and questions that help readers find things out for themselves.

Simon enjoys receiving letters from readers who have answered a question using one of his books. For him, sharing a reader's experience is "as much fun as the first time I found out something myself."

Story Questions & Activities

1. What are the two main groups of whales?
2. How are the two main groups of whales alike? What are the differences?
3. Why do we need to save the whales?
4. What is the main idea of this selection?
5. Compare this selection with a movie or a television program about another endangered animal. How are these animals alike? What are people trying to do to help them?

Write an Essay

Dolphins, like whales, are intelligent mammals that live in the ocean. Write an essay about dolphins. Name and describe different kinds of dolphins. Include information about where they can be found and what they eat. Use facts from different sources to support your ideas. Illustrate your essay with photos or drawings. Write a caption for each.

Create a Time Line

Today, laws prevent whaling in most places. Yet whaling played a large role in American history. Create a "history of American whaling" time line. Include these dates and facts.

1600	1650	1700	1750	1800	1850	1900	1950

pre-1600s Native Americans are first American whalers

1600s American colonists begin to hunt whales off the Atlantic

1820 Sperm whaling becomes an important industry

1865 The Civil War destroys sperm-whaling industry

1900 Petroleum is used instead of whale oil for lamps

1925 Whaling industry dies in U.S.

Write a Slogan

Write a slogan, or "catchy" phrase, that urges people to save the whales. First, brainstorm with your classmates to create a list of reasons for protecting these creatures. Then write a slogan about why we should save these gentle giants.

Find Out More

Why should we care if whales disappear? Use an encyclopedia or another reference book to discover the whale's role in the food chain. Use what you learn to tell why it is important for us to save the whales.

Use an Encyclopedia Index

Where would you go to find more information about whales? You might start by checking the index of an encyclopedia. The **encyclopedia index** is the last book, or volume. It helps you find your topic quickly. The index gives you the volume number in which the article appears. It also gives the page number on which the article begins. In addition, an index will tell you if the article has any pictures or tables.

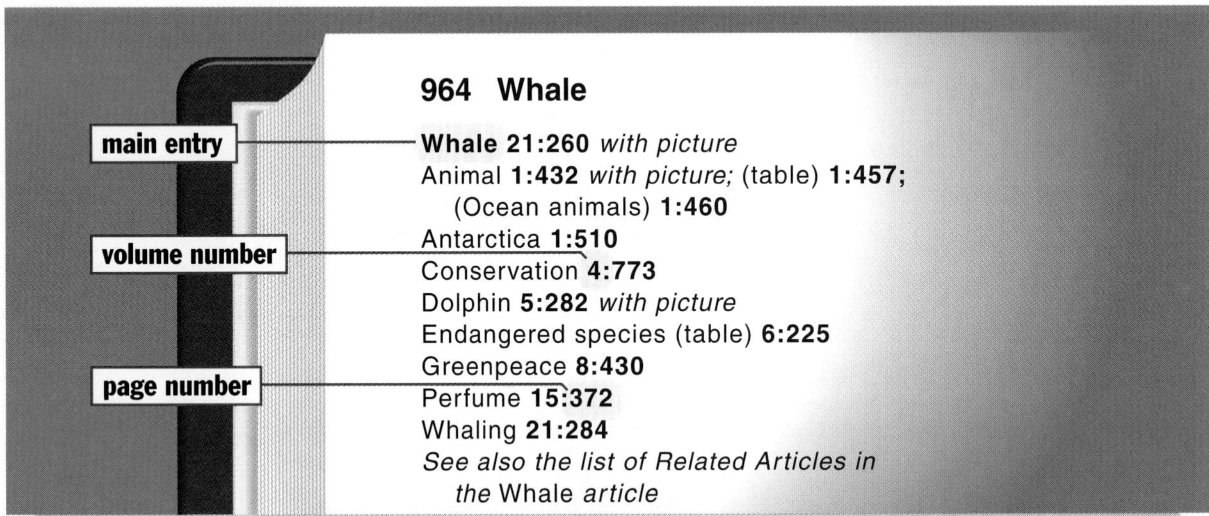

Use the sample index to answer these questions.

1. What is the main entry?
2. In which volume would you find special information about endangered animals?
3. On which page of Volume 5 would you begin to read about dolphins?
4. In which volume would you look to find general information about whales?
5. Why would you use the index of an encyclopedia?

TEST POWER

Test Tip

Answer the question in your own words before looking at the choices.

DIRECTIONS

Read the sample story. Then read each question about the story.

SAMPLE

The Essay

"How I spent my summer vacation" was the topic for Rita's first essay when school resumed. Her two best friends did exciting things during the summer. Shana went to Mexico, and Juan went to Montana. Since Rita didn't go anywhere, she thought that her vacation would sound dull.

During Rita's summer vacation, her Aunt Marta came to visit after Marta had surgery on her wrists. It took several weeks before Marta could even do simple jobs. Rita helped her aunt whenever she could. When Aunt Marta was ready to go home, she gave Rita a silver dollar for all her help. Remembering this gave Rita an excellent idea for her essay.

1 How did Rita feel about Marta?

A Angry

B Jealous

C Caring

D Miserable

2 What will Rita probably do next?

F Write about her trip

G Call her Aunt Marta

H Go back to school

J Write about helping her Aunt Marta

Like scientists, artists observe and study nature. They may even use the natural world to get their message across.

Look at the painting. What causes your eye to move around the picture? What effect does this have? How does it help you take in the whole scene?

Study the painting. How does the artist balance the picture? Does the wildlife seem to fit right into the landscape? What does this say about harmony in nature? What would happen if this balance were disturbed? Could saving the environment be the artist's message? Why or why not?

Caribbean Jungle
by Hilary Simon
Private Collection

TIME FOR KIDS

SPECIAL REPORT

SAVING THE EVERGLADES

Cleaning up pollution in Florida's Everglades means a better future for wildlife there, including baby alligators like this one.

Looking Out for 'Gators

Many of Florida's animals are being protected as the Everglades gets help from humans

Everglades National Park in Florida doesn't look like much from an airplane. A flat, soggy field of tall grass stretches toward the horizon. A few trees dot the landscape under the Florida sun.

But a closer look shows a busy natural world. Hundreds of kinds of animals live in the Everglades. Birds such as egrets and white ibis fly above the water. Lime-green tree frogs croak. Alligators lurk below the swamp's surface.

It's all very beautiful. But the Everglades is in serious trouble. After years of bad planning, the Everglades is dying. Dozens of its many kinds of animals are threatened. Some of its plants and flowers are disappearing. But help for the Everglades and its animals is under way. Humans are rescuing the Everglades and its wildlife from death by pollution.

GEORGIA
Atlantic Ocean
FLORIDA
Gulf of Mexico
Lake Okeechobee
EVERGLADES
Everglades National Park

The swamplike Everglades has been called a "river of grass."

COVER: MARTY CORDANO/DRK PHOTOS; RIGHT: GEORGE KUFRIN/FPG; FAR RIGHT: G.RANDALL/FPG

PEOPLE CAUSED THE PROBLEM

When large numbers of people first moved to Florida more than a century ago, the Everglades was thought to be nothing but swampland. No one paid much attention to the beauty of the area or its importance to the wildlife living there. Builders tried to drain the swamp. Farms and cities sprang up where alligators used to run freely.

In the 1920s, engineers straightened rivers. They built thousands of miles of canals and dikes. They hoped to stop flooding and keep water supplies stable for farms and cities. The plan worked.

But the changes also harmed the Everglades. The area shrank in size by half. Much of the fresh water disappeared. And the numbers of birds, alligators, and other animals shrank, too.

"Everything depends on the water," says Sandy Dayhoff, who works for Everglades National Park. "Not only having enough water, but the right amount at the right time." Dayhoff compares the Everglades to a giant bathtub. In the rainy season, the tub is full. In the dry season, it slowly drains. But humans are getting in the way of both parts of this natural cycle.

CHEMICALS POLLUTE

Farmers have caused another problem. They use fertilizers that help crops grow. But the fertilizers contain chemicals that have changed the balance of park plants. Cattails,

RIGHT: TONY ARRUZA/CORBIS; FAR RIGHT: KEVIN FLEMING/CORBIS

Canals keep flooding under control.

Sugar cane is an important Everglades crop.

Alligator or Crocodile?

American alligators and crocodiles are close cousins. They are both related to 50-foot reptiles that lived millions of years ago. And they look very much alike.

But there are some differences. The easiest way to tell whether the reptile you are looking at is a crocodile or an alligator is to look at the face. The alligator has a broader snout. The crocodile's is pointier. And when a crocodile's mouth is closed, you can see a long tooth sticking out. You can't see that tooth in an alligator when its mouth is closed.

The American crocodile, but not the alligator, is on the endangered list. The Everglades is the only place in the U.S. where alligators and crocodiles live together.

American crocodile

for instance, absorb the chemicals easily. So they are growing like mad. And they are pushing out some native plants, which provide food for the Everglades' animals.

Now everyone is aware of the importance of the Everglades. Farmers are aware of the dangers of the chemicals they are using. And engineers are putting rivers back on their old winding courses. It's a huge project that won't be finished until 2003 or later. In all, billions of dollars will be spent to help the Everglades.

For most people, that is money well spent. "There's no other place like this on Earth," says Dayhoff.

American alligator

CROCODILE: WILLIAM SILLIKER, JR./ANIMALS ANIMALS; ALLIGATOR: GALEN ROWELL/CORBIS

FIND OUT MORE
Visit our website:
www.mhschool.com/reading

*inter***NET**
CONNECTION

Based on an article in *TIME FOR KIDS*.

Story Questions & Activities

1. Where is the Everglades?
2. What is causing the Everglades to "die"?
3. What might happen to the Everglades if steps aren't taken to fix its problems?
4. How would you sum up this article in two sentences?
5. Compare this article with "Whales." How are the articles alike? What are the differences?

Write an Encyclopedia Article

Areas like the Everglades are called wetlands. In many areas, wetlands have been destroyed. Write an encyclopedia article on wetlands. Tell what wetlands are, where they can be found, and why they are important. Be sure to describe some ways people are working to protect wetlands.

Create a Mural

The Everglades is home to "a busy natural world." Make a mural of some of the Everglades' most interesting animals. Find pictures of the animals in magazines or on the Internet. Paste them on a long sheet of paper. Then label each animal under its picture to create a mural of the Everglades.

Write a Song

Write a song about the Everglades. Include lines about what happened to the area and what can be done to save it. Set your words to a tune you know.

Find Out More

The article says that the American crocodile is on the endangered list. What does this mean? Start by doing some research. Find out which other animals in your part of the country are threatened or in danger of disappearing. Share what you learn in a news broadcast to your class.

Use the Internet

When you want more information about a topic, you can search for it on the **Internet**. Below is a **home page** on the Internet for the Everglades National Park. The home page directs you to different topics that you can read by moving your pointer to the topic and clicking. Each topic will lead you to other topics until you find the one you want.

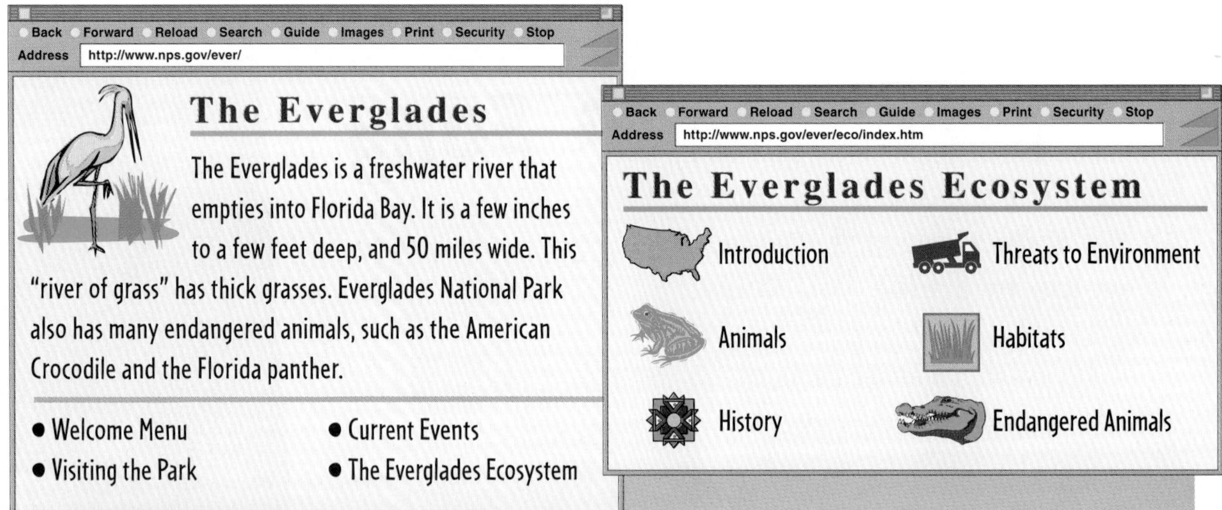

Use the screens above to answer these questions.

1. Which screen gives you the most general information about the park?
2. What would you click on to learn about the Everglades ecosystem?
3. If you wanted to know more about Native Americans in the Everglades, where would you look?
4. How would you find out more about the park's endangered animals?
5. Why would you use the Internet to learn about a topic?

TEST POWER

Test Tip

Rule out wrong answer choices.

DIRECTIONS

Read the sample story. Then read each question about the story.

SAMPLE

How to Make a Lion Mask

What you need: paper plate, scissors, glue, crayons, yarn, and 4 pipe cleaners

Step 1: Place the plate over your face and ask a grown-up to mark where your eyes are under the plate. Take the plate away from your face and cut holes for your eyes.

Step 2: Use crayons to draw the nose, mouth, and eyebrows.

Step 3: Glue the pipe cleaners to the mask for the lion's whiskers.

Step 4: To make the lion's mane, glue yarn around the lion's face.

Step 5: Fasten a piece of yarn to each side of the plate so that you can tie the two pieces together to wear the mask.

1 According to this passage, which of these objects is NOT used in making the lion mask?

A Colored paper

B Glue

C Paper plate

D Pipe cleaners

2 According to the steps, which of the following should be done first?

F Punch holes in the mask

G Glue on the whiskers

H Cut holes for the eyes

J Color the mask

Sometimes I have hard
decisions to make.
I must decide the road I
should take.
I must do the right thing
for me,
even if no one else agrees.

Sometimes the pathway
is dark and unclear,
and the crowd's angry
shouts make it hard
to hear
the clear, soft sound of a
heart that is true,
I must decide the right
thing to do.

Now is the time to face
my fears,
and leave behind all I
hold dear,
to throw open the gates
and fly away,
to discover new ideas
and a better day.

by Angela Shelf Medearis

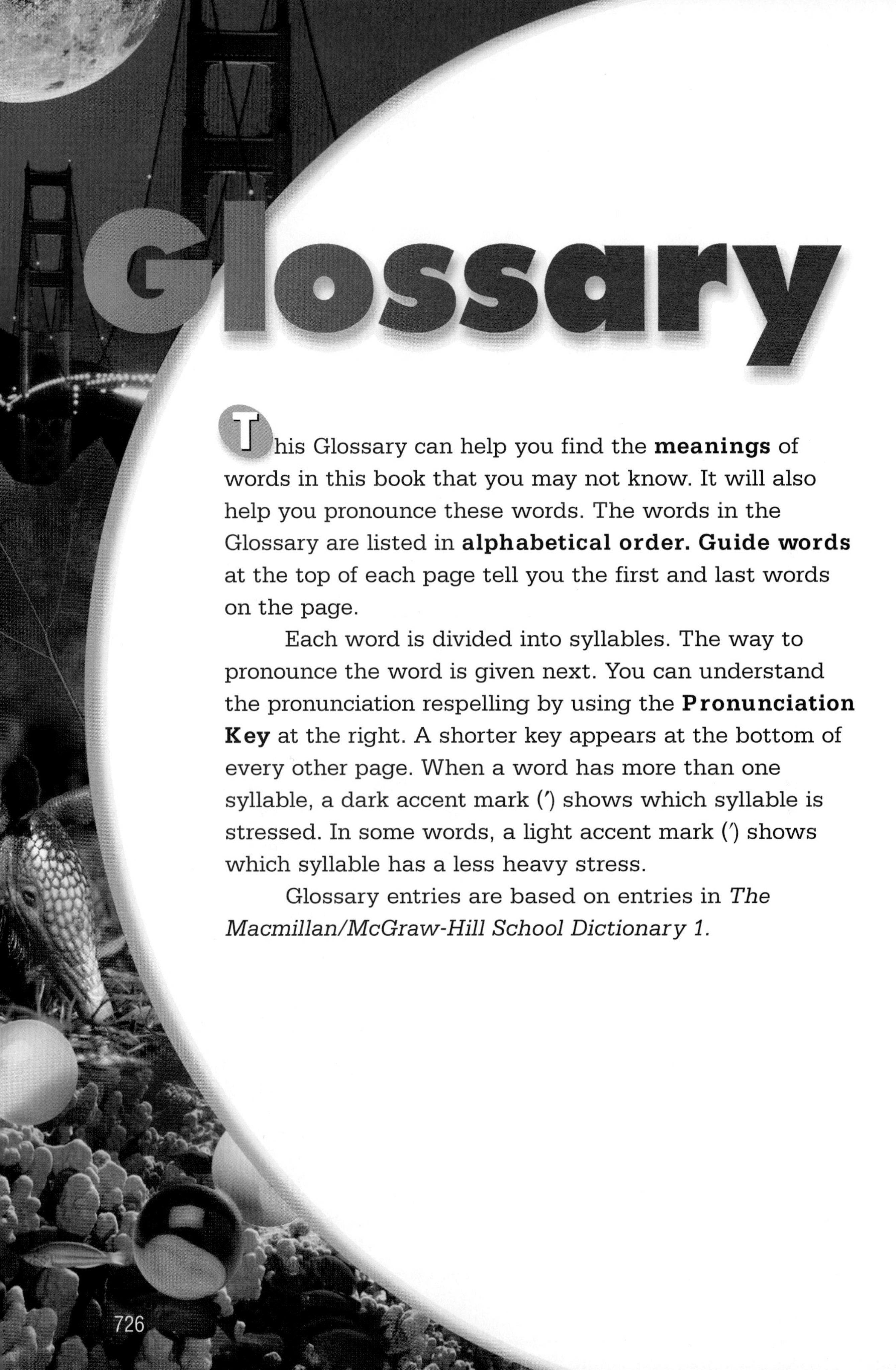

Glossary

This Glossary can help you find the **meanings** of words in this book that you may not know. It will also help you pronounce these words. The words in the Glossary are listed in **alphabetical order. Guide words** at the top of each page tell you the first and last words on the page.

Each word is divided into syllables. The way to pronounce the word is given next. You can understand the pronunciation respelling by using the **Pronunciation Key** at the right. A shorter key appears at the bottom of every other page. When a word has more than one syllable, a dark accent mark (ʹ) shows which syllable is stressed. In some words, a light accent mark (ʹ) shows which syllable has a less heavy stress.

Glossary entries are based on entries in *The Macmillan/McGraw-Hill School Dictionary 1.*

Guide Words

adobe/banner

First word on the page

Last word on the page

Sample Entry

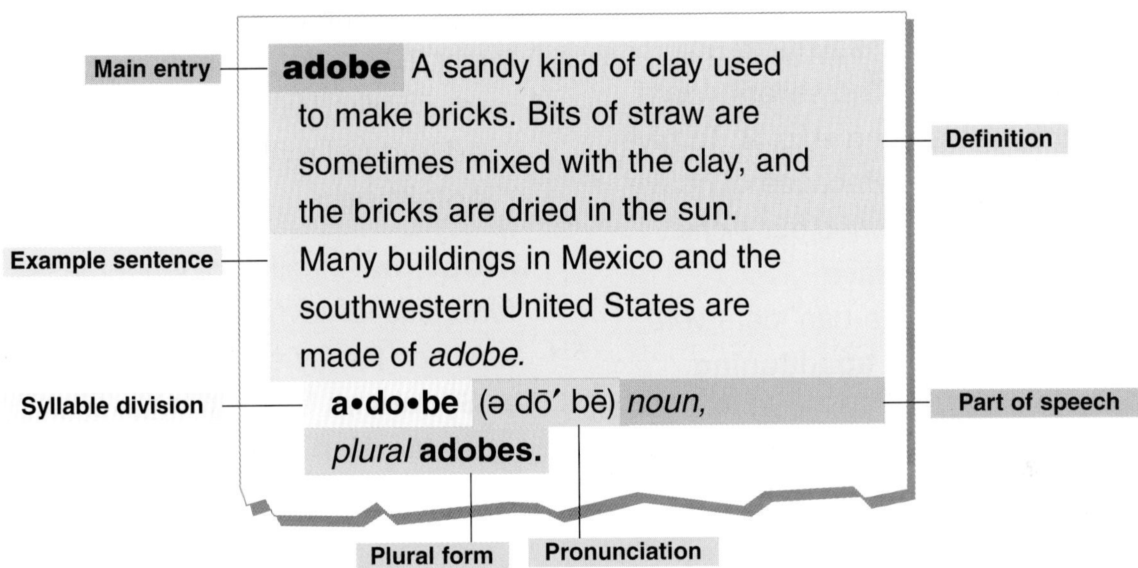

a	at, bad	**d**	dear, soda, bad
ā	ape, pain, day, break	**f**	five, defend, leaf, off, cough, elephant.
ä	father, car, heart	**g**	game, ago, fog, egg
âr	care, pair, bear, their, where	**h**	hat, ahead
e	end, pet, said, heaven, friend	**hw**	white, whether, which
ē	equal, me, feet, team, piece, key	**j**	joke, enjoy, gem, page, edge
i	it, big, English, hymn	**k**	kite, bakery, seek, tack, cat
ī	ice, fine, lie, my	**l**	lid, sailor, feel, ball, allow
îr	ear, deer, here, pierce	**m**	man, family, dream
o	odd, hot, watch	**n**	not, final, pan, knife
ō	old, oat, toe, low	**ng**	long, singer, pink
ô	coffee, all, taught, law, fought	**p**	pail, repair, soap, happy
ôr	order, fork, horse, story, pour	**r**	ride, parent, wear, more, marry
oi	oil, toy	**s**	sit, aside, pets, cent, pass
ou	out, now	**sh**	shoe, washer, fish, mission, nation
u	up, mud, love, double	**t**	tag, pretend, fat, button, dressed
ū	use, mule, cue, feud, few	**th**	thin, panther, both,
ü	rule, true, food	**<u>th</u>**	this, mother, smooth
u̇	put, wood, should	**v**	very, favor, wave
ûr	burn, hurry, term, bird, word, courage	**w**	wet, weather, reward
ə	about, taken, pencil, lemon, circus	**y**	yes, onion
b	bat, above, job	**z**	zoo, lazy, jazz, rose, dogs, houses
ch	chin, such, match	**zh**	vision, treasure, seizure

abandon 1. To leave and not return; desert. The sailors *abandoned* the sinking ship. **2.** To give up completely. Because of heavy rain, we *abandoned* our picnic.

▲ **Synonym:** leave

a•ban•don (ə ban′ dən) *verb,* **abandoned, abandoning.**

Language Note

A **synonym** is a word with the same meaning as another word. A synonym for *abandon* is *desert.*

absorb 1. To soak up or take in. A towel *absorbed* the spilled water. **2.** To hold the interest of. The book about animals *absorbed* me.

ab•sorb (ab sôrb′ *or* ab zôrb′) *verb,* **absorbed, absorbing.**

accidental Not planned or expected; happening by chance. We did not know we would see each other; our meeting was *accidental.*

ac•ci•den•tal (ak′si den′təl) *adjective; adverb* **accidentally**.

admit 1. To make known that something is true; confess. They *admitted* that they had broken the lamp. **2.**To allow to enter; let in. We were *admitted* to the club last week.

ad•mit (ad mit′) *verb,* **admitted, admitting.**

affection A feeling of tenderness, fondness, or love. I have deep *affection* for my sister.

▲ **Synonym:** liking

af•fec•tion (ə fek′shən) *noun, plural* **affections.**

amazement Great surprise or wonder; astonishment. The people watching the whales swim by were filled with *amazement.*

a•maze•ment (ə māz′mənt) *noun.*

ancestor A person from whom one is descended. Your grandparents and great-grandparents are among your *ancestors.*

an•ces•tor (an′ses tər) *noun, plural* **ancestors.**

assure 1. To give confidence to. We *assured* the child that the dog was friendly. **2.** To state positively. I *assure* you that I won't be late.
as•sure (ə shůr′) *verb,* **assured, assuring.**

attendant A person who takes care of someone or provides service to other people. The *attendant* at the park showed us where we could rent a canoe.
at•ten•dant (ə ten′dənt) *noun, plural* **attendants.**

available 1. Possible to get. There are still a few seats available for the game. Strawberries become *available* in early summer. **2.** Ready for use or service. The telephone is now *available.*
a•vail•a•ble (ə vā′lə bəl) *adjective.*

awkward 1. Difficult or embarrassing. It was an *awkward* moment when the teacher found out that I hadn't done my homework. **2.** Lacking grace or poise in movement or behavior; clumsy or uncomfortable. The *awkward* colt had trouble standing up.
▲ **Synonym:** troublesome
awk•ward (ôk′wərd) *adjective; adverb,* **awkwardly.**

Bb

background 1. A person's experience or learning. Her *background* is in physics. **2.** The part of a picture that appears in the distance.
back•ground (bak′ground′) *noun, plural* **backgrounds**

ballerina A woman or girl who dances ballet.
bal•le•ri•na (bal′ə rē′ nə) *noun, plural* **ballerinas.**

barracks The building or buildings where soldiers live. The *barracks* are inspected every week. The word **barracks** may be used with a singular or a plural verb.
bar•racks (bar′əks) *plural noun.*

at; āpe; fär; câre; end; mē; it; īce; pîerce; hot; ōld; sông; fôrk; oil; out; up; ūse; rüle; půll; tûrn; chin; sing; shop; thin; <u>th</u>is; hw in white; zh in treasure. The symbol ə stands for the unstressed vowel sound in about, taken, pencil, lemon, and circus.

beloved Loved very much. The dog was *beloved* by the whole neighborhood.
be•lov•ed (bi luv′id *or* bi luvd′) *adjective.*

bid To offer to pay. We *bid* thirty-five dollars for the old desk at the auction. *Verb.*— An offer to pay money. The rug was sold to the person who made the highest *bid. Noun.*
bid (bid) *verb,* **bid,** *or* **bidden, bidding;** *noun, plural* **bids.**

biscuit 1. A small cake of baked dough. For breakfast, he had eggs, bacon, juice, and a *biscuit.* **2.** A cracker. Every afternoon, she has tea and *biscuits.*
bis•cuit (bis′kit) *noun, plural* **biscuits.**

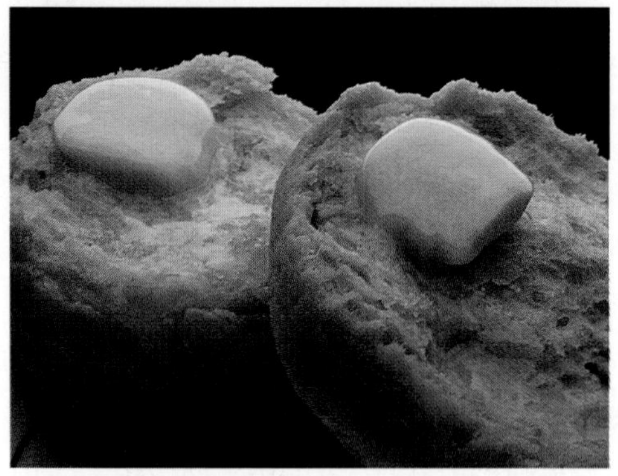

Word History
Cuit is the French word for "cooked." ***Biscuit*** comes from a 14th-century French word *bescuit,* meaning "twice-cooked bread."

brand-new Completely new. My aunt just bought a *brand-new* car.
brand-new (brand′nü *or* brand′nū) *adjective.*

brilliant 1. Very intelligent. That woman is a *brilliant* scientist. **2.** Very bright; sparkling. The North Star is a *brilliant* light in the sky.
bril•liant (bril′yənt) *adjective.*

brisk 1. Quick and lively. She walked at a *brisk* pace. **2.** Refreshing; keen; bracing. We walked in the *brisk* winter air.
brisk (brisk) *adjective,* **brisker, briskest.**

broad 1. Large from one side to the other side; wide. The side of the red barn is so *broad* that you can see it from a mile away. **2.** Wide in range; not limited. We have a *broad* knowledge of U.S. history.
broad (brôd) *adjective,* **broader, broadest.**

bulge To swell out. Because he put so many clothes in it, the suitcase *bulged. Verb.*— A rounded part that swells out. The rag made a *bulge* in the mechanic's back pocket. *Noun.*
bulge (bulj) *verb,* **bulged, bulging;** *noun, plural* **bulges;** *adjective,* **bulging.**

canoe To paddle or ride in a canoe. During the summer, they liked to go *canoeing* on the lake. *Verb.*— A light narrow boat, usually pointed at both ends and moved and steered with a paddle. The *canoe* tipped over when Eddie stood up. *Noun.*
ca•noe (kə nü′) *verb,* **canoed, canoeing;** *noun, plural* **canoes.**

captive A person or animal captured and held by force; prisoner. The police kept the *captive* in jail. *Noun.*—Held prisoner. The *captive* lion was kept in a cage. *Adjective.*
▲ **Synonym:** prisoner
cap•tive (kap′tiv) *noun, plural* **captives;** *adjective.*

captivity The state of being captive. Wolves live longer in *captivity* than in the wild.
cap•tiv•i•ty (kap ti′ və tē) *noun.*

celebration 1. The festivities carried on to observe or honor a special day or event. The wedding *celebration* is usually shared by friends and family. **2.** The act of celebrating. We went to the *celebration* of my cousin's graduation.
cel•e•bra•tion (sel′ ə brā′ shən) *noun, plural* **celebrations;** *adjective,* **celebratory.**

century A period of one hundred years. The time from 1651 to 1750 is one *century.*
century (sen′ chə rē) *noun, plural* **centuries**

challenge 1. Something calling for work, effort, and the use of one's talents. Chemistry is a real *challenge.* **2.** A call to take part in a contest or fight. In the days of duels, only a coward would refuse a *challenge. Noun.*—To question the truth or correctness of. They *challenged* my claim that bats are mammals. *Verb.*
chal•lenge (chal′ənj) *noun, plural* **challenges;** *verb,* **challenged, challenging.**

at; **ā**pe; f**ä**r; c**â**re; **e**nd; m**ē**; **i**t; **ī**ce; p**î**erce; h**o**t; **ō**ld; s**ô**ng; f**ô**rk; **oi**l; **ou**t; **u**p; **ū**se; r**ü**le; p**ů**ll; t**û**rn; **ch**in; si**ng**; **sh**op; **th**in; **th**is; **hw** in **wh**ite; **zh** in trea**s**ure. The symbol **ə** stands for the unstressed vowel sound in **a**bout, tak**e**n, penc**i**l, lem**o**n, and circ**u**s.

chant A singing or shouting of words over and over. *Chants* usually have a strong rhythm. *Noun.* — To sing or shout in a chant. At the election rally, the group *chanted* the name of their favorite candidate. *Verb.*

chant (chant) *noun, plural* **chants;** *verb,* **chanted, chanting.**

Word History

Chant, as it is spelled today, is based on the Middle English word *chaunten.* The Latin word *cantare,* which means "to sing," is the original basis of the word.

circulate 1. To pass from person to person. Bills and coins have *circulated* in the United States since Colonial times. **2.** To move around widely among different places. The window fan *circulates* air around the room.

cir•cu•late (sûr′kyə lāt′) *verb,* **circulated, circulating.**

climate The average weather conditions of a place or region through the year. Climate includes average temperature, rainfall, humidity, and wind conditions. Southern California has a warm, mild *climate.*

cli•mate (klī′mit) *noun, plural* **climates.**

cling To stick closely. The wet pants were *clinging* to her legs.

cling (kling) *verb,* **clung, clinging.**

clipper 1. A tool used for cutting. Use *clippers* to cut your fingernails. **2.** A fast sailing ship. American *clippers* sailed all over the world.

clip•per (klip′ər) *noun, plural* **clippers.**

clover A small plant with leaves of three leaflets and rounded, fragrant flowers of white, red, or purple.

clo•ver (klō′vər) *noun, plural* **clovers.**

cluster To grow or group in a cluster. We all *clustered* around the campfire. *Verb.*— A number of things of the same kind that grow or are grouped together. Grapes grow in *clusters. Noun.*

clus•ter (klus′tər) *verb,* **clustered, clustering;** *noun, plural* **clusters.**

combine To join together; unite. We *combined* eggs, flour, and milk to make the batter. *Verb.* — A farm machine that harvests and threshes grain. *Noun.*
com•bine (kəm bīn′ *for verb;* kom′bīn *for noun*) *verb,* **combined, combining;** *noun, plural* **combines.**

commercial An advertising message on radio or television. *Noun.*— Relating to business or trade. I plan to take *commercial* subjects in high school. *Adjective.*
com•mer•cial (kə mûr′shəl) *noun, plural* **commercials.**

communicate To exchange or pass along feelings, thoughts, or information. People *communicate* by speaking or writing. **com•mu•ni•cate** (kə mū′ni kāt′) *verb,* **communicated, communicating.**

compare 1. To say or think that something is like something else. The writer *compared* the boom of big guns to the sound of thunder. **2.** To study in order to find out how persons or things are alike or different. We *compared* our watches and saw that your watch was five minutes ahead of mine.
com•pare (kəm pâr′) *verb,* **compared, comparing.**

compass 1. An instrument for showing directions; it has a magnetic needle that points to the north. Pilots, sailors, and many other people use compasses. The camper was able to get home because his *compass* showed him which way was west. **2.** An instrument for drawing circles or measuring distances, made up of two arms joined together at the top. One arm ends in a point and the other holds a pencil. Using a *compass,* the student was able to create a perfect circle on her drawing paper.
com•pass (kum′pəs) *noun, plural* **compasses.**

at; āpe; fär; câre; end; mē; it; īce; pîerce; hot; ōld; sông; fôrk; oil; out; up; ūse; rüle; pu̇ll; tûrn; chin; sing; shop; thin; th̲is; hw in white; zh in treasure. The symbol ə stands for the unstressed vowel sound in about, taken, pencil, lemon, and circus.

complicated Hard to understand or do. The directions for putting together the bicycle were too *complicated* for me to follow.
▲ **Synonym:** difficult
com•pli•ca•ted (kom′pli kā′tid) *adjective.*

confusion 1. The condition of being confused; disorder. In my *confusion,* I gave the wrong answer. **2.** A mistaking of one person or thing for another. Mistaking John for his twin brother Tom is a common *confusion.*
con•fu•sion (kən fū′zhən) *noun, plural* **confusions.**

connect 1. To fasten or join together. *Connect* the trailer to the car. **2.** To consider as related; associate. We *connect* robins with spring.
con•nect (kə nekt′) *verb,* **connected, connecting.**

contain 1. To include as a part of. Candy *contains* sugar. **2.** To hold. The jar *contains* candy.
con•tain (kən tān′) *verb,* **contained, containing.**

coral A hard substance like stone, found in tropical seas. Coral is made up of the skeletons of tiny sea animals. *Coral* is beautiful when growing underwater, and it is very pretty as a decoration out of the water, too. *Noun.*— Having the color coral; pinkish red. She decided to use a *coral* nail polish. *Adjective.*
cor•al (kôr′əl) *noun, plural* **corals;** *adjective.*

county 1. One of the sections into which a state or country is divided. The longest bridge in the whole state is in that *county.* **2.** The people living in a county. Most of the *county* came to the fair.
coun•ty (koun′tē) *noun, plural* **counties.**

crate A box made of slats of wood. We broke up the old apple *crates* to use in our bonfire. *Noun.*
—To pack in a crate or crates. The farmer *crated* the lettuce. *Verb.*
crate (krāt) *noun, plural* **crates;** *verb,* **crated, crating.**

crate

crisscross To mark with crossing lines. The artist *crisscrossed* the paper with fine pencil marks.
criss•cross (kris′krôs) *verb,* **crisscrossed, crisscrossing.**

crumple 1. To press or crush into wrinkles or folds. He *crumpled* up the letter and threw it into the trash can. **2.** To fall down or collapse. The old shack *crumpled* when the bulldozer rammed it.
crum•ple (krum′pəl) *verb,* **crumpled, crumpling.**

cultured Having an appreciation of the arts, knowledge, and good taste and manners that are the result of education. The literature professor is a very *cultured* woman.
cul•tured (kul′chərd) *adjective.*

Dd

damage Harm that makes something less valuable or useful. The flood caused great *damage* to farms. *Noun.*— To harm or injure. Rain *damaged* the young plants. *Verb.*
dam•age (dam′ij) *noun, plural* **damages;** *verb,* **damaged, damaging.**

dart To move suddenly and quickly. The rabbit *darted* into the bushes. *Verb.*— A thin, pointed object that looks like a small arrow. He hit the target with each *dart* that he threw. *Noun.*
dart (därt) *verb,* **darted, darting;** *noun, plural* **darts.**

desire A longing; wish. I have always had a great *desire* to travel. *Noun.*—To wish for; long for. My sister *desires* a basketball more than anything. *Verb.*
de•sire (di zīr′) *noun, plural* **desires;** *verb,* **desired, desiring.**

at; **ā**pe; f**ä**r; c**â**re; **e**nd; m**ē**; **i**t; **ī**ce; p**î**erce; h**o**t; **ō**ld; s**ô**ng; f**ô**rk; **oi**l; **ou**t; **u**p; **ū**se; r**ü**le; p**u̇**ll; t**û**rn; **ch**in; si**ng**; **sh**op; **th**in; **th**is; **hw** in **wh**ite; **zh** in trea**s**ure. The symbol **ə** stands for the unstressed vowel sound in **a**bout, tak**e**n, penc**i**l, lem**o**n, and circ**u**s.

destroy To ruin completely; wreck. The earthquake *destroyed* the city.
▲ **Synonym:** ruin
de•stroy (di stroi′) *verb,* **destroyed, destroying.**

disaster 1. An event that causes much suffering or loss. The flood was a *disaster.* **2.** Something that does not go right. My birthday party was a *disaster* because it rained.
▲ **Synonym:** catastrophe
dis•as•ter (di zas′tər) *noun, plural* **disasters.**

display To show or exhibit. The art museum is now *displaying* some of Monet's paintings. *Verb.* —A show or exhibit. A hug is a *display* of affection. *Noun.*
dis•play (dis plā′) *verb,* **displayed, displaying;** *noun, plural* **displays.**

ditch A long, narrow hole dug in the ground. Ditches are used to drain off water. After the rain shower, the *ditch* was full. *Noun.*— To make an emergency landing in water. No pilot wants to have to *ditch* an airplane. *Verb.*
ditch (dich) *noun, plural* **ditches;** *verb,* **ditched, ditching.**

downstage Toward the front of a theatrical stage. The prop was supposed to land *downstage* left. *Adverb* or *adjective.*
down•stage (doun′stāj′) *adverb; adjective.*

editor 1. A person who edits. The *editor* made changes in the book after talking with its author. **2.** A person who writes editorials. The newspaper *editor* wrote an article in favor of raising city taxes.
ed•i•tor (ed′i tər) *noun, plural* **editors.**

eerie Strange in a scary way; making people frightened or nervous. Walking through that abandoned house was an *eerie* experience.
▲ **Synonym:** creepy
ee•rie (îr′ē) *adjective,* **eerier, eeriest.**

eldest Born first; oldest. I am the *eldest* of three children.
el•dest (el′dist) *adjective.*

elegant Rich and fine in quality. The museum has a major display of *elegant* costumes.
▲ **Synonym:** tasteful
el•e•gant (el′i gənt) *adjective; noun,* **elegance;** *adverb,* **elegantly.**

Word History

The word ***elegant*** first appeared in the English language in the 15th century. The word comes from the Latin *eligere,* which means "to select."

endanger 1. To threaten with becoming extinct. Pollution is *endangering* many different species of animals. **2.** To put in a dangerous situation. The flood *endangered* the lives of hundreds of people.
▲ **Synonym:** risk
en•dan•ger (en dān′jər) *verb,* **endangered, endangering.**

endless 1. Having no limit or end; going on forever. The drive across the desert seemed *endless.* **2.** Without ends. A circle is *endless.*
end•less (end′lis) *adjective.*

enterprise Something that a person plans or tries to do. An *enterprise* is often something difficult or important. The search for the treasure was an exciting *enterprise.*
en•ter•prise (en′tər prīz′) *noun, plural* **enterprises.**

entertain 1. To keep interested and amused. The clown *entertained* the children. **2.** To have as a guest. They often *entertain* people in their house in the country.
en•ter•tain (en′tər tān′) *verb,* **entertained, entertaining.**

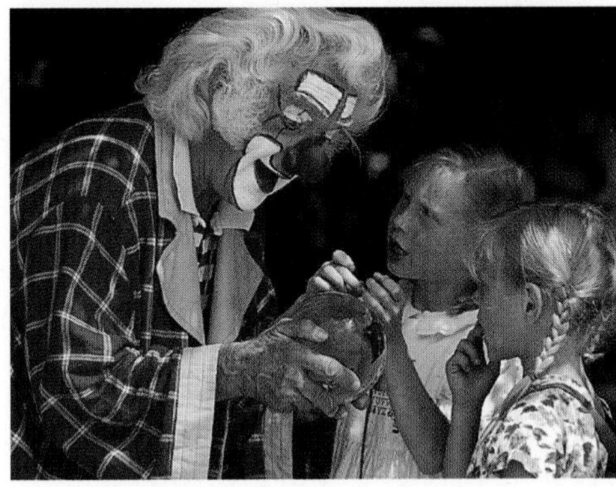

at; **ā**pe; f**ä**r; c**â**re; **e**nd; m**ē**; **i**t; **ī**ce; p**î**erce; h**o**t; **ō**ld; s**ô**ng; f**ô**rk; **oi**l; **ou**t; **u**p; **ū**se; r**ü**le; p**u**ll; t**û**rn; **ch**in; si**ng**; **sh**op; **th**in; **th**is; **hw** in **wh**ite; **zh** in trea**s**ure. The symbol **ə** stands for the unstressed vowel sound in **a**bout, tak**e**n, penc**i**l, lem**o**n, and circ**u**s.

errand **1.** A short trip to do something. I have to run several *errands* this morning. **2.** Something a person is sent to do; the purpose of such a trip. Our *errand* was to buy the newspaper.
er•rand (er′ənd) *noun, plural* **errands.**

exist **1.** To be found. Outside of zoos, polar bears *exist* only in arctic regions. **2.** To be real. I do not believe that ghosts *exist.*
ex•ist (eg zist′) *verb,* **existed, existing.**

expensive Having a high price; very costly. The town bought an *expensive* new fire engine.
▲ **Synonym:** costly
ex•pen•sive (ek spen′siv) *adjective.*

extinct **1.** No longer existing. The dodo became *extinct* because people hunted it for food. **2.** No longer active. The village is built over an *extinct* volcano.
ex•tinct (ek stingkt′) *adjective; noun,* **extinction.**

extraordinary Very unusual; remarkable. The teacher said my friend had *extraordinary* talent.
ex•tra•or•di•nar•y (ek strôr′də ner′ē *or* ek′strə ôr′də ner′ē) *adjective.*

fang A long, pointed tooth. When trying to look threatening, a wolf shows its *fangs.*
fang (fang) *noun, plural* **fangs.**

feeble Not strong; weak. That is a *feeble* excuse.
fee•ble (fē′bəl) *adjective,* **feebler, feeblest;** *noun,* **feebleness;** *adverb,* **feebly.**

festival **1.** A program of special activities or shows. We saw a foreign film at the film *festival.* **2.** A celebration or holiday. There were plenty of delicious foods to try at the street *festival.*
fes•ti•val (fes′tə vəl) *noun, plural* **festivals.**

foggy 1. Full of or hidden by fog; misty. Driving is dangerous on *foggy* days and nights. **2.** Confused or unclear. The ideas were *foggy* and the project needed more research to clear things up.
fog•gy (fôg′ē *or* fog′ē) *adjective,* **foggier, foggiest.**

footpath A trail or path for people to walk on. We walked on the *foot-path* beside the road.
foot•path (fu̇t′path) *noun, plural* **footpaths.**

foul Very unpleasant or dirty. The water in the old well looked *foul. Adjective.* —A violation of the rules. The basketball player committed a *foul. Noun.*
▲ Another word that sounds like this is **fowl.**
foul (foul) *adjective,* **fouler, foulest;** *noun, plural* **fouls.**

fowl One of a number of birds used for food. Chicken, turkey, and duck are kinds of *fowl.* We always eat *fowl* for Thanksgiving dinner.
▲ Another word that sounds like this is **foul.**
fowl (foul) *noun, plural* **fowl** *or* **fowls.**

fowl

fragrance A sweet or pleasing smell. Roses have a beautiful *fragrance.*
▲ **Synonym:** smell
fra•grance (frā′grəns) *noun, plural* **fragrances.**

fray To separate into loose threads. Many years of wear had *frayed* the cuffs of the coat.
fray (frā) *verb,* **frayed, fraying.**

freeze 1. To harden because of the cold. When water *freezes,* it becomes ice. **2.** To cover or block with ice. The cold weather *froze* the pipes.
freeze (frēz) *verb,* **froze, frozen, freezing.**

at; **ā**pe; f**ä**r; c**â**re; **e**nd; m**ē**; **i**t; **ī**ce; p**î**erce; h**o**t; **ō**ld; s**ô**ng; f**ô**rk; **oi**l; **ou**t; **u**p; **ū**se; r**ü**le; p**u̇**ll; t**û**rn; **ch**in; si**ng**; **sh**op; **th**in; **th**is; **hw** in **wh**ite; **zh** in trea**s**ure. The symbol **ə** stands for the unstressed vowel sound in **a**bout, tak**e**n, penc**i**l, lem**o**n, and circ**u**s.

fret To suffer emotional distress; irritation. My brother *frets* whenever he gets a low grade on a test. *Verb.* —One of the ridges fixed across the fingerboard of a stringed instrument such as a guitar. The notes get higher each time I move my finger up a *fret. Noun.*
fret (fret) *verb,* **fretted, fretting;** *noun, plural* **frets.**

gallon A unit of measure for liquids. A *gallon* equals four quarts, or about 3.8 liters.
gal•lon (gal′ən) *noun, plural* **gallons.**

garbage Things that are thrown out. All the spoiled food went into the *garbage.*
▲ **Synonym:** trash
gar•bage (gär′bij) *noun.*

generation 1. A group of persons born around the same time. My parents call us the younger *generation.* **2.** One step in the line of descent from a common ancestor. A grandparent, parent, and child make up three *generations.*
gen•er•a•tion (jen′ə rāsh′ən) *noun, plural* **generations.**

gild To cover with a thin layer of gold. The artist *gilded* the picture frame.
▲ Another word that sounds like this is **guild.**
gild (gild) *verb,* **gilded** *or* **gilt, gilding.**

girth The measurement around an object. The *girth* of the old redwood tree was tremendous.
girth (gûrth) *noun, plural* **girths.**

glint To sparkle or flash. Her eyes *glinted* with merriment.
glint (glint) *verb,* **glinted, glinting.**

glisten To shine with reflected light. The snow *glistened* in the sun.
glis•ten (glis′ən) *verb,* **glistened, glistening.**

glum Very unhappy or disappointed. Every member of the losing team looked *glum* after the game.
glum (glum) *adjective,* **glummer, glummest.**

gourd A rounded fruit related to the pumpkin or squash. Gourds grow on vines and have a hard outer rind. The hollow *gourd* hung above the tub of water.
gourd (gôrd) *noun, plural* **gourds.**

governess A woman who supervises and cares for a child, especially in a private household. The *governess* made sure the children were ready for bed.
gov•ern•ess (guv′ər nis) *noun, plural* **governesses.**

graze 1. To feed on growing grass. The sheep *grazed* on the hillside. **2.** To scrape or touch lightly in passing. The branch *grazed* the house when the wind blew.
graze (grāz) *verb,* **grazed, grazing.**

guilt 1. A feeling of having done something wrong; shame. I felt *guilt* because I got angry at a good friend. **2.** The condition or fact of having done something wrong or having broken the law. The evidence proved the robber's *guilt.*
▲ Another word that sounds like this is **gilt.**
guilt (gilt) *noun; adjective,* **guilty.**

Hh

harbor A sheltered place along a coast. Ships and boats often anchor in a *harbor. Noun.*—To give protection or shelter to. It is against the law to *harbor* a criminal. *Verb.*
har•bor (här′bər) *noun, plural* **harbors;** *verb,* **harbored, harboring.**

haul To pull or move with force; drag. We *hauled* the trunk up the stairs. *Verb.*— The act of hauling. It was an easy *haul* by truck. *Noun.*
▲ Another word that sounds like this is **hall.**
haul (hôl) *verb,* **hauled, hauling;** *noun, plural* **hauls.**

at; **ā**pe; f**ä**r; c**â**re; **e**nd; m**ē**; **i**t; **ī**ce; p**î**erce; h**o**t; **ō**ld; s**ô**ng; f**ô**rk; **oi**l; **ou**t; **u**p; **ū**se; r**ü**le; p**ů**ll; t**û**rn; **ch**in; si**ng**; **sh**op; **th**in; **th**is; **hw** in **wh**ite; **zh** in trea**s**ure. The symbol **ə** stands for the unstressed vowel sound in **a**bout, tak**e**n, penc**i**l, lem**o**n, and circ**u**s.

haze Mist, smoke, or dust in the air. The bridge was hidden in the *haze.*
haze (hāz) *noun, plural* **hazes.**

headlong 1. With the head first. The runner slid *headlong* into second base. **2.** In a reckless way; rashly. I rushed *headlong* into buying the bicycle.
head•long (hed′lông′) *adverb.*

healthy Having or showing good health. She has a *healthy* outlook on life.
health•y (hel′thē) *adjective,* **healthier, healthiest.**

heave 1. To lift, raise, pull, or throw using force or effort. I *heaved* a rock across the stream. **2.** To utter in an effortful way. I *heaved* a sigh of relief.
heave (hēv) *verb,* **heaved, heaving.**

hilltop The top of a hill. From the *hilltop,* the hikers could see the smoke from the campfire.
hill•top (hil′top′) *noun, plural* **hilltops.**

horizon 1. The line where the sky and the ground or the sea seem to meet. The fishing boat headed out to sea just as the sun rose above the *horizon.* **2.** The limit of a person's knowledge, interests, or experience. You can widen your *horizons* by reading books.
hor•i•zon (hə rī′zən) *noun, plural* **horizons.**

huddle To gather close together in a bunch. The scouts *huddled* around the campfire to keep warm. *Verb.*—A group of people or animals gathered close together. The football players formed a *huddle* to plan their next play. *Noun.*
hud•dle (hud′əl) *verb,* **huddled, huddling;** *noun, plural* **huddles.**

Ii

iceberg A very large piece of floating ice that has broken off from a glacier. Only the tip of the *iceberg* is visible above the surface of the water.
ice•berg (īs′bûrg′) *noun, plural* **icebergs.**

identify To find out or tell exactly who a person is or what a thing is; recognize. Can you *identify* this strange object?
▲ **Synonym:** recognize
i•den•ti•fy (ī den′tə fī′) *verb,* **identified, identifying.**

ignorant 1. Not informed or aware. I wasn't wearing my watch, so I was *ignorant* of the time. **2.** Showing a lack of knowledge. The young cowhands were *ignorant* at first of how to brand cattle, but they learned quickly.
ig•no•rant (ig′nər ənt) *adjective.*

image 1. A person who looks very similar to someone else. That girl is the *image* of her mother. **2.** A picture or other likeness of a person or thing. A penny has an *image* of Abraham Lincoln on one side of it.
im•age (im′ij) *noun, plural* **images.**

importance The state of being important; having great value or meaning. Rain is of great *importance* to farmers, since crops can't grow without water.
im•por•tance (im pôr′təns) *noun.*

ingredient Any one of the parts that go into a mixture. Flour, eggs, sugar, and butter are the main *ingredients* of this cake.
in•gre•di•ent (in grē′dē ənt) *noun, plural* **ingredients.**

injury Harm or damage done to a person or thing. The accident caused an *injury* to my leg.
in•ju•ry (in′jə rē) *noun, plural* **injuries.**

inning One of the parts into which a baseball or softball game is divided. Both teams bat during an inning until three players on each team are put out. Our team won the game by scoring five runs in the last *inning.*
in•ning (in′ing) *noun, plural* **innings.**

at; **ā**pe; f**ä**r; c**â**re; **e**nd; m**ē**; **i**t; **ī**ce; p**î**erce; h**o**t; **ō**ld; s**ô**ng; f**ô**rk; **oi**l; **ou**t; **u**p; **ū**se; r**ü**le; p**u̇**ll; t**û**rn; **ch**in; si**ng**; **sh**op; **th**in; **th**is; **hw** in **wh**ite; **zh** in trea**s**ure. The symbol **ə** stands for the unstressed vowel sound in **a**bout, tak**e**n, penc**i**l, lem**o**n, and circ**u**s.

inspect To look at closely and carefully. The official *inspected* our car and declared it safe to drive.
▲ **Synonym:** examine
in•spect (in spekt′) *verb,* **inspected, inspecting.**

inspire 1. To stir the mind, feelings, or imagination of. The senator's speech *inspired* the audience. **2.** To fill with a strong, encouraging feeling. Success in school *inspired* me with hope for the future.
▲ **Synonym:** encourage
in•spire (in spīr′) *verb,* **inspired, inspiring.**

instance An example; case. There are many *instances* of immigrants becoming famous Americans.
in•stance (in′stəns) *noun, plural* **instances.**

instinct A way of acting or behaving that a person or animal is born with and does not have to learn. Birds build nests by *instinct.*
in•stinct (in′stingkt′) *noun, plural* **instincts.**

jagged Having sharp points that stick out. Some eagles build nests on *jagged* cliffs.
jag•ged (jag′id) *adjective.*

keel To fall over suddenly; collapse. The heat in the crowded subway caused two people to *keel* over. *Verb.*— A wooden or metal piece that runs along the center of the bottom of many ships and boats. When we sailed through the shallow waters, the *keel* scraped along the bottom of the lake. *Noun.*
keel (kēl) *verb,* **keeled, keeling;** *noun, plural* **keels.**

knapsack A bag made of canvas, leather, nylon, or other material that is used for carrying clothes, books, equipment, or other supplies. A knapsack is strapped over the shoulders and carried on the back. Because she left her *knapsack* on the bus, she couldn't turn in her homework assignment.

▲ **Synonym:** backpack

knap•sack (nap′sak′) *noun, plural* **knapsacks.**

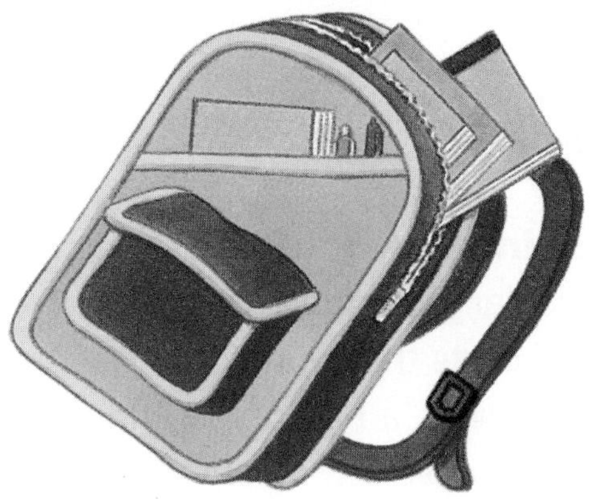

knowledge 1. An understanding that is gained through experience or study. I have enough *knowledge* of football to be able to follow a game. **2.** The fact of knowing. The *knowledge* that the car could slide on the icy road made the driver more careful.

knowl•edge (nol′ij) *noun.*

labor To do hard work. The two women *labored* over the quilt, hoping to finish it in time for the birthday party. *Verb.*—Hard work; toil. The farmers were tired after their *labor. Noun.*

la•bor (lā′bər) *verb,* **labored, laboring;** *noun, plural* **labors.**

launch To start something. The company *launched* its store with a big sale. *Verb.*—The act or process of launching. We watched the rocket *launch* on television. *Noun.*

launch (lônch) *verb,* **launched, launching;** *noun, plural* **launches.**

league 1. A number of people, groups, or countries joined together for a common purpose. Those two teams belong to the same *league.* **2.** A measure of distance used in the past, equal to about three miles. The army's camp was only two *leagues* from the city.

league (lēg) *noun, plural* **leagues.**

at; **ā**pe; f**ä**r; c**â**re; **e**nd; m**ē**; **i**t; **ī**ce; p**î**erce; h**o**t; **ō**ld; s**ô**ng; f**ô**rk; **oi**l; **ou**t; **u**p; **ū**se; r**ü**le; p**u̇**ll; t**û**rn; **ch**in; si**ng**; **sh**op; **th**in; **th**is; **hw** in **wh**ite; **zh** in trea**s**ure. The symbol **ə** stands for the unstressed vowel sound in **a**bout, tak**e**n, penc**i**l, lem**o**n, and circ**u**s.

linger To stay on as if not wanting to leave; move slowly. The fans *lingered* outside the stadium to see the team.
lin•ger (ling′gər) *verb,* **lingered, lingering.**

lodge A small house, cottage, or cabin. The hunters stayed at a *lodge* in the mountains. *Noun.*—To live in a place for a while. People *lodged* in the school during the flood. *Verb.*
lodge (loj) *noun, plural* **lodges;** *verb,* **lodged, lodging.**

loft 1. The upper floor, room, or space in a building. The artist cleaned his *loft.* **2.** An upper floor or balcony in a large hall or church. The choir sang in the choir *loft.*
loft (lôft) *noun, plural* **lofts.**

loosen 1. To make or become looser. *Loosen* your necktie. **2.** To set free or release. The dog had been *loosened* from its leash.
loosen (lü′sen) *verb,* **loosened, loosening.**

lurk 1. To lie hidden, especially in preparation for an attack. Snakes *lurk* under rocks. **2.** To move about quietly; sneak. Thieves *lurk* in the shadows.
lurk (lûrk) *verb,* **lurked, lurking.**

Mm

machine 1. A device that does a particular job, made up of a number of parts that work together. A lawn mower, a hair dryer, and a printing press are *machines.* **2.** A simple device that lessens the force needed to move an object. A lever and a pulley are simple *machines.*
ma•chine (mə shēn′) *noun, plural* **machines.**

malachite A green mineral that is used for making ornaments.
mal•a•chite (mal′ə kīt′) *noun.*

mammal A kind of animal that is warm-blooded and has a backbone. Human beings are *mammals.*
mam•mal (mam′əl) *noun, plural* **mammals.**

marine Having to do with or living in the sea. Whales are *marine* animals. *Adjective.*—A member of the Marine Corps. She joined the *Marines* after she graduated. *Noun.*
ma•rine (mə rēn′) *adjective; noun, plural* **marines.**

marketplace A place where food and other products are bought and sold. In old towns the *marketplace* was often in a square.
mar•ket•place (mär′kit plās′) *noun, plural* **marketplaces.**

marvel To feel wonder and astonishment. We *marveled* at the acrobat's skill. *Verb.*—A wonderful or astonishing thing. Space travel is one of the *marvels* of modern science. *Noun.*
mar•vel (mär′vəl) *verb,* **marveled, marveling;** *noun, plural* **marvels.**

mature Having reached full growth or development; ripe. When a puppy becomes *mature* it is called a dog. *Adjective.*—To become fully grown or developed. The tomatoes are *maturing* fast. *Verb.*
ma•ture (mə chůr′ *or* mə tůr′) *adjective; verb,* **matured, maturing.**

maze A confusing series of paths or passageways through which people may have a hard time finding their way. I got lost in the *maze* of hallways in my new school.
maze (māz) *noun, plural* **mazes.**

at; **ā**pe; f**ä**r; c**â**re; **e**nd; m**ē**; **i**t; **ī**ce; p**î**erce; h**o**t; **ō**ld; s**ô**ng; f**ô**rk; **oi**l; **ou**t; **u**p; **ū**se; r**ü**le; p**u̇**ll; t**û**rn; **ch**in; si**ng**; **sh**op; **th**in; **th**is; **hw** in **wh**ite; **zh** in trea**s**ure. The symbol **ə** stands for the unstressed vowel sound in **a**bout, tak**e**n, penc**i**l, lem**o**n, and circ**u**s.

memorize To learn by heart; fix in the memory. You can *memorize* the poem by reciting it over and over.
mem•o•rize (mem′ə rīz′) *verb,* **memorized, memorizing.**

merely Nothing more than; only. Your explanations are *merely* excuses.
mere•ly (mîr′lē) *adverb.*

messenger A person who delivers messages or runs errands. The *messenger* was delayed by traffic.
mes•sen•ger (mes′ən jər) *noun, plural* **messengers.**

method 1. A way of doing something. Speaking on the telephone is a *method* of communicating. **2.** Order or system. I could not find what I wanted because the books had been shelved without *method.*
meth•od (meth′əd) *noun, plural* **methods.**

microscope A device for looking at things that are too small to be seen with the naked eye. It has one or more lenses that produce an enlarged image of anything viewed through it.
mi•cro•scope (mī′krə skōp′) *noun, plural* **microscopes.**

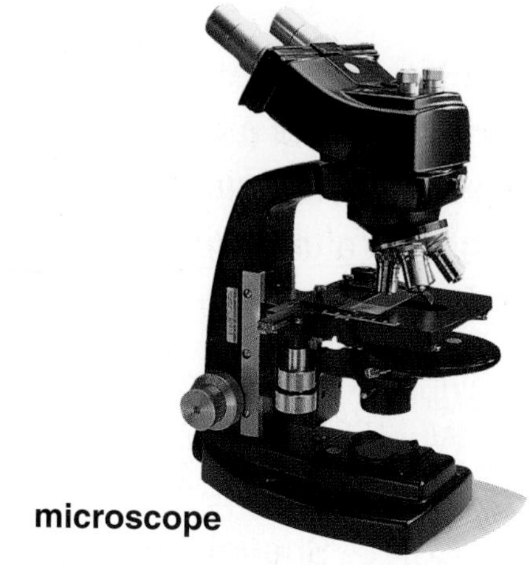
microscope

mingle 1. To put or come together; mix; join. This stream *mingles* with others to form a river. **2.** To move about freely; join; associate. We *mingled* with the other guests.
min•gle (ming′gəl) *verb,* **mingled, mingling.**

molar Any one of the large teeth at the back of the mouth. *Molars* have broad surfaces for grinding food.
mo•lar (mō′lər) *noun, plural* **molars.**

moonscape View of the surface of the moon.
moon•scape (mün′skāp′) *noun, plural* **moonscapes.**

mound A slightly raised area. The pitcher stands on the *mound* to pitch the ball. *Noun.*—To pile in a hill or heap. I like to *mound* ice cream on top of my pie. *Verb.*
mound (mound) *noun, plural* **mounds;** *verb,* **mounded, mounding.**

mug A large drinking cup with a handle, often made of pottery or metal. I drink tea out of my purple *mug. Noun.*—To attack and rob someone. A lady was *mugged* of all her belongings. *Verb.*

mug (mug) *noun, plural* **mugs;** *verb,* **mugged, mugging.**

mutter To speak in a low, unclear way with the mouth almost closed. I *muttered* to myself. *Verb.* —Oral sounds produced in a low, unclear way. There was a *mutter* of disapproval from the audience. *Noun.*

mut•ter (mut′ər) *verb,* **muttered, muttering;** *noun.*

native Originally living or growing in a region or country. Raccoons are *native* to America. *Adjective.* —A person who was born in a particular country or place. One of my classmates is a *native* of Germany. *Noun.*

na•tive (nā′tiv) *adjective; noun, plural* **natives.**

natural 1. Found in nature; not made by people; not artificial. *Natural* rock formations overlook the river. **2.** Existing from birth; not the result of teaching or training. Is your musical talent *natural,* or did you take lessons?

nat•u•ral (nach′ər əl) *adjective.*

neighbor A person, place, or thing that is next to or near another. Our *neighbor* took care of our dog while we were away.

neigh•bor (nā′bər) *noun, plural* **neighbors.**

newsletter A small publication containing news of interest to a special group of people. Our chess club publishes a monthly *newsletter.*

news•let•ter (nüz′let′ər) *noun, plural* **newsletters.**

at; **ā**pe; f**ä**r; c**â**re; **e**nd; m**ē**; **i**t; **ī**ce; p**î**erce; h**o**t; **ō**ld; s**ô**ng; f**ô**rk; **oi**l; **ou**t; **u**p; **ū**se; r**ü**le; p**ù**ll; t**û**rn; **ch**in; si**ng**; **sh**op; **th**in; **th**is; **hw** in **wh**ite; **zh** in trea**s**ure. The symbol **ə** stands for the unstressed vowel sound in **a**bout, tak**e**n, penc**i**l, lem**o**n, and circ**u**s.

nip 1. To bite or pinch quickly and not hard. The parrot *nipped* my finger. **2.** To cut off by pinching. The gardener *nipped* the dead leaves off the plants.

nip (nip) *verb,* **nipped, nipping.**

nursery 1. A baby's bedroom. The baby's *nursery* was painted pink and blue. **2.** A place where young children are taken care of during the day.

nurs•er•y (nûr′sə rē) *noun, plural* **nurseries.**

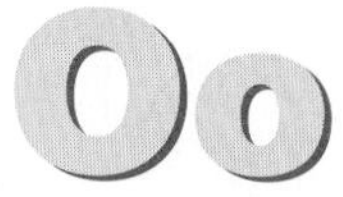

occasion 1. An important or special event. The baby's first birthday was an *occasion.* **2.** A time when something happens. I have met that person on several *occasions.*

oc•ca•sion (ə kā′zhən) *noun, plural* **occasions.**

opponent A person or group that is against another in a fight, contest, or discussion. The soccer team beat its *opponent.*

▲ **Synonym:** enemy

op•po•nent (ə pō′nənt) *noun, plural* **opponents.**

orchard An area of land where fruit trees are grown. We picked apples in the apple *orchard.*

or•chard (ôr′chərd) *noun, plural* **orchards.**

organization 1. A group of people joined together for a particular purpose. The Red Cross is an international *organization.* **2.** The act of organizing. Who is responsible for the *organization* of the school dance?

or•gan•i•za•tion (ôr′gə nə zā′shən) *noun, plural* **organizations.**

original Relating to or belonging to the origin or beginning of something; first. The *original* owner of the house still lives there. *Adjective.* —Something that is original; not a copy, imitation, or translation. That painting is an *original* by Monet. *Noun.*

o•rig•i•nal (ə rij′ə nəl) *adjective; noun, plural* **originals.**

orphan A child whose parents are dead. The little *orphan* was raised by her grandparents. *Noun.* —To make an orphan of. The war *orphaned* many children. *Verb.*
or•phan (ôr′fən) *noun, plural* **orphans;** *verb,* **orphaned, orphaning.**

overalls Loose-fitting trousers with a piece that covers the chest and attached suspenders.
o•ver•alls (ō′vər ôlz′) *plural noun.*

overcome 1. To get the better of; beat or conquer. The tired runner couldn't *overcome* the others in the race. **2.** To get over or deal with. I *overcame* my fear of small spaces.
▲ **Synonym:** defeat
o•ver•come (ō′vər kum′) *verb,* **overcame, overcome, overcoming.**

overflow To be so full that the contents spill over. The bathtub *overflowed. Verb.*— Something that flows over. We mopped up the *overflow. Noun.*
o•ver•flow (ō′vər flō′ *for verb;* ō′vər flō′ *for noun*) *verb,* **overflowed, overflowing;** *noun.*

oxygen A colorless, odorless gas that makes up about one fifth of our air.
ox•y•gen (ok′si jən) *noun.*

Pp

pathway A course or route taken to reach a particular place. This *pathway* leads to the rose garden.
path•way (path′wā′) *noun, plural* **pathways.**

patient A person under the care or treatment of a doctor. The pediatrician had many *patients* to see. *Noun.*—Having or showing an ability to put up with hardship, pain, trouble, or delay without getting angry or upset. I tried to be *patient* while I waited in the line at the post office. *Adjective.*
pa•tient (pā′shənt) *noun, plural* **patients;** *adjective.*

at; āpe; fär; câre; end; mē; it; īce; pîerce; hot; ōld; sông; fôrk; oil; out; up; ūse; rüle; pu̇ll; tûrn; chin; sing; shop; thin; th̲is; hw in white; zh in treasure. The symbol ə stands for the unstressed vowel sound in about, taken, pencil, lemon, and circus.

peddler One who carries goods from place to place and offers them for sale.
▲ **Synonym:** vendor
ped•dler (ped′lər) *noun, plural* **peddlers.**

percent The number of parts in every hundred. The symbol for *percent* when it is written with a number is %.
per•cent (pər sent′) *noun.*

permit To allow or let. My parents will not *permit* me to play outside after dark. *Verb.*—A written order giving permission to do something. You need a *permit* to fish here. *Noun.*
per•mit (pər mit′ *for verb;* pûr′mit *or* pər mit′ *for noun*) *verb,* **permitted, permitting;** *noun, plural* **permits.**

Word History
Permit comes from the Latin word *permittere,* "to let through."

pesky Troublesome or annoying. If that *pesky* fly does not stop buzzing in my ear, I'll swat it.
▲ **Synonym:** annoying
pes•ky (pes′kē) *adjective,* **peskier, peskiest.**

plantation A large estate or farm worked by laborers who live there. Cotton is grown on *plantations.*
plan•ta•tion (plan tā′shən) *noun, plural* **plantations.**

pod A part of a plant that holds a number of seeds as they grow. Beans and peas grow in *pods.*
pod (pod) *noun, plural* **pods.**

poisonous Containing a drug or other substance that harms or kills by chemical action. Many household chemicals are *poisonous.*
poi•son•ous (poi′zən əs) *adjective.*

poncho A cloak made of one piece of cloth or other material, with a hole in the middle for the head.
pon•cho (pon′chō) *noun, plural* **ponchos.**

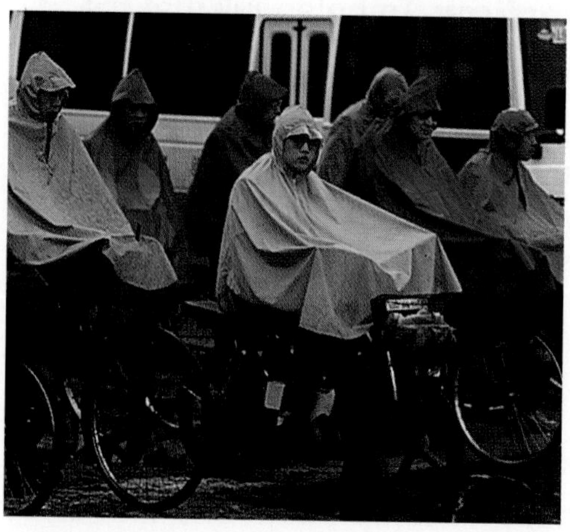

portable Easy to carry from place to place. *Portable* computers are very popular.
port•a•ble (pôr′tə bəl) *adjective.*

portfolio 1. A case for carrying loose pictures, pamphlets, or papers. I placed all the pictures in my *portfolio.* **2.** A set of drawings or pictures bound in a book or a folder. I must get my *portfolio* ready for the meeting
port•fo•lio (pôrt fō′lē ō′) *noun, plural* **portfolios.**

pottery Pots, bowls, dishes, and other things made from clay. I made a bowl in *pottery* class.
pot•ter•y (pot′ə rē) *noun.*

pouch 1. A bag; sack. The mail carrier took the letters out of her *pouch.* **2.** A pocket of skin in some animals. Kangaroos and opossums carry their young in *pouches.*
pouch (pouch) *noun, plural* **pouches.**

prairie Flat or rolling land covered with grass, and with few or no trees.
prai•rie (prâr′ē) *noun, plural* **prairies.**

prairie

praise An expression of high regard and approval. The teacher had nothing but *praise* for the student's drawing. *Noun.*—To worship. The minister *praised* God in her sermon. *Verb.*
praise (prāz) *noun, plural* **praises;** *verb,* **praised, praising.**

prance 1. To spring forward on the hind legs. The colt *pranced* and leaped about the field. **2.** To move in a proud, happy way. The children *pranced* around the house in their fancy costumes.
prance (prans) *verb,* **pranced, prancing.**

at; **ā**pe; f**ä**r; c**â**re; **e**nd; m**ē**; **i**t; **ī**ce; p**î**erce; h**o**t; **ō**ld; s**ô**ng; f**ô**rk; **oi**l; **ou**t; **u**p; **ū**se; r**ü**le; p**ů**ll; t**û**rn; **ch**in; si**ng**; **sh**op; **th**in; **th**is; **hw** in **wh**ite; **zh** in trea**s**ure. The symbol **ə** stands for the unstressed vowel sound in **a**bout, tak**e**n, penc**i**l, lem**o**n, and circ**u**s.

prejudice Hatred or unfair treatment of a particular group, such as members of a race or religion. *Noun.*—To cause to have prejudice. Being hurt once by a dentist *prejudiced* me against all dentists. *Verb.*
prej•u•dice (prej′ə dis) *noun, plural* **prejudices;** *verb,* **prejudiced, prejudicing.**

preserve To keep from being lost, damaged, or decayed; protect. It is important that we *preserve* our freedoms. *Verb.*—An area set aside for the protection of plants and animals. Rare birds and mammals breed in that nature *preserve. Noun.*
pre•serve (pri zûrv′) *verb,* **preserved, preserving;** *noun, plural* **preserves.**

pressure The force exerted by one thing pushing against another. The *pressure* of his foot on the gas pedal caused the car to go faster. *Noun.*—To urge strongly. The salesperson tried to *pressure* me into buying something I didn't need. *Verb.*
pres•sure (presh′ər) *noun, plural* **pressures;** *verb,* **pressured, pressuring.**

previously Before; at an earlier time. We had been introduced *previously.*
▲ **Synonym:** earlier
pre•vi•ous•ly (prē′vē əs lē) *adverb.*

quibble A minor dispute or disagreement. It's foolish to have a *quibble* over nothing. *Noun.* To engage in petty arguing. The two sisters *quibbled* for half an hour about who would take out the garbage. *Verb.*
quib•ble (kwi′bəl) *noun, plural* **quibbles;** *verb,* **quibbled, quibbling.**

Rr

racial Of or relating to a race of human beings. *Racial* prejudice is prejudice against people because of their race.
ra•cial (rā′shəl) *adjective; adverb,* **racially.**

ramp A sloping platform or passageway connecting two different levels.
ramp (ramp) *noun, plural* **ramps.**

reef A ridge of sand, rock, or coral at or near the surface of the ocean. We like to swim near the beautiful *reefs.*

reef (rēf) *noun, plural* **reefs.**

reference 1. A person or thing referred to; source of information. The encyclopedia was the *reference* for my report. **2.** A statement that calls or directs attention to something. The authors made a *reference* to their book.

ref•er•ence (ref′ər əns *or* ref′rəns) *noun, plural* **references.**

reflect 1. To give back an image of something. I saw myself *reflected* in the pond. **2.** To turn or throw back. Sand *reflects* light and heat from the sun.

re•flect (ri flekt′) *verb,* **reflected, reflecting.**

rein One of two or more narrow straps attached to a bridle or bit, used to guide and control a horse. The jockey held tightly to the horse's *reins. Noun.*—To guide, control, or hold back. The rider tried to *rein* in the galloping horse. *Verb.*

rein (rān) *noun, plural* **reins;** *verb,* **reined, reining.**

related 1. Belonging to the same family. You and your cousins are *related.* **2.** Having some connection. I have problems *related* to school.

re•la•ted (ri lā′tid) *adjective.*

at; **ā**pe; f**ä**r; c**â**re; **e**nd; m**ē**; **i**t; **ī**ce; p**î**erce; h**o**t; **ō**ld; s**ô**ng; f**ô**rk; **oi**l; **ou**t; **u**p; **ū**se; r**ü**le; p**ů**ll; t**û**rn; **ch**in; si**ng**; **sh**op; **th**in; **th**is; **hw** in **wh**ite; **zh** in trea**s**ure. The symbol **ə** stands for the unstressed vowel sound in **a**bout, tak**e**n, penc**i**l, lem**o**n, and circ**u**s.

release To set free; let go. The hostage was *released* after being held prisoner for ten days. *Verb.* —The act of releasing or the state of being released. The criminal's *release* from prison made headlines. *Noun.*
re•lease (ri lēs′) *verb,* **released, releasing;** *noun, plural* **releases.**

relieve 1. To free from discomfort or pain; comfort. The doctor gave me medicine to *relieve* my cough. **2.** To free from a job or duty. The lifeguards stayed on duty until they were *relieved.*
re•lieve (ri lēv′) *verb,* **relieved, relieving.**

reptile One of a class of cold-blooded animals with a backbone and dry, scaly skin, which move by crawling on their stomachs or creeping on short legs.
rep•tile (rep′təl *or* rep′tīl) *noun, plural* **reptiles.**

require 1. To have a need of. We all *require* food and sleep. **2.** To force, order, or demand. The law *requires* drivers to stop at a red light.
re•quire (ri kwīr′) *verb,* **required, requiring.**

research A careful study to find and learn facts. I did *research* in the library for my report. *Noun.* —To do research on or for. I *researched* my speech by reading many books on the subject. *Verb.*
re•search (ri sûrch′ *or* rē′sûrch′) *verb,* **researched, researching;** *noun, plural* **researches.**

resemble To be like or similar to. That hat *resembles* mine.
re•sem•ble (ri zem′bəl) *verb,* **resembled, resembling.**

resound 1. To be filled with sound. The stadium *resounded* with cheers. **2.** To make a loud, long, or echoing sound. Thunder *resounded* in the air.
re•sound (ri zound′) *verb,* **resounded, resounding.**

restless 1. Not able to rest. We got *restless* during the long speech. **2.** Not giving rest. The patient spent a *restless* night.
rest•less (rest′lis) *adjective; adverb,* **restlessly;** *noun,* **restlessness.**

rhythm A regular or orderly repeating of sounds or movements. We marched to the *rhythm* of drums.
rhythm (rith′əm) *noun, plural* **rhythms.**

roadblock A barrier or obstacle that prevents people or cars from passing through.
road•block (rōd′blok′) *noun, plural* **roadblocks.**

robot A machine that can do some of the same things that a human being can do.
ro•bot (rō′bət *or* rō′bot) *noun, plural* **robots.**

sacrifice The giving up of something for the sake of someone or something else. The parents made many *sacrifices* in order to send their children to college. *Noun.* —To offer as a sacrifice. Ancient peoples *sacrificed* animals to their gods. *Verb.*
sac•ri•fice (sak′rə fīs′) *noun, plural* **sacrifices;** *verb,* **sacrificed, sacrificing;** *adjective,* **sacrificial.**

sage A very wise person, usually old and respected. *Noun.*— Having or showing great wisdom and sound judgment. My grandparents often give me *sage* advice. *Adjective.*
sage (sāj) *noun, plural* **sages;** *adjective,* **sager, sagest.**

sagebrush A plant that grows on the dry plains of western North America.
sage•brush (sāj′brush′) *noun.*

scamper To run or move quickly. The rabbit *scampered* into the woods.
scam•per (skam′pər) *verb,* **scampered, scampering.**

at; āpe; fär; câre; end; mē; it; īce; pîerce; hot; ōld; sông; fôrk; oil; out; up; ūse; rüle; pu̇ll; tûrn; chin; sing; shop; thin; <u>th</u>is; hw in white; zh in treasure. The symbol ə stands for the unstressed vowel sound in about, taken, pencil, lemon, and circus.

scribble To write or draw quickly or carelessly. I *scribbled* a note to my friend. *Verb.*—Writing or drawing that is made by scribbling. The paper was covered with messy *scribbles. Noun.*
scrib•ble (skrib′əl) *verb,* **scribbled, scribbling;** *noun, plural* **scribbles;** *noun,* **scribbler.**

scuba (Self-Contained Underwater Breathing Apparatus) Equipment used for swimming underwater.
scu•ba (skü′bə) *noun.*

sediment 1. Rocks, dirt, or other solid matter carried and left by water, glaciers, or wind. **2.** Small pieces of matter that settle at the bottom of a liquid. There was *sediment* at the bottom of the bottle.
sed•i•ment (sed′ə mənt) *noun.*

segregation The practice of setting one group apart from another.
seg•re•ga•tion (seg′ri gā′shən) *noun.*

settlement 1. A small village or group of houses. During the 1800s, pioneers built many *settlements* in the American West. **2.** The act of settling or the condition of being settled. The *settlement* of Jamestown took place in 1607.
set•tle•ment (set′əl mənt) *noun, plural* **settlements.**

shanty A small, poorly built house; shack. During the Depression, many poor families lived in *shanties.*
▲ **Synonym:** shack
shan•ty (shan′tē) *noun, plural* **shanties.**

shoreline The line where a body of water and the land meet. My friend has a house near the *shoreline.*
shore•line (shôr′līn′) *noun.*

shortcut 1. A quicker way of reaching a place. I took a *shortcut* to school. **2.** A way of doing something faster. Don't use any *shortcuts* in your science experiment.
short•cut (shôrt′cut′) *noun, plural* **shortcuts.**

shriek A loud, sharp cry or sound. The child let out a *shriek* of laughter. *Noun.*—To utter a loud, sharp cry or sound. We all *shrieked* with laughter at her jokes. *Verb.*
shriek (shrēk) *noun, plural* **shrieks;** *verb,* **shrieked, shrieking.**

shutter 1. A movable cover for a window, usually attached to the frame by hinges. *Shutters* are used to shut out light **2.** The part of a camera that snaps open and shuts quickly to let light onto the film when a picture is taken.
shut•ter (shut′ər) *noun, plural* **shutters.**

siren A device that makes a loud, shrill sound, used as a signal or warning. Ambulances and police cars have *sirens.*
si•ren (sī′rən) *noun, plural* **sirens.**

sketch A rough, quick drawing. The artist made several *sketches* of the model before starting the painting. *Noun.*—To make a sketch of. I *sketched* an old barn for my art class. *Verb.*
sketch (skech) *verb,* **sketched, sketching;** *noun, plural* **sketches.**

Word History

Sketch comes from the Dutch word *schets* and the Italian word *schizzo,* meaning "splash." A sketch is often a rough drawing, a splash of an idea that will later become a detailed finished product.

skill The power or ability to do something. *Skill* comes with practice and experience.
skill (skil) *noun, plural* **skills.**

skillet A shallow pan with a handle. A *skillet* is used for frying.
skil•let (skil′it) *noun, plural* **skillets.**

skim 1. To remove from the surface of a liquid. The cook *skimmed* the fat from the soup. **2.** To read quickly. *Skim* the paper for the scores.
skim (skim) *verb,* **skimmed, skimming.**

at; **ā**pe; f**ä**r; c**â**re; **e**nd; m**ē**; **i**t; **ī**ce; p**î**erce; h**o**t; **ō**ld; s**ô**ng; f**ô**rk; **oi**l; **ou**t; **u**p; **ū**se; r**ü**le; p**u̇**ll; t**û**rn; **ch**in; si**ng**; **sh**op; **th**in; **th**is; **hw** in **wh**ite; **zh** in trea**s**ure. The symbol **ə** stands for the unstressed vowel sound in **a**bout, tak**e**n, penc**i**l, lem**o**n, and circ**u**s.

smog A combination of smoke and fog in the air. *Smog* is found especially over cities where there are factories and many cars.
smog (smog) *noun.*

Word History
The word ***smog*** was made using the first two letters of *smoke* and the last two letters of *fog.*

snout The front part of an animal's head, including nose, mouth, and jaws. My dog has a cute *snout.*
snout (snout) *noun, plural* **snouts.**

soapsuds Water that is bubbly with soap. I like my bath to be filled with *soapsuds.*
soap•suds (sōp′sudz′) *plural noun.*

soggy Very wet or damp; soaked. The soil was *soggy* after the rain.
sog•gy (sog′ē) *adjective,* **soggier, soggiest.**

soot A black, greasy powder that forms when such fuels as wood, coal, and oil are burned. The old chimney was caked with *soot.*
soot (su̇t *or* süt) *noun; adjective,* **sooty.**

spice The seeds or other parts of certain plants used to flavor food. Pepper, cloves, and cinnamon are spices. *Noun.*—To flavor with a spice or spices. I *spiced* the hamburgers. *Verb.*
spice (spīs) *noun, plural* **spices;** *verb,* **spiced, spicing;** *adjective,* **spicy.**

spike **1.** Any sharp, pointed object or part that sticks out. Baseball shoes have *spikes* on the soles. **2.** A large, heavy nail used to hold rails to railroad ties. It was difficult to hammer in the railroad *spike.*
spike (spīk) *noun, plural* **spikes.**

sponge A simple water animal that has a body that is full of holes and absorbs water easily. The dried skeletons of some *sponge* colonies are used for cleaning and washing. *Noun.*—To clean with a sponge. We *sponged* and dried the dirty walls. *Verb.*
sponge (spunj) *noun, plural* **sponges;** *verb,* **sponged, sponging.**

squall A strong gust of wind that arises very suddenly. Squalls often bring rain, snow, or sleet. We were forced indoors by a *squall* of snow.
squall (skwôl) *noun, plural* **squalls.**

Word History
The word ***squall*** first appeared in the English language in 1699. It is probably based on the Swedish word *skval,* which means "rushing water."

squeal To make a loud, shrill cry or sound. The little pigs *squealed* with excitement. *Verb.* —A loud, shrill cry or sound. The *squeal* of the brakes hurt my ears. *Noun.*
squeal (skwēl) *verb,* **squealed, squealing;** *noun, plural* **squeals.**

stake A stick or post pointed at one end so that it can be driven into the ground. The campers drove in *stakes* and tied the corners of the tent to them. *Noun.* — To fasten or hold up with a stake. The gardener *staked* the beans. *Verb.*
▲ Another word that sounds like this is **steak.**
stake (stāk) *noun, plural* **stakes;** *verb,* **staked, staking.**

sterilize To make free of bacteria and microorganisms. The nurse *sterilized* the scalpels before the operation.
ster•il•ize (ster′ə līz′) *verb,* **sterilized, sterilizing.**

stitch To make, fasten, or mend with stitches; sew. I *stitched* up the tear in my shirt. *Verb.*—One complete movement made with a needle and thread. *Noun.*
stitch (stich) *verb,* **stitched, stitching;** *noun, plural* **stitches.**

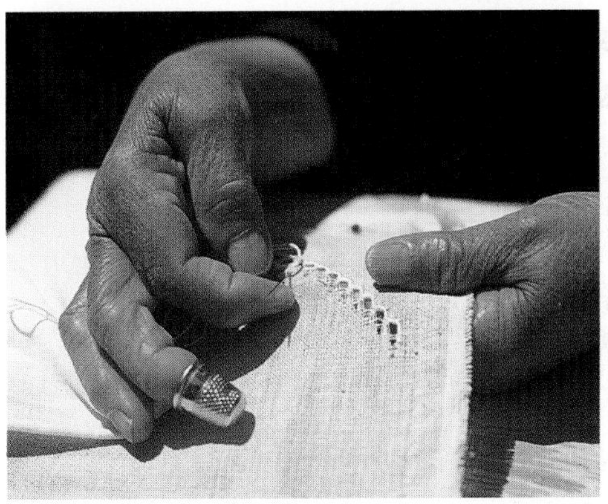

strew To spread by scattering. I have to clean my room because my clothes are *strewn* all over the place.
strew (strü) *verb,* **strewed, strewn, strewing.**

at; **ā**pe; f**ä**r; c**â**re; **e**nd; m**ē**; **i**t; **ī**ce; p**î**erce; h**o**t; **ō**ld; s**ô**ng; f**ô**rk; **oi**l; **ou**t; **u**p; **ū**se; r**ü**le; p**u̇**ll; t**û**rn; **ch**in; si**ng**; **sh**op; **th**in; **th**is; **hw** in **wh**ite; **zh** in trea**s**ure. The symbol **ə** stands for the unstressed vowel sound in **a**bout, tak**e**n, penc**i**l, lem**o**n, and circ**u**s.

stroll To walk in a slow, relaxed way. We *strolled* through the park. *Verb.* —A slow, relaxed walk. After dinner we took a *stroll. Noun.*
stroll (strōl) *verb,* **strolled, strolling;** *noun, plural* **strolls.**

sturdy Strong; hardy. Heavy trucks can drive on the *sturdy* bridge.
stur•dy (stûr′dē) *adjective,* **sturdier, sturdiest;** *adverb,* **sturdily;** *noun,* **sturdiness.**

success 1. A result hoped for; favorable end. The coach was pleased with the *success* of the game. **2.** A person or thing that does or goes well. The party was a big *success.*
suc•cess (sək ses′) *noun, plural* **successes;** *adjective,* **successful.**

sunrise The rising of the sun. We went to the beach to watch the *sunrise.*
sunrise (sun′rīz′) *noun, plural* **sunrises.**

swamp An area of wet land. The *swamp* looked scary and creepy. *Noun.* —To fill with water. High waves *swamped* the boat. *Verb.*
swamp (swomp) *noun, plural* **swamps;** *verb,* **swamped, swamping.**

swamp

talker One who exchanges spoken words in conversation. The two friends were great *talkers.*
talk•er (tôk′ ər) *noun, plural* **talkers.**

teammate A person who is a member of the same team. We're basketball *teammates.*
team•mate (tēm′māt′) *noun, plural* **teammates.**

threat 1. A person or thing that might cause harm; danger. The outbreak of flu was a *threat* to the community. **2.** A statement of something that will be done to hurt or punish. The trespassers heeded our *threat.*
threat (thret) *noun, plural* **threats.**

ton A measure of weight equal to 2,000 pounds in the United States and Canada, and 2,240 pounds in Great Britain.
ton (tun) *noun, plural* **tons.**

tractor A vehicle with heavy tires or tracks. *Tractors* are used to pull heavy loads over rough ground.
trac•tor (trak′tər) *noun, plural* **tractors.**

tradition A custom or belief that is passed on from one generation to another.
tra•di•tion (trə dish′ən) *noun, plural* **traditions;** *adjective,* **traditional.**

travel To go from one place to another; to make a trip. We *traveled* through England. *Verb.* —The act of traveling. Camels are used for desert *travel. Noun.*
trav•el (trav′əl) *verb,* **traveled, traveling;** *noun, plural* **travels.**

tricorn A hat with the brim turned up on three sides.
tri•corn (trī′kôrn′) *noun, plural* **tricorns.**

tube A container of soft metal or plastic from which the contents are removed by squeezing. I need a new *tube* of toothpaste.
tube (tüb) *noun, plural* **tubes.**

tusk A long, pointed tooth that sticks out of each side of the mouth in certain animals. Elephants and walruses have *tusks.*
tusk (tusk) *noun, plural* **tusks.**

waddle To walk or move with short steps, swaying the body from side to side. The duck *waddled* across the yard. *Verb.*—A swaying or rocking walk. The audience laughed at the clown's *waddle. Noun.*
wad•dle (wod′əl) *verb,* **waddled, waddling;** *noun, plural* **waddles.**

at; **ā**pe; f**ä**r; c**â**re; **e**nd; m**ē**; **i**t; **ī**ce; p**î**erce; h**o**t; **ō**ld; s**ô**ng; f**ô**rk; **oi**l; **ou**t; **u**p; **ū**se; r**ü**le; p**u̇**ll; t**û**rn; **ch**in; si**ng**; **sh**op; **th**in; **th**is; **hw** in **wh**ite; **zh** in trea**s**ure. The symbol **ə** stands for the unstressed vowel sound in **a**bout, tak**e**n, penc**i**l, lem**o**n, and circ**u**s.

weary Very tired. The carpenter was *weary* after the day's hard work. *Adjective.*—To make or become weary; tire. The long walk *wearied* the children. *Verb.*
wea•ry (wîr′ē) *adjective,* **wearier, weariest;** *verb,* **wearied, weary-ing;** *adverb,* **wearily;** *noun,* **weariness.**

weird Strange or mysterious; odd. A *weird* sound came from the deserted old house.
▲ **Synonym:** peculiar
weird (wîrd) *adjective,* **weirder, weirdest;** *adverb,* **weirdly;** *noun,* **weirdness.**

wharf A structure built along a shore as a landing place for boats and ships; dock. We had to unload the boat once we reached the *wharf.*
wharf (hworf *or* wôrf) *noun, plural* **wharves** *or* **wharfs.**

whicker To neigh or whinny. The horse began *whickering* at the kids. *Verb.*—A neigh or whinny. The horse let out a *whicker. Noun.*
whick•er (hwi′kər) *verb,* **whickered, whickering;** *noun, plural* **whickers.**

whinny A soft neigh. We heard the *whinnies* of the horses. *Noun.* —To neigh in a low, gentle way. My horse *whinnied* when he saw me. *Verb.*
whin•ny (hwin′ē *or* win′ē) *verb,* **whinnied, whinnying;** *noun, plural* **whinnies.**

wildlife Wild animals that live naturally in an area. My favorite part of hiking is observing the *wildlife.*
wild•life (wīld′līf′) *noun.*

windowpane A framed sheet of glass in a window. I placed my candles by the *windowpane.*
win•dow•pane (win′dō pān′) *noun, plural* **windowpanes.**

wondrous Extraordinary; wonderful. The local theater put on a *wondrous* performance.
▲ **Synonym:** marvelous
won•drous (wun′drəs) *adjective; adverb,* **wondrously;** *noun,* **wondrousness.**

wrestle 1. To force by grasping. The champion *wrestled* his opponent to the mat. **2.** To struggle by grasping and trying to force and hold one's opponent to the ground, without punching. The children *wrestled* on the lawn.

wres•tle (res′əl) *verb,* **wrestled, wrestling.**

wriggle 1. To twist or turn from side to side with short, quick moves; squirm. The bored children *wriggled* in their seats. **2.** To get into or out of a position by tricky means. You always try to *wriggle* out of having to wash the dishes.

wrig•gle (rig′əl) *verb,* **wriggled, wriggling;** *adjective,* **wriggly.**

Word History

The word ***wriggle*** comes from the Old English word *wrigian,* which means "to turn."

at; **ā**pe; f**ä**r; c**â**re; **e**nd; m**ē**; **i**t; **ī**ce; p**î**erce; h**o**t; **ō**ld; s**ô**ng; f**ô**rk; **oi**l; **ou**t; **u**p; **ū**se; r**ü**le; p**ů**ll; t**û**rn; **ch**in; si**ng**; **sh**op; **th**in; <u>**th**</u>is; **hw** in **wh**ite; **zh** in trea**s**ure. The symbol **ə** stands for the unstressed vowel sound in **a**bout, tak**e**n, penc**i**l, lem**o**n, and circ**u**s.

ACKNOWLEDGMENTS

The publisher gratefully acknowledges permission to reprint the following copyrighted material.

"Amelia's Road" by Linda Jacobs Altman, illustrated by Enrique O. Sanchez. Text copyright © 1993 by Linda Jacobs Altman. Illustrations copyright © 1993 by Enrique O. Sanchez. Permission granted by Lee & Low Books Inc., 95 Madison Avenue, New York, NY 10016.

"August 8" by Norman Jordan. From MY BLACK ME: A Beginning Book of Black Poetry, edited by Arnold Adoff. Copyright © 1974. Used by permission of Dutton Books, a division of Penguin Putnam, Inc.

"Baseball Saved Us" by Ken Mochizuki, illustrated by Dom Lee. Text copyright © 1993 by Ken Mochizuki. Illustrations copyright © 1993 by Dom Lee. Permission granted by Lee & Low Books Inc., 95 Madison Avenue, New York, NY 10016.

"Final Curve" by Langston Hughes from MY BLACK ME: A Beginning Book of Black Poetry, edited by Arnold Adoff. Copyright © 1974. Used by permission of Dutton Books, a division of Penguin Putnam, Inc.

"The Fox and the Guinea Pig"/"El zorro y el cuy" A traditional Folk Tale translated by Mary Ann Newman, illustrated by Kevin Hawkes. Copyright © 1997 Macmillan/McGraw-Hill, a Division of the Educational and Professional Publishing Group of the McGraw-Hill Companies, Inc.

"The Garden We Planted Together" by Anuruddha Bose from A WORLD IN OUR HANDS. Reprinted with permission of A WORLD IN OUR HANDS by Peace Child Charitable Trust, illustrated by Sanjay Sinha ($15.95). Copyright © 1995 Tricycle Press (800-841-BOOK).

"Gluskabe and the Snow Bird" from GLUSKABE AND THE FOUR WISHES retold by Joseph Bruchac. Copyright © 1995 Cobblehill Books/Dutton.

"Grass Sandals/The Travels of Basho" by Dawnine Spivak, illustrated by Demi. Text copyright © 1997 by Dawnine Spivak, illustrations copyright © 1997 by Demi. Reprinted by permission of Atheneum Books for Young Readers, Simon and Schuster Children's Publishing Division. All rights reserved.

"The Hatmaker's Sign" by Candace Fleming, illustrated by Robert Andrew Parker. Text copyright © 1998 by Candace Fleming. Illustrations copyright © 1998 by Robert Andrew Parker. All rights reserved. Reprinted by permission by Orchard Books, New York.

"How to Tell the Top of a Hill" by John Ciardi from THE REASON FOR THE PELICAN. Copyright © 1959 by John Ciardi. Reprinted by permission of the Estate of John Ciardi.

"I Ask My Mother to Sing" by Li-Young Lee. Copyright © 1986 by Li-Young Lee. Reprinted from *Rose* with the permission of BOA Editions, Ltd., 260 East Ave., Rochester, NY 14604.

"Just a Dream" is from JUST A DREAM by Chris Van Allsburg. Copyright © 1990 by Chris Van Allsburg. Reprinted by permission of Houghton Mifflin Company.

"Justin and the Best Biscuits in the World" is from JUSTIN AND THE BEST BISCUITS IN THE WORLD by Mildred Pitts Walter. Copyright © 1986 by Mildred Pitts Walter. Published by Lothrop, Lee & Shepard Books and used by permission of William Morrow & Company, Inc. Publishers, New York.

"Leah's Pony" by Elizabeth Friedrich, illustrated by Michael Garland. Text copyright © 1996 by Elizabeth Friedrich. Illustrations copyright © 1996 by Michael Garland. Used by permission of Boyds Mills Press.

"The Lost Lake" by Allen Say. Copyright © 1989 by Allen Say. Reprinted by permission of Houghton Mifflin Company. All rights reserved.

"The Malachite Palace" by Alma Flor Ada, translated by Rosa Zubizarreta, illustrated by Leonid Gore. Text copyright © 1998 by Alma Flor Ada, illustrations copyright © 1998 by Leonid Gore. Reprinted by permission by of Atheneum Books for Young Readers, Simon and Schuster Children's Publishing Division. All rights reserved.

"Meet an Underwater Explorer" by Luise Woelflein. Reprinted from the June 1994 issue of RANGER RICK magazine, with the permission of the publisher, the National Wildlife Federation. Copyright © 1994 by the National Wildlife Federation.

"Mom's Best Friend" by Sally Hobart Alexander, photographs by George Ancona. Text copyright ©1992 by Sally Hobart Alexander. Photographs copyright © 1992 by George Ancona. Reprinted with permission of Simon & Schuster Books for Young Readers, Simon & Schuster Children's Publishing Division.

"My Poems" by Alan Barlow. From RISING VOICES: WRITINGS OF YOUNG NATIVE AMERICANS selected by Arlene B. Hirschfelder and Beverly R. Singer. Copyright © 1992. Published by Scribner's. Used by permission.

"On the Bus with Joanna Cole" excerpt from *On the Bus with Joanna Cole: A Creative Autobiography* by Joanna Cole with Wendy Saul. Copyright © 1996 by Joanna Cole. Published by Heinemann, a division of Reed Elsevier Inc. Reprinted by permission of the Publisher. Illustration on page 447 by Bruce Degen from THE MAGIC SCHOOL BUS INSIDE THE HUMAN BODY by Joanna Cole. Illustration copyright © 1989 by Bruce Degen. Reprinted with permission of Scholastic, Inc. THE MAGIC SCHOOL BUS is a registered trademark of Scholastic, Inc.

"Pat Cummings: My Story" reprinted with the permission of Simon & Schuster Books for Young Readers from TALKING WITH ARTISTS compiled and edited by Pat Cummings. Jacket illustration copyright © 1992 Pat Cummings. Copyright © 1992 Pat Cummings.

"A Place Called Freedom" by Scott Russell Sanders, illustrated by Thomas B. Allen. Text copyright © 1997 by Scott Russell Sanders, illustrations copyright © 1997 by Thomas B. Allen. Reprinted by permission of Atheneum Books for Young Readers, Simon and Schuster Children's Publishing Division. All rights reserved.

"The Poet Pencil" by Jesús Carlos Soto Morfín, translated by Judith Infante. From THE TREE IS OLDER THAN YOU ARE: A Bilingual Gathering of Poems and Stories from Mexico, selected by Naomi Shihab Nye. Copyright © 1995 Reprinted by permission of the author.

"The Rajah's Rice" from THE RAJAH'S RICE by David Barry, illustrated by Donna Perrone. Text Copyright © 1994 by David Barry. Art copyright © 1994 by Donna Perrone. Used with permission of W. H. Freeman and Company.

"Sarah, Plain and Tall" text excerpt from SARAH, PLAIN AND TALL by Patricia MacLachlan. Copyright © 1985 by Patricia MacLachlan. Reprinted by permission of HarperCollins Publishers. Cover permission for the Trophy Edition used by permission of HarperCollins Publishers.

"Scruffy: A Wolf Finds His Place in the Pack" by Jim Brandenburg. Copyright © 1996 by Jim Brandenburg. Published by arrangement with Walker Publishing Company, Inc.

"Seal Journey" From SEAL JOURNEY by Richard and Jonah Sobol. Copyright © 1993 Richard Sobol, text and photographs. Used by permission of Cobblehill Books, an affiliate of Dutton Children's Press, a division of Penguin USA, Inc.

"Teammates" from TEAMMATES by Peter Golenbock, text copyright © 1990 by Golenbock Communications, reprinted by permission of Harcourt, Inc.

"To" by Lee Bennett Hopkins from BEEN TO YESTERDAYS: Poems of a Life. Text copyright © 1995 by Lee Bennett Hopkins. Published by Wordsong/Boyds Mills Press. Reprinted by permission.

"The Toothpaste Millionaire" by Jean Merrill. Copyright © 1972 by Houghton Mifflin Company. Adapted and reprinted by permission of Houghton Mifflin Company. All rights reserved.

"Tortillas Like Africa" from CANTO FAMILIAR by Gary Soto. Copyright © 1995 Harcourt, Inc.

"Whales" excerpt from WHALES by Seymour Simon. Copyright © 1989 by Seymour Simon. Reprinted by permission of HarperCollins Publishers.

"Yeh-Shen: A Cinderella Story from China" is from YEH-SHEN: A CINDERELLA STORY FROM CHINA by Ai-Ling Louie. Text copyright © 1982 by Ai-Ling Louie. Illustrations copyright © 1982 by Ed Young. Reprinted by permission of Philomel Books. Introductory comments by Ai-Ling Louie and used with her permission.

"Your World" by Georgia Douglas Johnson appeared originally in HOLD FAST TO DREAMS selected by Arna Bontemps. Extensive research has failed to locate the author and/or copyright holder of this work.

Cover Illustration
Terry Widener

Illustration
Roberta Ludlow, 16-17; Jean and Mou-Sien Tseng, 128-129; David Ridley, 130-131; Elizabeth Rosen, 252-253; J. W. Stewart, 254-255; Bruno Paciulli, 372-373; Stefano Vitale, 408-419; Amy Vangsgard, 482-483; Susan Leopold, 484-485; Yoshi Miyake, 612-613; David Catrow, 666-687; B. J. Faulkner, 724-725; George Thompson, 728, 749; Rodica Prato, 732, 739; John Carrozza, 745, 759, 763.

Photography
18-19: c. Fine Art Photographic Library, London/Art Resource, NY. 42-43: c. The Bridgeman Art Library International Ltd. 66: c. Superstock. 94-95: c. Shelburne Museum. 118-119: c. E. A. Barton Collection, England. 132-133: c. Jerry Jacka. 158-159: c. MPTV. 190-191: c. The Museum of Modern Art, New York. 216-217: c. The Bridgeman Art Library International Ltd. 242-243: c. The Bridgeman Art Library International Ltd. 256-257: c. Richard Estes. 282-283: c. Superstock. 298-299: c. The Bridgeman Art Library International Ltd. 332-333: c. The Phillips Collection. The Bridgeman Art Library International Ltd. 360-361: c. Cordon Art B. V. 406-407: c. The Heard Museum. 374-375: c. 424-425: c. Corbis/Bettmann. 444-445: c. Private Collection. 472-473: c. The Bridgeman Art Library International Ltd. 486-487: c. Christies Images. 516-517: c. Millennium Pictures. 536-537: c. Art Resource. 568-569: c. Omni-Photo Communications. 600-601: c. The Bridgeman Art Library Ltd. 614-615: c. Jonathan Green. 632-633: c. Chester Beatty Library, Dublin. 664-665: c. Motion Picture and Television Archives. 692/693: c. Superstock. 714-715: c. The Bridgeman Art Library Ltd.